Prentice Hall

Algebra 2

Student Companion

PEARSON

Boston, Massachusetts • Chandler, Arizona • Glenview, Illinois • Upper Saddle River, New Jersey

Acknowledgements   Photo: All photographs not listed are the property of Pearson Education
Back Cover: Klein J.-L & Hube/Biosphoto; 180, ©Bob Krist/CORBIS; 353 t, Steve Gorton/Dorling Kindersley;
352 b, European Space/Photo Researchers Inc.

ISBN-13: 978-0-13-318612-3
ISBN-10: 0-13-318612-1
14   16

PEARSON

Contents

Contents

Contents

Welcome *to* **Algebra 2!**

Your *Prentice Hall Algebra 2* program is designed to help you achieve mastery of Algebra 2 topics. Your *Prentice Hall Algebra 2 Student Companion* is written to support you as you study. Your Student Companion is designed to work with your Student Edition textbook and PowerAlgebra.com by providing a place to practice the concepts, skills, and vocabulary you'll learn in each lesson.

Using the Algebra 2 Student Companion

Your Student Companion provides daily support for each lesson by targeting the following areas:

- **Vocabulary** Building your math vocabulary is an important part of success this year. You'll use your Student Companion to learn and understand the vocabulary words you need for algebra.

- **Got It?** You'll use your Student Companion to check your understanding of example problems from your Student Edition.

- **Lesson Check** You'll use your Student Companion to make sure you're ready to tackle your homework.

Together, these sections will help you prepare to master the topics covered in your Student Edition—and lead to a successful year in Algebra 2.

Using PowerAlgebra.com

All your Student Companion pages are available for downloading and printing from PowerAlgebra.com.

Vocabulary

● Review

Write the correct word to continue each *pattern*.

1. Monday, Wednesday, Friday, Sunday, Tuesday, . . .

2. January, April, July, October, January, . . .

3. red, blue, red, yellow, red, blue, . . .

4. circle, square, triangle, circle, square, . . .

Write the next number in each *pattern*.

5. 2, 4, 6, 8, ▢

6. 6, 3, 0, −3, ▢

7. 2, 8, 32, 128, ▢

● Vocabulary Builder

> *x* and *y*
> are often used as
> **variables**

variable (noun) VERH **ee uh bul**

Related Words: vary

Main Idea: A **variable** is usually a letter that can change or vary.

Definition: A **variable** is a symbol that can represent one or more numbers.

Math Usage: A **variable** represents an unknown number in equations and inequalities.

● Use Your Vocabulary

8. Write **N** if the expression is a *numerical expression*. Write **A** if the expression is an *algebraic expression*.

   $5x$ ___ $3 + \frac{5}{2}$ ___ $9 - z \cdot 5$ ___ $\frac{6}{r} + 7$ ___

9. Circle the *variables* in each algebraic expression below.

   $3 - x$ $4w + d$ $8 \cdot v$ $k + 2q - 7$

Problem 1 Identifying a Pattern

Got It? Look at the figures from left to right. What is the pattern?
Draw the next figure in the pattern.

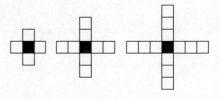

10. There are [ ] white squares in the first figure.

11. There are [ ] more white squares in the second figure.

12. Describe the pattern.

_____

_____

13. Draw the next figure in the pattern.

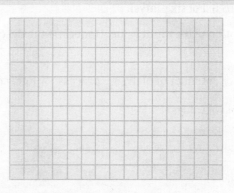

Problem 2 Expressing a Pattern with Algebra

Got It? How many tiles are in the 25th figure in this pattern?
Use a table of values with a process column.

14. Complete the table of values.

Figure Number (Input)	Process Column	Number of Tiles (Output)
1	$1 + (2 \cdot 1 + 1)$	4
2	$1 + \left(2 \cdot \boxed{} + 1\right)$	[ ]
3	$1 + \left(2 \cdot \boxed{} + 1\right)$	[ ]
4	$1 + \left(2 \cdot \boxed{} + 1\right)$	10
⋮	⋮	⋮
n	[ ]	[ ]

15. There are $25\left(\boxed{}\right) + 2$, or [ ], tiles in the 25th figure of this pattern.

3

Lesson 1-1

16. Explain how the table of values helps you find the number of tiles in the 25th figure.

_____

_____

_____

Problem 3 **Using a Graph**

Got It? The graph shows the total cost of platys at the aquarium shop. Use a table to find the cost of six platys.

Cost of Platys

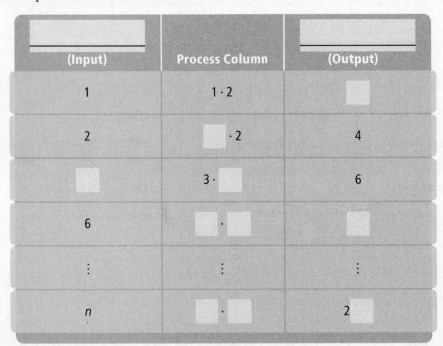

17. Circle the description of the input value. Underline the description of the output value.

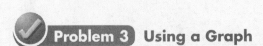

cost of platys   number of platys   process   total cost

18. Complete the table of values.

(Input)	Process Column	(Output)
1	1 · 2	☐
2	☐ · 2	4
☐	3 · ☐	6
6	☐ · ☐	☐
⋮	⋮	⋮
n	☐ · ☐	2

Underline a number or expression to complete each sentence.

19. In the table, when the input value is 6, the output value is 2 / 6 / 12 .

20. The expression n / $2n$ / $3n$ describes the cost of 1 / 2 / n platys.

21. At the aquarium shop, six platys cost $ ☐ .

Lesson Check • Do you know HOW?

Make a table to represent each pattern. Use a process column.

22. 2, 4, 6, 8

23.

Lesson Check • Do you UNDERSTAND?

Error Analysis Your friend looks for a pattern in the table at the right and claims that the output equals the input divided by 2. Is your friend correct? Explain.

Input	3	6.8	8	10	25
Output	2	3.4	4	5	12.5

24. Circle the rule that applies to most of the input and output values.

Output = Input ÷ 3   Output = Input · 2   Output = Input ÷ 2

25. Does the input value of 3 follow this rule?   Yes / No

26. Does the table represent a pattern? Explain.

_____

_____

_____

Math Success

Check off the vocabulary words that you understand.

☐ variable   ☐ algebraic expression

Rate how well you can *determine patterns.*

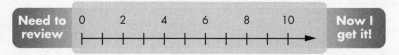

Need to review   0   2   4   6   8   10   Now I get it!

Lesson 1-1

Vocabulary

● Review

1. Circle the pairs of numbers that are *opposites*.

7 and $\frac{1}{7}$	−4 and 4	1.2 and 2.1	5 and −5	4 and $|4|$

2. Write the opposite of each number.

$|-3|$	1	−17	$\frac{1}{2}$	$\sqrt{16}$	0
□	□	□	□	□	□

● Vocabulary Builder

real numbers (noun) **reel NUM burz**

Definition: The set of **real numbers** includes all rational and irrational numbers.

Related Words: natural numbers, whole numbers, integers, rational numbers, irrational numbers

Real Numbers

$-5, \frac{1}{3}, \sqrt{8}, 0,$ 1.55, and 4

● Use Your Vocabulary

3. Circle the *real numbers*.

−3	$\sqrt{5}$	$\sqrt{-1}$	0	$\frac{7}{8}$

4. Circle the *real numbers* that are integers.

−3	$\sqrt{5}$	$\sqrt{-1}$	0	$\frac{7}{8}$

5. How does the set of *real numbers* differ from the set of integers?

_____

_____

Problem 1 Classifying a Variable

Got It? Your school is sponsoring a charity race. If each participant made a donation d of $15.50 to a local charity, which subset of real numbers best describes the amount of money raised?

6. Circle the values below that could represent the number of participants making a donation.

$$\sqrt{5} \qquad 0 \qquad \frac{3}{8} \qquad 2.7 \qquad 10 \qquad 150$$

7. Circle the set of numbers that best describes the numbers you chose in Exercise 6.

counting numbers   rational numbers   real numbers   whole numbers

Problem 2 Graphing Numbers on the Number Line

Got It? What is the graph of the numbers $\sqrt{3}$, $-1.\overline{4}$, and $\frac{1}{3}$?

8. Find the integers each number is between.

Use a calculator and round to one decimal place:

Because $\sqrt{3} \approx$ ☐ , $\sqrt{3}$ is between 1 and 2.

Think of the fraction form: $-1.\overline{4} \approx -1.4 \approx$ ☐ ,

so $-1.\overline{4}$ is between ☐ and ☐ .

Think: $\frac{1}{3}$ is between ☐ and ☐ .

9. How can you estimate $\sqrt{3}$ without using a calculator?

_____

10. Graph the numbers $\sqrt{3}$, $-1.\overline{4}$, and $\frac{1}{3}$ on the number line.

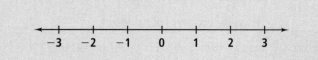

Problem 3 Ordering Real Numbers

Got It? How do $\sqrt{26}$ and 6.25 compare? Use > or <.

11. Find a perfect square close to 26.

☐ $^2 =$ ☐

12. Find a square root of a perfect square close to 6.25.

$\sqrt{☐} =$ ☐

Lesson 1-2

13. Use $<$ or $>$ twice to compare your answers to Exercises 11 and 12.

$\sqrt{}\ \square\ \sqrt{}\ \square$ 6.25

14. Now write $>$ or $<$ to compare $\sqrt{26}$ and 6.25.

$\sqrt{26}\ \square$ 6.25

take note

Key Concept   Properties of Real Numbers

Let a, b, and c represent real numbers.

Property	Addition	Multiplication
Closure	$a + b$ is a real number.	ab is a real number.
Commutative	$a + b = b + a$	$ab = ba$
Associative	$(a + b) + c = a + (b + c)$	$(ab)c = a(bc)$
Identity	$a + 0 = a, 0 + a = a$ 0 is the additive identity	$a \cdot 1 = 1, 1 \cdot a = a$ 1 is the multiplicative identity
Inverse	$a + (-a) = 0$	$a \cdot \dfrac{1}{a} = 1, a \neq 0$
Distributive	$a(b + c) = ab + bc$	

15. Draw a line from the expression in Column A to the property that it illustrates in Column B.

Column A

$2(3x + 7) = (3x + 7)(2)$

$(x + y) + 5 = x + (y + 5)$

$x + 0 = x$

$x \cdot 1 = x$

$8 + (-8) = 0$

$5(2x + 1) = 5 \cdot 2x + 5 \cdot 1$

Column B

Inverse Property of Addition

Commutative Property of Multiplication

Associative Property of Addition

Distributive Property

Identity Property of Multiplication

Identity Property of Addition

Problem 4   Identifying Properties of Real Numbers

Got It? Which property does the equation $3(g + h) + 2g = (3g + 3h) + 2g$ illustrate?

16. Circle the operations used in the equation.

division	addition	multiplication	subtraction

17. Circle the algebraic equation that models $3(g + h) = 3g + 3h$.

$hg = gh$	$h + g = g + h$	$a(g + h) = ag + ah$	$a + (g - h) = (g - h) + a$

18. The equation $3(g - h) + 2g = 3g - 3h + 2g$ illustrates the __?__ Property.

Lesson Check • Do you UNDERSTAND?

Reasoning There are grouping symbols in the equation $(5 + w) + 8 = (w + 5) + 8$, but it does not illustrate the Associative Property of Addition. Explain.

19. Circle the equation below that illustrates the Associative Property of Addition.

$a + b + c = b + a + c$ $a + (b + c) = ab + ac$ $(a + b) + c = a + (b + c)$

20. The Associative Property of Addition is a rule about the order / grouping of the terms of an addition statement.

21. Write the terms grouped on each side of the equation.

Left side: ☐ and ☐   Right side: ☐ and ☐

22. Now explain why $(5 + w) + 8 = (w + 5) + 8$ does NOT illustrate the Associative Property of Addition.

_____

_____

_____

_____

23. Circle the property that the equation illustrates.

Closure Property of Addition   Commutative Property of Addition

Inverse Property of Addition   Distributive Property

 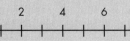

Math Success

Check off the vocabulary words that you understand.

☐ additive inverse   ☐ multiplicative inverse   ☐ opposite   ☐ reciprocal   ☐ squares

Rate how well you _understand the properties of real numbers_.

Need to review   0   2   4   6   8   10   Now I get it!

Vocabulary

Review

Simplify each numerical expression.

1. $6(5 - 2) + 7 =$ ▢

2. $\dfrac{7 + 5 \cdot (-3)}{4} =$ ▢

3. $(-5)^2 - (4)^2 =$ ▢

Vocabulary Builder

> **evaluate**   (noun)   ee VAL you ayt
>
> **Definition:** To **evaluate** an expression means to substitute a number for each variable and then simplify to get a value.
>
> **Example:** To **evaluate** xy for $x = 2$ and $y = 3$, substitute 2 for x and 3 for y; $xy = (2)(3) = 6$.

Use Your Vocabulary

Evaluate each expression for the given values of the variables.

4. $a + \dfrac{b}{4}$ for $a = -2$ and $b = 8$

5. $x - x^2 y$ for $x = 3$ and $y = -4$

Key Concept   **Properties for Simplifying Algebraic Expressions**

6. Draw a line from each property in Column A to an algebraic example of the property in Column B. Let a, b, and c represent real numbers.

Column A	Column B
Distributive Property for Subtraction	$-(a + b) = -a + (-b) = -a - b$
Multiplication by 0	$-(-a) = a$
Multiplication by -1	$-1 \cdot a = -a$
Opposite of a Sum	$a(b - c) = ab - ac$
Opposite of a Difference	$0 \cdot a = 0$
Opposite of an Opposite	$-(a - b) = -a + b = b - a$

Problem 1 Modeling Words With Algebraic Expressions

Got It? Which algebraic expression models the word phrase *two times the sum of a and b*?

7. The word "times" means you should use multiplication / addition / division .

8. The word "sum" means you should use multiplication / addition / division .

9. Now write the expression.

Complete each numerical or algebraic expression by writing a letter, number or operation sign in each box.

10. The difference of 7 and 4.　　　　　7 ☐ 4

11. The product of 3 and *x*.　　　　　3 ☐ *x*

12. The number *y* increased by 2.　　*y* ☐ ☐

13. The quotient of 48 and 3.　　　　48 ☐ 3

14. The number *t* is doubled then decreased by 1.　　☐ *t* ☐ 1

15. Five taken away from *q*.　　　　☐ – ☐

Problem 2 Modeling a Situation

Got It? You had $150, but you are spending $2 each day. What algebraic expression models this situation?

16. Define the variable. Let *d* = _____.

17. Complete the model to write the algebraic expression.

Relate	Starting amount	−	the amount spent per day	·	the number of days
Write	☐	−	☐	·	☐

18. Now write the expression.

Problem 3 Evaluating Algebraic Expressions

Got It? What is the value of the expression $\frac{2(x^2 - y^2)}{3}$ for $x = 6$ and $y = -3$?

19. Substitute the given values for each variable into the expression.

$$\frac{2(x^2 - y^2)}{3} = \frac{2\left(\boxed{}^2 - \boxed{}^2\right)}{3}$$

Lesson 1-3

20. Now simplify the numerical expression.

Problem 4 **Writing and Evaluating an Expression**

Got It? In basketball, teams can score by making two-point shots, three-point shots, and one-point free throws. What algebraic expression models the total number of points that a basketball team scores in a game? If a team makes 10 two-point shots, 5 three-point shots, and 7 free throws, how many points does it score in all?

21. Define the variables.

Let t = the number of two-point shots,

Let h = _____, and

Let f = _____.

22. Complete the expression for the total number of points a team can score in one game.

2 ☐ + 3 ☐ + ☐

23. Evaluate the expression for $t = 10$, $h = 5$, and $f = 7$.

24. The team scored ☐ points.

The expression $5ax + 6y - 7$ has three *terms*: $5ax$, $6y$, and -7.

The *coefficient* is the numerical factor of a term: 5, 6

The *constant term* is the term with no variables: -7.

Identify the *coefficients* and the *constant term* in each expression.

25. $2x^2 - 3x + 5$

Coefficients: ☐ and ☐

Constant: ☐

26. $-4yx + 8x - 3$

Coefficients: ☐ and ☐

Constant: ☐

Got It? Combine like terms. What is a simpler form of the expression $-4j^2 - 7k + 5j + j^2$?

At the right is one student's solution.

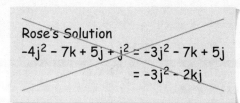

Rose's Solution
$-4j^2 - 7k + 5j + j^2 = -3j^2 - 7k + 5j$
$= -3j^2 - 2kj$

27. What error did Rose make?

_____

_____

28. Simplify the expression correctly.

Lesson Check • Do you UNDERSTAND?

Compare and Contrast How are algebraic expressions and numerical expressions alike? How are they different? Include examples to justify your reasoning.

29. How is an algebraic expression different from a numerical expression?

_____

_____

30. Put an **N** next to each *numerical expression*. Put an **A** next to each *algebraic expression*.

$3x + 2$ ____ $6 \cdot 4$ ____ $a - 7$ ____ $4 \cdot 1 + 10$ ____ $\frac{5g}{3} + h$ ____

Math Success

Check off the vocabulary words that you understand.

☐ term ☐ evaluate ☐ coefficient ☐ constant ☐ terms ☐ like terms

Rate how well you can *write and evaluate algebraic expressions*.

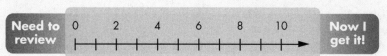

Need to review   0   2   4   6   8   10   Now I get it!

1-4 Solving Equations

Vocabulary

● **Review**

Circle the equations.

$$2(3x + 7) = 10 \qquad 3x + 14 \qquad 3x + 2y = 6 \qquad 4x + (y + 5)$$

● **Vocabulary Builder**

inverse operations (noun) IN vurs ahp uh RAY shunz

Related Words: opposite, reverse

Main Idea: **Inverse operations** undo each other.

Example: Addition and subtraction are **inverse operations.**

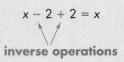

$$x - 2 + 2 = x$$

inverse operations

● **Use Your Vocabulary**

1. Write each *inverse operation.*

Add 7.	Subtract 4.	Divide by 5.	Multiply by 3.
_____	_____	_____	_____

take note

Key Concepts   Properties of Equality

Assume *a*, *b*, and *c* represent real numbers.

Property	Definition	Example
Reflexive	$a = a$	$5 = 5$
Symmetric	If $a = b$, then $b = a$.	$(4)(2) = 8$, so $8 = (4)(2)$
Transitive	If $a = b$ and $b = c$, then $a = c$.	$6 = (2)(3)$ and $(2)(3) = (3)(2)$, so $6 = (3)(2)$
Substitution	If $a = b$, then you can replace a with b and vice versa.	If $a = b$ and $9 + a = 15$, then $9 + b = 15$

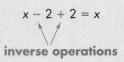

Draw a line from each example in Column A to the property that it illustrates in Column B.

Column A

2. $a = 4$ and $a + b = 5$, so $4 + b = 5$

3. $2 + (x + 8) = 2 + (x + 8)$

4. $x + y = z$ and $z = 4$, so $x + y = 4$

5. $y + 12 = 9$, so $9 = y + 12$

Column B

Reflexive Property

Symmetric Property

Transitive Property

Substitution Property

Key Concepts   Properties of Equality, Continued

Assume a, b, and c represent real numbers.

Property	Definition	Example
Addition	If $a = b$, then $a + c = b + c$.	If $x = 12$, then $x + 3 = 12 + 3$.
Subtraction	If $a = b$, then $a - c = b - c$.	If $x = 12$, then $x - 3 = 12 - 3$.
Multiplication	If $a = b$, then $a \cdot c = b \cdot c$.	If $x = 12$, then $x \cdot 3 = 12 \cdot 3$.
Division	If $a = b$, then $a \div c = b \div c$ (with $c \neq 0$).	If $x = 12$, then $x \div 3 = 12 \div 3$.

Write the Property of Equality that justifies each statement.

6. If $x + 2 = 5$, then $x + 2 - 2 = 5 - 2$.

_____ Property of Equality

7. If $4x = 12$, then $\frac{4x}{4} = \frac{12}{4}$.

_____ Property of Equality

8. If $-20 = \frac{x}{5}$ then $-20 \cdot 5 = \frac{x}{5} \cdot 5$.

_____ Property of Equality

9. If $y - 3 = -12$ then $y - 3 + 3 = -12 + 3$.

_____ Property of Equality

Problem 1   Solving a One-Step Equation

Got It? What is the solution of $12b = 18$?

10. Circle the multiplicative inverse of 12.

$\frac{1}{12}$	-12	$-\frac{1}{12}$	1

11. Use the multiplicative inverse to solve the equation and check your solution.

Lesson 1-4

Problem 2 **Solving a Multi-Step Equation**

Got It? What is the solution of $3(2x - 1) - 2(3x + 4) = 11x$?

12. The equation has been solved below. Use one of the reasons in the box to justify each step.

$$3(2x - 1) - 2(3x + 4) = 11x$$

$$6x - 3 - 6x - 8 = 11x$$

$$-11 = 11x$$

$$-\frac{11}{11} = \frac{11x}{11}$$

$$-1 = x$$

 Problem 3 **Using Properties of Equations to Solve Problems**

Got It? The carpet at the right has perimeter 320 feet. What are the dimensions of the carpet?

13. Let $x = $ the width of the carpet. Then ☐ = length of the carpet.

14. Use the formula for perimeter of a rectangle, $P = 2w + 2\ell$. Write an equation for the perimeter of the carpet.

15. Solve for x.

16. The width of the carpet is ☐ ft, and the length of the carpet is ☐ ft.

 Problem 4 **Equations With No Solutions and Identities**

Got It? Is the equation $7x + 6 - 4x = 12 + 3x - 8$ *always*, *sometimes*, or *never* true?

17. Combine like terms on each side of the equation.

☐ $+ 6 = 3x + $ ☐

18. Now solve the equation.

19. The equation is 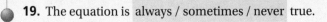 always / sometimes / never true.

Problem 5 **Solving a Literal Equation**

Got It? The equation $S = 3F - 24$ relates shoe size S and length of a foot in inches F. What is F in terms of S?

20. What two operations will you undo?

21. Now solve the equation for F.

Lesson Check • **Do you UNDERSTAND?**

Reasoning Suppose you solve an equation and find that your school needs 4.3 buses for a class trip. Explain how to interpret this solution.

22. Why does the solution 4.3 not make sense as a solution to this problem?

23. What is the minimum number of buses that are needed for the trip? Explain.

Math Success

Check off the vocabulary words that you understand.

☐ equation   ☐ solution   ☐ inverse operations

Rate how well you can *solve equations*.

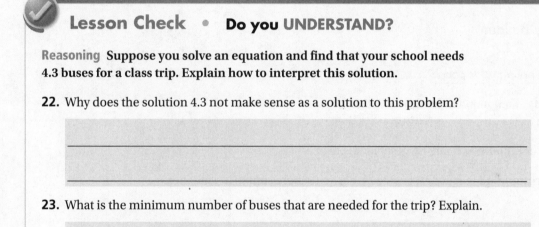

Lesson 1-4

Vocabulary

● Review

1. Write **I** if the math sentence is an *inequality*. Write **E** if it is an *equation*.

_____ $15 > 32x$ _____ $45 < 46$ _____ $-27 \neq 3x$ _____ $17x = 34$

Complete each statement with $<$, $>$, or $=$.

2. $\frac{9}{2}$ ☐ 4   **3.** $5(2 + 3)$ ☐ 27   **4.** $0.\overline{6}$ ☐ $\frac{2}{3}$ **5.** -6 ☐ 4

● Vocabulary Builder

> **compound inequality**
> $x \leq 7$ or $x \geq 5$

compound (noun) KAHM **pound**

Related Words: compound inequality, less than, greater than

Definition: A **compound** is made up of separate parts.

Example: A **compound** inequality is made up of two or more simple inequalities joined by *and* or *or*.

● Use Your Vocabulary

6. A student uses the word *compound* in three different sentences. Place a ✓ next to the sentences that use the word correctly. Place an ✗ next to those that do not.

☐ In chemistry class we learn about various chemical *compounds*.

☐ *Compound* inequalities contain more than one inequality symbol.

☐ To simplify an expression, you can *compound* like terms.

Write an *inequality* for each verbal description.

7. x is at most 25   **8.** x is not equal to 25   **9.** x is greater than 25   **10.** x is less than 25

_____   _____   _____   _____

Problem 1 Writing an Inequality From a Sentence

Got It? What inequality represents the sentence *The quotient of a number and 3 is no more than 15?*

11. Circle the expression that represents the phrase "the quotient of a number and 3."

$$n - 3 \qquad \frac{n}{3} \qquad \frac{3}{n} \qquad 3n$$

12. The symbol $<\,/\,>\,/\,\geq\,/\,\leq$ represents the phrase "no more than".

13. Now write the inequality.

 Problem 2 Solving and Graphing an Inequality

Got It? What is the solution of $-2(x + 9) + 5 \geq 3$? Graph the solution.

14. Solve the inequality for x.

15. Underline the correct word or number to complete each sentence.

The graph includes all numbers less / greater than $-8\,/\,-2\,/\,3\,/\,5\,/\,9\,/\,10$.

The graph will include a closed / an open circle at $-8\,/\,-2\,/\,3\,/\,5\,/\,9\,/\,10$.

16. Graph the solution.

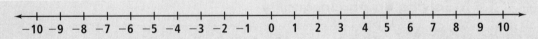

Problem 3 Using an Inequality

Got It? A digital music service offers two subscription plans. The first has a $9 membership fee and charges $1 per download. The second has a $25 membership fee and charges $.50 per download. How many songs must you download for the second plan to cost less than the first plan?

17. Define the variables.

Let ____ = the number of songs downloaded.

Let C_1 = cost of the first plan.

Let C_2 = _____.

Lesson 1-5

Write an algebraic expression to describe the cost of the first plan and the cost of the second plan.

18. $C_1 = \boxed{} + 1 \boxed{}$ **19.** $C_2 = \boxed{} + 0.5 \boxed{}$

20. Write an inequality to represent the situation. Then solve.

21. You must download $\boxed{}$ songs for the second plan to cost less than the first plan.

 Problem 4   No Solution or All Real Numbers as Solution

Got It? Is $4(2x - 3) < 8(x + 1)$ *always*, *sometimes*, or *never* true?

22. Complete the solution.

$4(2x - 3) < 8(x + 1)$ Write the original inequality.

       Distributive Property

       Subtract 8 from each side.

       Subtract $8x$ from each side.

23. The inequality is always / sometimes / never true.

24. Describe the solution set of the inequality.

 Problem 5   Solving an *And* Inequality

Got It? What is the solution of $8 \le 3x - 1$ and $2x < 12$? Graph the solution.

25. Solve each inequality.

26. Graph each inequality.

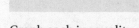

27. Graph the solution set. Then write the solution as a compound inequality.

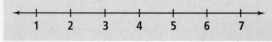

Problem 6 Solving an *Or* Inequality

Got It? What is the solution of $7w + 3 > 11$ or $4w - 1 < -13$? Graph the solution.

28. Cross out the inequality that is NOT a solution to either $7w + 3 > 11$ or $4w - 1 < -13$.

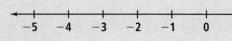

$$w < -3 \qquad\qquad w > 1\tfrac{1}{7} \qquad\qquad w > 1$$

29. Graph the solution.

30. The solution to $7w + 3 > 11$ or $4w - 1 < -13$ is all real numbers

less than ☐ or greater than ☐.

Lesson Check • Do you UNDERSTAND?

Reasoning Make up an example to help explain why you must reverse the inequality symbol when you multiply or divide by a negative number.

Write T for *true* or F for *false*.

____ **31.** $5 > -4$

____ **32.** $(-1)5 > (-1)(-4)$

____ **33.** $\dfrac{5}{-1} < \dfrac{-4}{-1}$

34. Explain what to do to multiply or divide an inequality by a negative number.

Math Success

Check off the vocabulary words that you understand.

☐ compound inequality   ☐ *"and"* inequality   ☐ *"or"* inequality

Rate how well you can *solve and graph inequalities*.

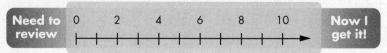

Lesson 1-5

Vocabulary

● **Review**

1. Circle the *solution* of $3x + 8 = -4$.

$x = -9$	$x = -4$	$x = 4$	$x = \frac{4}{3}$

● **Vocabulary Builder**

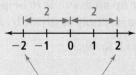

absolute value (noun) AB **suh loot** VAL **yoo**

Definition: The **absolute value** of a real number x is its distance from zero on the number line.

Main Idea: If x is positive, then $|x| = x$. If x is negative, then $|x| = -x$.

Examples: $|5| = 5$, $|-5| = 5$

● **Use Your Vocabulary**

Graph each absolute value on the number line.

2. $|3|$ **3.** $|-2|$ **4.** $-|1|$ **5.** $2|-2|$

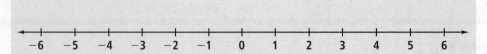

Complete each graph.

6. $|x| = 4$ **7.** $|x| = 5$

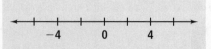   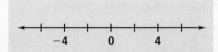

Problem 1 Solving an Absolute Value Equation

Got It? What is the solution of $|3x + 2| = 4$? Graph the solution.

8. Write as two equations.

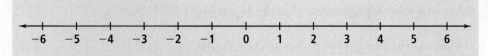

or

9. Complete the steps to find x.

	Write the two equations from Exercise 8.
	Subtract 2 from each side.
	Divide each side by 3.

10. Graph the solution.

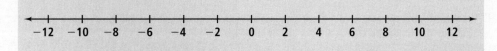

-6 -5 -4 -3 -2 -1 0 1 2 3 4 5 6

 Problem 2 Solving a Multi-Step Absolute Value Equation

Got It? What is the solution of $2|x + 9| + 3 = 7$? Graph the solution.

11. Complete the steps to find x.

$2|x + 9| + 3 = 7$ Write the original equation.

$2|x + 9| = \boxed{}$ Subtract 3 from each side.

$|x + 9| = \boxed{}$ Divide each side by 2.

12. Write as two equations.

     or

13. Solve for x.

	Write the two equations from Exercise 12.
	Subtract 9 from each side.

14. Graph the solution.

-12 -10 -8 -6 -4 -2 0 2 4 6 8 10 12

Lesson 1-6

Problem 3 **Solving for Extraneous Solutions**

Got It? What is the solution of $|5x - 2| = 7x + 14$? Check for extraneous solutions.

15. Solving the equation yields $x = -1$ and $x = -8$. Substitute each value into the original equation.

$$|5 \cdot \boxed{} - 2| = 7 \cdot \boxed{} + 14 \qquad\qquad |5 \cdot \boxed{} - 2| = 7 \cdot \boxed{} + 14$$

$$|\boxed{}| = \boxed{} \qquad\qquad\qquad\qquad |\boxed{}| = \boxed{}$$

16. Which, if any, solutions are extraneous? Explain.

_____

 Problem 4 **Solving the Absolute Value Inequality $|A| < b$**

Got It? What is the solution of $|3x - 4| \le 8$? Graph the solution.

17. The inequality is solved below. Use the justifications to complete each step.

$-8 \le \boxed{} \le 8$ Write the compound inequality.

$\boxed{} \le \boxed{} \le \boxed{}$ Add 4 to each part.

$\boxed{} \le \boxed{} \le \boxed{}$ Divide each part by 3.

18. The endpoints of the graph are $\boxed{}$ and $\boxed{}$.

The endpoints are indicated on the graph with open / closed dots.

19. Now graph the solution.

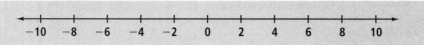

 Problem 5 **Solving the Absolute Value Inequality $|A| \ge b$**

Got It? What is the solution of $|5x + 10| > 15$? Graph the solution.

20. Write the absolute value inequality as a compound inequality.

$5x + 10 < -15$ or 

21. Solve each inequality for x.

22. Now graph the solution.

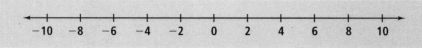

Problem 6 Using an Absolute Value Inequality

Got It? Suppose the smallest allowable height of a racecar is 52 in. and the desirable height is 52.5 in. What absolute value inequality describes heights of a racecar within an indicated tolerance?

23. Find the difference between the desirable height and the smallest allowable height.

$$52.5 - \boxed{} = \boxed{}$$

24. Circle the expression that models the difference between the desirable height and the actual height h.

$$52.0 - h \qquad\qquad 52.5 - h$$

25. Write a compound inequality.

$$-0.5 \leq \boxed{} \leq 0.5$$

26. Rewrite the compound inequality as an absolute value inequality.

$$\left| \boxed{} \right| \leq \boxed{}$$

Lesson Check • Do you UNDERSTAND?

Reasoning When is the absolute value of a number equal to itself?

27. The absolute value of 0 is equal to __?__ .

28. When a number is negative, its absolute value is equal to __?__ .

29. When a number is positive, its absolute value is equal to __?__ .

30. Now answer the question.

Math Success

Check off the vocabulary words that you understand.

☐ absolute value   ☐ graph   ☐ inequality   ☐ equation

Rate how well you can *use absolute value to solve equations and inequalities.*

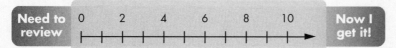

Lesson 1-6

Relations and Functions

Vocabulary

● **Review**

1. For every input of a *function* there is exactly / at least / at most one output.

● **Vocabulary Builder**

relation   (noun)   **ree LAY shun**

Related Words: input, output, domain, range, function

Definition: A **relation** is a set of ordered pairs of input and output values.

Examples: {(0, 1), (2, 3), (0, 4)}, $f(x) = x^2$

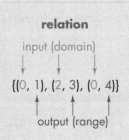

relation

input (domain)

{(0, 1), (2, 3), (0, 4)}

output (range)

● **Use Your Vocabulary**

2. Circle the output values in the *relation*.

{(1, 0),   (−2, 3),   (3, 2),   (5, −4)}

3. Write the domain of the *relation* {(−2, 3), (−2, 1), (5, 4)}.

 Problem 1 **Representing a Relation**

Got It? The average water temperature of the Gulf of Mexico in Key West, Florida varies during the year. In January, the average water temperature is 69° F; in February, 70° F; in March, 75° F; and in April, 78° F. How can you represent this relation in four different ways?

Complete each representation of the relation.

4. Mapping Diagram

Jan. ⟶ 69
Feb. ⟶
Mar. ⟶
Apr. ⟶

5. Ordered Pairs

$\left\{ \Big(\text{Jan., } 69\Big), \Big(\text{Feb., } \Big), \Big(\text{Mar., } \Big), \Big(\text{Apr., } \Big) \right\}$

6. Table

x (Month)	y (°F)
Jan.	69
Feb.	
Mar.	
Apr.	

7. Graph

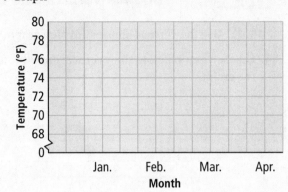

Problem 2 Finding Domain and Range

Got It? What are the domain and range of this relation?

$\{(-3, 14), (0, 7), (2, 0), (9, -18), (23, -99)\}$

8. Complete the reasoning model below.

Think	Write
First, I write the set of x-coordinates.	{ −3, , , , }
Then I write the set of y-coordinates.	{ 14, , , , }

Complete each sentence with the word *domain* or *range*.

9. The set of x-coordinates is the __?__ of the relation.

10. The set of y-coordinates is the __?__ of the relation.

Problem 3 Identifying Functions

Got It? Is the relation a function?

11. Circle the range value(s) that correspond to domain value 2.

−3	−1	3	6

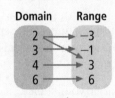

Write T for *true* or F for *false*.

____ **12.** Every element of the input corresponds to exactly one element of the range.

____ **13.** The relation is a function.

Lesson 2-1

 **Problem 4** Using the Vertical-Line Test

Got It? Use the vertical-line test. Which graph(s) represent(s) a function?

14. On each graph below, draw vertical lines through at least five different *x*-values on the graph.

A 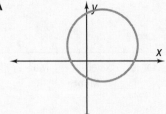 B 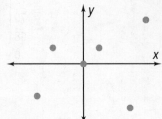 C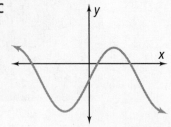

15. Underline the correct word(s) to complete the sentence.

If a vertical line passes through more than one point on a graph, the graph represents / does not represent a function.

16. Cross out each graph that is NOT a function.

Graph A   Graph B   Graph C

 Problem 5 Using Function Notation

Got It? For $f(x) = -4x + 1$, what is $f(-2)$?

17. Circle the given input.

| 2 | −2 | *x* | −*x* |

18. Substitute the input into the function rule and simplify.

$$f\left(\boxed{}\right) = -4\left(\boxed{}\right) + 1$$
$$= \boxed{}$$

 Problem 6 Writing and Evaluating a Function

Got It? You are buying bottles of a sports drink mix for a softball team. Each bottle costs $1.19. What function rule models the total cost of a purchase? Evaluate the function for 15 bottles.

19. Let $c = \underline{\ ?\ }$. Circle your choice.

| cost per bottle | cost of 15 bottles | number of bottles bought | total cost |

20. Then $f(c) = \underline{\ ?\ }$. Circle your choice.

| cost per bottle | cost of 15 bottles | number of bottles bought | total cost |

Chapter 2   28

21. Complete the model to write the function.

Relate | total cost | is | cost per bottle | times | number of bottles bought

Write $f\left(\right)$ = .

22. Now evaluate the function for 15 bottles.

Lesson Check • Do you UNDERSTAND?

Error Analysis Your friend writes, "In a function, every vertical line must intersect the graph in exactly one point." Explain your friend's error and rewrite his statement so that it is correct.

23. Draw a vertical line on each graph that does not intersect the function.

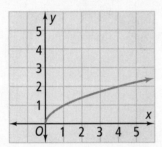 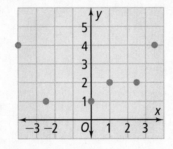 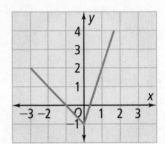

24. Now rewrite your friend's statement.

In a function, a vertical line _?_ .

_____

_____

Math Success

Check off the vocabulary words that you understand.

☐ relation   ☐ function   ☐ domain   ☐ range

Rate how well you can *represent and interpret functions.*

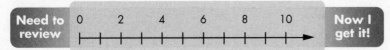

Vocabulary

Review

1. Cross out the *ratio* that is NOT equal to the others.

$$\frac{3.5}{1} \qquad \frac{7}{2} \qquad \frac{10.5}{3} \qquad \frac{9}{4}$$

Solve each *proportion*.

2. $\frac{3}{2} = \frac{9}{x}$

$x =$ ⬚

3. $\frac{x}{3} = \frac{16}{12}$

$x =$ ⬚

4. $\frac{x}{2} = \frac{5}{7}$

$x =$ ⬚

5. $\frac{2}{9} = \frac{x}{18}$

$x =$ ⬚

Vocabulary Builder

direct (adjective) **duh** REKT

Other Word Forms: directly (adverb), directions (plural noun)

Main Idea: **Direct** describes two quantities that vary in the same way: increasing together or decreasing together.

Definition: Something that is **direct** is proceeding from one point to another, in time or space, without interruption.

Use Your Vocabulary

Choose the correct word from the list to complete each sentence.

directly   direct   directions

6. Tomás gave the visitor __?__ to the stadium.

7. The fans went __?__ to their seats.

8. There was a __?__ connection between the team's scoring and the fans' cheering.

Problem 1 Identifying Direct Variation From Tables

Got It? For the table at the right, determine whether y varies directly with x.
If so, what are the constant of variation and the function rule?

x	3	2	1
y	−21	−14	−7

9. Write the ratio of the input-output pairs in simplest form.

Input-Output Pair	(3, −21)	(2, −14)	(1, −7)
Ratio	$\frac{-21}{3} = \boxed{}$	$\frac{}{2} = \boxed{}$	$\frac{}{} = \boxed{}$

10. Underline the correct word(s) to complete the sentence.

Since the ratio $\frac{y}{x}$ is / is not the same for all of the input-output pairs,

the function is / is not a direct variation.

11. If possible, identify the constant of variation and write a function rule.

$k = \boxed{}$ $\qquad\qquad\qquad\qquad$ $y = \boxed{}\, x$

 Problem 2 Identifying Direct Variation From Equations

Got It? For the function $5x + 3y = 0$, determine whether y varies directly with x.
If so, what is the constant of variation?

12. Solve the equation for y.

13. Circle the constant of variation.

$\qquad\qquad -\frac{5}{3} \qquad\qquad \frac{3}{5} \qquad\qquad \frac{5}{3} \qquad\qquad$ None

 Problem 3 Using a Proportion to Solve a Direct Variation

Got It? Suppose y varies directly with x, and $y = 15$ when $x = 3$.
What is y when $x = 12$?

14. Complete the proportion below.

$\dfrac{\boxed{}}{\boxed{}} = \dfrac{y}{\boxed{}}$

15. Simplify the proportion you wrote in Exercise 14.

16. When $x = 12$, the value of y is $\boxed{}$.

Lesson 2-2

Problem 4 Using a Proportion to Solve a Problem

Got It? The number of Calories varies directly with the mass of cheese. If 50 grams of cheese contain 200 Calories, how many Calories are in 70 grams of cheese?

17. Complete the model below. Let c = Calories.

Relate | the ratio of 200 Calories to 50 grams | is the same as | the ratio of c Calories to 70 grams

Write $\dfrac{200}{}$ = $\dfrac{}{}$

18. Solve the proportion for c.

19. There are about _____ Calories in 70 grams of cheese.

 Problem 5 Graphing Direct Variation Equations

Got It? What is the graph of the direct variation equation $y = -\frac{2}{3}x$?

20. Complete the table.

x	−3	0	3
y			

21. Graph the direct variation.

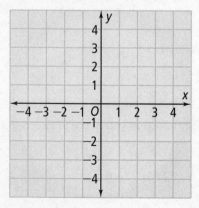

Lesson Check • Do you UNDERSTAND?

Reasoning Explain why the graph of a direct variation function always passes through the origin.

22. Write *direct variation* if the graph is a direct variation. Write *linear* if the graph is a linear function that is not a direct variation.

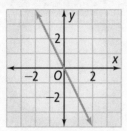   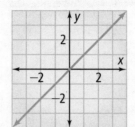   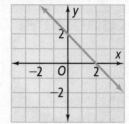

_____   _____   _____

23. Write **D** if the equation describes a direct variation. Write **L** if the equation describes a linear function that is not a direct variation.

_____ $y = -2x$ _____ $y = x$ _____ $y = -x + 2$

24. Circle the true statement.

A linear function is always a direct variation.   A direct variation is always a linear function.

25. Write the direct variation equation of a function with constant of variation k.

26. Evaluate the function you wrote in Exercise 25 for $x = 0$.

27. Why does the graph of a direct variation function always pass through the origin?

_____

Math Success

Check off the vocabulary words that you understand.

☐ direct variation   ☐ constant of variation

Rate how well you can *identify and use direct variation functions.*

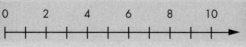

2-3 Linear Functions and Slope-Intercept Form

Vocabulary

● Review

1. Circle the relation that is also a *function*.

$\{(0, 1), (-1, 3), (0, 4)\}$

x	y
2	5
3	3
4	1

Input | Output
-2 → 4
3 → 7
→ 0

● Vocabulary Builder

slope (noun) slohp

$$\text{slope} = \frac{\text{rise}}{\text{run}}$$

Definition: **Slope** is the ratio of the vertical change to the horizontal change between two points.

Main Idea: **Slope** describes the steepness of a line in the coordinate plane.

Example: The **slope** of a hill is its steepness.

● Use Your Vocabulary

2. Use the graph at the right. Draw a line from the *slope* in Column A to the line with that slope in Column B.

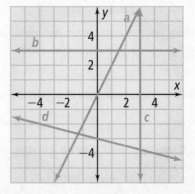

Column A	Column B
positive	line *a*
negative	line *b*
zero	line *c*
undefined	line *d*

Key Concept   Slope

The **slope** of a non-vertical line is the ratio of the vertical change to a corresponding horizontal change.

$$\text{slope} = \frac{\text{vertical change (rise)}}{\text{horizontal change (run)}} = \frac{y_2 - y_1}{x_2 - x_1}, \text{ where } x_2 - x_1 \neq 0$$

Underline the correct word to complete each sentence.

3. If x_1 is less than x_2, and y_1 is less than y_2, then the slope is positive / negative .

4. If x_1 is less than x_2, and y_1 is greater than y_2, then the slope is positive / negative .

Problem 1   Finding Slope

Got It? What is the slope of the line that passes through the points (5, 4) and (8, 1)?

5. Let $x_1 = 5$ and $x_2 = 8$. Then $y_1 = \boxed{}$ and $y_2 = \boxed{}$.

6. Complete the model below to find the slope.

$$\text{slope} = \frac{\underline{\qquad}\text{ change}}{\underline{\qquad}\text{ change}} = \frac{\boxed{}_2 - y_1}{\boxed{}_2 - x_1}$$

$$= \frac{1 - \boxed{}}{\boxed{} - \boxed{}} = \boxed{}$$

7. The slope of the line through the points (5, 4) and (8, 1) is $\boxed{}$.

Summary   Slope of a Line

8. Label each graph *positive*, *negative*, *zero*, or *undefined* slope.

Horizontal line

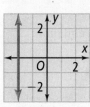
Vertical line

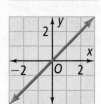
Line rises from left to right

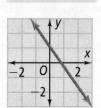
Line falls from left to right

Underline the correct word to complete each sentence.

9. A line that has *zero slope* is horizontal / vertical .

10. A line that has *undefined slope* is horizontal / vertical .

Lesson 2-3

Key Concept Slope-Intercept Form

The **slope-intercept form** of an equation of a line is $y = mx + b$, where m is the slope of the line and $(0, b)$ is the y-intercept.

11. Place a ✓ in the box if the equation is in slope-intercept form. Place an ✗ if it is not.

$\quad\square\quad y = 3x + 7$ $\qquad\qquad\square\quad 8y = x - 11$ $\qquad\qquad\square\quad y = x$

12. The slope of the line with equation $y = 4x + 2$ is $\square$.

13. The y-intercept of the line with equation $y = -2x - 3$ is $\left(0, \boxed{}\right)$.

14. Circle the graph that can be represented by the equation $y = -2x + 3$.

  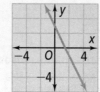

✓ **Problem 2** **Writing Linear Equations**

Got It? What is the equation of the line with $m = 6$ and y-intercept $(0, 5)$?

15. Write a phrase to describe each constant value.

$m = $ _____ , $b = $ _____

16. The equation of the line in slope-intercept form is _____ .

✓ **Problem 3** **Writing Equations in Slope-Intercept Form**

Got It? Write the equation $3x + 2y = 18$ in slope-intercept form. What are the slope and y-intercept?

17. Use the justifications at the right to solve the equation for y.

$3x + 2y = 18$ $\qquad\qquad$ Write the original equation.

$2y = 18 - \square$ $\qquad\qquad$ Subtract $\square$ from each side.

$y = \dfrac{18 - \square}{\square}$ $\qquad\qquad$ Divide each side by $\square$.

$y = 9 - \square\, x$ $\qquad\qquad$ Simplify.

18. In slope-intercept form, the equation is $y = \boxed{}$.

19. The slope is $\boxed{}$, and the y-intercept is $\boxed{}$.

Problem 4 Graphing a Linear Equation

Got It? What is the graph of $4x - 7y = 14$?

20. Write the equation in slope-intercept form.

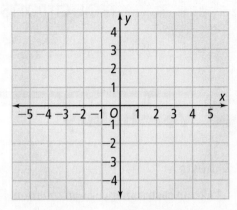

21. Graph the function on the coordinate plane at the right.

 Lesson Check • **Do you UNDERSTAND?**

Explain why the slope of a vertical line is called "undefined."

22. Cross out the points below that are NOT on the line at the right.

$(0, 4)$ $(4, 1)$ $(3, 4)$ $(4, -3)$

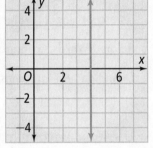

23. Find the slope of the line at the right.

$$ m = \frac{y_2 - y_1}{x_2 - x_1} = \frac{\boxed{} - \left(\boxed{}\right)}{\boxed{} - \boxed{}} = \frac{\boxed{}}{\boxed{}} $$

24. The x-coordinate of all of the points on this line is $\boxed{}$.

The difference $x_2 - x_1$ always equals $\boxed{}$ for this line.

25. Now explain why the slope of a vertical line is undefined.

_____

_____

Math Success

Check off the vocabulary words that you understand.

☐ linear function   ☐ slope-intercept form

Rate how well you can *write and graph equations of lines.*

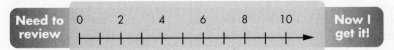

Lesson 2-3

2-4 More About Linear Equations

Vocabulary

● Review

1. Write each sentence as an *equation*.

The sum of *x* and *y* is eight.   The product of *p* and *q* is seven.   The square root of *y*, cubed, is two.

● Vocabulary Builder

intercept (noun) IN **tur sept**

Related Words: *x*-intercept, *y*-intercept

Definition: An **intercept** of a line is a point where the line crosses an axis.

intercepts

● Use Your Vocabulary

Use the graph at the right. Write T for *true* or F for *false*.

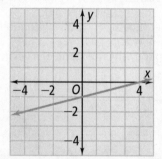

_____ **2.** The *x*-intercept of the line is (4, 0).

_____ **3.** The *x*-intercept of the line is (0, 4).

_____ **4.** The *y*-intercept of the line is (−1, 0).

_____ **5.** The *y*-intercept of the line is (0, −1).

---

take note

Concept Summary   Writing Equations of Lines

Slope-Intercept Form	Point-Slope Form	Standard Form
$y = mx + b$	$y - y_1 = m(x - x_1)$	$Ax + By = C$
Use this form when you know the slope and the *y*-intercept.	Use this form when you know the slope and a point, or when you know two points.	*A*, *B*, and *C* are real numbers. *A* and *B* cannot both be zero.

6. Write **I** if the equation is in *slope-intercept form,* **P** if it is in *point-slope form,* or **S** if it is in *standard form.*

_____ $r = 5s + 7$ _____ $8m + 6n = 2$ _____ $y - 3 = x - 1$ _____ $p = q + 9$

 Problem 1 **Writing an Equation Given a Point and the Slope**

Got It? What is an equation of the line through $(-7, 1)$ with slope -3?

7. Complete the model to write the equation in point-slope form.

Point-Slope Form $\left(y - \boxed{y_1} \right) = \boxed{m} \cdot \left(x - \boxed{x_1} \right)$

Write $\left(y - \boxed{} \right) = \boxed{} \cdot \left(x - \boxed{} \right)$

8. Now write the equation.

 Problem 2 **Writing an Equation Given Two Points**

Got It? A line passes through $(-5, 0)$ and $(0, 7)$. What is an equation of the line in point-slope form?

9. Circle the slope of the line through the points $(-5, 0)$ and $(0, 7)$.

$\dfrac{-7}{5}$ $\dfrac{5}{-7}$ $\dfrac{5}{7}$ $\dfrac{7}{5}$

10. Now write the equation of the line in point-slope form.

 Problem 3 **Writing an Equation in Standard Form**

Got It? What is an equation of the line $y = 9.1x + 3.6$ in standard form?

11. **Error Analysis** Karina made two errors while writing $y = 9.1x + 3.6$ in standard form without decimals. What are Karina's errors? Explain how to correct them.

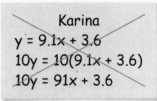

Karina
$y = 9.1x + 3.6$
$10y = 10(9.1x + 3.6)$
$10y = 91x + 3.6$

Lesson 2-4

12. Now write the equation in standard form.

 Problem 4 Graphing an Equation Using Intercepts

Got It? What are the intercepts of $2x - 4y = 8$?

13. Find each intercept.

$2x - 4y = 8$ ⟵ Write the original equation. ⟶ ⬚ = ⬚

$2x - 4 \cdot$ ⬚ $= 8$ ⟵ Substitute 0 for the variable. ⟶ $2 \cdot$ ⬚ $- 4y = 8$

$2x =$ ⬚ ⟵ Simplify. ⟶ ⬚ $= 8$

$x =$ ⬚ ⟵ Simplify. ⟶ $y =$ ⬚

14. Now plot the intercepts and draw the line.

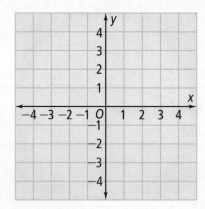

 Problem 5 Drawing and Interpreting a Linear Graph

Got It? The office manager of a small office ordered 140 packs of printer paper. Based on average daily use, she knows that the paper will last about 80 days. What graph represents this situation?

15. Complete the table of values.

Days	Packs of Printer Paper Used
0	⬚
⬚	140

16. Graph the situation. Label the graph.

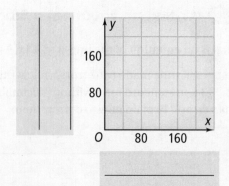

Problem 6 **Writing Equations of Parallel and Perpendicular Lines**

Got It? What is the equation, in slope-intercept form, of the line through $(-4, 2)$ and parallel to $4x + 2y = 7$?

17. Circle the slope of the line $4x + 2y = 7$.

| $-\dfrac{7}{2}$ | -2 | 2 | $\dfrac{7}{2}$ |

18. Circle the form you will use to write the equation.

Slope-Intercept Form	Point-Slope Form	Standard Form
$y = mx + b$	$y - y_1 = m(x - x_1)$	$Ax + By = C$

19. Now write and simplify the equation.

Lesson Check • **Do you UNDERSTAND?**

If the intercepts of a line are $(a, 0)$ and $(0, b)$, what is the slope of the line?

20. Use the points to calculate the slope.

$$\text{slope} = \frac{y_2 - y_1}{x_2 - x_1} = \frac{\left(b - \boxed{}\right)}{\left(0 - \boxed{}\right)} = \frac{\boxed{}}{\boxed{}}$$

21. The slope of the line through $(a, 0)$ and $(0, b)$ is $\boxed{}$.

Math Success

Check off the vocabulary words that you understand.

☐ point-slope form   ☐ slope-intercept form   ☐ standard form

Rate how well you can *write forms of linear equations*.

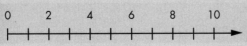

Need to review 0 2 4 6 8 10 Now I get it!

Lesson 2-4

2-5 Using Linear Models

Vocabulary

● **Review**

1. Circle the set(s) of data that you can model with a *linear* function.

3, 6, 9, 12, . . .   birthdays of your classmates   amount of rain each day of the week

2. Cross out the graphs that do NOT show a *linear* function.

     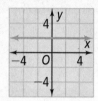   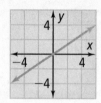   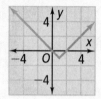

● **Vocabulary Builder**

correlation   (noun) **kawr uh LAY shun**

Related Words: correspond, relate, correlation coefficient

Definition: A **correlation** is a relationship between two sets of data points.

● **Use Your Vocabulary**

Choose the *correlation* that most closely represents each situation below. Write the letter of your choice in the box. Use each letter once.

A   **B**   **C**
Positive   Negative   No
Correlation   Correlation   Correlation

3. the age of a used car and the car's value

4. the color of your hair and the weather in Venezuela

5. the number of hours you work at an after-school job and the amount of your paycheck

Problem 1 Using a Scatter Plot

Got It? The table shows the number of hours students spent online the day before a test, and the scores on the test. Make a scatter plot. How would you describe the correlation?

Computer Use and Test Scores											
Number of Hours Online	0	0	1	1	1.5	1.75	2	2	3	4	4.5	5
Test Score	100	94	98	88	92	89	75	70	78	72	57	60

6. Plot the data pairs on the coordinate plane at the right. Label the graph.

7. Place a ✔ in the box if the statement is correct. Place an ✘ if it is incorrect.

   ☐ The data pairs are tightly clustered around a line.

   ☐ As online time increases, test scores increase.

8. Underline the correct word(s) to complete the sentence.

   There is a strong positive / weak positive / strong negative correlation between hours online and test scores.

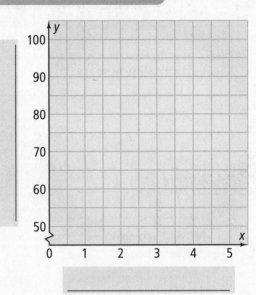

Problem 2 Writing the Equation of a Trend Line

Got It? The table shows median home prices in California. What is an equation for a trend line that models the relationship between time and home prices?

California Median Home Prices							
Year	1940	1950	1960	1970	1980	1990	2000
Median Price ($)	36,700	57,900	74,400	88,700	167,300	249,800	211,500

9. Graph the data on the coordinate plane at the right. (*Hint*: Use 0 to represent 1940.)

10. Choose two data points on the graph through which to draw a trend line. About half of the points should be above the line and about half should be below it.

   Point 1

   Point 2

11. Draw the trend line on the graph.

California Median Home Prices

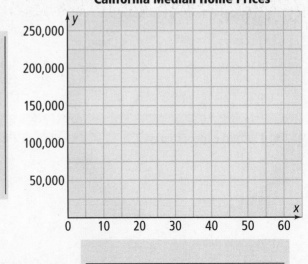

Lesson 2-5

12. Now write an equation for the line in point-slope form.

 Problem 3 **Finding the Line of Best Fit**

Got It? The table lists the cost of 2% milk. Use a table to find the equation of the line of best fit. Based on your linear model, how much would you expect to pay for a gallon of 2% milk in 2025?

Cost of 2% Milk						
Year	1998	2000	2002	2004	2006	2008
Average cost for one gallon ($)	2.56	2.82	2.89	2.93	3.11	3.67

13. Use the information in the table and the STAT screen below to complete each sentence.

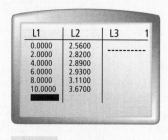

_____ is year 0.

2025 is year _____ .

14. Use the LinReg screen below to write an equation for the line of best fit. Round to the nearest hundredth if necessary.

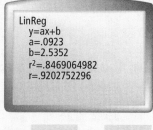

$y = $ _____ $x + $ _____

15. Use your equation from Exercise 14 to estimate how much you will pay for a gallon of 2% milk in 2025.

16. I would expect to pay _____ for a gallon of 2% milk in the year 2025.

Lesson Check • Do you UNDERSTAND?

Compare and Contrast What is the difference between a positive correlation and a negative correlation? How might you relate positive correlation with direct variation?

17. Use the situations in the box at the right. Write each situation in the correct oval.

Positive Correlations   **Negative Correlations**

- As the value of one variable increases, the other decreases.
- As the value of one variable increases, the other increases.
- Example: As absences increase, test scores decrease.
- Example: As study time increases, test scores increase.
- Data points are clustered around a trend line with negative slope.
- Data points are clustered around a trend line with positive slope.

18. Underline the correct words to complete each sentence.

The equation of a trend line showing direct variation will look like $y = kx$.

If there is a positive correlation, k will be positive / negative , and if there is

a negative correlation, k will be positive / negative .

Math Success

Check off the vocabulary words that you understand.

☐ scatter plot   ☐ correlation   ☐ line of best fit   ☐ correlation coefficient

Rate how well you can make a scatter plot.

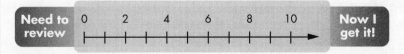

Need to review   0   2   4   6   8   10   Now I get it!

Families of Functions

Vocabulary

● Review

1. Cross out the item(s) that are NOT *vertical*.

| the *y*-axis | the *x*-axis | the horizon | columns | rows |

● Vocabulary Builder

translation (noun) **trans LAY shun**

Other Word Forms: translate (verb), translatable (adjective), translation (noun)

Definition: A **translation** is a change from one form, state, or appearance to another.

Math Usage: A **translation** shifts the graph of a parent function horizontally, vertically, or both without changing its size or shape.

● Use Your Vocabulary

2. Complete each statement with the correct form of the word *translation*.

NOUN The graph shows a vertical __?__ of the function.

ADJECTIVE The toddler's language was not __?__ .

VERB The Spanish teacher helped the town mayor __?__ the letter.

3. Complete the graphic organizer below.

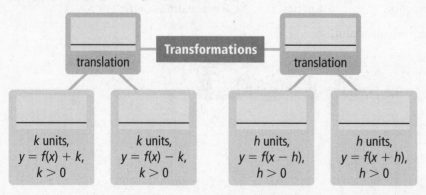

Problem 1 Vertical Translation

Got It? How are the functions $y = 2x$ and $y = 2x - 3$ related? How are their graphs related?

4. Complete the table of values.

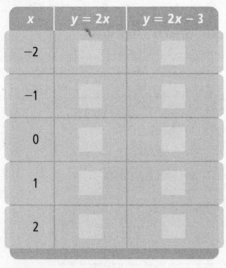

x	y = 2x	y = 2x − 3
−2		
−1		
0		
1		
2		

5. Draw the graphs on the coordinate plane below.

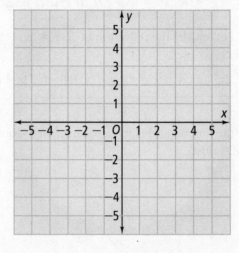

6. Write T for *true* or F for *false*.

_____ Each output value for $y = 2x - 3$ is three less than the corresponding output value for $y = 2x$.

_____ The graph of $y = 2x - 3$ is the graph of $y = 2x$ stretched vertically two units.

_____ The graph of $y = 2x - 3$ is the graph of $y = 2x$ translated down three units.

_____ The graphs of $y = 2x - 3$ and $y = 2x$ are parallel.

Problem 2 Horizontal Translation

Got It? The graph shows the projected altitude $f(x)$ of an airplane scheduled to depart an airport at noon. If the plane leaves 30 minutes early, what function represents this transformation?

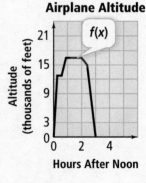

Airplane Altitude

7. Circle the graph below that shows the plane leaving 30 minutes early.

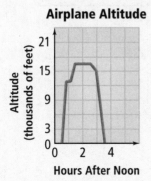

Airplane Altitude

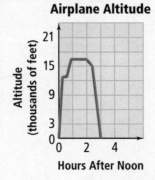

Airplane Altitude

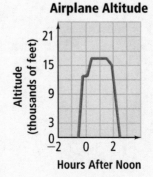

Airplane Altitude

Lesson 2-6

8. Circle the function that represents this transformation.

$$f(x + 30) \qquad f(x - 30) \qquad f\left(x + \tfrac{1}{2}\right) \qquad f\left(x - \tfrac{1}{2}\right)$$

 Problem 3 Reflecting a Function Algebraically

Got It? Let $h(x)$ be the reflection of $f(x) = 3x + 3$ in the x-axis. What is a function rule for $h(x)$?

9. Circle the function that shows $f(x)$ reflected in the x-axis.

$$f(-x) \qquad\qquad -f(x)$$

10. Write the function rule for $h(x)$ below. Then graph $h(x)$ and $f(x)$ to check the reflection.

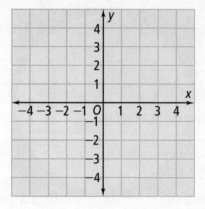

 Problem 4 Stretch and Compression

Got It? For the function $f(x)$ in the table below, what are the corresponding table and graph for the transformation $h(x) = \tfrac{1}{3}f(x)$?

11. Complete the table of output values.

x	f(x)	h(x)
−5	2	$\frac{2}{3}$
−2	2	
0	−3	
3	1	
5	−2	

12. Graph $h(x)$ on the coordinate plane below.

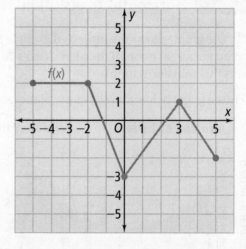

Got It? The function $f(x) = x$. The graph of $g(x)$ is $f(x)$ stretched vertically by a factor of 2 and translated down 3 units. What is the function rule for $g(x)$?

13. Underline the correct word or expression to complete each sentence.

    The function $f(x) = x$ stretched vertically by a factor of 2 is

    $x + 2 \,/\, x - 2 \,/\, 2x \,/\, -2x$.

    The function $f(x) = x$ stretched vertically by a factor of 2 and then translated down 3 units is $-2x + 3 \,/\, 2x - 3 \,/\, -2x - 3 \,/\, 2x + 3$.

14. The function rule for the combined transformation is   .

Lesson Check • Do you UNDERSTAND?

Compare and Contrast The graph below shows $f(x) = 0.5x - 1$. Graph $g(x)$ by translating $f(x)$ up 2 units and then stretching it vertically by a factor of 2. Graph $h(x)$ by stretching $f(x)$ by a factor of 2 and then translating it up 2 units. Compare the graphs of $g(x)$ and $h(x)$.

15. Graph $g(x)$ and $h(x)$.

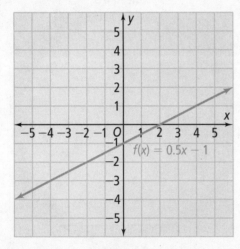

16. Underline the correct word(s) or expression to complete each sentence or equation.

    $g(x)$ and $h(x)$ are / are not the same function.

    $g(x) = x + 2 \,/\, x - 2 \,/\, x \,/\, -x$

    $h(x) = x + 2 \,/\, x - 2 \,/\, x \,/\, -x$

    $g(x)$ and $h(x)$ are

    the same / parallel / perpendicular lines.

Math Success

Check off the vocabulary words that you understand.

☐ translation ☐ reflection ☐ transformation ☐ stretch ☐ compression

Rate how well you can *transform linear functions*.

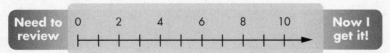

2-7 Absolute Value Functions and Graphs

Vocabulary

● Review

Simplify each *absolute value* expression.

1. $|3(5 - 7)| = $ ☐ **2.** $-|-8| = $ ☐ **3.** $|4| - |9| = $ ☐ **4.** $|2 - |5|| = $ ☐

5. Absolute values are always negative / non-negative / zero .

● Vocabulary Builder

symmetry (noun) SIM **uh tree**

Related Words: axis of symmetry, symmetrical, symmetric

Definition: **Symmetry** is a correspondence in size, shape, and relative position of parts on opposite sides of an axis of symmetry.

Math Usage: The graph of $y = |x|$ is a mirror image of itself over its *axis of* **symmetry**, $x = 0$.

The Ms in
**SYMMETRY are
symmetric.**

SYMMETRY

● Use Your Vocabulary

6. Draw a line of *symmetry* through each figure.

  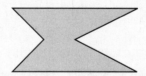

7. Cross out the graph that does NOT show *symmetry* around the *y*-axis.

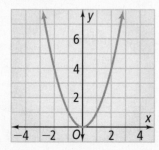 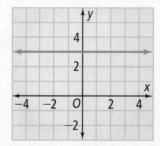 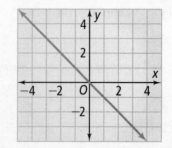

Problem 1 Graphing an Absolute Value Function

Got It? What is the graph of the function $y = |x| + 2$? How is this graph different from the parent function $f(x) = |x|$?

8. Complete the table of values.

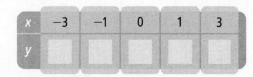

x	−3	−1	0	1	3
y					

9. Use the table from Exercise 8. Circle the graph of $y = |x| + 2$.

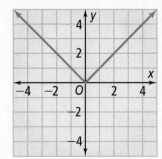 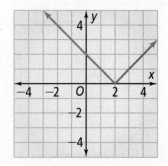 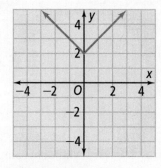

10. Describe how the graph of $y = |x| + 2$ differs from the graph of the parent function.

---

take note

Key Concept The Family of Absolute Value Functions

Parent Function $y = |x|$

Vertical Translation

Translation up k units, $k > 0$
$$y = |x| + k$$

Translation down k units, $k > 0$
$$y = |x| - k$$

Horizontal Translation

Translation right h units, $h > 0$
$$y = |x - h|$$

Translation left h units, $h > 0$
$$y = |x + h|$$

Vertical Stretch and Compression

Vertical stretch, $a > 0$
$$y = a|x|$$

Vertical compression, $0 < a < 1$
$$y = a|x|$$

Reflection

In the x-axis
$$y = -|x|$$

In the y-axis
$$y = |-x|$$

11. Place a ✓ in the box if the statement describes a transformation of the parent function $y = |x|$ for $g(x) = -\frac{1}{3}|x + 5| + 2$. Place an ✗ if it does not.

☐ translation right 5 units ☐ translation left 5 units ☐ compression by a factor of $\frac{1}{3}$

☐ reflection in the x-axis ☐ translation up 2 units ☐ reflection in the y-axis

Lesson 2-7

Got It? What is the graph of the function $y = 2|x|$?

12. Complete the table of values.

x	y
−2	
−1	
0	
1	
2	

13. Plot the points and connect them.

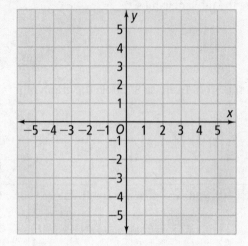

14. Error Analysis A student compares the shapes of the graphs of $y = |x| + 2$ and $y = 2|x|$. She concludes that when a graph is compressed, the value of its slope increases. Explain her error.

Got It? What are the vertex, axis of symmetry, and transformations of the function $y = -2|x - 1| - 3$?

15. Compare $y = -2|x - 1| - 3$ with the general form $y = a|x - h| + k$. Write the values of a, h, and k.

$a = $ ⬚ $h = $ ⬚ $k = $ ⬚

Underline the correct equation, point, value, or word to complete each sentence.

16. In the function $y = -2|x - 1| - 3$, the vertex is $(1, 3) / (0, 0) / (1, -3)$.

17. The axis of symmetry is $y = 1 / x = 0 / y = -3 / x = 1$.

18. The function is translated $1 / 2 / 3$ unit(s) to the right and $1 / 2 / 3$ unit(s) up / down.

19. The function is stretched / compressed by a factor of $1 / 2 / -2$ and reflected across the x-axis / y-axis.

Problem 5 Writing an Absolute Value Function

Got It? What is the equation of the absolute value function?

20. Complete the model to write the equation.

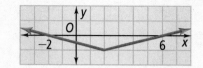

1 Identify the stretch or compression.

$a =$

↓

2 Identify the vertex.

$(h, k) = \left(\quad , \quad\right)$

↓

3 Substitute the values of a, h, and k into the general form, $y = a\,|x - h| + k$.

$y = \quad |x - \quad| +$

21. The equation of the absolute value function is

 ## Lesson Check • Do you UNDERSTAND?

Is it true that, without making a graph of an absolute value function, you can describe its position on a graph? Explain with an example.

Circle each function.

22. The function $y = |x|$ reflected across the x-axis.

$y = -|x|$ $\qquad$ $y = |-x|$ $\qquad$ $y = |x| - 1$ $\qquad$ $-y = -|x|$

23. The function $y = |x|$ translated 3 units to the left and 2 units up.

$y = |x - 2| + 3$ $\quad$ $y = |x + 2| - 3$ $\quad$ $y = |x + 3| + 2$ $\quad$ $y = |x - 3| - 2$

 ## Math Success

Check off the vocabulary words that you understand.

☐ absolute value function $\qquad$ ☐ axis of symmetry $\qquad$ ☐ vertex

Rate how well you can *graph absolute value functions*.

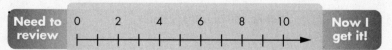

Need to review $\quad$ 0 $\quad$ 2 $\quad$ 4 $\quad$ 6 $\quad$ 8 $\quad$ 10 $\quad$ Now I get it!

Lesson 2-7

Vocabulary

● Review

1. Circle each *inequality*.

$$15 < 32 \qquad 45 < 46 \qquad -27 \neq 3x \qquad 17x = 34$$

Complete each *inequality* with **<** or **>**.

2. -2 ☐ 1 **3.** 0.05 ☐ 0.5 **4.** $\dfrac{8}{6}$ ☐ $\dfrac{16}{6}$ **5.** $2\dfrac{2}{5}$ ☐ $\dfrac{7}{4}$

● Vocabulary Builder

boundary (noun) BOWN dree

Math Usage: A **boundary** is the line that separates the coordinate plane into two half-planes, one of which consists of the solutions of an inequality.

Example: $y = 2x + 1$ is the **boundary** of $y \leq 2x + 4$.

● Use Your Vocabulary

6. Circle the inequalities that have a dashed *boundary line*. Underline the inequalities that have a solid *boundary line*.

$$y < 3x \qquad 2y - 3x \leq 9 \qquad 4y \geq x - 1 \qquad y > -5x + 4$$

Problem 1   **Graphing a Linear Inequality**

Got It? What is the graph of the inequality $y \geq -2x + 1$?

Underline the correct word(s) to complete each sentence.

7. The boundary line of the graph is a   solid / dashed   line.

8. The test point $(0, 0)$ satisfies / does not satisfy   the inequality.

9. The graph of the solution should be shaded   above / below   the boundary line.

10. Graph the inequality.

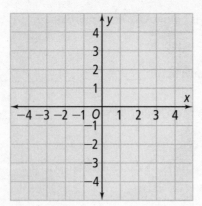

 Problem 2 Using a Linear Inequality

Got It? The sign shows the number of tickets needed for small or large rides at the fair. You would like to get on both types of rides. You can buy 60 tickets with $15. You decide to spend no more than $30 for tickets. What are the possible combinations of small and large rides that you can take? Use a graph to find your answer.

> **Tickets to Ride**
>
> Small Rides
> 3 Tickets
>
> Large Rides
> 5 Tickets

11. Circle the greatest number of tickets you can buy with $30.

| 30 | 60 | 120 |

12. Circle the symbol that represents *no more than*.

$<$ $>$ $\leq$ $\geq$

13. Complete the model below.

Relate   the number of tickets for small rides   plus   the number of tickets for large rides   is no more than   120

Define   Let x = the number of tickets for small rides.

Let y = _____

Write x + y $\leq$ 120

14. Graph the inequality that represents the combinations of rides.

Tickets to Ride

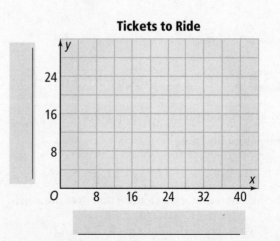

Lesson 2-8

15. Complete the sentence with the words below. Use each word once.

combinations   shaded   whole

All points with __?__ number coordinates in the __?__

region represent possible __?__ of small and large rides.

Problem 3 Graphing an Absolute Value Inequality

Got It? What is the graph of $y - 4 \geq 2|x - 1|$?

16. Complete the reasoning model at the right.

Think	Write
I need to solve the inequality for *y*.	$y = $
Now I can compare the boundary line of the inequality with the parent function.	The boundary line is narrower. It is shifted ☐ unit right and ☐ units up.
I need to pick a test point to decide which half of the plane to shade.	Point (1, 5) is / is not a solution of the inequality. Shade above / below the boundary line.

17. Graph the absolute value inequality $y - 4 \geq 2|x - 1|$.

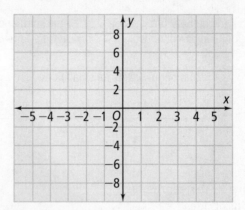

Problem 4 Writing an Inequality Based on a Graph

Got It? What inequality does this graph represent?

18. Circle the parent function.

$y = |x|$ $y = -|x|$

19. Circle the function that shows a reflection over the *x*-axis.

$y = |x|$ $y = -|x|$

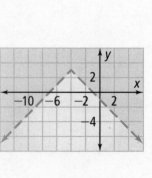

20. Underline the correct word(s) to complete each sentence.

The graph is / is not stretched.

The graph is / is not compressed.

21. Circle the function rule that completes the sentence.

Transformations of the parent function are shown by __?__.

$$f(x) = -a|x + h| + k \qquad f(x) = a|x - h| + k \qquad f(x) = -a|x - h| - k$$

22. The vertex of the function is $(-4, 3)$. Choose from the words *left of, right of, up from,* or *down from* to complete each description.

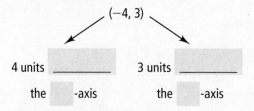

4 units _____   3 units _____

the ☐ -axis   the ☐ -axis

23. Use your answers to Exercises 18–22 to write the function.

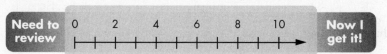

Lesson Check • Do you UNDERSTAND?

Reasoning Is the ordered pair $\left(\frac{3}{4}, 0\right)$ a solution of $3x + y > 3$? Explain.

Underline the word(s) or number(s) to complete each sentence.

24. The value of $3x + y$ when $x = \frac{3}{4}$ and $y = 0$ is $\frac{6}{4} / \frac{9}{4} / \frac{9}{12}$.

25. Substituting $\left(\frac{3}{4}, 0\right)$ into $3x + y > 3$ results / does not result in a true inequality.

26. The ordered pair $\left(\frac{3}{4}, 0\right)$ is / is not a solution of $3x + y > 3$.

Math Success

Check off the vocabulary words that you understand.

☐ absolute value inequality ☐ linear inequality ☐ boundary

Rate how well you can *graph two-variable inequalities.*

Need to review 0 2 4 6 8 10 Now I get it!

Lesson 2-8

Vocabulary

● Review

1. Cross out the equation that is NOT in *slope-intercept* form.

$$y = -\frac{1}{7}x \qquad r = s \qquad a = \sqrt{3}b + 5 \qquad 3x + 7y = 13$$

● Vocabulary Builder

linear system (noun) LIN ee ur SIS tum

Related Words: independent system, dependent system

Definition: A **linear system** is a collection of linear equations involving the same set of variables. The system above is two equations in two variables.

> **linear system**
> $5x + 7y = 1$
> $4x - y = 9$

● Use Your Vocabulary

The graphs below show the possible types of solutions for a system of two equations in two variables. Write T for *true* or F for *false*.

Intersecting Lines	**Coinciding Lines**	**Parallel Lines**
		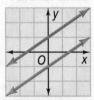
one solution Consistent Independent	infinitely many solutions Consistent Dependent	no solution Inconsistent

_____ **2.** Inconsistent *linear systems* intersect at two points.

_____ **3.** An independent *linear system* has one solution.

_____ **4.** A dependent *linear system* has no solutions.

_____ **5.** Two unique lines with the same slope form an inconsistent system.

Problem 1 Using a Graph or Table to Solve a System

Got It? What is the solution of the system? $\begin{cases} x - 2y = 4 \\ 3x + y = 5 \end{cases}$

6. Circle the graph of the equations.

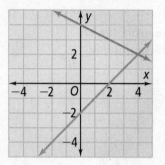 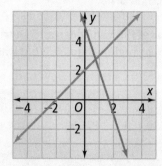 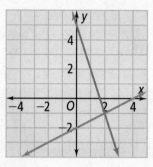

7. Circle the row in the calculator screen that contains the solution of the system.

X	Y1	Y2
0	−2	5
1	−1.5	2
2	−1	−1
3	−.5	−4
4	0	−7

8. The solution of the system of equations is ([   ] , [   ]).

Problem 2 Using a Table to Solve a Problem

Got It? Biology The equation $y_1 = 1.5x + 22$ models the length, in centimeters, of a Spiny Dogfish shark x years old. The equation $y_2 = 0.75x + 37$ models the length, in centimeters, of a Greenland shark x years old. If the growth rates continue, how long will each shark be when it is 25 years old?

9. Reasoning Which shark will be longer at age 25? How do you know?

10. Underline the correct phrase to complete the sentence.

To solve the problem, I need to find

an x-value / a y-value / two x-values / two y-values .

11. Complete the table for $x = 25$.

x	$y_1 = 1.5x + 22$	$y_1 = 0.75x + 37$
25		

Lesson 3-1

12. Spiny Dogfish sharks will be [   ] cm long and Greenland sharks will be [   ] cm long when they are 25 years old.

 Problem 3 **Using Linear Regression**

Got It? The table shows the populations of the San Diego and Detroit metropolitan regions. When were the populations of these regions equal? What was that population?

Populations of San Diego and Detroit (1950–2000)

	1950	1960	1970	1980	1990	2000
San Diego	334,387	573,224	696,769	875,538	1,110,549	1,223,400
Detroit	1,849,568	1,670,144	1,511,482	1,203,339	1,027,974	951,270

Source: U.S. Census Bureau

13. Circle the first calculator step in solving the problem.

Calculate the intersection.   Enter the data into lists.   Enter y_1.

14. Write the name of the list you will use (L_1, L_2, or L_3) next to the data type.

[   ] population of San Diego   [   ] population of Detroit   [   ] years since 1950

15. Circle the pair of equations you will graph.

$y_1 = 17816.597\ldots x + 356896.238\ldots$ $y_1 = -17816.597x\ldots + 356896.238\ldots$

$y_2 = -19217.551\ldots x + 1849401.619\ldots$ $y_2 = 19217.551x\ldots + 1849401.619\ldots$

16. Cross out the graph that does NOT show the regression lines.

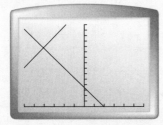 

17. Underline the correct word to complete each sentence.

The *x*-axis / *y*-axis corresponds to the number of years since 1950.

The *x*-axis / *y*-axis corresponds to the populations of San Diego and Detroit.

18. The scale of the graphs is $-60 \leq x \leq 60$ by 10s and $0 \leq y \leq 1{,}500{,}000$ by 100,000s. Use the scale to estimate the coordinates of the point of intersection.

The coordinates are $\left(\rule{1.5cm}{0.4pt} , \rule{3cm}{0.4pt} \right)$.

The populations of San Diego and Detroit were equal sometime during the year [   ].

The population was about [   ].

Got It? Without graphing, is the system $\begin{cases} -3x + y = 4 \\ x - \frac{1}{3}y = 1 \end{cases}$ *independent, dependent, or inconsistent?*

19. Write each equation in slope-intercept form.

$-3x + y = 4$ $\qquad\qquad\qquad\qquad\qquad$ $x - \frac{1}{3}y = 1$

20. The slope of $-3x + y = 4$ is $\quad$ and the slope of $x - \frac{1}{3}y = 1$ is $\quad$.

21. The y-intercept of $-3x + y = 4$ is $\quad$ and the y-intercept of $x - \frac{1}{3}y = 1$ is $\quad$.

22. Underline the correct words to complete the sentence.

Because the slopes of the lines are equal / not equal and the y-intercepts are

the same / different , the system is inconsistent / independent / dependent .

Lesson Check • Do you UNDERSTAND?

Vocabulary Is it possible for a system of equations to be both *independent* and *inconsistent*? Explain.

Write T for *true* or F for *false*.

_____ **23.** The graphs of an inconsistent system are parallel.

_____ **24.** The graphs of an independent system intersect at one point.

25. Now answer the question.

Math Success

Check off the vocabulary words that you understand.

☐ system of equations ☐ dependent ☐ independent ☐ consistent ☐ inconsistent

Rate how well you can *solve a linear system using a graph or table*.

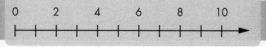

Need to review 0   2   4   6   8   10   Now I get it!

3-2 Solving Systems Algebraically

Vocabulary

● Review

1. Circle the equations that are in *standard form*.

$$4x + 3y = 2 \qquad y = 3x - 5 \qquad 4x - 3 = 2y \qquad 2x + 5y = 0$$

Write each equation in *standard form*.

2. $y = 5x - 3$

3. $y - 4 = 6x$

4. $-y + 3x - 12 = 0$

● Vocabulary Builder

solution (noun) suh LOO shun

Main Idea: If two numbers are substituted for x and y in a system of equations and they make both equations true, then the ordered pair (x, y) is a solution of the system.

Definition: A solution is any ordered pair that makes an equation in two variables true.

> $(2, 1)$ is a **solution** of
> $y = 3x - 5$ because
> $1 = 3(2) - 5.$

● Use Your Vocabulary

5. Write three ordered pairs that are *solutions* of the equation $y = -5x - 2$.

$(\;\;\;,\;\;\;)$ $\qquad$ $(\;\;\;,\;\;\;)$ $\qquad$ $(\;\;\;,\;\;\;)$

Use the system at the right. Write T for *true* or F for *false*.

$\begin{cases} 2x + \frac{y}{2} = 3 \\ 4x + y = 2 \end{cases}$

_____ **6.** The system has a unique *solution*.

_____ **7.** The system has infinitely many *solutions*.

_____ **8.** The system has no *solution*.

_____ **9.** The solution is $(0, 0)$.

_____ **10.** The *solution* of a system can be found by graphing the equations of the system.

Problem 1 Solving by Substitution

Got It? What is the solution of the system of equations? $\begin{cases} x + 3y = 5 \\ -2x - 4y = -5 \end{cases}$

11. Follow the steps to find the solution.

1 Solve the first equation for x. $x + 3y = 5$

$$x = \boxed{} + 5$$

2 Substitute the expression for x in the second equation. Then solve for y.

$-2x - 4y = -5$

$-2\left(\boxed{}\right) - 4y = -5$

$\boxed{} - 4y = -5$

$\boxed{}\, y = 5$

$y = \boxed{}$

3 Substitute the value for y in either equation. Solve for x.

$x + 3y = 5$

$x + 3\left(\boxed{}\right) = 5$

$x + \boxed{} = 5$

$x = \boxed{}$

12. The solution of the system is $\left(\boxed{} , \boxed{} \right)$.

Problem 2 Using Substitution to Solve a Problem

Got It? Music An online music company offers 15 downloads for $19.75 and 40 downloads for $43.50. Each price includes a one-time registration fee. What is the cost of each download and the registration fee?

13. Complete the model to write a system of equations.

Relate	total cost	is	number of downloads	times	cost of one download	plus	registration fee

Define Let c = the cost of one download and let r = the registration fee.

Write

$\$19.75 = \boxed{} \cdot c + r$

$\$\boxed{} = 40 \cdot \boxed{} + \boxed{}$

63

Lesson 3-2

14. Circle the equation that expresses r in terms of c in the first equation.

$$r = -15c + 19.75 \qquad r = 15c + 19.75 \qquad r = -15c - 19.75$$

15. Substitute the equation you chose in Exercise 14 into the second equation of the system and solve for c.

$43.5 = 40c + r$	Write the original equation.
$43.5 = 40c + \boxed{}\ c + \boxed{}$	Substitute for r.
$43.5 = \boxed{}\ c + 19.75$	Simplify.
$\boxed{} = \boxed{}\ c$	Use the Addition Property of Equality.
$\boxed{} = c$	Divide.

16. Now substitute the value of c into one of the equations of the system and solve for r.

 17. The cost of each download is $\$\boxed{}$ and the registration fee is $\$\boxed{}$.

Problem 3 Solving by Elimination

Got It? What is the solution of the system of equations? $\begin{cases} -2x + 8y = -8 \\ 5x - 8y = 20 \end{cases}$

18. Add the equations.

$$\begin{array}{rcrcr} -2x & + & 8y & = & -8 \\ 5x & - & 8y & = & 20 \\ \hline \boxed{} & + & \boxed{} & = & \boxed{} \\ & & \boxed{} & = & \boxed{} \end{array}$$ Simplify.

19. Now choose one of the original equations. Substitute and solve.

20. Circle the ordered pair that is the solution of the system of equations.

$$(-4, -2) \qquad (4, -2) \qquad (4, 0)$$

Problem 4 Solving an Equivalent System

Got It? What is the solution of the system of equations? $\begin{cases} 3x + 7y = 15 \\ 5x + 2y = -4 \end{cases}$

21. Underline the correct values to complete the sentence.

To get additive inverses for the x-term, multiply the first equation by $2 / 3 / 5$

and the second equation by $-2 / -3 / -7$.

22. Circle the equivalent system that shows additive inverses for the x-term.

$$\begin{cases} 3x + 7y = 15 \\ 5x + 2y = -4 \end{cases} \qquad \begin{cases} 6x + 14y = 3c \\ -35x - 14y = 28 \end{cases} \qquad \begin{cases} 15x + 35y = 75 \\ -15x - 6y = 12 \end{cases}$$

23. Solve the system for y.

24. Then substitute and solve for x.

25. The solution of the system is $\left(\boxed{} , \boxed{} \right)$.

 Problem 5 Solving Systems Without Unique Solutions

Got It? What is the solution of the system of equations? Explain. $\begin{cases} -x + y = -2 \\ 2x - 2y = 0 \end{cases}$

26. Circle the first step in solving the system.

Multiply $-x + y = -2$ by -1.   Multiply $-x + y = -2$ by 2.

27. Add $-2x + 2y = -4$ and $2x - 2y = 0$.

$$\begin{array}{ccccc} -2x & + & 2y & = & -4 \\ 2x & - & 2y & = & 0 \\ \hline & & \boxed{} & = & \boxed{} \end{array}$$

28. What is the solution of the system?
Place a ✓ in the box if the response is correct.
Place an ✗ if it is incorrect.

$\boxed{}$ The system has no solution.

$\boxed{}$ The system has infinitely many solutions.

 Lesson Check • **Do you UNDERSTAND?**

Vocabulary Give an example of two equivalent systems.

29. Cross out the system of equations that is NOT equivalent to the others.

$$\begin{cases} 4y + 5x = 13 \\ 4y - x = 3 \end{cases} \qquad \begin{cases} y + 5x = 12 \\ 4y - x = 3 \end{cases} \qquad \begin{cases} 8y + 40x = 96 \\ 8y - 2x = 6 \end{cases}$$

 Math Success

Check off the vocabulary words that you understand.

☐ substitution   ☐ elimination   ☐ equivalent equation   ☐ unique solutions

Rate how well you can *solve linear systems algebraically*.

| Need to review | 0 | 2 | 4 | 6 | 8 | 10 | Now I get it! |

Vocabulary

Review

Complete each statement with the correct word or phrase from the list below.
Use each word or phrase only once.

minimum   greater than or equal to   at least   at most

1. The Florida football team needs __?__ two more wins to clinch the division title.

2. The __?__ speed a car may travel on the Florida freeway is 40 miles per hour.

3. If you have $45 and sweaters sell for $20 each, you can buy __?__ two sweaters.

4. The height of a rider must be __?__ 42 inches in order to ride the Summit Plummet.

Vocabulary Builder

inequality (noun) in ee KWAL uh tee

inequality symbols
$<, >, \leq, \geq, \neq$

Definition: An **inequality** is a mathematical statement indicating that one quantity is less than or less than or equal to a second quantity.

Use Your Vocabulary

5. Place a ✓ next to the math statements that are *inequalities*. Place an ✗ next to the math statements that are not.

   ☐ $15x > 3y$ ☐ $y \leq x$ ☐ $r \neq s$ ☐ $p = t - 17$

Complete each inequality with <, >, ≤, or ≥.

6. $y < 6$, so 6 ☐ y

7. $b \geq 10$, so 10 ☐ b

8. $r \leq s + t$, so $s + t$ ☐ r

9. Write an *inequality* symbol to represent each verbal expression.

   p is at most 10 u is greater than m z is at least 9

   p ☐ 10 u ☐ m z ☐ 9

Problem 1 Solving a System by Using a Table

Got It? Assume that x and y are whole numbers. What is the solution of the system of inequalities? $\begin{cases} x + y > 4 \\ 3x + 7y \le 21 \end{cases}$

10. Circle the inequality that has a finite number of whole-number solutions.

$x + y > 4$	$3x + 7y \le 21$

11. Use the inequality you circled in Exercise 10 and whole numbers to complete the table of values.

x	y
0	0, 1, 2, 3
1	0, 1, ☐
☐	0, ☐, ☐
	☐, ☐
☐	☐
☐	☐
☐	☐
7	☐

12. Write the ordered pairs of values from the table that satisfy the first inequality.

Problem 2 Solving a System by Graphing

Got It? What is the solution of the system of inequalities? $\begin{cases} x + 2y \le 4 \\ y \ge -x - 1 \end{cases}$

13. Circle the equivalent system that shows the equations in slope-intercept form.

$\begin{cases} y \ge -0.5x + 2 \\ y \ge -x - 1 \end{cases}$	$\begin{cases} 2y \le 4 + x \\ y \ge -x - 1 \end{cases}$	$\begin{cases} y \le -0.5x + 2 \\ y \ge -x - 1 \end{cases}$	$\begin{cases} y \ge -2 + 0.5x \\ y \ge -x - 1 \end{cases}$

Lesson 3-3

14. Circle the graph of the solution of the system.

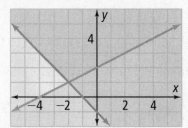 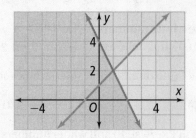 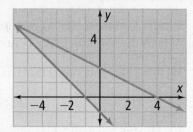

 Problem 3 Using a System of Inequalities

Got It? A pizza parlor charges $1 for each vegetable topping and $2 for each meat topping. You want at least five toppings on your pizza. You have $10 to spend on toppings. How many of each type of topping can you get on your pizza?

15. Complete the model to write a system of inequalities.

Relate

number of vegetable toppings	plus	number of meat toppings		is at least	
cost of vegetable toppings	plus	cost of _____		is _____	10

Define   Let v = the number of vegetable toppings.
Let m = the number of meat toppings.

Write

$$\begin{cases} v + \boxed{} + \boxed{} \geq \boxed{} \\ \boxed{} + \boxed{} \boxed{} \boxed{} \end{cases}$$

16. Circle the system of inequalities that is equivalent to the system in Exercise 15.

$$\begin{cases} v + m \geq 5 \\ 2m \leq 10 + v \end{cases} \qquad \begin{cases} m \leq 5 - v \\ m \geq 5 + v \end{cases} \qquad \begin{cases} m \geq 5 - v \\ m \leq -\frac{1}{2}v + 5 \end{cases}$$

17. Number Sense Circle the types of numbers that can represent the number of toppings you can get on your pizza.

rational numbers   integers   whole numbers   real numbers

18. Use the graph of the system at the right. Underline the correct number to complete each sentence.

If you order 0 vegetable toppings, you can order at most

0 / 5 / 10 meat toppings.

If you order 10 vegetable toppings, you can order at most

0 / 5 / 10 meat toppings.

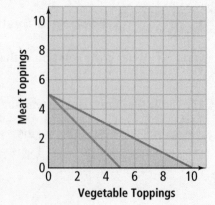

Got It? What is the solution of the system of inequalities? $\begin{cases} y < -\frac{1}{3}x + 1 \\ y > 2|x - 1| \end{cases}$

19. The graph at the right shows the boundaries of the system. Shade $y < -\frac{1}{3}x + 1$ vertically. Shade $y > 2|x - 1|$ horizontally. Darken the region of overlap. Then label each inequality.

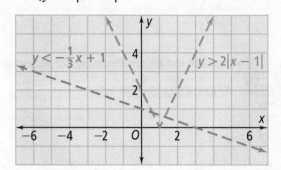

 ## Lesson Check • Do you UNDERSTAND?

Reasoning Is the solution of a system of linear inequalities a *union* or an *intersection* of the solutions of the two inequalities? Justify your answer.

Write T for *true* or F for *false*.

20. Systems of inequalities are similar to systems of equations.

21. The solution of a system of equations is the union of all points on the graphs of the lines.

22. The solution of a system of inequalities is the union of all points in the graphs of the inequalities.

23. Now answer the question.

_____

_____

_____

Math Success

Check off the vocabulary words that you understand.

☐ linear inequalities   ☐ overlap   ☐ absolute-value system

Rate how well you can *solve systems of linear inequalities.*

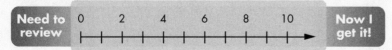

Linear Programming

Vocabulary

● Review

1. Draw a line from each polygon in Column A to the number of vertices it has in Column B.

Column A	Column B
pentagon	5
quadrilateral	8
octagon	4

2. Write the letter of each *vertex* of the quadrilateral at the right.

(6, 4)   (3, 5)   (4, −1)   (1, 2)

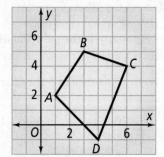

● Vocabulary Builder

constraint (noun) **kun STRAYNT**

Related Words: constrain, restrict, limit, feasible region

Main Idea: The **constraints** in a linear programming situation form a system of inequalities. The graph of this system is the feasible region and contains all the points that satisfy the **constraints**.

Definition: A **constraint** is a restriction or limitation.

● Use Your Vocabulary

Complete each statement with a word from the list. Use each word only once.

constraint   constrain   constrained

3. Weight is one __?__ on vehicles allowed on the bridge.

4. An injury can cause __?__ motion.

5. The rules of a game __?__ how you play.

Linear programming is a method for finding the minimum or maximum value of some quantity, given a set of constraints. The constraints form a system of linear inequalities. The graph of the solutions is the *feasible region*.

Key Concept   Vertex Principle of Linear Programming

If there is a maximum or a minimum value of a linear objective function, it occurs at one or more vertices of the feasible region.

6. The graph at the right shows a feasible region. Write the coordinates at which a maximum or minimum value of a linear objective function could occur.

$$\left(\boxed{}, \boxed{}\right) \left(\boxed{}, \boxed{}\right) \left(\boxed{}, \boxed{}\right)$$

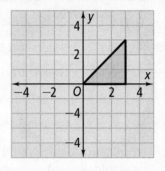

Problem 1   Testing Vertices

Got It? Use the graph and the constraints below. What values of *x* and *y* in the feasible region maximize *P* for the objective function $P = x + 3y$?

7. Label the vertices of the feasible region with their coordinates.

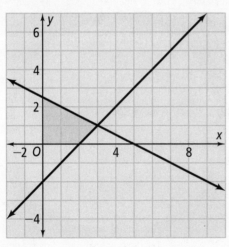

Constraints:
$$\begin{cases} x + 2y \le 5 \\ x - y \le 2 \\ x \ge 0, y \ge 0 \end{cases}$$

8. Evaluate $P = x + 3y$ at each vertex.

9. *P* has a maximum value of $\boxed{}$ when $x = \boxed{}$ and $y = \boxed{}$.

Lesson 3-4

Problem 2 Using Linear Programming to Maximize Profit

Got It? Business You are screen-printing T-shirts and sweatshirts to sell at the Polk County Blues Festival and are working with the following constraints.

- It takes 10 min to make a 1-color T-shirt.

- It takes 20 min to make a 3-color sweatshirt.

- You have 20 hours at most to make shirts.

- Supplies for a T-shirt cost $4.

- Supplies for a sweatshirt cost $20.

- You want to spend no more than $600 on supplies.

- You want to have at least 50 items to sell.

The profit on a T-shirt is $6. The profit on a sweatshirt is $20. How many of each type of shirt should you make to maximize your profit?

10. Complete the inequalities that describe the constraints.

$$\text{constraints} \begin{cases} 10x + 20y \leq \boxed{} \\ x + y \geq \boxed{} \\ \boxed{}\ x + 20y \leq \boxed{} \\ x \geq \boxed{} \\ y \geq \boxed{} \end{cases}$$

11. Circle the objective function that models the situation.

$$P = 10x + y \qquad P = 10x + 20y \qquad P = 4x + 20y \qquad P = 6x + 20y$$

12. Shade the feasible region on the graph.

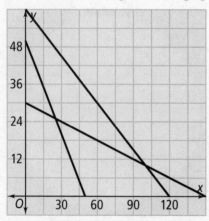

13. The vertices of the feasible region are

$$\left(\boxed{}, 0\right), \left(\boxed{}, 0\right),$$

$$\left(100, \boxed{}\right), \text{ and } \left(25, \boxed{}\right).$$

14. Evaluate P at each vertex.

15. How many of each type of shirt should you make to maximize your profit?

T-shirts = [ ]   sweatshirts = [ ]

 Lesson Check • **Do you UNDERSTAND?**

Write a system of constraints whose graphs determine a trapezoid.
Write an objective function and evaluate it at each vertex.

16. Write the constraints that produce the feasible region below.

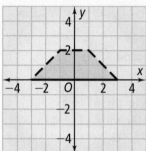

$y \geq 0$

17. Use the objective function $P = -3x + 2y$. Evaluate the function at each vertex of the feasible region.

(−3, 0)   (−1, 2)   (1, 2)   (3, 0)

 Math Success

Check off the vocabulary words that you understand.

☐ constraint   ☐ linear programming   ☐ objective function   ☐ feasible region

Rate how well you can *solve linear programming problems*.

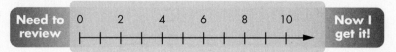

Lesson 3-4

Vocabulary

● **Review**

1. Circle the number of points that determine a *plane*.

| 1 | 2 | 3 | 4 |

● **Vocabulary Builder**

ordered triple (noun) AWR durd TRIP ul

Definition: An **ordered triple** (x, y, z) has three coordinates and describes a point in three-dimensional space.

Main Idea: The first coordinate of an ordered triple represents the point's location along the x-axis, the second coordinate its location along the y-axis, and the third coordinate its location along the z-axis.

● **Use Your Vocabulary**

2. Circle the *ordered triple* that has x-coordinate 0.

| $(1, 0, 1)$ | $(1, 1, 0)$ | $(0, 1, 1)$ | $(1, 0, 0)$ |

 Problem 1 Solving a System Using Elimination

Got It? What is the solution of the system at the right? Use elimination. Check your answer in all three original equations.

① $\begin{cases} x - y + z = -1 \\ ② \quad x + y + 3z = -3 \\ ③ \quad 2x - y + 2z = 0 \end{cases}$

3. How can you combine ① and ② to eliminate y?

| add ② to ① | subtract ② from ① |

4. How can you combine ② and ③ to eliminate y?

| add ② to ③ | subtract ② from ③ |

5. Combine ① and ② to eliminate y.

$$
\begin{array}{rrr}
x - & y + & z = -1 \\
x + & y + & 3z = -3 \\
\hline
x + & \ y + & \ z =
\end{array}
$$

6. Combine ② and ③ to eliminate y.

$$
\begin{array}{rrr}
x + & y + & 3z = -3 \\
2x - & y + & 2z = 0 \\
\hline
x + & \ y + & \ z =
\end{array}
$$

7. Use the equations from Exercises 5 and 6 to write and solve a system of two equations in two variables.

8. Use the solutions from Exercise 7 and ① to substitute and solve for y.

9. The solution of the original system is

$$\left(\boxed{}, \boxed{}, \boxed{}\right).$$

10. Now check your answer in all three original equations.

$x - y + z = -1$ $x + y + 3z = -3$ $2x - y + 2z = 0$

Problem 2   Solving an Equivalent System

Got It? What is the solution of the system at the right? Use elimination.

$$\begin{array}{l} ① \\ ② \\ ③ \end{array} \begin{cases} x - 2y + 3z = 12 \\ 2x - y - 2z = 5 \\ 2x + 2y - z = 4 \end{cases}$$

11. First, add a multiple of ① to ② to eliminate x. Circle the number you will use to multiply ①.

-1	1	-2	2

12. Next, add a multiple of ② to ③ to eliminate x. Circle the number you will use to multiply ②.

-1	1	-2	2

13. Write the two equations you get by eliminating x.

$\boxed{}\, y + \boxed{}\, z = \boxed{}$ $\boxed{}\, y + \boxed{}\, z = \boxed{}$

14. Now find the solution of the two-variable system of equations.

15. Substitute the values of y and z into ① to solve for x.

Lesson 3-5

Problem 3 Solving a System Using Substitution

Got It? What is the solution of the system? Use substitution.

① $\begin{cases} x - 2y + z = -4 \\ -4x + y - 2z = 1 \\ 2x + 2y - z = 10 \end{cases}$
②
③

16. **Reasoning** Why should you choose ① to solve for x? Place a ✓ in the box if the response is correct. Place an ✗ if it is incorrect.

☐ The coefficient of x is 1.

☐ The coefficient of x is negative.

☐ The coefficients of x and y are equal.

17. Now solve the system.

18. The solution of the system is $\left(\boxed{}, \boxed{}, \boxed{} \right)$.

 Problem 4 Solving a Real-World Problem

Got It? **Business** You manage a clothing store and budget $5400 to restock 200 shirts. You can buy T-shirts for $12 each, polo shirts for $24 each, and rugby shirts for $36 each. If you want to have the same number of T-shirts as polo shirts, how many of each type of shirt should you buy?

19. Use the information in the problem to complete the model below.

| T-shirts | + | polo shirts | + | rugby shirts | = | $\boxed{}$ |

Relate

T-shirts = $\boxed{}$
_____

$12 · T-shirts + $ $\boxed{}$ · polo shirts + $ $\boxed{}$ · rugby shirts = $ $\boxed{}$

Define Let $\begin{cases} x = \text{the number of T-shirts} \\ y = \text{the number of polo shirts} \\ z = \text{the number of rugby shirts} \end{cases}$

Write
① $\begin{cases} x + y + \boxed{} = \boxed{} \\ x = \boxed{} \\ 12x + 24\boxed{} + \boxed{} = \boxed{} \end{cases}$
②
③

20. Circle the method(s) you will use to solve the system.

> elimination   equivalent system   substitution

21. Now solve the system.

22. You should buy [____] T-shirts, [____] polo shirts, and [____] rugby shirts.

Lesson Check • Do you UNDERSTAND?

Writing How many solutions does the system at the right have?
Explain your answer in terms of intersecting planes.

$$\begin{array}{l} ① \\ ② \\ ③ \end{array} \begin{cases} 2x - 3y + z = 5 \\ 2x - 3y + z = -2 \\ -4x + 6y - 2z = 10 \end{cases}$$

23. Solve the system by adding ① and ② and then adding ③.

24. The system has zero / one / infinitely many solution(s). The graphs of the three

equations are intersecting / parallel / perpendicular planes.

Math Success

Check off the vocabulary words that you understand.

☐ linear system   ☐ elimination   ☐ substitution

Rate how well you can *solve systems with three variables.*

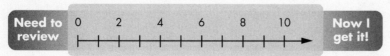

Lesson 3-5

3-6 Solving Systems Using Matrices

Vocabulary

● Review

1. Underline the correct word to complete the sentence.

The partial solution of the system of equations at the right uses

substitution / elimination / equivalent systems.

$$2x + 3y - z = 4$$
$$\underline{-x + 2y + z = -3}$$
$$x + 5y = 1$$

● Vocabulary Builder

rref (noun)

Definition: The **rref** (reduced **r**ow **e**chelon **f**orm) function on a calculator generates the matrix that represents the solution of a system of equations.

Example: $\begin{bmatrix} 1 & 0 & 0 & | & 5 \\ 0 & 1 & 0 & | & -8 \\ 0 & 0 & 1 & | & 4 \end{bmatrix}$ is a matrix in reduced row echelon form representing

the solution $(5, -8, 4)$.

● Use Your Vocabulary

2. Draw a line from each *rref* matrix in Column A to the solution it represents in Column B.

Column A

$\begin{bmatrix} 1 & 0 & 0 & | & 2 \\ 0 & 1 & 0 & | & 0 \\ 0 & 0 & 1 & | & 3 \end{bmatrix}$

$\begin{bmatrix} 1 & 0 & 0 & | & 0 \\ 0 & 1 & 0 & | & 2 \\ 0 & 0 & 1 & | & 3 \end{bmatrix}$

$\begin{bmatrix} 1 & 0 & 0 & | & 2 \\ 0 & 1 & 0 & | & 3 \\ 0 & 0 & 1 & | & 0 \end{bmatrix}$

Column B

$(0, 2, 3)$

$(2, 0, 3)$

$(2, 3, 0)$

Problem 1 Identifying a Matrix Element

Got It? What is element a_{13} in matrix A?

$$A = \begin{bmatrix} 4 & -9 & 17 & | & 1 \\ 0 & 5 & 8 & | & 6 \\ -3 & -2 & 10 & | & 0 \end{bmatrix}$$

3. Underline the correct words to complete the sentence.

The matrix has 3 rows / columns and 4 rows / columns .

4. The element a_{13} is in row ⬜ and column ⬜ .

5. Use the matrix below. Circle element a_{13}.

$$A = \begin{bmatrix} 4 & -9 & 17 & | & 1 \\ 0 & 5 & 8 & | & 6 \\ -3 & -2 & 10 & | & 0 \end{bmatrix}$$

 Problem 2 Representing Systems With Matrices

Got It? How can you represent the system of equations at the right with a matrix?

$$\begin{cases} -4x - 2y = 7 \\ 3x + y = -5 \end{cases}$$

6. How many *rows* and *columns* will the matrix have?

number of rows = ⬜   number of columns = ⬜

7. Write the matrix.

 Problem 3 Writing a System from a Matrix

Got It? What linear system does $\begin{bmatrix} 2 & 0 & | & 6 \\ 5 & -2 & | & 1 \end{bmatrix}$ represent?

8. Underline the correct numbers to complete the sentence.

The matrix represents a system of 2 / 3 / 4 equations in 2 / 3 / 4 variables.

9. Complete the system of equations.

⬜ $x +$ ⬜ $y =$ ⬜

⬜ $x +$ ⬜ $y =$ ⬜

Lesson 3-6

10. Use the row operation indicated to complete each matrix.

Switch any two rows.

Switch Rows 1 and 2. $\begin{bmatrix} 4 & 5 & 3 \\ 3 & 2 & 6 \end{bmatrix}$ becomes $\begin{bmatrix} 3 & 2 & \square \\ \square & \square & \square \end{bmatrix}$

Multiply a row by a constant.

Multiply Row 2 by 3. $\begin{bmatrix} 4 & 5 & 3 \\ 3 & 2 & 6 \end{bmatrix}$ becomes $\begin{bmatrix} 4 & 5 & \square \\ 3 \cdot \square & 3 \cdot \square & 3 \cdot \square \end{bmatrix} = \begin{bmatrix} 4 & \square & \square \\ \square & \square & \square \end{bmatrix}$

Add one row to another.

Add Row 2 to Row 1. $\begin{bmatrix} 4 & 5 & 3 \\ 3 & 2 & 6 \end{bmatrix}$ becomes $\begin{bmatrix} 4+3 & 5+\square & \square + \square \\ 3 & 2 & \square \end{bmatrix} = \begin{bmatrix} 7 & \square & \square \\ \square & \square & \square \end{bmatrix}$

You can combine any of these steps to solve a system using a matrix.

Problem 4 Solving a System Using a Matrix

Got It? What is the solution of the system of equations? $\begin{cases} 9x - 2y = 5 \\ 3x + 7y = 17 \end{cases}$

11. The system is solved below. Write a justification for each step.

Write the matrix for the system.

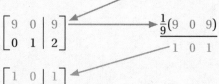

12. Circle the solution of the system.

(1, 0)   (0, 1)   (1, 2)

Got It? What is the solution of the system of equations?

$$\begin{cases} a + 4b + 6c = 21 \\ 2a - 2b + c = 4 \\ -8b + c = -1 \end{cases}$$

13. Circle the matrix that models the system.

$$\begin{bmatrix} 1 & 4 & 6 & | & 21 \\ 2 & 2 & 1 & | & 4 \\ 0 & 8 & 1 & | & -1 \end{bmatrix} \qquad \begin{bmatrix} 1 & 4 & 6 & | & 21 \\ 2 & -2 & 1 & | & 4 \\ 0 & -8 & 1 & | & -1 \end{bmatrix} \qquad \begin{bmatrix} 1 & 2 & 0 & | & 21 \\ 4 & -2 & -8 & | & 4 \\ 6 & 1 & 1 & | & -1 \end{bmatrix}$$

14. Use the rref() function on your calculator to find the solution.

$a = $ $\qquad\qquad b = $ $\qquad\qquad c = $

15. Check the solution.

$a + 4b + 6c = 21$ $\qquad\qquad 2a - 2b + c = 4$ $\qquad\qquad -8b + c = -1$

 Lesson Check • **Do you UNDERSTAND?**

How many elements are in a 4 × 4 matrix?

16. There are rows, and each row has elements.

17. A 4 × 4 matrix has × , or elements.

 Math Success

Check off the vocabulary words that you understand.

☐ matrix ☐ matrix element ☐ row operation

Rate how well you can *use matrices to solve systems of equations.*

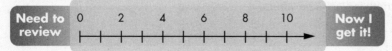

4-1 Quadratic Functions and Transformations

Vocabulary

● **Review**

1. Circle the *vertex* of each absolute value graph.

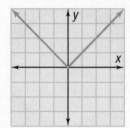   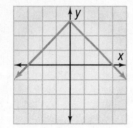   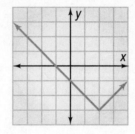

● **Vocabulary Builder**

parabola (noun) puh RAB uh luh

Related Words: vertex, axis of symmetry, quadratic function

Definition: A **parabola** is the graph of a *quadratic function,* a function of the form $y = ax^2 + bx + c$.

Main Idea: A **parabola** is symmetrical around its *axis of symmetry,* a line passing through the *vertex.* A **parabola** can open upward or downward.

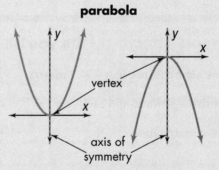

parabola

vertex

axis of symmetry

● **Use Your Vocabulary**

2. Circle each function whose graph is a *parabola*.

$$y = -6x + 9 \qquad y = -2x^2 - 15x - 18 \qquad y = x^2 + 4x + 4 \qquad y = 16x - 22$$

3. Cross out the function(s) whose graph is NOT a *parabola*.

$$y = 5x^2 - 3x + 6 \qquad y = x - 3 \qquad y = 2x^2 + 6x - 7 \qquad y = 0.2x + 7$$

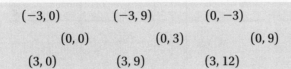 **Problem 2** Graphing Translations of $f(x) = x^2$

Got It? Graph $g(x) = x^2 + 3$. How is it a translation of $f(x) = x^2$?

Use the graphs of $f(x) = x^2$ and $g(x) = x^2 + 3$ at the right for Exercises 4 and 5.

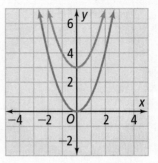

4. Circle the ordered pairs that are solutions of $g(x) = x^2 + 3$. Underline the ordered pairs that are solutions of $f(x) = x^2$.

$(-3, 0)$	$(-3, 9)$	$(0, -3)$
$(0, 0)$	$(0, 3)$	$(0, 9)$
$(3, 0)$	$(3, 9)$	$(3, 12)$

5. Underline the correct word to complete each sentence.

For each value of x, the value of $g(x) = x^2 + 3$ is 3 more / less than the value of $f(x) = x^2$.

The graph of $g(x) = x^2 + 3$ is a translation 3 units up / down of the graph of $f(x) = x^2$.

The graph shows $f(x) = x^2$ in red / blue and $g(x) = x^2 + 3$ in red / blue .

 Problem 3 Interpreting Vertex Form

Got It? What are the vertex, axis of symmetry, minimum or maximum, and domain and range of the function $y = -2(x + 1)^2 + 4$?

6. Compare $y = 2(x - 1)^2 + 4$ with the vertex form $y = a(x - h)^2 + k$. Identify a, h, and k.

$a = $ ____ $h = $ ____ $k = $ ____

7. The vertex of the parabola is $(h, k) = \left(\underline{}, \underline{} \right)$.

8. The axis of symmetry is the line $x = $ ____ .

9. Underline the correct word or symbol to complete each sentence.

Since a is $<$ / $>$ 0, the parabola opens upward / downward .

The parabola has a maximum / minimum value of ____ when $x = $ ____ .

10. Circle the domain.

all real numbers	$x \leq -1$	$x \leq 4$	$x \geq 4$

11. Circle the range.

all real numbers	$x \leq -1$	$x \leq 4$	$x \geq 4$

Lesson 4-1

12. Use one of the functions below to label each graph.

$$y = (x + 3)^2 \qquad y = x^2 - 1 \qquad y = (x - 2)^2 + 3 \qquad y = (x + 1)^2 - 2$$

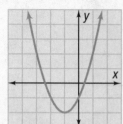 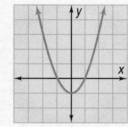 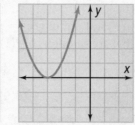 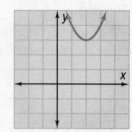

Problem 4 **Using Vertex Form**

Got It? What is the graph of $f(x) = 2(x + 2)^2 - 5$?

13. Multiple Choice What steps transform the graph of $y = x^2$ to $y = 2(x + 2)^2 - 5$?

(A) Reflect across the x-axis, stretch by the factor 2, and translate 2 units to the left and 5 units up.

(B) Stretch by the factor 2 and translate 2 units to the right and 5 units up.

(C) Stretch by the factor 2 and translate 2 units to the left and 5 units down.

(D) Reflect across the x-axis, stretch by the factor 2, and translate 2 units to the left and 5 units down.

14. Circle the graph of $f(x) = 2(x + 2)^2 - 5$.

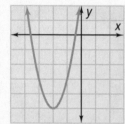 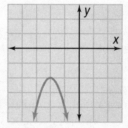 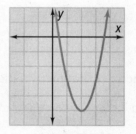 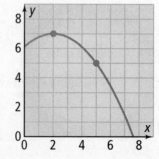

Problem 5 **Writing a Quadratic Function in Vertex Form**

Got It? The graph shows the jump of a dolphin. The axis of symmetry is $x = 2$, and the height is 7. If the path of the jump passes through the point (5, 5), what quadratic function models the path of the jump?

15. The vertex is $\left(\boxed{}, \boxed{} \right)$.

16. Substitute h and k in the vertex form $f(x) = a(x - h)^2 + k$.

$$y = a\left(x - \boxed{}\right)^2 + \boxed{}$$

17. Substitute $(5, 5)$ for (x, y) and solve for a.

18. Write the quadratic function that models the path of the water.

Lesson Check • Do you UNDERSTAND?

Vocabulary When does the graph of a quadratic function have a minimum value?

19. Circle the parabola that has a minimum value.

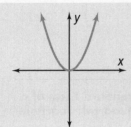 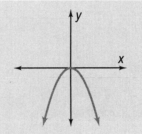

20. The graph of $y = x^2$ is a parabola that opens upward / downward .

21. The graph of $y = -x^2$ is a parabola that opens upward / downward .

22. When does the graph of a quadratic function have a minimum value?

_____

_____

Math Success

Check off the vocabulary words that you understand.

☐ parabola   ☐ vertex form   ☐ quadratic function   ☐ axis of symmetry

Rate how well you can *graph a quadratic function in vertex form.*

Need to review 0 2 4 6 8 10 Now I get it!

Lesson 4-1

4-2   Standard Form of a Quadratic Function

Vocabulary

● **Review**

1. Circle the functions in *standard form*.

$$y = 2x^2 - 4x + 2 \qquad y = \frac{1}{3}(x - 4) \qquad y = -4x + 1 \qquad y = -\frac{2}{3}x - \frac{5}{3}x + 4$$

Write each equation in *standard form*.

2. $x + 2y = 17$

3. $2x = 5$

4. $5 - x = y + 2$

● **Vocabulary Builder**

> **Standard Form of a Quadratic Function**
> $$y = ax^2 + bx + c,$$
> $$a \neq 0$$

quadratic   (adjective)   **kwah DRAT ik**

Related Words: parabola, vertex, axis of symmetry

Definition: A **quadratic** function is a function that can be written in the form $y = ax^2 + bx + c$ where $a \neq 0$. The graph of a **quadratic** function is a *parabola*.

Examples: **quadratic** functions, $y = x^2$, $y = -3x^2 + 7$, $f(x) = 2x^2 + 5x - 4$, $g(x) = \frac{1}{2}(x - 4)^2 + 5$

Nonexamples: *not* **quadratic** functions, $y = \dfrac{1}{2x^2 + 4x + 5}, \dfrac{x^2 + 5x + 10}{3x}$

● **Use Your Vocabulary**

5. Circle the graphs of *quadratic* functions.

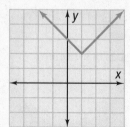 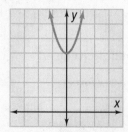 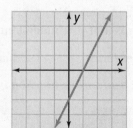 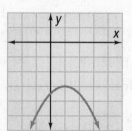

Problem 1 Finding the Features of a Quadratic Function

Got It? What are the vertex, axis of symmetry, maximum and minimum values, and range of $y = -3x^2 - 4x + 6$?

6. Circle the graph of $y = -3x^2 - 4x + 6$.

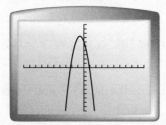 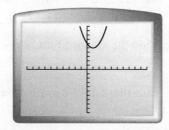 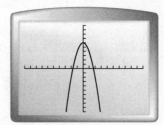

7. Draw and label the axis of symmetry on the graph you circled in Exercise 6.

8. Circle and label the maximum or minimum value on the graph.

9. Circle the range of the function.

$y \geq 5.0$ $y \leq 6.0$ all real numbers $\leq 7.\overline{3}$ all real numbers ≤ 9.2

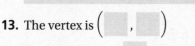

Properties Quadratic Function in Standard Form

- The graph of $f(x) = ax^2 + bx + c$, $a \neq 0$, is a parabola.

- If $a > 0$, the parabola opens upward. If $a < 0$, the parabola opens downward.

- The axis of symmetry is the line $x = -\frac{b}{2a}$.

- The x-coordinate of the vertex is $-\frac{b}{2a}$. The y-coordinate of the vertex is $f\left(-\frac{b}{2a}\right)$.

- The y-intercept is $(0, c)$.

10. The y-intercept of the graph of $f(x) = 5x^2 - 3x - 4$ is $\left(\boxed{}, \boxed{}\right)$.

 Problem 2 Graphing a Function of the Form $y = ax^2 + bx + c$

Got It? What is the graph of $y = -2x^2 + 2x - 5$?

11. The axis of symmetry is $x = -\frac{b}{2a} = -\dfrac{\boxed{}}{2 \cdot \boxed{}} = \boxed{}$.

12. Substitute to find the y-coordinate of the vertex.

13. The vertex is $\left(\boxed{}, \boxed{}\right)$

14. The y-intercept is $\boxed{}$. The reflection of the y-intercept across the axis of symmetry is $\left(\boxed{}, \boxed{}\right)$.

15. Plot the points from Exercises 13 and 14. Draw a smooth curve.

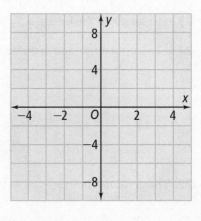

Lesson 4-2

Problem 3 Converting Standard Form to Vertex Form

Got It? What is the vertex form of $y = -x^2 + 4x - 5$?

16. Use the justifications at the right to find the vertex.

$y = \left(\boxed{}\right)x^2 + \left(\boxed{}\right)x + \left(\boxed{}\right)$ Write the function in the form $y = ax^2 + bx + c$.

$x = -\dfrac{b}{2a} = -\dfrac{\boxed{}}{2 \cdot \boxed{}} = \boxed{}$ Find the x-coordinate of the vertex.

$\boxed{}$ Substitute the x-coordinate value into the equation and simplify.

$y = \boxed{}$

17. The vertex is $\left(\boxed{}, \boxed{}\right)$.

18. Use the general form of the equation, $y = a(x - h)^2 + k$. Substitute for a, h, and k.

$y = \boxed{}\left[x - \left(\boxed{}\right)\right]^2 + \left(\boxed{}\right)$

19. The vertex form of the function is $\boxed{}$.

 Problem 4 Interpreting a Quadratic Graph

Got It? The Zhaozhou Bridge in China is the oldest known arch bridge, dating to 605 A.D. You can model the support arch with the function $f(x) = -0.001075x^2 + 0.131148x$, where x and y are measured in feet. How high is the arch above its supports?

20. What point on the parabola gives the height of the arch above its supports?

$\boxed{}$

21. Find the x-coordinate of the vertex.

$x = -\dfrac{b}{2a} = -\dfrac{\boxed{}}{2 \cdot \boxed{}} = \boxed{}$

22. The axis of symmetry of the parabola is $x = \boxed{}$.

23. The length of the bridge is $\boxed{}$ ft.

24. Use the x-coordinate of the vertex to find the y-coordinate.

$\boxed{}$

25. The vertex is about $\left(\boxed{}, \boxed{}\right)$, so the arch is $\boxed{}$ feet above its support.

Lesson Check • Do you UNDERSTAND?

Error Analysis A student graphed the function $y = 2x^2 - 4x - 3$. **Find and correct the error.**

26. The vertex of $y = ax^2 + bx + c$ is $\left(-\dfrac{b}{2a}, f\left(-\dfrac{b}{2a}\right)\right)$. Find the x- and y-coordinates of the vertex of $y = 2x^2 - 4x - 3$.

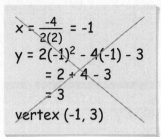

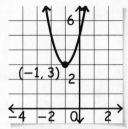

27. Find the y-intercept of $y = 2x^2 - 4x - 3$.

28. Describe the student's error and graph the function correctly.

_____

_____

Math Success

Check off the vocabulary words that you understand.

☐ quadratic ☐ standard form ☐ vertex ☐ axis of symmetry ☐ y-intercept

Rate how well you can *graph quadratic functions written in standard form.*

Need to review 0 2 4 6 8 10 Now I get it!

Lesson 4-2

Vocabulary

● Review

1. Cross out the graphs that are NOT parabolas.

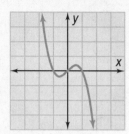 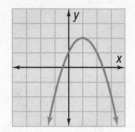 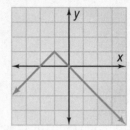 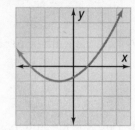

● Vocabulary Builder

model (verb) MAH dul

Main Idea: **Modeling** is a way of using math to describe a real-world situation.

Definition: A function or equation **models** an action or relationship by describing its behavior or the data associated with that relationship.

Example: The equation $a = 3g$ **models** the relationship between the number of apples, a, and the number of oranges, g, when the number of apples is triple the number of oranges.

● Use Your Vocabulary

Draw a line from each description in Column A to the equation that *models* it in Column B.

Column A	Column B
2. The string section of the orchestra has twice as many violins as cellos.	$y = 2x + 1$
3. There are two eggs per person with one extra for good measure.	$y = 100 - 2x$
4. There were 100 shin guards in the closet, and each player took two.	$y = 2x$

Problem 1 Writing an Equation of a Parabola

Got It? What is the equation of a parabola containing the points $(0, 0)$, $(1, -2)$, and $(-1, -4)$?

5. Substitute the three points one at a time into $y = ax^2 + bx + c$ to write a system of equations.

Use $(0, 0)$. $\quad\boxed{} = a\left(\boxed{}\right)^2 + b\left(\boxed{}\right) + c$

Use $(1, -2)$. $\quad\boxed{} = a\left(\boxed{}\right)^2 + b\left(\boxed{}\right) + c$

Use $(-1, -4)$. $\quad\boxed{} = a\left(\boxed{}\right)^2 + b\left(\boxed{}\right) + c$

6. Solve the system of equations.

7. The equation of the parabola is $y = \boxed{}\, x^2 + \boxed{}\, x + \boxed{}$.

 Problem 2 Using a Quadratic Model

Got It? The parabolic path of a thrown ball can be modeled by the table. The top of a wall is at $(5, 6)$. Will the ball go over the wall? If not, will it hit the wall on the way up, or the way down?

x	y
1	3
2	5
3	6

8. Circle the system of equations you find by substituting the three given points that are on the parabola.

$1 = 9a + 3b + c$	$3 = a + b + c$	$3 = a + b + c$
$2 = 25a + 5b + c$	$5 = 2a + 2b + c$	$5 = 4a + 2b + c$
$3 = 36a + 6b + c$	$6 = 9a - 3b + c$	$6 = 9a + 3b + c$

9. Now, solve the system of equations.

10. The solution of the system is $a = \boxed{}$, $b = \boxed{}$, $c = \boxed{}$.

11. The quadratic model for the ball's path is $\boxed{}$.

12. How can you determine whether the ball goes over the wall? Place a ✓ if the statement is correct. Place an ✗ if it is not.

$\boxed{}$ The value of the model at $x = 5$ is at least 6.

$\boxed{}$ The value of the model at $x = 6$ is at least 5.

Lesson 4-3

13. Will the ball go over the wall? Explain.

_____

_____

14. The value of the model at $x = 6$ is less than / greater than value of the model at

$x = 5$, therefore the ball was on its way down / up as it approached the wall.

 Problem 3 **Using Quadratic Regression**

Got It? The table shows a meteorologist's predicted temperatures for a summer day in Denver, Colorado. What is a quadratic model for the data? Predict the high temperature for the day. At what time does the high temperature occur?

Time	Predicted Temperature (°F)
6 A.M.	63
9 A.M.	76
12 P.M.	86
3 P.M.	89
6 P.M.	85
9 P.M.	76

15. Using the LIST feature on a graphing calculator, identify the data that you will enter.

$L_1 = $ _____

$L_2 = $ _____

16. Using a 24-hour clock, write the values for the L_1 column.

6 A.M.: ☐   3 A.M.: ☐

9 A.M.: ☐   6 P.M.: ☐

12 P.M.: ☐   9 P.M.: ☐

17. Circle the calculator screen that shows the correct data entry.

L1	L2	L3
6	63	
9	76	
12	86	
3	89	
6	85	
9	76	

L2(6)=76

L1	L2	L3
6	63	
9	76	
12	86	
15	89	
18	85	
21	76	

L2(6)=76

L1	L2	L3
6	76	
9	86	
12	89	
15	85	
18	76	
21	63	

L2(6)=63

18. Enter the data from the table into your calculator. Use the QuadReg function. Your screen should look like the one at the right.

Write the quadratic model for temperature.

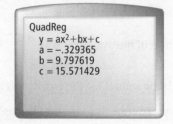

QuadReg
$y = ax^2 + bx + c$
a = −.329365
b = 9.797619
c = 15.571429

_____

19. Use your calculator to find the maximum value of the model. The vertex of the parabola is ([   ] , [   ]).

20. The high temperature will be [   ] °F.

21. At what time will the high temperature occur?

_____

Lesson Check • Do you UNDERSTAND?

Error Analysis Your classmate says he can write the equation of a quadratic function that passes through the points $(3, 4)$, $(5, -2)$, and $(3, 0)$. Explain his error.

22. Graph the points $(3, 4)$, $(5, -2)$, and $(3, 0)$.

23. Underline the correct words to complete the rule for finding a quadratic model.

Two / Three noncollinear points, no two / three of which are in line horizontally / vertically , are on the graph of exactly one quadratic function.

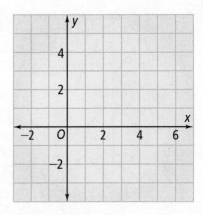

24. What is your classmate's error?

_____

_____

_____

Math Success

Check off the vocabulary words that you understand.

☐ model   ☐ quadratic model

Rate how well you can _use a quadratic model_.

Need to review 0 2 4 6 8 10 Now I get it!

4-4 Factoring Quadratic Expressions

Vocabulary

● Review

1. Complete each *factor* tree.

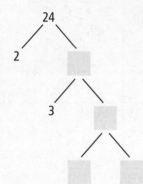

● Vocabulary Builder

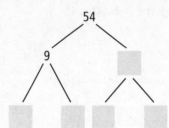

$$\underbrace{2x^2 - x - 10}_{\text{expression}} = \underbrace{(2x - 5)(x + 2)}_{\text{factors}}$$

factor (noun) **FAK tur**

Other Word Forms: factor (verb)

Main Idea: The **factors** of an expression are similar to the **factors** of a number.

Definition: The **factors** of a given expression are expressions whose product equals the given expression. When you **factor** an expression, you break it into smaller expressions whose product equals the given expression.

Example: The **factors** of the expression $2x^2 - x - 10$ are $2x - 5$ and $x + 2$.

● Use Your Vocabulary

2. Circle the prime *factors* of $24xy$.

$24 \cdot x \cdot y$	$2 \cdot 4 \cdot x \cdot y$	$2^3 \cdot 3 \cdot x \cdot y$

3. Circle the prime factors of $54a^2b$.

$54 \cdot a^2 \cdot b$	$5 \cdot 4 \cdot a^2 \cdot b$	$2 \cdot 3^3 \cdot a^2 \cdot b$

Problem 1 Factoring $ax^2 + bx + c$ when $a = \pm 1$

Got It? What is the expression $x^2 + 14x + 40$ in factored form?

4. Complete the factor table. Then circle the pair of factors whose sum is 14.

Factors of 40	1, 40	2,		
Sum of Factors				

5. Circle the expression written as the product of two binomials.

$(x + 1)(x + 40)$ $(x + 2)(x + 20)$ $(x + 4)(x + 10)$ $(x + 5)(x + 8)$

Got It? What is the expression $x^2 - 11x + 30$ in factored form?

6. Underline the correct word(s) to complete each sentence.

I need to find factors that multiply / sum to 30 and multiply / sum to −11.

At least one of the factors that sum to −11 must be positive / negative .

The two factors that multiply to 30 must both be positive / negative .

7. Circle the factors of 30 that sum to −11.

1 and 30	2 and 15	3 and 10	5 and 6
−1 and −30	−2 and −15	−3 and −10	−5 and −6

8. Factor the expression.

$$x^2 - 11x + 30 = \left(x \quad \right)\left(x \quad \right)$$

Got It? What is the expression $-x^2 + 14x + 32$ in factored form?

9. Rewrite the expression to show a trinomial with a leading coefficient 1.

$-x^2 + 14x + 32 = $

10. **Reasoning** You are looking for factors of −32 that sum to −14. Which of the factors has the greater absolute value, the negative factor or the positive factor? How do you know?

11. Circle the factors of −32 that sum to −14.

−1 and 32	−2 and 16	−4 and 8
1 and −32	2 and −16	4 and −8

12. Write the factored form of the expression.

Lesson 4-4

Problem 2 Finding Common Factors

Got It? What is the expression $7n^2 - 21$ in factored form?

13. The GCF of $7n^2$ and 21 is ☐.

14. Use the Distributive Property to factor the expression.

$7n^2 + 21 =$ ☐ $\left(\right.$ ☐ $+$ ☐ $\left.\right)$

Problem 3 Factoring $ax^2 + bx + c$ when $|a| \neq 1$

Got It? What is the expression $4x^2 + 7x + 3$ in factored form? Check your answers.

15. Complete the diagram below.

$$4x^2 + 7x + 3$$

☐ • ☐ $= 12$

16. Complete the factor pairs of ac. Then circle the pair that sums to 7.

$\left(1, \text{☐}\right)$ $\qquad$ $\left(2, \text{☐}\right)$ $\qquad$ $\left(3, \text{☐}\right)$

17. Use your answer to Exercise 16 to complete the diagram below.

$$4x^2 \quad + \quad 7x \quad + \quad 3$$

☐ $+$ ☐

$= \quad 4x^2 + (4x) \quad + \quad$ ☐ $+$ ☐

$= 4x\left(\text{☐} + \text{☐}\right) + 3\left(\text{☐} + \text{☐}\right)$

The expressions inside the parentheses must be equal.

Use the Distributive Property to factor out the GCF, the part inside the parentheses.

$= \left(4x + 3\right)\left(\text{☐} + \text{☐}\right)$

Problem 4 Factoring a Perfect Square Trinomial

Got It? What is $64x^2 - 16x + 1$ in factored form?

18. Circle the form your answer will have.

$$(a + b)^2 \qquad\qquad\qquad (a - b)^2$$

19. Use the justifications to complete each step.

$64x^2 - 16x + 1$ Write the original expression.

$\left(\boxed{}\,x\right)^2 - 16x + \left(\boxed{}\right)^2$ Write the first and third terms as squares.

$\left(\boxed{}\,x\right)^2 - 2\left(\boxed{}\right)\left(\boxed{}\right)x + \left(\boxed{}\right)^2$ Write the middle term as $(2ac)x$.

20. Write the expression as the square of a binomial.

Lesson Check • Do you UNDERSTAND?

Reasoning Explain how to rewrite the expression $a^2 - 2ab + b^2 - 25$ as the product of two trinomial factors. (*Hint:* Group the first three terms. What type of expression are they?)

21. Complete: The first three terms of the expression are a ___?___.

| perfect square trinomial | difference of two squares |

22. Factor the first three terms of the expression.

23. Rewrite the original expression using the factored form of the first three terms.

24. Complete: The expression you wrote in Exercise 23 is a ___?___.

| perfect square trinomial | difference of two squares |

25. Circle the expression written as the product of two trinomial factors.

$a^2 - 2ab + b^2 \qquad (a - b)^2 - 25 \qquad (a - b)(-25) \qquad (a - b - 5)(a - b + 5)$

Math Success

Check off the vocabulary words that you understand.

☐ factor of an expression ☐ perfect square trinomial ☐ difference of two squares

Rate how well you can *factor quadratic expressions*.

 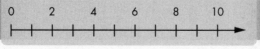

Lesson 4-4

Quadratic Equations

Vocabulary

● Review

1. Cross out the equation below that is *not* a function.

$$f(x) = 2x - 7 \qquad y^2 = 3x^2 - 4x \qquad y = -x^2 + 14x - 7 \qquad g(x) = |x^3|$$

● Vocabulary Builder

zero of a function (noun) ZEER oh

Main Idea: Wherever the graph of a function $y = f(x)$ intersects the x axis, $f(x) = 0$. The value of x at any of these intersection points is called a **zero** of the function.

Definition: A value of x for which $f(x) = 0$ is a **zero** of the function $f(x)$.

Example: $x = 2$ is a zero of $f(x) = 3x - 6$, because $f(2) = 3(2) - 6 = 0$.

● Use Your Vocabulary

Write the *zero(s)* of each function.

2.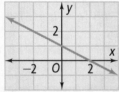

Zero(s):

3.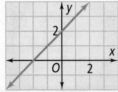

Zero(s):

4.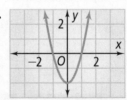

Zero(s):

Key Concept Zero-Product Property

If $ab = 0$, then $a = 0$ or $b = 0$.

Example: If $(x + 7)(x - 2) = 0$, then $(x + 7) = 0$ or $(x - 2) = 0$.

5. If either $x + 7 = 0$ or $x - 2 = 0$, circle all of the possible values of x.

$$-7 \qquad\qquad -2 \qquad\qquad 2 \qquad\qquad -7$$

Problem 1 Solving Quadratic Equations by Factoring

Got It? What are the solutions of the quadratic equation $x^2 - 7x = -12$?

6. The equation is solved below. Write a justification for each step.

$x^2 - 7x = -12$ — Write the original equation.

$x^2 - 7x + 12 = 0$

$(x - 3)(x - 4) = 0$

$x - 3 = 0 \text{ or } x - 4 = 0$

$x = 3 \text{ or } x = 4$

 Problem 2 Solving Quadratic Equations With Tables

Got It? What are the solutions of the quadratic equation $4x^2 - 14x + 7 = 4 - x$?

7. Write the equation in standard form.

$\boxed{} x^2 + \boxed{} x + \boxed{} = 0$

8. Enter the equation into your calculator. Use the results to complete the table below.

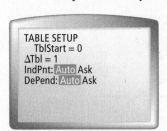

x	0	1	2	3	4
y_1					

9. Based on the table, one solution of the equation is $x = \boxed{}$.

10. Another solution occurs between $\boxed{}$ and $\boxed{}$. Change the x-interval to 0.05. Complete the table.

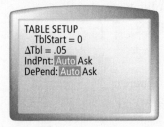

x	0.1	0.15	0.2	0.25	0.3
y_1					

11. Based on the table, the other solution to the equation is $x = \boxed{}$.

Lesson 4-5

Problem 3 Solving a Quadratic Equation by Graphing

Got It? What are the solutions of the quadratic equation $x^2 + 2x - 24 = 0$?

12. The graph at the right shows the equation. Circle the zeros of the function.

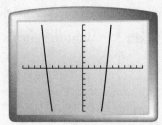

13. The solutions of the quadratic equation

are [ ] and [ ] .

Problem 4 Using a Quadratic Equation

Got It? The function $y = -0.03x^2 + 1.60x$ models the path of a kicked soccer ball. The height is y, the distance is x, and the units are meters. How far does the soccer ball travel? How high does the soccer ball go? Describe a reasonable domain and range for the function.

14. The graph below shows the function. Circle the point on the graph where the soccer ball is at its highest point and the point where the soccer ball lands. Label each point with its coordinates.

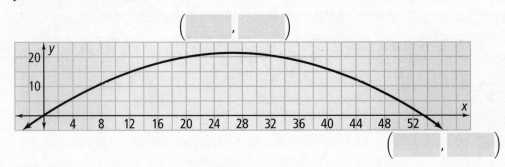

Reasoning Circle the phrase that completes each sentence.

15. The distance the soccer ball travels is the __?__ .

x-coordinate of the vertex	y-intercept	x-coordinate of the positive zero	y-coordinate of the vertex

16. The maximum height of the soccer ball is the __?__ .

x-coordinate of the vertex	y-intercept	x-coordinate of the positive zero	y-coordinate of the vertex

17. Underline the correct word to complete each sentence.

The domain should include positive / negative numbers only.

The range should include positive / negative numbers only.

18. Complete.

Domain: [ ] $\leq x \leq$ [ ]   Range: [ ] $\leq y \leq$ [ ]

Lesson Check • Do you know HOW?

Solve the equation $x^2 - 9 = 0$ by factoring.

19. Circle the phrase that *best* describes the expression on the left side of the equals sign.

binomial   difference of two squares   parabola   quadratic expression

20. Factor the expression on the left side of the equal sign.

21. The solutions of the equation are ☐ and ☐ .

Lesson Check • Do you UNDERSTAND?

Vocabulary If 5 is a zero of the function $y = x^2 + bx - 20$, what is the value of b? Explain.

22. If 5 is a zero of the function then whenever ☐ = 5,

☐ = 0.

23. Substitute ☐ for x and solve for ☐ .

24. The coefficient $b =$ ☐ .

Math Success

Check off the vocabulary words that you understand.

☐ zero of a function   ☐ Zero-Product property

Rate how well you can *find the zeros of quadratic equations.*

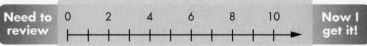

4-6 Completing the Square

Vocabulary

● Review

Draw a line from each expression to its *square root*.

1. $25x^2$	$x + 2$
2. $x^2 + 4x + 4$	$6x - 3$
3. $36x^2 - 36x + 9$	$2x - 5y$
4. $4x^2 - 20xy + 25y^2$	$\pm 5x$

● Vocabulary Builder

> **trinomial** (noun) **try NOH mee ul**
>
> **Related Words:** perfect square
>
> **Definition:** A **trinomial** is an expression consisting of three terms.
>
> **Main Idea:** You can use *perfect square* **trinomials** to solve quadratic equations.
>
> **Examples:** $4x^2 - 7x + 5$, $ax^2 + bx + c$, and $2x - 5y + 4z$ are all **trinomials**.
> $x^2 + 4x + 4$ is a *perfect square* **trinomial** because it is the square of the binomial $x + 2$.

● Use Your Vocabulary

5. Write the number of terms in each expression.

$x + 1$	$t^2 - 2t - 6$	y^3	$p^2 - 6p + 9$

6. Put a **T** next to each expression that is a *trinomial*. Put an **N** next to each expression that is *not* a *trinomial*.

_____ x^2	_____ $g^3 + g - 4$	_____ $x^2 - 2x + 5$	_____ $x^2 - 4x$

7. Cross out the expression that is NOT a perfect square *trinomial*.

$x^2 + 2x + 1$	$9x^2 - 6x + 1$	$4x^2 - 4x - 4$	$25x^2 - 30x + 9$

Problem 2 Determining Dimensions

Got It? The lengths of the sides of a rectangular window have the ratio 1.6 to 1. The area of the window is 2822.4 in^2. What are the window dimensions?

8. Circle the equation that represents this situation.

$$x(1.6x) = 2822.4 \qquad 1.6x^2 + x = 2822.4^2 \qquad (1 + 1.6)x^2 = 2822.4$$

9. The equation is solved below. Write a justification from the box for each step.

Divide each side by 1.6.	Simplify.
Simplify the left side.	Take the square root of each side.

$x(1.6x) = 2822.4$ Write the original equation.

$1.6x^2 = 2822.4$ _____

$\dfrac{1.6x^2}{1.6} = \dfrac{2822.4}{1.6}$ _____

$x^2 = 1764$ _____

$x = \pm 42$ _____

10. One side of the window measures [ ] in. The other side measures

1.6([ ]), or [ ] in.

Problem 3 Solving a Perfect Square Trinomial Equation

Got It? What is the solution of $x^2 - 14x + 49 = 25$?

11. Use the justifications at the right to solve the equation.

$x^2 - 14x + 49 = 25$ Write the original equation.

$\left(x - \boxed{}\right)^2 = 25$ Factor the perfect square trinomial.

$\left(x - \boxed{}\right) = \pm\,\boxed{}$ Take the square root of each side.

$x - \boxed{} = \boxed{}$ or $x - \boxed{} = \boxed{}$ Write as two equations.

$x = \boxed{}$ or $x = \boxed{}$ Solve for x.

take note

Key Concept Completing the Square

You can turn the expression $x^2 + bx$ into a perfect square trinomial by adding $\left(\dfrac{b}{2}\right)^2$.

$$x^2 + bx + \left(\dfrac{b}{2}\right)^2 = \left(x + \dfrac{b}{2}\right)^2$$

Lesson 4-6

12. Circle the value that completes the square for $x^2 + 16x$.

| 4 | −4 | −16 | 64 |

Problem 4 Completing the Square

Got It? What value completes the square for $x^2 + 6x$?

13. In the expression, the value $b = $ ☐.

14. Circle the expression for the value that completes the square.

| 6^2 | $-\dfrac{6}{2}$ | $\dfrac{6^2}{2}$ | $\left(\dfrac{6}{2}\right)^2$ |

15. Complete the square and write the expression as a perfect square.

Problem 5 Solving by Completing the Square

Got It? What is the solution of $2x^2 - x + 3 = x + 7$?

16. Use the justifications at the right to solve the equation.

$$2x^2 - x + 3 = x + 7$$ Write the original equation.

$$x^2 + \boxed{}\, x = \boxed{}$$ Rewrite so that all terms with x on one side of the equation.

$$x^2 + \left(\dfrac{\boxed{}}{\boxed{}}\right) x = \dfrac{\boxed{}}{\boxed{}}$$ Divide each side by a so that the coefficient of x^2 is 1.

$$x^2 + \boxed{}\, x = \boxed{}$$ Simplify.

$$\left(\dfrac{b}{2}\right)^2 = \left(\dfrac{\boxed{}}{2}\right)^2 = \boxed{}$$ Find $\left(\dfrac{b}{2}\right)^2$.

$$x^2 + \boxed{}\, x + \boxed{} = \dfrac{\boxed{}}{\boxed{}}$$ Add $\left(\dfrac{b}{2}\right)^2$ to each side.

$$\left(x + \boxed{}\right)^2 = \dfrac{\boxed{}}{\boxed{}}$$ Factor the trinomial.

$$x + \boxed{} = \boxed{}$$ Take the square root of each side.

$$x = \boxed{}$$ Solve for x.

Problem 6 Writing in Vertex Form

Got It? What is $y = x^2 + 3x - 6$ in vertex form? Name the vertex and y-intercept.

17. Circle the equation that you can use to complete the square.

$$y = x^2 + 3x + \left(\tfrac{3}{2}\right)^2 - 6 - \left(\tfrac{3}{2}\right)^2 \qquad\qquad y = x^2 + 3x - \tfrac{3}{2} - 6 + \tfrac{3}{2}$$

$$y = x^2 + 3x - \tfrac{3}{2} - 6 \qquad\qquad y = x^2 + 3x - \left(\tfrac{3}{2}\right)^2$$

18. Simplify the equation.

$$y = \left(x + \boxed{}\right)^2 - 6 + \boxed{} = \left(x + \boxed{}\right)^2 + \boxed{}$$

19. The vertex is $\left(\boxed{}, \boxed{}\right)$.

20. The y-intercept is $\boxed{}$.

Lesson Check • Do you UNDERSTAND?

How can you rewrite the equation $x^2 + 12x + 5 = 3$ so that the left side of the equation is in the form $(x + a)^2$?

21. Use the justifications at the right to rewrite the equation.

$$x^2 + 12x + 5 = 3 \qquad\qquad\text{Write the original equation.}$$

$$x^2 + 12x = \boxed{} \qquad\qquad\text{Rewrite the equation as } x^2 + bx = c.$$

$$x^2 + 12x + \left(\frac{\boxed{}}{2}\right)^2 = \boxed{} + \left(\frac{\boxed{}}{2}\right)^2 \qquad\qquad\text{Complete the square.}$$

$$x^2 + 12x + \boxed{} = \boxed{} + \boxed{} \qquad\qquad\text{Simplify powers.}$$

$$x^2 + 12x + \boxed{} = \boxed{} \qquad\qquad\text{Add.}$$

$$\left(x + \boxed{}\right)^2 = \boxed{} \qquad\qquad\text{Write as } (x + a)^2 = c.$$

Math Success

Check off the vocabulary words that you understand.

☐ trinomial   ☐ perfect square trinomial   ☐ completing the square

Rate how well you can *simplify quadratic expressions by completing the square.*

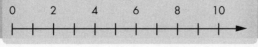

Lesson 4-6

The Quadratic Formula

Vocabulary

● **Review**

Draw a line from each *formula* to its description.

1. $a = s^2$ area of a circle

2. $c = 2\pi r$ circumference of a circle

3. $p = 2(l + w)$ area of a square

4. $a = \pi r^2$ perimeter of a rectangle

● **Vocabulary Builder**

discriminant (noun) **dih SKRIM uh nunt**

Definition: The **discriminant** of a quadratic
equation in the form $ax^2 + bx + c = 0$
is the value of the expression $b^2 - 4ac$.

Main Idea: The **discriminant** helps you determine how many real solutions
a quadratic function has.

discriminant

$b^2 - 4ac > 0$ means 2 real solutions.
$b^2 - 4ac = 0$ means 1 real solution.
$b^2 - 4ac < 0$ means 0 real solutions.

● **Use Your Vocabulary**

Circle the *discriminant* of each equation.

5. $2x^2 + (-7x) - 4 = 0$

| $7^2 - 4(2)-4$ | $7 - 4(-4)$ | $(-7)^2 - 4(2)(-4)$ |

6. $3x^2 + 4x + 2 = 0$

| $4 - 4(3)(2)$ | $12 + 4(3)(2)$ | $4^2 - 4(3)(2)$ |

7. $x^2 + x - 1 = 0$

| $1^2 - 4(1)(-1)$ | $2 - 4(1)(1)$ | $1(2) - (1)(1)$ |

8. $4x^2 + (-12x) + 9 = 0$

| $12 - 4(4)(9)$ | $(-12)^2 - 4(4)(9)$ | $(-12)^2 + 4(4)(9)$ |

Key Concept The Quadratic Formula

To solve the quadratic equation $ax^2 + bx + c = 0$, use the **Quadratic Formula**.

$$x = \frac{-b \pm \sqrt{b^2 - 4ac}}{2a}$$

9. Cross out the value of a that does NOT give a solution to the quadratic formula.

| $a = 4$ | $a = -1$ | $a = 1$ | $a = 0$ |

 **Problem 1** Using the Quadratic Formula

Got It? What are the solutions to $x^2 + 4x = -4$? Use the Quadratic Formula.

10. Circle the standard form of the equation.

| $x^2 + 4x = -4$ | $x^2 + 4x - 4 = 0$ | $x^2 + 4x + 4 = 0$ |

11. Identify the values of a, b, and c.

$a = \boxed{}$ $\qquad b = \boxed{}$ $\qquad c = \boxed{}$

12. Substitute the values of a, b, and c into the Quadratic Formula. Use the justifications to solve the equation.

$x = \dfrac{-b \pm \sqrt{\left(\boxed{}\right)^2 - 4\left(\boxed{}\right)c}}{2\left(\boxed{}\right)}$ $\qquad$ Write the Quadratic Formula.

$= \dfrac{\boxed{} \pm \sqrt{\left(\boxed{}\right)^2 - 4\left(\boxed{}\right)\left(\boxed{}\right)}}{2\left(\boxed{}\right)}$ $\qquad$ Substitute for a, b, and c.

$= \dfrac{\boxed{} \pm \sqrt{\boxed{}}}{\boxed{}}$ $\qquad$ Simplify under the radical.

$= \boxed{}$ $\qquad$ Simplify.

13. Substitute the value you found in Exercise 12 into the original equation to check your solution.

$x^2 + 4x + 4 = 0$ $\qquad$ Write the original equation.

$\left(\boxed{}\right)^2 + 4\left(\boxed{}\right) + 4 \stackrel{?}{=} 0$ $\qquad$ Substitute for x.

$\boxed{} = 0$ ✓ $\qquad$ Check for equality.

Lesson 4-7

Problem 2 Applying the Quadratic Formula

Got It? Fundraising Your School's jazz band is selling CDs as a fundraiser. The total profit p depends on the amount x that your band charges for each CD. The equation $p = -x^2 + 48x - 300$ models the profit of the fundraiser. What's the least amount, in dollars, you can charge for a CD to make a profit of $100?

14. Circle the equation that represents the situation.

$$0 = -x^2 + 48x - 200 \qquad 0 = x^2 + 48x + 500 \qquad 0 = -x^2 + 48x - 400$$

15. Cross out the value that will NOT be substituted into the Quadratic Formula to solve the problem.

$$-1 \qquad\qquad 1 \qquad\qquad 48 \qquad\qquad -400$$

16. Substitute values for a, b, and c into the Quadratic Formula and simplify.

$$x = \frac{\boxed{} \pm \sqrt{\left(\boxed{}\right)^2 - 4\left(\boxed{}\right)\left(\boxed{}\right)}}{2\left(\boxed{}\right)}$$

$$x = \frac{\boxed{} \pm \sqrt{\boxed{}}}{\boxed{}} \approx \boxed{} \text{ or } x \approx \boxed{}$$

17. The smallest amount you can charge is $\boxed{}$ for each CD to make a profit of $100.

 Problem 3 Using the Discriminant

Got It? What is the number of real solutions of $2x^2 - 3x + 7 = 0$?

18. Complete the reasoning model below.

Think	Write
Find the values of a, b, and c.	$a = \boxed{}$, $b = \boxed{}$, $c = \boxed{}$
Evaluate $b^2 - 4ac$.	$b^2 - 4ac = \left(\boxed{}\right)^2 - 4\left(\boxed{}\right)\left(\boxed{}\right) = \boxed{}$
Interpret the discriminant.	The discriminant is positive / negative / zero . The equation has 2 / 1 / 0 real solution(s).

 Problem 4 Using the Discriminant to Solve a Problem

Got It? Reasoning You hit a golf ball into the air from a height of 1 in. above the ground with an initial vertical velocity of 85 ft/s. The function $h = -16t^2 + 85t + \frac{1}{12}$ models the height, in feet, of the ball at time t in seconds. Will the ball reach a height of 120 ft? Explain.

Chapter 4   108

19. Circle the correct strategy to solve the problem.

Evaluate the discriminant using the values $a = -16$, $b = 85$, $c = \frac{1}{12}$.	Substitute 120 for h in the equation and evaluate the discriminant to check for real solutions.	Substitute 120 for t in the equation and solve for h.

20. Write the equation in standard form.   **21.** Evaluate the discriminant.

$$\boxed{}\, t^2 + \boxed{}\, t + \boxed{} = 0$$

22. The discriminant is positive / negative / zero , so the equation has 2 / 1 / 0 real solutions.

23. The golf ball will / will not reach a height of 120 feet.

Lesson Check • Do you UNDERSTAND?

Reasoning For what values of k does the equation $x^2 + kx + 9 = 0$ have one real solution? two real solutions?

24. If 9 completes the square, then $\left(\frac{k}{2}\right)^2 = \boxed{}$, so $\frac{k}{2} = \boxed{}$ and $k = \boxed{}$.

25. Place a ✓ if you can use the equation or inequality to solve this problem. Place an ✗ if you cannot.

$\boxed{}\; k^2 - 36 = 0$ $\boxed{}\; k^2 - 36 < 0$ $\boxed{}\; k^2 - 36 > 0$ $\boxed{}\; k^2 = 36^2$

26. Now answer the question.

Math Success

Check off the vocabulary words that you understand.

☐ quadratic formula   ☐ discriminant   ☐ real solutions

Rate how well you can *use the quadratic formula to solve problems.*

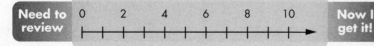

Lesson 4-7

4-8   Complex Numbers

Vocabulary

● Review

1. Circle the square root that is not a *real number*.

$$\sqrt{64} \qquad \sqrt{6 - (2)(4)} \qquad \sqrt{4 - (2)(-6)} \qquad \sqrt{(-5)^2}$$

● Vocabulary Builder

> **conjugate** (adjective) KAHN juh gut
>
> **Related Words:** complex numbers, pairs, roots, imaginary solutions
>
> **Math Usage:** The **conjugate** of the complex number $a + bi$ is $a - bi$.
>
> **Main Idea:** Complex solutions occur in **conjugate** pairs of the form $a + bi$ and $a - bi$. The product of complex **conjugates** is always a real number. You can use complex **conjugates** to simplify division of complex numbers.

● Use Your Vocabulary

Write C if the number pairs are complex conjugate or N if they are not.

_____ **2.** $4 + 3i, 4 - 3i$

_____ **3.** $5 + \sqrt{2}, 5 - \sqrt{2}$

_____ **4.** $\sqrt{5} - \sqrt{3}i, \sqrt{5} + \sqrt{3}i$

_____ **5.** $3 + \sqrt{5}i, 3 + \sqrt{-5}i$

➤ take note

Key Concept   Square Root of a Negative Real Number

The **imaginary unit** i is the complex number whose square is -1. So, $i^2 = -1$, and $i = \sqrt{-1}$.

For any positive real number a, $\sqrt{-a} = \sqrt{-1 \cdot a} = \sqrt{-1} \cdot \sqrt{a} = i\sqrt{a}$.   **Example:** $\sqrt{-5} = i\sqrt{5}$

Note that $\left(\sqrt{-5}\right)^2 = (i\sqrt{5})^2 = i^2(\sqrt{5})^2 = -1 \cdot 5 = -5$ (not 5).

6. Use $\sqrt{-1} = i$ to complete each equation.

$\sqrt{-2} = \boxed{}\,\sqrt{2}$ $\qquad$ $\sqrt{-3} = i\sqrt{\boxed{}}$ $\qquad$ $\sqrt{-6} = \boxed{}$ $\qquad$ $\sqrt{\boxed{}} = i\sqrt{8}$

 Problem 1 Simplifying a Number Using i

Got It? How do you write the number $\sqrt{-12}$ using the imaginary unit i?

7. Circle the expression that is equivalent to $\sqrt{-12}$.

$$\sqrt{-1 \cdot 4(-3)} \qquad 4\sqrt{-1} \cdot \sqrt{3} \qquad \sqrt{-1 \cdot 4 \cdot 3} \qquad -2\sqrt{3}$$

8. Simplify the expression you circled in Exercise 7.

9. Using the imaginary unit i, $\sqrt{-12} = \blacksquare$.

$$2\sqrt{3}i \qquad\qquad 4\sqrt{i} \qquad\qquad 6i \qquad\qquad 4\sqrt{3}i$$

 Problem 2 Graphing in the Complex Number Plane

Got It? What are the graph and absolute value of $5 - i$?

10. Underline the correct words to complete the sentence.

The graph of $5 - i$ is 5 units left / right and 1 unit up / down.

11. Graph the point.

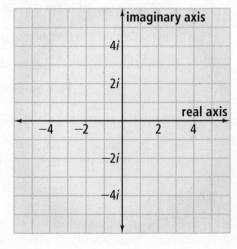

12. Find the absolute value.

$|5 - i| = \sqrt{\left(\boxed{}\right)^2 + \left(\boxed{}\right)^2}$ $\qquad$ Use the Distance Formula.

$= \sqrt{\boxed{} + \boxed{}}$ $\qquad$ Simplify powers.

$= \sqrt{\boxed{}}$ $\qquad$ Add.

 Problem 3 Adding and Subtracting Complex Numbers

Got It? What is the sum $(7 - 2i) + (-3 + i)$?

Lesson 4-8

13. The sum is found below. Write the justification for each step.

$(7 - 2i) + (-3 + i)$ Write the original expression.

$7 + (-2i - 3) + i$ _____ Property

$7 + (-3 - 2i) + i$ _____ Property

$(7 - 3) + (-2i + i)$ _____ Property

$4 - i$ _____

Problem 4 Multiplying Complex Numbers

Got It? What is the product $(7i)(3i)$?

14. Complete the solution. Justifications are given.

$(7i)(3i)$ Write the original expression.

[ ] i^2 Multiply.

([ ])([ ])   Substitute -1 for i^2.

[ ]   Simplify.

Problem 5 Dividing Complex Numbers

Got It? What is the quotient $\frac{5 - 2i}{3 + 4i}$?

15. Circle the first step in simplifying the fraction.

Find the complex conjugate of $5 - 2i$.	Find the complex conjugate of $3 + 4i$.
Find the absolute value of $5 - 2i$.	Find the absolute value of $3 + 4i$.

16. Cross out the expression that is NOT equivalent to the quotient.

$$\frac{15 - 20i - 6i + 8i^2}{9 - 12i + 12i - 16i^2} \qquad \frac{15 - 26i + 8i^2}{25} \qquad \frac{25 + 10i - 10i - 16i^2}{9 - 12i + 12i - 16i^2}$$

17. Simplify.

18. $\frac{5 - 2i}{3 + 4i} =$ [ ]

Problem 6 Factoring using Complex Conjugates

Got It? What are the factors of each expression?

19. $5x^2 + 20$

What is the GCF of 5 and 20? ____   Write as a product using the GCF. _____

Rewrite $x^2 + 4$ as $a^2 + b^2$. $a =$ ____ $b =$ ____ _____

Use $a^2 + b^2 = (a + bi)(a - bi)$.   _____

_____

What are the factors of $5x^2 + 20$?   _____

20. $x^2 + 81$ Rewrite $x^2 + 81$ in terms of $a^2 + b^2$. ____

Use $a^2 + b^2 = (a + bi)(a - bi)$.   _____

 Lesson Check • **Do you UNDERSTAND?**

Error Analysis Describe and correct the error made in simplifying the expression $(4 - 7i)(4 + 7i)$.

$(4 - 7i)(4 + 7i) = 16 + 28i - 28i + 49i^2$
$= 16 - 49$
$= -33$

21. Simplify the expression.

22. Explain the error shown above.

_____

_____

 Math Success

Check off the vocabulary words that you understand.

☐ imaginary number   ☐ complex number   ☐ complex conjugates

Rate how well you can *find complex-number solutions to quadratic equations.*

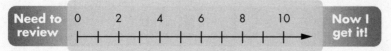

Need to review   0   2   4   6   8   10   Now I get it!

Vocabulary

● Review

Write T for true or F for false.

_____ **1.** The solution of system $y = 3x + 2$ and $y = 5x$ is the point where the two lines *intersect*.

_____ **2.** The solution of a system of 2 linear equations has at most 2 points of *intersection*.

_____ **3.** The solution of a system of inequalities is the point where the lines *intersect* with the *y*-axis.

_____ **4.** The solution of a system of inequalities is the region where the graphs of the inequalities overlap.

● Vocabulary Builder

Quadratic-Linear System (noun) kwah DRAT ik LIN ee ur SIS tum

Related Words: System of equations, system of inequalities.

Main Idea: A system of equations can include an equation with a graph that is not a line. Such a system can have more than one solution.

Definition: A **quadratic-linear system** is a system of one quadratic equation and one linear equation. The system can have two, one, or no solutions (points of intersection).

● Use Your Vocabulary

5. Cross out the graph that does NOT illustrate a *quadratic-linear system*.

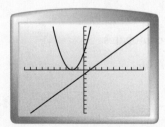
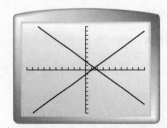
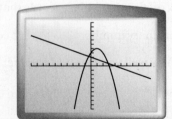

 **Problem 1** Solving a Linear-Quadratic System by Graphing

Got It? What is the solution of the system? $\begin{cases} y = x^2 + 6x + 9 \\ y = x + 3 \end{cases}$

6. Complete the table of values for both equations.

x	$x^2 + 6x + 9$	$x + 3$
−4		
−3		
−2		
−1		
0		
1		

7. Use the points from the table to graph the two equations.

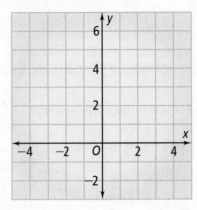

8. The solutions are $\left(\boxed{}, \boxed{} \right)$ and $\left(\boxed{}, \boxed{} \right)$.

9. Substitute into both equations to check the solutions.

 Problem 2 Solving Using Substitution

Got It? What is the solution of the system? $\begin{cases} y = -x^2 - 3x + 10 \\ y = x + 5 \end{cases}$

10. Use the justifications at the right to solve the system.

$x + \boxed{} = \boxed{} x^2 + \boxed{} x + \boxed{}$ Substitute $x + 5$ for y in the quadratic equation.

$\boxed{} x^2 + \boxed{} x + \boxed{} = 0$ Write in standard form.

$\left(x + \boxed{} \right)\left(x + \boxed{} \right) = 0$ Factor.

$x = \boxed{}$ or $x = \boxed{}$ Solve for x.

$x = \boxed{} \rightarrow y = \boxed{} + 5 = \boxed{}$ Substitute for x in $y = x + 5$.

$x = \boxed{} \rightarrow y = \boxed{} + 5 = \boxed{}$

Lesson 4-9

11. Check the solutions.

Solution 1 $\left(\boxed{}, \boxed{} \right)$

$y = -x^2 - 3x + 10$

$\boxed{} = -\left(\boxed{} \right)^2 - 3\left(\boxed{} \right) + 10$

$\boxed{} = \boxed{}$

Solution 2 $\left(\boxed{}, \boxed{} \right)$

$y = -x^2 - 3x + 10$

$\boxed{} = -\left(\boxed{} \right)^2 - 3\left(\boxed{} \right) + 10$

$\boxed{} = \boxed{}$

Problem 3 Solving a Quadratic System of Equations

Got It? What is the solution of the system? $\begin{cases} y = x^2 - 4x + 5 \\ y = -x^2 + 5 \end{cases}$

12. Circle the graph of the system. Each graph shows the standard viewing window.

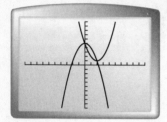 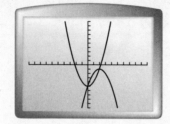 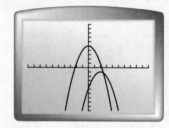

13. Use the graph you circled. Circle the solution of the system.

| $(-2, 1)$ | $(-1, 4)$ | $(0, 5)$ | $(1, 2)$ | $(2, 1)$ | $(3, -4)$ |

Problem 4 Solving a Quadratic System of Inequalities

Got It? What is the solution of this system of inequalities? $\begin{cases} y \le -x^2 - 4x + 3 \\ y > x^2 + 3 \end{cases}$

The graph at the right shows the boundaries of the inequalities.

14. Shade the region that represents $y \le -x^2 - 4x + 3$.

15. Shade the region that represents $y > x^2 + 3$ in another color.

16. Outline the region that represents the solution of the system of inequalities.

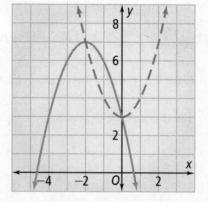

Lesson Check • **Do you know HOW?**

Solve the system by substitution. $\begin{cases} y = x^2 - 2x + 3 \\ y = x + 1 \end{cases}$

17. Complete the solution. Justifications are given.

$x + 1 = x^2 - 2x + 3$ Substitute $x + 1$ for y.

$0 = x^2 \boxed{} x + \boxed{}$ Addition property of equality.

$0 = \left(x - \boxed{}\right)\left(x \boxed{}\right)$ Factor.

$x = \boxed{}$ or $x = \boxed{}$ Solve for x.

$y = 1 + 1 = \boxed{}$ or $y = \boxed{} + 1 = \boxed{}$ Substitute for x in $y = x + 1$ and solve for y.

The solutions are $\left(1, \boxed{}\right)$ and $\left(\boxed{}, \boxed{}\right)$.

Lesson Check • Do you UNDERSTAND?

Reasoning How many points of intersection can you have between a linear function and a quadratic function? Draw graphs to justify your answers.

18. If possible, draw linear function and a quadratic function with the number of intersections specified.

0 points of intersection

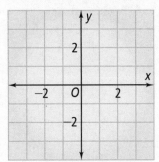

1 point of intersection

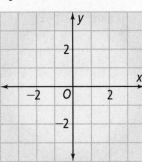

2 points of intersection

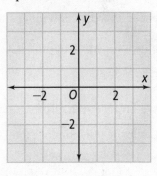

19. Circle the number(s) of points of intersection you can have between a linear function and a quadratic function.

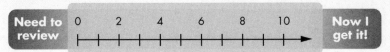

    0   1   2   3   4

Math Success

Check off the vocabulary words that you understand.

☐ quadratic-linear system   ☐ system of equations   ☐ system of inequalities

Rate how well you can *solve and graph systems of equations and inequalities.*

Need to review   0   2   4   6   8   10   Now I get it!

Lesson 4-9

5-1 Polynomial Functions

Vocabulary

● **Review**

1. Write **S** if the expression is in *standard form*. Write **N** if it is not.

$5 + 7x - 13x^2$ _____ $47y^2 - 2y - 1$ _____ $3m^2 + 4m$ _____

● **Vocabulary Builder**

polynomial (noun) **pahl ah NOH mee ul**

Related Words: monomial, binomial, trinomial

Definition: A **polynomial** is a monomial or the sum of monomials.

polynomial

$$3t - rt + r^3$$

monomials

● **Use Your Vocabulary**

2. Circle the polynomial expression(s).

$-t^4 - 5t + \dfrac{3}{t}$ $7g^3 + 8g^2 - 5$ $\dfrac{3x^2 - 5x + 2}{x}$

3. Circle the graph(s) that can be represented by a polynomial.

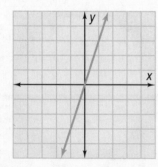   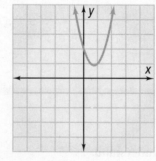   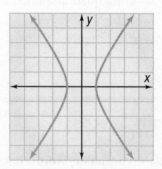

Write the number of terms in each *polynomial.*

4. $6 - 7x^2 + 3x$ **5.** $4b^5 - 3b^4 + 7b^3 + 8b^2 - b$ **6.** $3qr^2 + q^3r^2 - q^2r + 7$

The degree of a polynomial function affects the shape of its graph and determines the maximum number of **turning points**, or places where the graph changes direction. It affects the **end behavior**, or the directions of the graph to the far left and to the far right. A function is *increasing* when the *y*-values increase as *x*-values increase. A function is *decreasing* when the *y*-values decrease as *x*-values increase.

Key Concepts   Polynomial Functions

$$y = 4x^4 + 6x^3 - x$$

End Behavior: Up and Up

Turning Points: $(-1.07, -1.04)$, $(-0.27, 0.17)$, and $(0.22, -0.15)$

The function is decreasing when $x < -1.07$ and $-0.27 < x < 0.22$. The function increases when $-1.07 < x < -0.27$ and $x > 0.22$.

$$y = -x^2 + 2x$$

End Behavior: Down and Down

Turning Point: $(1, 1)$

The function is increasing when $x < 1$ and is decreasing when $x > 1$.

$$y = x^3$$

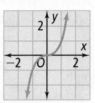

End Behavior: Down and Up

Zero turning points.

The function is increasing for all x.

$$y = -x^3 + 2x$$

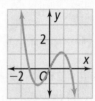

End Behavior: Up and Down

Turning Points: $(-0.82, -1.09)$ and $(0.82, 1.09)$

The function is decreasing when $x < -0.82$ and when $x > 0.82$. The function is increasing when $-0.82 < x < 0.82$.

You can determine the end behavior of a polynomial function of degree n from the leading term ax^n of the standard form.

End Behavior of a Polynomial Function of Degree *n* with Leading Term *ax^n*

	n Even ($n \neq 0$)	*n* Odd
a **Positive**	Up and Up	Down and Up
a **Negative**	Down and Down	Up and Down

Lesson 5-1

Problem 2 Describing End Behavior of Polynomial Functions

Got It? Consider the leading term of $y = -4x^3 + 2x^2 + 7$. What is the end behavior of the graph?

7. Circle the leading term, ax^n, in the polynomial.

$$y = -4x^3 + 2x^2 + 7$$

8. In this polynomial, $a = \boxed{}$ is positive / negative , and $n = \boxed{}$ is even / odd .

9. Circle the graph that illustrates the end behavior of this polynomial.

The end behavior is down and up.

The end behavior is down and down.

The end behavior is up and down.

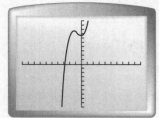
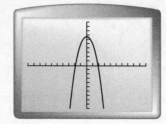
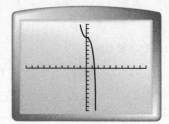

10. Circle the letter of the graph that is continuously decreasing. Underline the letter of the graph that is increasing and then decreasing only.

Graph A   Graph B   Graph C

Problem 3 Graphing Cubic Functions

Got It? What is the graph of $y = -x^3 + 2x^2 - x - 2$? Describe the graph.

Underline the correct word to complete each sentence.

11. The coefficient of the leading term is positive / negative .

12. The exponent of the leading term is even / odd .

13. The end behavior is down / up and down / up .

14. Circle the graph that shows $y = -x^3 + 2x^2 - x - 2$.

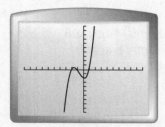
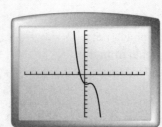

15. The end behavior of $y = -x^3 + 2x^2 - x - 2$ is down / up and down / up , and there are 1 / 2 / 3 turning points.

Problem 4 Using Differences to Determine Degree

Got It? What is the degree of the polynomial function that generates the data shown in the table at the right?

x	y
−3	23
−2	−16
−1	−15
0	−10
1	−13
2	−12
3	29

16. Complete the flowchart to find the differences of the *y*-values.

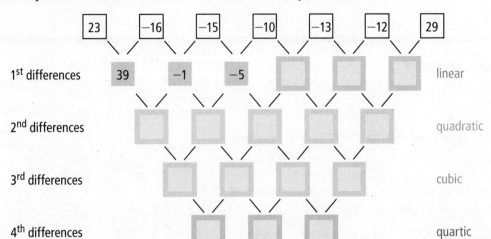

23   −16   −15   −10   −13   −12   29

1ˢᵗ differences   39   −1   −5   ☐   ☐   ☐   linear

2ⁿᵈ differences   ☐   ☐   ☐   ☐   ☐   quadratic

3ʳᵈ differences   ☐   ☐   ☐   ☐   cubic

4ᵗʰ differences   ☐   ☐   ☐   quartic

17. The degree of the polynomial is ☐ .

Lesson Check • **Do you UNDERSTAND?**

Vocabulary Describe the end behavior of the graph of $y = -2x^7 - 8x$.

18. Underline the correct word(s) to complete each sentence.

The value of *a* in $-2x^7$ is positive / negative . The exponent in $-2x^7$ is even / odd .

The end behavior is up and up / down and up / up and down / down and down .

Math Success

Check off the vocabulary words that you understand.

☐ polynomial   ☐ polynomial function   ☐ turning point   ☐ end behavior

Rate how well you can *describe the graph of a polynomial function.*

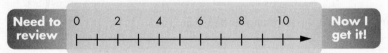

Need to review   0   2   4   6   8   10   Now I get it!

Lesson 5-1

5-2 Polynomials, Linear Factors, and Zeros

Vocabulary

● Review

1. Cross out the expression that does NOT have x^4 as a *factor*.

| x^5 | $2x^3$ | x^3xy | $(3x^2)^2$ |

2. Circle the *factor* tree that shows the prime factorization of $14x^2$.

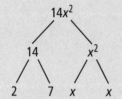 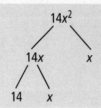

● Vocabulary Builder

turning point (noun) TUR **ning poynt**

Related Words: relative maximum, relative minimum

Math Usage: A **turning point** is where the graph of a function changes from going up to going down, or from going down to going up.

● Use Your Vocabulary

3. Write the letters of the points that describe each *turning point* and intercept.

relative maximum   relative minimum   *x*-intercept   *y*-intercept

4. Place a ✓ if the sentence shows a correct use of the word *turning point*. Place an ✗ if it does not.

The turning point in the story was when the hero chose the book instead of the sword.

The function has a turning point at $x = 17$.

A function has a turning point when it crosses the *x*-axis.

Problem 1 Writing a Polynomial in Factored Form

Got It? What is the factored form of $x^3 - x^2 - 12x$?

5. Factor an x from each term.

$$x^3 - x^2 - 12x = x\left(\boxed{} - \boxed{} - \boxed{} \right)$$

6. Complete the factor table. Then circle the pair of factors that have a sum equal to -1.

Factors of -12	Sum of Factors
1, -12	$1 + \boxed{} = -11$
-1,	$\boxed{} + \boxed{} = 11$
2,	$\boxed{} + \boxed{} = -4$
-2,	$\boxed{} + \boxed{} = \boxed{}$
3,	$\boxed{} + \boxed{} = \boxed{}$
,	$\boxed{} + \boxed{} = \boxed{}$

7. Complete the factorization using the factors you circled in Exercise 6. Check your answer using *FOIL*.

$$x^3 - x^2 - 12x$$

$$= \boxed{}\left(\boxed{} - \boxed{} - \boxed{} \right)$$

$$= \boxed{}\left(\boxed{} + \boxed{} \right)\left(\boxed{} - \boxed{} \right)$$

Problem 2 Finding Zeros of a Polynomial Function

Got It? What are the zeros of $y = x(x - 3)(x + 5)$? Graph the function.

8. Use the Zero-Product Property to find the value of x in each factor.

x

$(x - 3)$

$(x + 5)$

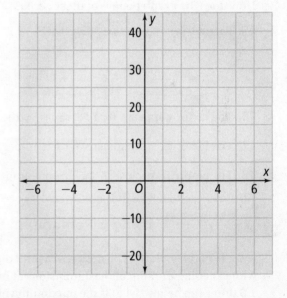

9. The zeros of $y = x(x - 3)(x + 5)$ are $\boxed{}$, $\boxed{}$, and $\boxed{}$.

10. The graph of $y = x(x - 3)(x + 5)$ crosses the x-axis at $\left(\boxed{}, \boxed{} \right)$, $\left(\boxed{}, \boxed{} \right)$, and $\left(\boxed{}, \boxed{} \right)$.

11. Now graph the function.

Theorem Factor Theorem

The expression $x - a$ is a factor of a polynomial if and only if the value a is a zero of the related polynomial function.

12. Circle the zeros of the polynomial function $y = (x - 2)(x + 3)(x + 4)$.

-4	-3	-2	2	3	4

Lesson 5-2

13. A polynomial equation $Q(x) = 0$ has a solution of -2. Cross out the statement that is NOT true.

| One root of the equation is -2. | There is an x-intercept on the graph of the equation at -2. | A factor of the polynomial is $x - 2$. |

 Problem 3 Writing a Polynomial Function From Its Zeros

Got It? What is a quadratic polynomial function with zeros 3 and -3?

14. The polynomial is found below. Use one of the reasons in the blue box to justify each step.

$P(x) = (x - 3)(x + 3)$

_____

$= x^2 - 3x + 3x - 9$

_____

$= x^2 - 9$

_____

Combine like terms.
Distributive Property
Zero-Product Property

 Problem 4 Finding the Multiplicity of a Zero

Got It? What are the zeros of $f(x) = x^3 - 4x^2 + 4x$? What are their multiplicities? How does the graph behave at these zeros?

15. Factor $f(x) = x^3 - 4x^2 + 4x$.

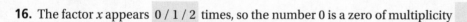

16. The factor x appears $0\,/\,1\,/\,2$ times, so the number 0 is a zero of multiplicity [   ].

17. The factor $(x - 2)$ appears $0\,/\,1\,/\,2$ times, so the number 2 is a zero of multiplicity [   ].

18. The graph looks close to linear / quadratic at 0 and close to linear / quadratic at 2.

 Problem 5 Using a Polynomial Function to Maximize Volume

Got It? Technology The design of a mini digital box camera maximizes the volume while keeping the sum of the dimensions at most 4 inches. If the length must be 1.5 times the height, what is the maximum volume?

19. Complete the reasoning model below to find the volume.

| **Relate** | the volume of the camera | = | the _____ of the camera | · | the length of the camera | · | the _____ of the camera |

Define   Let $x =$ the height of the camera.

Write V = x · $\Big(\quad\Big)x$ · $(4 - (x + 1.5x))$

20. Each graphing calculator screen shows the standard viewing window. Circle the graph of the function.

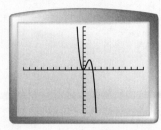 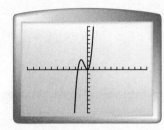

21. Use the *maximum* feature on your calculator. The *maximum* volume is

⬚ in.³ for a height of ⬚ in.

22. Now find the length and the width.

Length | Width

23. The dimensions should be approximately

⬚ in. high by ⬚ in. long by ⬚ in. wide.

Lesson Check • Do you UNDERSTAND?

Vocabulary Write a polynomial function *h* that has 3 and −5 as zeros of multiplicity 2.

24. The expressions $(x − 3)$ and $(x + 5)$ are / are not factors of the polynomial *h*.

25. Write the polynomial in factored form.

Math Success

Check off the vocabulary words that you understand.

☐ zero ☐ multiplicity ☐ relative maximum ☐ relative minimum

Rate how well you can *find zeros of a polynomial function*.

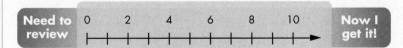

Need to review 0 2 4 6 8 10 Now I get it!

Lesson 5-2

5-3 Solving Polynomial Equations

Vocabulary

● **Review**

1. Complete the graphic organizer.

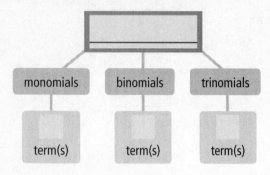

monomials	binomials	trinomials
term(s)	term(s)	term(s)

● **Vocabulary Builder**

cubic (adjective) KYOOB ik

Related Words: cube, cubic expression, cubic function, cubic equation

Main Idea: A **cubic** expression is an expression whose highest-power term is to the third power when written as a polynomial.

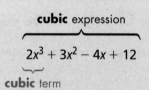

cubic expression

$$2x^3 + 3x^2 - 4x + 12$$

cubic term

● **Use Your Vocabulary**

2. Cross out the polynomial that is NOT a *cubic* expression.

$$x(x + 1)(x - 2) \qquad x^3 - 2x^2 + 4x \qquad x^2 - 2x + 4 \qquad x^3 - 8$$

3. Circle each *cubic* expression.

$$\frac{x^3 + 2x^2 + 3x + 5}{x + 1} \qquad \frac{1}{x^3 + 6} \qquad \frac{x^4 + 16x}{x} \qquad x^3 - 1$$

4. Write the coefficient of each *cubic* term.

$$-3x^4 + 2x^3 - 3 \qquad\qquad x^3 - 2x \qquad\qquad -5x^3 + 6$$

Problem 1 Solving Polynomial Equations Using Factors

Got It? What are the real or imaginary solutions of the equation $(x^2 - 1)(x^2 + 4) = 0$?

5. The equation is solved below. Write a justification for each step.

$$(x^2 - 1)(x^2 + 4) = 0 \qquad \text{Write the original equation.}$$

$$(x + 1)(x - 1)(x^2 + 4) = 0 \qquad \underline{\hspace{6cm}}$$

$$x + 1 = 0 \ \text{ or } \ x - 1 = 0 \ \text{ or } \ x^2 + 4 = 0 \qquad \underline{\hspace{5cm}}$$

$$x = -1 \qquad x = 1 \qquad x^2 = -4 \qquad \underline{\hspace{5cm}}$$

$$x = \pm 2i \qquad \underline{\hspace{5cm}}$$

take note

Summary Polynomial Factoring Techniques

Factoring Out the GCF: Factor out the greatest common factor of all the terms.

6. $12x^6 + 8x^4 - 48x^3 = \boxed{} \left(3x^3 + \boxed{} - \boxed{}\right)$

Quadratic Trinomials
For $ax^2 + bx + c$, find factors with product ac and sum b.

7. $2x^2 + 11x + 15 = \left(2x + \boxed{}\right)\left(x + \boxed{}\right)$

Perfect Square Trinomials
$a^2 + 2ab + b^2 = (a + b)^2$
$a^2 - 2ab + b^2 = (a - b)^2$

8. $x^2 - \boxed{} + 49 = \left(x - \boxed{}\right)^2$

Difference of Squares
$a^2 - b^2 = (a + b)(a - b)$

9. $16x^2 - 11 = \left(\boxed{} + \sqrt{11}\right)\left(4x - \boxed{}\right)$

Factoring by Grouping: $ax + ay + bx + by = a(x + y) + b(x + y) = (a + b)(x + y)$

10. $x^3 - 3x^2 + x - 3 = \boxed{}(x - 3) + \boxed{}(x - 3) = \left(\boxed{} + 1\right)\left(x - \boxed{}\right)$

Sum or Difference of Cubes
$a^3 + b^3 = (a + b)(a^2 - ab + b^2)$
$a^3 - b^3 = (a - b)(a^2 + ab + b^2)$

11. $8x^3 + 27 = \left(\boxed{} + 3\right)\left(4x^2 - \boxed{} + \boxed{}\right)$

Problem 2 Solving Polynomial Equations by Factoring

Got It? What are the real or imaginary solutions of the polynomial equation $x^4 = 16$?

12. Use the justifications below to find the roots of $x^4 = 16$.

$$x^4 - \boxed{} = 0 \qquad \text{Rewrite in the form } P(x) = 0.$$

$$\boxed{} - \boxed{} = 0 \qquad \text{Let } a = x^2.$$

$$\left(a - \boxed{}\right)\left(a + \boxed{}\right) = 0 \qquad \text{Factor.}$$

$$\left(x^2 - \boxed{}\right)\left(\boxed{} + 4\right) = 0 \qquad \text{Replace } a \text{ with } x^2.$$

$$\left(x - \boxed{}\right)\left(x + \boxed{}\right)\left(x^2 + \boxed{}\right) = 0 \qquad \text{Factor.}$$

Lesson 5-3

13. Cross out the equation that does NOT follow the Zero-Product Property for $x^4 = 16$.

| $x + 2 = 0$ | $x^2 + 2 = 0$ | $x^2 + 4 = 0$ |

14. The solutions of $x^4 = 16$ are ☐ , ☐ , ☐ , and $-2i$.

  Problem 3 **Finding Real Roots by Graphing**

Got It? What are the real solutions of the equation $x^3 + x^2 = x - 1$?

15. Write the equation in standard form.

16. The related function $y_1 = x^3 + x^2 - x + 1$ is graphed below. Circle the zero(s) and write each approximate x-value.

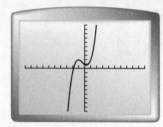

zero(s) $\approx$ ☐

17. **Reasoning** What does this graph tell you about the solutions of $x^3 + x^2 = x - 1$? Place a ✓ in the box if the statement is correct. Place an ✗ if it is incorrect.

☐ The equation $x^3 + x^2 = x - 1$ has three real solutions.

☐ The y-coordinate of the x-intercept corresponds to a zero of the function $y = x^3 + x^2 - x + 1$.

18. The approximate solution of $x^3 + x^2 = x - 1$ is ☐ .

Problem 4 **Modeling a Problem Situation**

Got It? What are three consecutive integers whose product is 480 more than their sum?

19. Complete the model to write the equation.

Relate | the product of three consecutive integers | = | the sum of the three integers | + | 480 |

Define Let x = the first integer.

Then $x + 1 = $ _____ ,

and ☐ = the third integer.

Write ☐ = ☐ + ☐

20. Rewrite the equation as a function in calculator-ready form.

21. Circle the graph of the function. Each graph shows the standard viewing window.

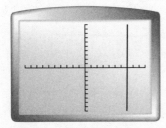 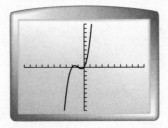 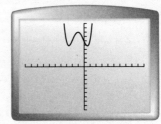

22. The value of x is [ ] .

23. Three consecutive integers whose product is 480 more than their sum are

[ ] , [ ] , and [ ] .

Lesson Check • Do you UNDERSTAND?

Vocabulary Identify $x^2 - 64$ as a sum of cubes, difference of cubes, or difference of squares.

24. Circle the rule you use to factor $x^2 - 64$.

$$a^3 + b^3 = (a + b)(a^2 - ab + b^2) \qquad a^2 - b^2 = (a + b)(a - b)$$
$$a^3 - b^3 = (a - b)(a^2 + ab + b^2)$$

25. $x^2 - 64$ is a sum of cubes / a difference of cubes / a difference of squares .

Math Success

Check off the vocabulary words that you understand.

☐ sum of cubes ☐ difference of cubes

Rate how well you can *solve polynomial equations.*

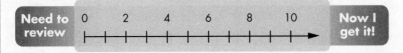

5-4 Dividing Polynomials

Vocabulary

● Review

1. Circle the *factors* of $x^3 - 4x^2$.

| x^2 | x^3 | $x - 4$ | $-4x^2$ |

2. Cross out the expression that is NOT a *factor* of $2x^5 + 8x^3$.

| x^2 | $2x^3$ | $2x^2 + 8$ | $8x^3$ |

● Vocabulary Builder

> $$6 \leftarrow \text{quotient}$$
> $$\text{divisor} \longrightarrow 3\overline{)19} \leftarrow \text{dividend}$$
> $$\underline{18}$$
> $$1 \leftarrow \text{remainder}$$

quotient (noun) KWOH shunt

Related Words: dividend, divisor, remainder

Main Idea: A **quotient** is the simplification of a division expression.

● Use Your Vocabulary

3. Circle the dividend and underline the divisor in each *quotient*.

| $\frac{x}{5}$ | $3.2 \div 16$ | $15\overline{)100}$ | two divided by seven |

 Problem 1 **Polynomial Long Division**

Got It? Use polynomial long division to divide $3x^2 - 29x + 56$ by $x - 7$. What are the quotient and remainder?

4. Use the justifications to divide the expressions.

$$
\begin{array}{r}
3x - \boxed{} \\
x - 7 \overline{)3x^2 - 29x + 56} \\
-\left(3x^2 - \boxed{}x\right) \\
\hline
-8x + 56 \\
\boxed{} + \boxed{} \\
\hline
\boxed{}
\end{array}
$$

Divide the first term in the dividend by the first term in the divisor to get the first term in the quotient: $3x^2 \div x = 3x$.

Multiply the first term in the quotient by the divisor: $3x(x - 7)$.

Subtract to get $-8x$. Bring down 56.

Divide $-8x$ by x.

Subtract to find the remainder.

5. Identify each part of the problem.

Dividend

Divisor

Quotient

Remainder

6. Check your solution.

take note

Key Concept   The Division Algorithm for Polynomials

You can divide polynomial $P(x)$ by polynomial $D(x)$ to get polynomial quotient $Q(x)$ and polynomial remainder $R(x)$. The result is $P(x) = D(x)Q(x) + R(x)$.

$$D(x)\overline{)P(x)}^{\,Q(x)}$$

If $R(x) = 0$, then $P(x) = D(x)Q(x)$ and $D(x)$ and $Q(x)$ are factors of $P(x)$.

*

*

*

$R(x)$

To use long division, $P(x)$ and $D(x)$ should be in standard form with zero coefficients where appropriate. The process stops when the degree of the remainder, $R(x)$, is less than the degree of the divisor, $D(x)$.

7. Cross out the polynomials that are NOT in the correct form for long division.

$$x^3 - 7x + 2 \qquad 2x^4 + 3x \qquad 4x^3 + 9x^2 + 0x - 12$$

Problem 2 Checking Factors

Got It? Is $x^4 - 1$ a factor of $P(x) = x^5 + 5x^4 - x - 5$? If it is, write $P(x)$ as a product of two factors.

8. Divide.

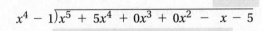

$$x^4 - 1\overline{)x^5 + 5x^4 + 0x^3 + 0x^2 - x - 5}$$

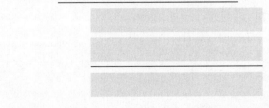

9. Write $P(x)$ as a product of two factors.

Underline the correct word(s), number, or expression to complete each sentence.

10. The remainder of the quotient is $0 \,/\, x + 5 \,/\, x - 5$.

11. The expression $x^4 - 1$ is / is not a factor of $P(x) = x^5 + 5x^4 - x - 5$.

131

Lesson 5-4

Problem 3 Using Synthetic Division

Got It? Use synthetic division to divide $x^3 - 57x + 56$ by $x - 7$. What are the quotient and remainder?

12. Do the synthetic division. Remember that the sign of the number in the divisor is reversed.

$$7 \,\rvert\, \quad 1 \quad 0 \quad \Box \quad \Box$$

Write the coefficients of the polynomial.

Bring down the first coefficient. Multiply the coefficient by the divisor.

Add to the next coefficient. Continue multiplying and adding through the last coefficient.

13. The quotient is ⬚⬚⬚⬚, and the remainder is ⬚.

Problem 4 Using Synthetic Division to Solve a Problem

Got It? Crafts If the polynomial $x^3 + 6x^2 + 11x + 6$ expresses the volume, in cubic inches, of a shadow box, and the width is $(x + 1)$ in., what are the dimensions of the box?

14. Use synthetic division.

15. Factor the quotient.

16. The height of the box is ⬚⬚⬚ in., the width of the box is ⬚⬚⬚ in., and the length of the box is ⬚⬚⬚ in.

Theorem The Remainder Theorem

If you divide a polynomial $P(x)$ of degree $n \geq 1$ by $x - a$, then the remainder is $P(a)$.

17. If you divide $3x^2 + x - 5$ by $x - 1$, the remainder is $P\left(\boxed{}\right)$.

18. If you divide $2x^2 + x + 6$ by $x + 1$, the remainder is $P\left(\boxed{}\right)$.

Problem 5 Evaluating a Polynomial

Got It? What is $P(-4)$, given $P(x) = x^5 - 3x^4 - 28x^3 + 5x + 20$?

19. $P(-4)$ is the remainder when you divide

$x^5 - 3x^4 - 28x^3 + 5x + 20$ by $x - 4 \,/\, 4 - x \,/\, x + 4$

20. Use synthetic division. Circle the remainder.

21. $P(-4) =$

 Lesson Check • **Do you UNDERSTAND?**

Reasoning A polynomial $P(x)$ is divided by a binomial $x - a$. The remainder is zero. What conclusion can you draw? Explain.

Write T for *true* or F for *false*.

_____ **22.** One factor of the polynomial is $x - a$.

_____ **23.** One root of the polynomial is $-a$.

_____ **24.** An x-intercept of the graph of $y = P(x)$ is a.

25. If $P(x)$ is divided by $x - a$ then $P(a) =$ the remainder and $P(x) = (x - a)(Q(x))$.

This illustrates the Division Algorithm / Remainder Theorem / Factor Theorem .

26. If the remainder of $P(x)$ divided by $x - a$ is zero, what do you know about the factors and roots of $P(x)$?

_____

_____

_____

Math Success

Check off the vocabulary words that you understand.

☐ polynomial   ☐ synthetic division   ☐ Remainder Theorem

Rate how well you can *divide polynomials*.

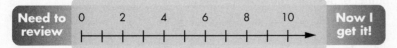

5-5 Theorems About Roots of Polynomial Equations

Vocabulary

Review

1. Write **L** if the polynomial is *linear*, **Q** if it is *quadratic*, or **C** if it is *cubic*.

$3x + x^2$ _____ $2x^3 - 7x^2 + x$ _____ $14 - x$ _____

Vocabulary Builder

root (noun) root

Related Words: factor, solution, zero, x-intercept

Definition: A **root** of an equation is a value that, when substituted for the unknown quantity, satisfies the equation.

Main Idea: A **root** is a solution of an equation. It is an x-intercept of the related function, which is why it can be called a *zero*. If $(x - a)$ is a factor of a polynomial, then a is a root of that polynomial.

Use Your Vocabulary

Write **T** for *true* or **F** for *false*.

_____ **2.** 1 and -1 are *roots* of the equation $x^2 = 1$.

_____ **3.** The equation $x^2 - 4x + 4 = 0$ has *roots* 4 and -4.

Write the number of *roots* each polynomial has.

4. $3x^4 - 2x^2 + 17x - 4$ [ ]   **5.** $12x^5 + x^7 - 8 + 4x^2$ [ ]   **6.** $15 + 6x$ [ ]

take note

Theorem Rational Root Theorem

Let $P(x) = a_n x^n + a_{n-1} x^{n-1} + \ldots + a_1 x + a_0$ be a polynomial with integer coefficients. Then there are a limited number of possible roots of $P(x) = 0$.

Integer roots must be factors of a_0.

Rational roots must have a reduced form $\frac{p}{q}$, where p is an integer factor of a_0 and q is an integer factor of a_n.

What are the possible rational roots of $15x^4 - 3x + 8$?

7. Identify a_0 and a_n.　　$a_0 = \boxed{}$　　$a_n = \boxed{}$

8. List the factors of the constant, a_0.

$\pm \boxed{} , \pm \boxed{} , \pm \boxed{} , \pm \boxed{} ,$

9. List the factors of the leading coefficient, a_n.

$\pm \boxed{} , \pm \boxed{} , \pm \boxed{} , \pm \boxed{} ,$

10. Circle the possible rational roots.

$$\frac{2}{5} \qquad\qquad \frac{5}{4} \qquad\qquad -\frac{1}{5} \qquad\qquad \frac{2}{3}$$

Problem 2 Using the Rational Root Theorem

Got It? What are the rational roots of $2x^3 + x^2 - 7x - 6 = 0$?

Underline the correct number(s) to complete each sentence.

11. The leading coefficient is $0 / 2 / 1 / 7 / -6$.

12. The constant is $0 / 2 / 1 / 7 / -6$.

13. The factors of the leading coefficient are $0 / -1 / 1 / -2 / 2 / -3 / 3 / -6 / 6$.

14. The factors of the constant are $0 / -1 / 1 / -2 / 2 / -3 / 3 / -6 / 6$.

15. Cross out the numbers that are NOT possible rational roots.

$$0 \qquad\qquad -1 \qquad\qquad \frac{1}{3} \qquad\qquad \frac{1}{2}$$

16. Try the easiest possible roots.

$P(1) = \boxed{}$　　　　$P(-1) = \boxed{}$

17. Since $1 / -1$ is a root, $x + 1 / x - 1$ is a factor of $2x^3 + x^2 - 7x - 6 = 0$.

18. Use synthetic division to find another factor.　　**19.**　The quotient is $\boxed{}$.

$$-1 \, | \begin{array}{cccc} 2 & 1 & -7 & -6 \end{array}$$

$$\begin{array}{cccc} & \boxed{} & \boxed{} & \boxed{} \\ \hline 2 & \boxed{} & \boxed{} & \boxed{} \end{array}$$

20. Use the quadratic formula to find the remaining factors.

$$\frac{-b \pm \sqrt{b^2 - 4ac}}{2a} = \frac{\boxed{} \pm \sqrt{\boxed{} - 4(\boxed{})(\boxed{})}}{\boxed{}} = \frac{\boxed{} \pm \sqrt{\boxed{} - \boxed{}}}{\boxed{}}$$

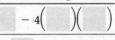 

$$= \frac{\boxed{} \pm \boxed{}}{\boxed{}} = \boxed{} \text{ or } \boxed{}$$

21. The rational roots of $2x^3 + x^2 - 7x - 6 = 0$ are $\boxed{}$, $\boxed{}$, and $\boxed{}$.

135

Theorem Conjugate Root Theorem

If $P(x)$ is a polynomial with rational coefficients, then the irrational roots of $P(x) = 0$ occur in conjugate pairs. That is, if $a + \sqrt{b}$ is an irrational root with a and b rational, then $a - \sqrt{b}$ is also a root.

If $P(x)$ is a polynomial with real coefficients, then the complex roots of $P(x) = 0$ occur in conjugate pairs. That is, if $a + bi$ is a complex root with a and b real, then $a - bi$ is also a root.

22. Write the conjugate of each root.

$1 + 3i$ $\qquad\qquad$ $4 - \sqrt{7}$ $\qquad\qquad$ $-2 - 9i$ $\qquad\qquad$ $15 + \sqrt{10}$

Problem 3 Using the Conjugate Root Theorem to Identify Roots

Got It? A cubic polynomial $P(x)$ has real coefficients. If $3 - 2i$ and $\frac{5}{2}$ are two roots of $P(x) = 0$, what is one additional root?

23. Place a ✓ if the Conjugate Root Theorem could be applied to the following types of roots. Place an ✗ if it could not be.

Rational $\qquad\qquad$ Irrational $\qquad\qquad$ Complex

24. Write **R** if the root is rational, **I** if it is irrational, or **C** if it is complex.

_____ $3 - 2i$ $\qquad\qquad$ _____ $\frac{5}{2}$

25. By the Conjugate Root Theorem, _____ is an additional root.

Problem 4 Using Conjugates to Construct a Polynomial

Got It? What is a quartic polynomial function with rational coefficients for the roots $2 - 3i, 8, 2$?

Underline the correct word or number to complete each sentence.

26. A quartic polynomial has $1 / 2 / 3 / 4$ roots.

27. Since $2 - 3i$ is a root, _____ is also a root.

28. Write $P(x)$ as the product of four binomials.

$P(x) = \left(x \quad (2 - 3i)\right)\left(x \quad 8\right)\left(x \quad 2\right)\left(x \quad \quad\right)$

29. Circle the simplified form of the polynomial.

$x^4 - 14x^3 + 37x^2 - 66x - 208$ $\qquad$ $x^4 - 14x^3 + 69x^2 - 194x + 208$

$-13x^3 + 37x^2 - 194x + 208$

Theorem   Descartes's Rule of Signs

Let $P(x)$ be a polynomial with real coefficients written in standard form.

The number of positive real roots of $P(x) = 0$ is either equal to the number of sign changes between consecutive coefficients of $P(x)$ or less than that by an even number.

The number of negative real roots of $P(x) = 0$ is either equal to the number of sign changes between consecutive coefficients of $P(-x)$ or less than that by an even number.

30. A possible number of positive real roots for $x^4 - x^3 + x^2 - x + 1$ is $1 / 2 / 3 / 5$.

 Problem 5 Using Descartes's Rule of Signs

Got It? What does Descartes's Rule of Signs tell you about the real roots of $2x^4 - x^3 + 3x^2 - 1 = 0$?

31. The number of sign changes is 3, and the number of positive real roots is ☐ or ☐ .

32. $P(-x) = 2\left(\boxed{}\right)^4 - \boxed{}^3 + 3\left(\boxed{}\right)^2 - 1 = $ ☐

The number of sign changes is ☐ , and the number of negative real roots is ☐ .

Lesson Check   •   Do you UNDERSTAND?

Reasoning In the statement below, r and s represent integers. Is the statement *sometimes*, *always*, or *never* true? Explain.

A root of the equation $3x^3 + rx^2 + sx + 8 = 0$ could be 5.

33. Write the factors of 8.   **34.** Write the factors of 3.

35. Because there are / are no factors of 5, the statement

is always / sometimes / never true.

Math Success

Check off the vocabulary words that you understand.

☐ Rational Root Theorem   ☐ Conjugate Root Theorem   ☐ Descartes's Rule of Signs

Rate how well you can *solve polynomial equations.*

Need to review 0 2 4 6 8 10 Now I get it!

Lesson 5-5

Vocabulary

● **Review**

1. Circle the expressions that are *trinomials*.

$$7x^2 + 4x - 5 \qquad\qquad x^4 - 3x + 1$$

$$x^3 + 9x \qquad\qquad 3x^3 + x^2 - x + 10$$

● **Vocabulary Builder**

fundamental (adjective) **fun duh MENT ul**

Related Words: basic, essential

Definition: Something is **fundamental** if it serves as the foundation of a system.

Main Idea: The **Fundamental** Theorem of Algebra is the central idea of algebra.

● **Use Your Vocabulary**

Write T for *true* or F for *false*.

2. The *fundamental* idea of geometry is the study of the provable properties of shapes.

3. A *fundamental* idea in the Declaration of Independence is that all people have the right to life, liberty, and the pursuit of happiness.

4. A *fundamental* rule of history is that kings are always right.

Theorem   The Fundamental Theorem of Algebra

If $P(x)$ is a polynomial of degree $n \geq 1$, then $P(x) = 0$ has exactly n roots, including multiple and complex roots.

Write the degree and the number of complex roots of each equation.

Equation	Degree	Number of Complex Roots
5. $7x^6 - 4x^3 + x + 5 = 0$		
6. $4x^5 + 5x^3 - 9x^2 + 2 = 0$		
7. $17x^{12} + x^7 - x^3 - 8 = 0$		

 Problem 1 Using the Fundamental Theorem of Algebra

Got It? What are all the complex roots of the equation $x^4 + 2x^3 = 13x^2 - 10x$?

8. Write the polynomial equation in standard form.

9. Factor out an x.

10. A rational root of the polynomial is [ ] .

11. Use the Rational Root Theorem on the cubic factor. List the possible rational roots.

12. Underline the correct word(s) or number to complete each sentence.

When you substitute 1 for x, the value of the cubic factor is 0 / 1 / 3 .

Therefore, 1 is / is not a root, and $x - 1$ is / is not a factor.

13. Use synthetic division to factor out $x - 1$ from the cubic factor.

14. Factor the resulting quadratic trinomial.

[   ] = ([   ])([   ])

15. Write all the roots of $x^4 + 2x^3 = 13x^2 - 10x$.

Lesson 5-6

Got It? What are all the zeros of the function $g(x) = 2x^4 - 3x^3 - x - 6$?

16. Use the graph of the function at the right to write the real zeros of the function.

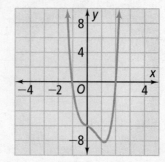

17. Write the linear factors.

[   ] and [   ]

18. Use synthetic division to factor out the first linear factor.

19. Factor out the second linear factor from the quotient you found in Exercise 18.

20. The remaining quadratic factor is [   ].

21. Use the Quadratic Formula to factor your answer to Exercise 20.

22. The four zeros of the function $g(x) = 2x^4 - 3x^3 - x - 6$ are

[   ], [   ], [   ], and [   ].

Lesson Check • Do you know HOW?

Find the number of roots of the equation $5x^4 + 12x^3 - x^2 + 3x + 5 = 0$.

23. The degree of the polynomial is ____.

24. The number of roots is ____.

Lesson Check • Do you UNDERSTAND?

Open-Ended Write a polynomial function of degree 4 with two complex roots of multiplicity 2.

25. Write a complex number.

Write its conjugate.

26. Now use the numbers you wrote in Exercise 25 to write a polynomial function of degree 4 with two complex roots of multiplicity 2.

$$f(x) = \left(\underline{} \right)^2 \left(\underline{} \right)^2$$

Math Success

Check off the vocabulary words that you understand.

☐ Fundamental Theorem of Algebra   ☐ polynomial equation

Rate how well you can *solve polynomial equations*.

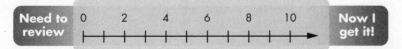

Lesson 5-6

the Binomial Theorem

...e next number in each *pattern*.

...1,

...5, 7, 9,

...00, 90, 80, 70, 60,

Vocabulary Builder

expand (verb) **ek SPAND**

Definition: You **expand** something by increasing it, stretching it out, or giving it more detail.

Math Usage: You **expand** a power of a polynomial by doing the multiplying to find all the terms.

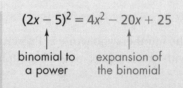

$(2x - 5)^2 = 4x^2 - 20x + 25$

binomial to   expansion of
a power   the binomial

Use Your Vocabulary

2. Place a ✓ if the sentence shows the correct use of *expand*. Place an ✗ if it does not.

☐ The writer expanded the short story into a novel.

☐ Heat expands most metals.

☐ The balloon expanded as all of the air was let out of it.

☐ The bird expanded its wings.

☐ The expanded form of $(3x^2 - 4)^2$ is $9x^4 - 24x^2 + 16$.

3. Circle a rule for squaring binomials that you could use to *expand* $(a - b)^2$.

$(a - b)^2 = (a + b)(a - b)$ $(a - b)^2 = a^2 - 2ab + b^2$ $(a - b)^2 = a^2 + 2ab + b^2$

4. The expression $25 - 10x + x^2$ is the *expansion* of which power of a binomial? Circle your answer.

$5^2 - x^2$ $(25 - x)^2$ $(5 - x)^2$ $(5 + x)^2$

Pascal's Triangle is a triangular array of numbers. The first and last number of each row is 1. Each of the other numbers in the row is the sum of the two numbers above it.

5. Use the description above to complete Pascal's Triangle.

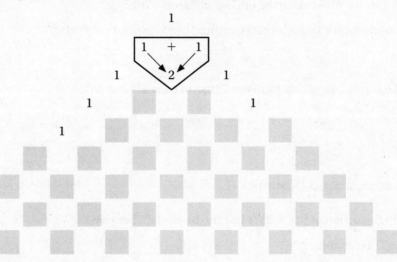

 **Problem 1** **Using Pascal's Triangle**

Got It? What is the expansion of $(a + b)^8$? Use Pascal's Triangle.

6. Circle the row of Pascal's Triangle that you would use to expand $(a + b)^8$.

Pascal's Triangle

					1					
				1		1				
			1		2		1			
		1		3		3		1		
	1		4		6		4		1	
1		5		10		10		5		1
1	6	15	20	15	6	1
1	7	21	35	35	21	7	1
1	8	28	56	70	56	28	8	1
1	9	36	84	126	126	84	36	9	1

7. Use the row you circled to complete the expansion.

$(a + b)^8 = \boxed{} a^8 + \boxed{} a^7b + \boxed{} a^6b^2 + \boxed{} a^5b^3 + \boxed{} a^4b^4 + \boxed{} a^3b^5$

$\qquad + \boxed{} a^2b^6 + \boxed{} ab^7 + \boxed{} b^8$

Lesson 5-7

Theorem   Binomial Theorem

For every positive integer n, $(a + b)^n = P_0a^n + P_1a^{n-1}b + P_2a^{n-2}b^2 + \cdots + P_{n-1}ab^{n-1} + P_nb^n$, where $P_0, P_1, \ldots, P_n$ are the numbers in the nth row of Pascal's Triangle.

8. Complete the row of Pascal's Triangle that you would use to expand $(a + b)^5$.

   1   5   ▢   ▢   ▢   ▢

9. Write the row of Pascal's Triangle that you would use to expand $(a + b)^6$.

Problem 2   Expanding a Binomial

Got It? What is the expansion of $(2x - 3)^4$? Use the Binomial Theorem.

10. Identify the values of a, b, and n.

    $a =$ ▢ $b =$ ▢ $n =$ ▢

11. Write the expression in the form $(a + b)^n$.

    $(2x - 3)^4 = \left(\,▢\, + \,▢\,\right)$

12. Circle the row of Pascal's Triangle that you would use to expand $(2x - 3)^4$.

Pascal's Triangle

```
                1
             1     1
          1     2     1
       1     3     3     1
    1     4     6     4     1
 1     5    10    10     5     1
```

13. Use the row you circled to complete the expansion of $(2x - 3)^4$. Simplify the result.

$(2x - 3)^4 = ▢\left(▢\right)^4 + ▢(2x)^3\left(▢\right) + ▢(2x)^2\left(▢\right)^2 + ▢(2x)\left(▢\right)^3 + ▢\left(▢\right)^4$

$\qquad = ▢x^4 - ▢x^3 + ▢x^2 - ▢x + ▢$

Lesson Check • Do you UNDERSTAND?

Vocabulary Tell whether each expression can be expanded using the Binomial Theorem.

$(2a - 6)^4$ $(5x^2 + 1)^5$ $(x^2 - 3x - 4)^3$

14. Circle the expressions that are written in the form $(a + b)^n$.

    $(2a - 6)^4$ $(5x^2 + 1)^5$ $(x^2 - 3x - 4)^3$

15. Place a ✓ if you can use the Binomial Theorem to expand the expression. Place an ✗ if you cannot.

  $(2a - 6)^4$ $(5x^2 + 1)^5$ $(x^2 - 3x - 4)^3$

Reasoning Using Pascal's Triangle, determine the number of terms in the expansion of $(x + a)^{12}$. How many terms are there in the expansion of $(x + a)^n$?

16. Circle the row of Pascal's Triangle you would use to expand $(x + a)^3$.

```
            1
        1       1
      1     2     1
    1    3     3    1
  1    4    6    4    1
```

17. Write the expansion of $(x + a)^3$.

  +   +   +

18. Compare. Write $<$, $>$, or $=$. Then complete the last expression.

the number of terms in the row of Pascal's Triangle		the number of terms in the expansion of $(x + a)^3$	$= 3 +$

19. Circle the number of terms in the row of Pascal's Triangle you would use to expand $(x + a)^{12}$.

1   2   10   11   12   13

20. Circle the number of terms in the expansion of $(x + a)^{12}$.

1   2   10   11   12   13

21. Circle the number of terms in the expansion of $(x + a)^n$.

1   2   10 $n - 1$ n $n + 1$

Math Success

Check off the vocabulary words that you understand.

☐ binomial   ☐ Pascal's Triangle   ☐ Binomial Theorem

Rate how well you can *expand a binomial*.

Need to review   0   2   4   6   8   10   Now I get it!

Lesson 5-7

Polynomial Models in the Real World

Vocabulary

● Review

1. Draw a line from each item in Column A to a corresponding *model* in Column B.

Column A	Column B
numerical data	floor plan
airplane	equation
house	model airplane

● Vocabulary Builder

extrapolate (verb) **ek STRAP uh layt**

Related Words: interpolate, model

Definition: When you **extrapolate,** you estimate unknown information from known information.

Math Usage: You can **extrapolate** data by using a model to predict values outside the data set.

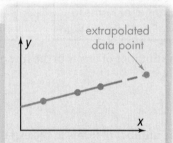

● Use Your Vocabulary

2. The points (1, 3) and (2, 6) are collinear. *Extrapolate* the y-value of the point on the same line when $x = 4$.

The point (4, ⬜) is also on the line.

take note

Key Concept   The (n + 1) Point Principle

For any set of $n + 1$ points in the coordinate plane that pass the vertical line test, there is a unique polynomial of degree at most n that fits the points perfectly.

3. For a set of 6 points, a unique polynomial of degree ⬜ fits the points perfectly.

4. For a set of ⬜ points, a unique polynomial of degree 8 fits the points perfectly.

 **Problem 1** Using a Polynomial Function to Model Data

Got It? What polynomial function has a graph that passes through the four points $(-2, 1)$, $(0, 5)$, $(2, 9)$, and $(3, 36)$?

5. There is a unique polynomial of degree 1 / 2 / 3 / 4 that passes through the three points.

6. Substitute the four points into the cubic $ax^3 + bx^2 + cx + d$ and simplify.

$$1 = a(-2)^3 + b(-2)^2 + c\left(\boxed{}\right) + d \qquad\qquad 5 = a(0)^3 + b(0)^2 + c\left(\boxed{}\right) + d$$

$$= -8a + \boxed{}\,b + \boxed{}\,c + d \qquad\qquad = \boxed{}\,a + \boxed{}\,b + \boxed{}\,c + d$$

$$9 = a\left(\boxed{}\right)^3 + b\left(\boxed{}\right)^2 + c\left(\boxed{}\right) + d \qquad 36 = a\left(\boxed{}\right)^3 + b\left(\boxed{}\right)^2 + c\left(\boxed{}\right) + d$$

$$= \boxed{}\,a + \boxed{}\,b + \boxed{}\,c + d \qquad\qquad = \boxed{}\,a + \boxed{}\,b + \boxed{}\,c + d$$

7. From the second equation, the value of d is $\boxed{}$.

8. Rewrite the other equations, substituting the value for d.

9. Solve the system of equations.

10. The values of the coefficients are $a = \boxed{}$, $b = \boxed{}$, $c = \boxed{}$, and $d = \boxed{}$.

11. The polynomial function is $y = \boxed{}$.

 Problem 2 Choosing a Model

Got It? The chart shows the amount of milk that Wisconsin dairy farms produced from 1945 to 2005. A linear function model of the data is $f(x) = 0.167x + 6.83$. Use the linear model to estimate Wisconsin milk production in 1995.

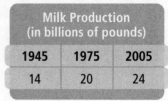

Milk Production (in billions of pounds)		
1945	1975	2005
14	20	24

12. To model the data with a function, the year is the

dependent / independent variable, and the amount

of milk is the dependent / independent variable.

13. Use the calculator screens to estimate Wisconsin milk production in 1995. Draw a point on the graph where you would estimate the milk production in 1995.

  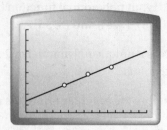

14. An estimate of milk production in Wisconsin in 1995 is ▢ billion pounds of milk.

 Problem 3 **Comparing Models**

Got It? The graph shows the quadratic model for the milk production data in Problem 2. If four data points were given, would a cubic function be the best model for the data? Explain your answer.

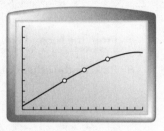

15. According to the $(n + 1)$ Point Principle, there is a polynomial of degree

▢ that fits the four points perfectly.

16. Does a cubic model match the situation for positive values of x? Explain.

Problem 4 **Interpolation and Extrapolation**

Got It? The table shows the annual consumption of cheese per person in the U. S. for selected years from 1910 to 2001. Use LinReg to find a linear model for cheese consumption. Graph it with a scatter plot. Use the model to estimate consumption for 1980, 2000, and 2012. In which of these estimates do you have the most confidence? The least confidence? Explain.

Cheese Consumption

Year	Pounds Consumed
1910	4
1940	5
1970	8
1975	10
1995	25
2001	30

17. Let x be the number of years since 1900. The linear regression and the scatter plot of the data are shown below.

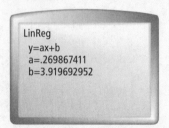 

A linear equation modeling the data is $y = $ ▢ $x + $ ▢ .

18. The x-values 80, ▢ , and ▢ represent the years 1980, 2000, and 2012.

19. Use the *x*-values to estimate cheese consumption in each year.

20. The cheese consumption in 1980 was about ☐ pounds, in 2000 was about ☐ pounds, and in 2012 will be about ☐ pounds.

Underline the correct number(s) and word to complete each sentence.

21. The estimates for 1980 / 2000 / 2012 are likely close to the actual numbers because they are interpolations / extrapolations of the given data.

22. The estimate for 1980/ 2000 / 2012 may not be close to the actual numbers because it is an interpolation / extrapolation of the given data.

Lesson Check • Do you UNDERSTAND?

Vocabulary Explain which form of estimation, *interpolation* or *extrapolation*, is more reliable.

23. Suppose you have census data about the number of people who live in your state. You have the population of your state for every 10 years from 1950 to 2000. Circle the years below that you would be able to *interpolate* the population. Underline the years that you would have to *extrapolate* the population.

| 1920 | 1975 | 1988 | 2010 | 2022 |

24. Is *interpolation* or *extrapolation* more reliable to estimate the population during a given year? Explain.

_____

_____

Math Success

Check off the vocabulary words that you understand.

☐ polynomial function ☐ polynomial model

Rate how well you can *model data with a polynomial function*.

Need to review 0 2 4 6 8 10 Now I get it!

Lesson 5-8

Vocabulary

● Review

1. Circle the value of the *constant* term in $2x^2 - 3x + 1$.

−3	1	2	3

2. Cross out the expressions that do NOT include a *constant* term.

$x^3 + 1$	$3x^3 + 3x$	$x^2 + 3$	$4x^4$

● Vocabulary Builder

transformation (noun) **trans fur MAY shun**

Related Words: translation, reflection, dilation, stretch, compression

Definition: A **transformation** is a change in form, appearance, nature, or character.

Math Usage: A **transformation** changes a function in a plane by shifting it, reflecting it, or changing its size.

transformations

stretch

reflection | noɪʇɔǝⅼɟǝɹ

translation ⟶ translation

● Use Your Vocabulary

Label each as a *translation*, *reflection*, *stretch*, or *compression* of the word *Algebra*.

3. Algebra

_____

4. Algebra
ɐɹqǝƃl∀

_____

5. Algebra
↘ **Algebra**

_____

6. Algebra

_____

The graph of the function $y = a \cdot f(x - h) + k$ is a vertical stretch or compression by a factor $|a|$, a horizontal shift of h units, and a vertical shift of k units of the graph of $y = f(x)$.

7. Cross out the functions that are NOT transformations of $y = x^2$.

$$y = -7x^2 \qquad y = 4x^3 + x^2 \qquad y = x^2 + 5 \qquad y = (x + 3)^2 - 5 \qquad y = 2x$$

 Problem 1 Transforming $y = x^3$

Got It? What is an equation of the graph of $y = x^3$ under a vertical stretch by the factor 2 followed by a horizontal translation 3 units to the left, and a vertical translation 4 units down?

8. Use the words *vertical stretch*, *vertical translation*, and *horizontal translation* to complete the diagram below. Then write the equation.

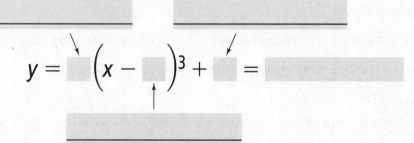

 Problem 2 Finding Zeros of a Transformed Cubic Function

Got It? What are all the real zeros of the function $y = 3(x - 1)^3 + 6$?

9. Use one of the reasons in the shaded box to justify each step of the solution.

> Addition Property of Equality
> Division Property of Equality
> Subtraction Property of Equality
> Set the function equal to 0 to find a root.
> Take the cube root of each side.

$$0 = 3(x - 1)^3 + 6$$

$$-6 = 3(x - 1)^3$$

$$-\frac{6}{3} = (x - 1)^3$$

$$\sqrt[3]{-2} = x - 1$$

$$1 - \sqrt[3]{2} = x$$

10. The real zero of the function is _____ .

Lesson 5-9

Problem 3 Constructing a Quartic Function With Two Real Zeros

Got It? What is a quartic function with only two real zeros, $x = 0$ and $x = 6$?

Method 1 Use transformations.

11. A quartic function with zeros at $x = 0$ and $x = 6$ has zeros ☐ units apart.

12. Translate the basic function $y = x^4 3^4$, or ☐ , units down.

13. The zeros of that function are $x = $ ☐ and $x = 3$.

14. The zero $x = 6$ is ☐ units to the right of 3.

15. Translate the function ☐ units to the right / left .

$$y = x^4 \rightarrow y = x^4 - \boxed{} \rightarrow y = \left(x - \boxed{}\right)^4 - \boxed{}$$

16. A quartic function with only two real zeros at $x = 0$ and $x = 6$ is $y = $ _____ .

Method 2 Use algebraic methods.

17. Having zeros at $x = 0$ and $x = 6$ means that x and ☐ are factors of the function.

18. Since $x = 0$ and $x = 6$ are the only two real zeros, the other zeros of the function are irrational / complex .

19. Multiply the two linear factors by a quadratic factor with no real zeros, such as $x^2 + 1$.

20. Another quartic function with only two real zeros at $x = 0$ and $x = 6$ is $y = $ _____ .

Key Concept Power Function

A **power function** is a function of the form $y = a \cdot x^b$, where a and b are nonzero real numbers.

If the exponent b in $y = ax^b$ is a positive integer, the function is also a *monomial function*.

If $y = ax^b$ describes y as power function of x, then y *varies directly with*, or *is proportional to*, the bth power of x. The constant a is the *constant of proportionality*.

21. Cross out the function(s) that are NOT power functions.

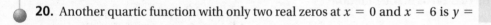

$$y = 0.36x^9 \qquad y = 2 + 4x^8 \qquad y = 43x^9 - x^2 \qquad y = -12x^{53}$$

Problem 4 Modeling with a Power Function

Got It? The power P (in kilowatts) generated by a wind turbine varies directly as the cube of the wind speed v. A turbine generates 210 kW of power in a 12 mi/h wind. How much power does this turbine generate in a 20 mi/h wind?

Chapter 5

152

22. Substitute the known pair of values for P and v in the function $P = a \cdot V^3$.

$\boxed{} = a \boxed{}^3$

23. Write a power function to model the situation.

24. When the wind is 20 mi/h, the turbine generates

$\boxed{} \left(\boxed{} \right) = \boxed{}$ kW of power.

Lesson Check • Do you UNDERSTAND?

Compare and Contrast How are the graphs of $y = x^3$ and $y = 4x^3$ alike? How are they different? What transformation was used to get the second equation?

25. Both functions are __?__ functions. Circle all that apply.

cubic	monomial	power

26. Graph each function.

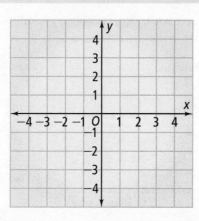 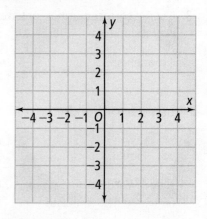

27. Describe how the shape of the graphs are similar and how they are different.

Math Success

Check off the vocabulary words that you understand.

☐ power function   ☐ constant of proportionality   ☐ transformation

Rate how well you can *transform polynomial equations*.

Roots and Radical Expressions

Vocabulary

● Review

1. Circle the *exponents* in each expression.

$$21^7 \qquad -3t^2 \qquad 4a^7b^{12} \qquad \frac{-3x^5}{4y^0}$$

2. Underline the expression that is read *five to the second power*.

$$2^5 \qquad 5^2 \qquad 5 \times 2 \qquad 2 \times 5$$

3. List the correct numbers or letters described by the vocabulary words for the expression $-4x^{54} + 2r^2 - 5s^5 + 7w^3$ in the correct space.

Exponents: _____ Coefficients: _____ Bases: _____

● Vocabulary Builder

root (noun) **root**

Related Words: square **root**, cube **root**, *n*th **root**, power, radical, index, radicand

Definition: The *n*th **root** of a given number is a specific number that when it is used as a factor *n* times, equals the given number.

Using Symbols: $2 \times 2 \times 2 = 8$, so $\sqrt[3]{8} = 2$.

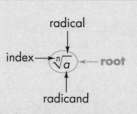

● Use Your Vocabulary

4. Draw a line from the number or symbol in Column A to each term in Column B that best describes a part of $\sqrt[4]{81} = 3$.

Column A	Column B
4	radical
81	root
$\sqrt{}$	index
3	radicand

Key Concept   The *n*th Root

If $a^n = b$, with a and b real numbers and n a positive integer, then a is an **nth** root of b.

If *n* is odd . . .
there is one real *n*th root of b, denoted in radical form as $\sqrt[n]{b}$.

If *n* is even . . .
- and b is positive, there are two real *n*th roots of b. The positive root is the **principal root** (or principal *n*th root). Its symbol is $\sqrt[n]{b}$. The negative root is its opposite, or $-\sqrt[n]{b}$.
- and b is negative, there are no real *n*th roots of b.

The only *n*th root of 0 is 0.

5. Underline the correct words to complete the sentence.

Since the index of $\sqrt[4]{81}$ is   even / odd   and the radicand is   negative / positive , there

are   two real fourth roots / no real fourth roots   of 81.

Problem 1 Finding All Real Roots

Got It? What are the real fifth roots of 0, -1, and 32?

6. Cross out the question that will NOT help you find the roots.

What number is the index?		Is the radicand negative or positive?
	What number times 5 equals -1?	How many real roots of 0 are there?

7. Complete the equation to find the fifth root of 0.

☐ × 0 × ☐ × 0 × ☐ = 0

8. The fifth root of 0 is ☐ .

9. Complete the equation to find the fifth root of -1.

☐ × ☐ × ☐ × ☐ × ☐ = -1

10. The fifth root of -1 is ☐ .

11. Complete the equation to find the fifth root of 32.

☐ × ☐ × ☐ × ☐ × ☐ = 32

12. The fifth root of 32 is ☐ .

Problem 2 Finding Roots

Got It? What is each real-number root?

$\sqrt[3]{-27}$ $\sqrt[4]{-81}$ $\sqrt{(-7)^2}$ $\sqrt{-49}$

Lesson 6-1

13. Circle the true equation.

$$(-2)^3 = 27 \qquad (-3)^3 = 27 \qquad (-3)^3 = -27$$

Underline the correct words to complete each sentence.

14. The index of $\sqrt[4]{-81}$ is even / odd and the radicand is positive / negative , so there

is one real root / are no real roots .

15. The index of $\sqrt{-49}$ is even / odd , and the radicand is positive / negative ,

so there is one real root / are no real roots .

16. What is the principal square root of the square of a number?

_____

_____

17. Simplify each root.

$\sqrt[3]{-27}$ $\qquad$ $\sqrt[4]{-81}$ $\qquad$ $\sqrt{(-7)^2}$ $\qquad$ $\sqrt{-49}$

Key Concept *n*th Roots of *n*th Powers

For any real number a, $\sqrt[n]{a^n} = \begin{cases} a \text{ if } n \text{ is odd} \\ |a| \text{ if } n \text{ is even} \end{cases}$.

18. The index of $\sqrt[3]{(-2)^3}$ is even / odd , so $\sqrt[3]{(-2)^3} = -2$.

Problem 3 **Simplifying Radical Expressions**

Got It? What is the simplified form of the radical expression $\sqrt{81x^4}$?

19. Complete the equation to simplify the radical expression.

$$\sqrt{81x^4} = \sqrt{9^2\left(\right)^2}$$

$$= 9 $$

Problem 4 **Using a Radical Expression**

Got It? Some teachers adjust test scores when a test is difficult. One teacher's formula for adjusting scores is $A = 10\sqrt{R}$, where A is the adjusted score and R is the raw score. What are the adjusted scores for raw scores of 0 and 100?

20. Circle the first thing you should do to solve this problem.

Evaluate $A = 10\sqrt{R}$ for $R = 0$ and $R = 100$. $\qquad$ Solve $A = 10\sqrt{R}$ for R.

Chapter 6

156

Underline the correct number to complete each sentence.

21. The lowest possible *raw score* is 0 / 10 / 15 / 100 .

The lowest possible *adjusted score* is 0 / 10 / 15 / 100 .

22. The highest possible *raw score* is 0 / 10 / 15 / 100 .

The highest possible *adjusted score* is 0 / 10 / 15 / 100 .

23. So, the curved scores for raw scores of 0 and 100 are [ ] and [ ] .

Lesson Check • Do you UNDERSTAND?

Error Analysis A student said *the only fourth root of 16 is 2.* Describe and correct his error.

24. If *a* is a fourth root of 16, which statement is true?

(A) $a \cdot a \cdot a \cdot a = 16$ (B) $a = 16^4$ (C) $4a = 16$ (D) $a = \frac{16}{4}$

25. Look at the statement you circled in Exercise 24. Circle the values of *a* below that make the statement true.

$$-64 \qquad -4 \qquad -2 \qquad 2 \qquad 4 \qquad 64$$

26. There are 1 / 2 / 3 / 4 values of *a* that satisfy the statement you circled in Exercise 24.

Therefore, the number of fourth roots of 16 is 1 / 2 / 3 / 4 .

27. Describe the error the student made.

_____

_____

_____

28. Complete the sentence to correct the error the student made.

The fourth root of 16 is [ ] or [ ] .

Math Success

Check off the vocabulary words that you understand.

☐ *n*th root   ☐ principal root   ☐ radicand   ☐ index

Rate how well you can *find nth roots*.

Need to review 0 2 4 6 8 10 Now I get it!

Vocabulary

● **Review**

Write T for *true* or F for *false*.

_____ **1.** All mathematical expressions can be written as an equivalent expression with a *denominator* of 1.

_____ **2.** An expression can have a *denominator* equal to zero.

_____ **3.** The expression above the fraction bar is the *numerator*.

_____ **4.** Multiplying both the *numerator* and the *denominator* by the same nonzero number results in an equivalent fraction.

Circle the *numerator* and underline the *denominator* in each expression.

5. $\dfrac{5}{6}$

6. $\dfrac{-5r^2}{16}$

7. $\dfrac{r^2 + s^2}{c - 16}$

● **Vocabulary Builder**

combine (verb) **kum** BYN

Main Idea: **Combine** means to put things together or to get a total.

Math Usage: To **combine** means to put together or add two like terms to get one term.

Example: The like terms $-2x^3$ and $7x^3$ can be **combined** to get $5x^3$.

● **Use Your Vocabulary**

8. Circle the expression that shows the like terms in $3x^2 + 1 + 4x^2 - 5$ *combined*.

$4x^2 - 1x^2$ $\qquad\qquad$ $7x^2 - 4$ $\qquad\qquad$ $3x^2 - 4x^2 + 1 - 5$

take note

Property **Combining Radical Expressions: Products**

If $\sqrt[n]{a}$ and $\sqrt[n]{b}$ are real numbers, then $\sqrt[n]{a} \cdot \sqrt[n]{b} = \sqrt[n]{ab}$.

_____ **9.** $\left(\sqrt[3]{4}\right)\left(\sqrt[3]{6}\right) = \left(\sqrt[4]{24}\right)$ _____ **10.** $\left(\sqrt[3]{36}\right) = \left(\sqrt[3]{4}\right)\left(\sqrt[3]{9}\right)$ _____ **11.** $\left(\sqrt[4]{3}\right)\left(\sqrt[4]{8}\right) = \left(\sqrt[4]{24}\right)$

Problem 1 Multiplying Radical Expressions

Got It? Can you simplify the product of the radical expression? Explain.

$\sqrt[4]{7} \cdot \sqrt[5]{7}$ $\sqrt[5]{-5} \cdot \sqrt[5]{-2}$

12. Circle the indexes in $\sqrt[4]{7} \cdot \sqrt[5]{7}$.   **13.** Circle the indexes in $\sqrt[5]{-5} \cdot \sqrt[5]{-2}$.

14. The indexes above are the same / different.   **15.** The indexes above are the same / different.

16. Can you simplify the product? Yes / No   **17.** Can you simplify the product? Yes / No

If yes, write the product. _____   If yes, write the product. _____

Problem 2 Simplifying a Radical Expression

Got It? What is the simplest form of $\sqrt[3]{128x^7}$? $\left(\textit{Hint: Remember } \sqrt[3]{b^3} = b.\right)$

18. The index of $\sqrt[3]{128x^7}$ is 3 / 7 / 128.

19. Circle the perfect cube factors.

$$\sqrt[3]{128x^7} = \sqrt[3]{4^3 \cdot 4 \cdot x^3 \cdot x^3 \cdot x}$$

20. The simplest form of $\sqrt[3]{128x^7}$ is _____ .

Problem 3 Simplifying a Product

Got It? What is the simplest form of $\sqrt{45x^5y^3} \cdot \sqrt{35xy^4}$?

21. Complete the steps to simplify $\sqrt{45x^5y^3} \cdot \sqrt{35xy^4}$.

$$\sqrt{45x^5y^3} \cdot \sqrt{35xy^4} = \sqrt{(45x^5y^3) \cdot \left(\boxed{}\right)}$$

$$= \sqrt{\left(45 \cdot \boxed{}\right)\left(x^5y^3 \cdot \boxed{}\right)}$$

$$= \sqrt{\left(9 \cdot 5 \cdot 5 \cdot \boxed{}\right)\left(x^6 \cdot \boxed{}\right)}$$

$$= \sqrt{\left(3^2 \cdot \boxed{}^2 \cdot 7\right)\left(x^3\right)^2 \cdot \left(\boxed{}\right)^2 \cdot y}$$

$$= 3 \cdot \boxed{} \cdot x^3 \cdot \boxed{} \cdot \sqrt{7y}$$

$$= \boxed{} \sqrt{7y}$$

Lesson 6-2

Property Combining Radical Expressions: Quotients

If $\sqrt[n]{a}$ and $\sqrt[n]{b}$ are real numbers and $b \neq 0$, then $\dfrac{\sqrt[n]{a}}{\sqrt[n]{b}} = \sqrt[n]{\dfrac{a}{b}}$.

22. Multiple Choice Which expression is equivalent to $\dfrac{\sqrt[3]{7}}{\sqrt[3]{4x^2}}$?

Ⓐ $\left(2\sqrt[3]{1}\right)\left(x\sqrt[3]{1}\right)$ Ⓑ $x\sqrt[3]{\dfrac{7}{4}}$ Ⓒ $\sqrt[3]{\dfrac{7}{4x^2}}$ Ⓓ $21x^2$

Problem 4 Dividing Radical Expressions

Got It? What is the simplest form of $\dfrac{\left(\sqrt{50x^6}\right)}{\left(\sqrt{2x^4}\right)}$?

23. Complete the expression.

$$\dfrac{\left(\sqrt{50x^6}\right)}{\left(\sqrt{2x^4}\right)} = \sqrt{\dfrac{\boxed{}}{\boxed{}}}$$ Use the Combining Radicals Property for Quotients.

$$= \sqrt{\boxed{}}$$ Simplify under the radical sign.

$$= \boxed{}$$ Simplify the square root.

Problem 5 Rationalizing the Denominator

Got It? What is the simplest form of $\dfrac{\sqrt[3]{7x}}{\sqrt[3]{5y^2}}$?

24. The radicand in the *denominator* needs a 5^2 and a $\boxed{}$ to make $5y^2$ a perfect cube.

25. You will need to multiply *both* the numerator and the denominator by the expression $\sqrt[3]{\boxed{}}$ to rationalize the denominator.

26. Complete to show the rationalization of the denominator.

$$\dfrac{\sqrt[3]{7x}}{\sqrt[3]{5y^2}} = \dfrac{\sqrt[3]{7x}}{\sqrt[3]{5y^2}} \cdot \dfrac{\sqrt[3]{\boxed{}}}{\sqrt[3]{\boxed{}}}$$ Rationalize the denominator.

$$= \dfrac{\sqrt[3]{\boxed{}\ xy}}{\sqrt[3]{5^3 \cdot \boxed{}}}$$ Multiply.

$$= \dfrac{\sqrt[3]{\boxed{}\ xy}}{5 \cdot \boxed{}}$$ Find the cube root of the denominator.

$$= \dfrac{\sqrt[3]{\boxed{}}}{\boxed{}}$$ Simplify.

Chapter 6

160

27. Explain why *both* the numerator and the denominator are multiplied by the expression used to rationalize the denominator.

_____

_____

_____

 Lesson Check • **Do you know HOW?**

Divide and simplify $\dfrac{\sqrt{21x^{10}}}{\sqrt{7x^5}}$.

28. Circle the first step in simplifying the fraction. Underline the second step.

| Combine radical expressions. | Divide out common factors. | Rationalize the denominator. | Simplify each root. |

29. Now divide and simplify.

 Lesson Check • **Do you UNDERSTAND?**

Vocabulary Write the simplest form of $\sqrt[3]{32x^4}$.

30. Complete to simplify.

$$\sqrt[3]{32x^4} = \sqrt[3]{2^3 \cdot \boxed{} \cdot \boxed{} \cdot x}$$

$$= \boxed{} \sqrt[3]{\boxed{}}$$

 Math Success

Check off the vocabulary words that you understand.

☐ simplest form of a radical   ☐ rationalize the denominator

Rate how well you can *multiply and divide radical expressions*.

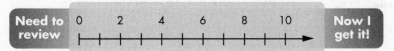

Lesson 6-2

6-3 Binomial Radical Expressions

Vocabulary

● Review

Circle the *like terms* in each group.

1. $3y^2$ $2y$ $2y^2$ **2.** b bc $4bc$ c **3.** 5 18 $5a$

● Vocabulary Builder

> **binomial** (adjective) **by NOH mee ul**
>
> **Definition:** A binomial expression is an expression made up of two terms.
>
> **Related Words:** monomial, binomial expression, trinomial
>
> **Examples:** monomial: $a, x^2, -3, 17c^3, \sqrt{5}$
>
>   binomial: $a - 7, x^2 + 0.9, -3 - ab, 17c^3 + 1, b - \sqrt{5}$
>
>   trinomial: $a - 7 + x, x^2 + x + 0.9, -3 - ab + a, 17c^3 = c^2 + 1,$
> $b^3 + b - \sqrt{5}$

● Use Your Vocabulary

Write M if the expression is a *monomial*, B if the expression is a *binomial*, or T if
the expression is a *trinomial*.

4. $37 - 100x^3y + r$ **5.** $-57t^6$

6. $s + 0.91r$ **7.** $18a - 1.4b^7 + 3.85c^{14}$

Property   Combining Radical Expressions: Sums and Differences

Use the Distributive Property to add or subtract like radicals.

$$a\sqrt[n]{x} + b\sqrt[n]{x} = (a + b)\sqrt[n]{x} \qquad a\sqrt[n]{x} - b\sqrt[n]{x} = (a - b)\sqrt[n]{x}$$

8. Underline the words that make each sentence true.

To be like radicals, their indexes must be the same / different , and their radicands must be the same / different .

To add or subtract two like radicals, you add or subtract their radicands / coefficients .

 Problem 1 Adding and Subtracting Radical Expressions

Got It? What is the simplified form of each expression?

$7\sqrt[3]{5} - 4\sqrt{5}$ $3x\sqrt{xy} + 4x\sqrt{xy}$

9. Are the radicals in $7\sqrt[3]{5} - 4\sqrt{5}$ like radicals?

Yes / No

10. Are the radicals in $3x\sqrt{xy} + 4x\sqrt{xy}$ like radicals?

Yes / No

11. Is $7\sqrt[3]{5} - 4\sqrt{5}$ simplified?

Yes / No

12. Is $3x\sqrt{xy} + 4x\sqrt{xy}$ simplified?

Yes / No

13. Write the simplified form of each expression.

$7\sqrt[3]{5} - 4\sqrt{5}$ $3x\sqrt{xy} + 4x\sqrt{xy}$

Problem 2 Using Radical Expressions

Got It? In the stained-glass window design, the side of each small square is 6 in. Find the perimeter of the window to the nearest tenth of an inch.

14. The length of the window is made up of the diagonals / sides of three squares.

15. The width of the window is made up of the diagonals / sides of two squares.

16. Multiple Choice Which is the length of the diagonal of a square with side s?

Ⓐ $2s$ Ⓑ $\sqrt{2}s$ Ⓒ $s\sqrt{3}$ Ⓓ $s\sqrt{2}$

17. Write the length of the diagonal of a square with side 6 in.

18. Complete the following to find the length and the width of the window.

Length of the window: Width of the window:

$\ell = 3\left(\right) = $ $w = 2\left(\right) = $

Lesson 6-3

19. Complete the steps to find the perimeter of the window.

Perimeter $= 2\ell + 2w$

$= 2\left(\boxed{}\right) + 2\left(\boxed{}\right)$ Substitute for length and width.

$= \boxed{} + \boxed{}$ Simplify.

$= \boxed{}$ Add the coefficients of the like radicals.

$= \boxed{}$ Use a calculator to approximate to the nearest tenth.

 Problem 3 Simplifying Before Adding or Subtracting

Got It? What is the simplified form of the expression $\sqrt[3]{250} + \sqrt[3]{54} - \sqrt[3]{16}$?

20. Complete each factor tree to factor each radicand.

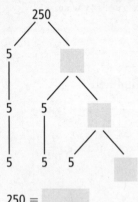 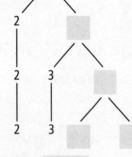 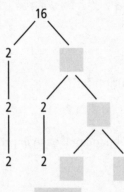

$250 = \boxed{}$ $54 = \boxed{}$ $16 = \boxed{}$

21. Complete the following by substituting the prime factorizations for 250, 54, and 16.

$$\sqrt[3]{250} + \sqrt[3]{54} - \sqrt[3]{16} = \sqrt[3]{\boxed{}} + \sqrt[3]{\boxed{}} - \sqrt[3]{\boxed{}}$$

22. Circle the simplified form of the expression $\sqrt[3]{250} + \sqrt[3]{54} - \sqrt[3]{16}$.

$5\sqrt[3]{2} + 3\sqrt[3]{3} - 2\sqrt[3]{2}$ $6\sqrt[3]{2}$ $3\sqrt[3]{2} + 3\sqrt[3]{3}$

 Problem 4 Multiplying Binomial Radical Expressions

Got It? What is the product $(3 + 2\sqrt{5})(2 + 4\sqrt{5})$?

23. Circle the expression that shows the FOIL method.

$(3 + 2\sqrt{5})(2 + 4\sqrt{5})$ $(3 + 2\sqrt{5})(2 + 4\sqrt{5})$

$3 \cdot 2 + 3 \cdot 4\sqrt{5} + 2\sqrt{5} \cdot 2 + 2\sqrt{5} \cdot 4\sqrt{5}$ $3 \cdot 2 + 3 \cdot 4\sqrt{5} + 2\sqrt{5} \cdot 4\sqrt{5}$

24. The product $(3 + 2\sqrt{5})(2 + 4\sqrt{5}) = \boxed{}$.

Problem 5 Multiplying Conjugates

Got It? What is the product of the expression $(6 - \sqrt{12})(6 + \sqrt{12})$?

25. Use the FOIL method to find the product.

 Problem 6 Rationalizing the Denominator

Got It? How can you write the expression $\dfrac{2\sqrt{7}}{\sqrt{3} - \sqrt{5}}$ with a rationalized denominator?

26. Circle the conjugate of the denominator. $\sqrt{5} - \sqrt{3}$ / $\sqrt{3} + \sqrt{5}$

27. Use the conjugate of the denominator to write $\dfrac{2\sqrt{7}}{\sqrt{3} - \sqrt{5}}$ with a rational denominator.

 Lesson Check • **Do you UNDERSTAND?**

Vocabulary Determine whether each of the following is a pair of like radicals. If so, combine them.

$3x\sqrt{11}$ and $3x\sqrt{10}$ $2\sqrt{3xy}$ and $7\sqrt{3xy}$ $12\sqrt{13y}$ and $12\sqrt{6y}$

28. Cross out the pairs that do NOT have the same index and the same radicand.

$3x\sqrt{11}$ and $3x\sqrt{10}$ $2\sqrt{3xy}$ and $7\sqrt{3xy}$ $12\sqrt{13y}$ and $12\sqrt{6y}$

29. The sum of the like radicals is   .

 Math Success

Check off the vocabulary words that you understand.

☐ like radicals   ☐ binomial radical expressions

Rate how well you can *add and subtract radical expressions*.

Need to review   0   2   4   6   8   10   Now I get it!

Lesson 6-3

Vocabulary

● Review

1. Use the terms in the box to complete the diagram. Then, give examples.

Irrational Numbers	Integers	Natural Numbers
	Rational Numbers	Whole Numbers

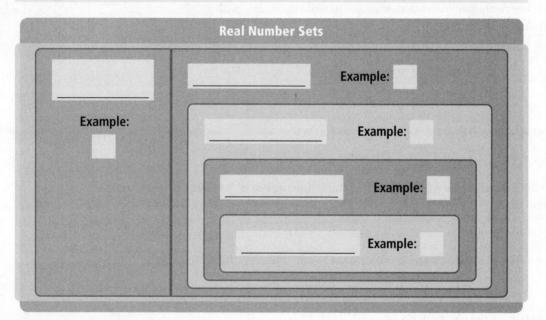

Real Number Sets

_____

Example: ☐

_____   Example: ☐

_____   Example: ☐

_____   Example: ☐

_____   Example: ☐

● Vocabulary Builder

convert (verb) **kun VURT**

Related Words: conversion (noun), convertible (adjective)

Definition: To **convert** is to rewrite or change to another form.

● Use Your Vocabulary

2. Circle the expression that shows $\frac{3}{4}$ _converted_ to a decimal.

$1.3\overline{3}$	0.75	0.34

Complete each sentence with the correct form of the word *convert*.

3. NOUN Travelers to Europe calculate the __?__ of dollars to euros. _____

4. ADJECTIVE A __?__ sofa is a couch by day and a bed by night. _____

5. VERB To __?__ fractions to decimals, divide the numerator by the denominator. _____

 **Problem 1** **Simplifying Expressions With Rational Exponents**

Got It? What is the simplified form of the expression $64^{\frac{1}{2}}$?

6. Circle the expression that shows $64^{\frac{1}{2}}$ rewritten as a radical. (*Hint:* $x^{\frac{1}{n}} = \sqrt[n]{x}$)

$$\sqrt{64} \qquad\qquad \sqrt[\frac{1}{2}]{64} \qquad\qquad \frac{1}{2}\sqrt{64}$$

7. The simplified form of $64^{\frac{1}{2}}$ is [ ] .

---

take note

Key Concept **Rational Exponent**

If the nth root of a is a real number and m is an integer, then
$$a^{\frac{1}{n}} = \sqrt[n]{a} \ \text{ and } \ a^{\frac{m}{n}} = \sqrt[n]{a^m} = (\sqrt[n]{a})^m. \qquad \text{If } m \text{ is negative, } a \neq 0.$$

8. Draw a line from each expression in Column A to its exponent form in Column B.

Column A	Column B
$4\sqrt[3]{x}$	$4x^{\frac{1}{3}}$
$\sqrt[4]{x^3}$	$x^{\frac{3}{4}}$

 Problem 2 **Converting Between Exponential and Radical Form**

Got It? What are the expressions $w^{-\frac{5}{8}}$ and $w^{0.2}$ in radical form?

9. Is the exponent in $w^{-\frac{5}{8}}$ in lowest terms? Yes / No

10. Identify the values of a, m, and n for $w^{-\frac{5}{8}}$ using the rule $a^{\frac{m}{n}} = \sqrt[n]{a^m}$.

$a = $ [ ] $\qquad m = $ [ ] $\qquad n = $ [ ]

11. Use your values for a, m, and n to write $w^{-\frac{5}{8}}$ in radical form.

12. Convert $w^{0.2}$ to w raised to a power that is a fraction in lowest terms.

13. Identify the values of a, m, and n for $w^{0.2}$ using the rule $a^{\frac{m}{n}} = \sqrt[n]{a^m}$.

$a = $ [ ] $\qquad m = $ [ ] $\qquad n = $ [ ]

14. Use your values for a, m, and n to write $w^{0.2}$ in radical form.

Lesson 6-4

Problem 3 **Using Rational Exponents**

Got It? Kepler's third law of orbital motion states that you can approximate the period P (in Earth years) it takes a planet to complete one orbit of the sun using the function $P = d^{\frac{3}{2}}$, where d is the distance (in astronomical units, AU) from the planet to the sun. Find the approximate length (in Earth years) of a Venusian year if Venus is 0.72 AU from the sun.

15. Complete the problem-solving model below.

Know	Need	Plan

16. Use the formula to find the length of a Venusian year.

  Key Concept **Properties of Rational Exponents**

Let m and n represent rational numbers. Assume that no denominator equals 0.

$$a^m \cdot a^n = a^{m+n} \qquad (a^m)^n = a^{mn} \qquad (ab)^m = a^m b^m$$

$$a^{-m} = \frac{1}{a^m} \qquad \frac{a^m}{a^n} = a^{m-n} \qquad \left(\frac{a}{b}\right)^m = \frac{a^m}{b^m}$$

Complete each example below.

17. $g^3 \cdot g^4 = g^{3+\boxed{}} = g^{\boxed{}}$

18. $(h^3)^4 = h^{3\cdot\boxed{}} = h^{\boxed{}}$

19. $(5y)^2 = 5^{\boxed{}} \cdot y^{\boxed{}}$

20. $2^{-6} = \dfrac{1}{2^{\boxed{}}} = \dfrac{1}{\boxed{}}$

21. $\dfrac{d^8}{d^3} = d^{8-\boxed{}} = d^{\boxed{}}$

22. $\left(\dfrac{3}{4}\right)^2 = \dfrac{3^2}{4^{\boxed{}}} = \dfrac{\boxed{}}{\boxed{}}$

 Problem 4 **Combining Radicals With Like Radicands**

Got It? What is $\sqrt{3}(\sqrt[4]{3})$ in simplest form?

23. Convert $\sqrt{3}(\sqrt[4]{3})$ to exponential form.

24. The bases of the factors are the same / different , so the Property you should use to simplify the exponential form is $(ab)^m = a^m b^m \,/\, a^m \cdot a^n = a^{m+n}$.

25. In simplest form, $\sqrt{3}(\sqrt[4]{3}) = \boxed{}$.

Got It? What is $32^{-\frac{3}{5}}$ in simplest form?

26. Solve using two different methods. Complete each method.

Method 1

$32^{-\frac{3}{5}} = (2^{})^{-\frac{3}{5}}$

$\phantom{32^{-\frac{3}{5}}} = (2)^{\cdot\,-\frac{3}{5}}$

$\phantom{32^{-\frac{3}{5}}} = (2)^{}$

$\phantom{32^{-\frac{3}{5}}} = $

Method 2

$32^{-\frac{3}{5}} = \dfrac{1}{32^{}}$

$\phantom{32^{-\frac{3}{5}}} = \dfrac{1}{\left(\sqrt[5]{}\,\right)^{}}$

$\phantom{32^{-\frac{3}{5}}} = \dfrac{1}{\left(\right)^{}}$

$\phantom{32^{-\frac{3}{5}}} = $

Lesson Check • Do you UNDERSTAND?

Error Analysis Explain why this simplification is incorrect.

27. The radical form of $5^{\frac{1}{2}}$ is ▢ .

The radical form of $5(5^{\frac{1}{2}})$ is ▢ .

The radical form of $25^{\frac{1}{2}}$ is ▢ .

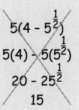

$$5(4 - 5^{\frac{1}{2}})$$
$$5(4) - 5(5^{\frac{1}{2}})$$
$$20 - 25^{\frac{1}{2}}$$
$$15$$

28. Explain why the simplification shown is incorrect.

_____

_____

Math Success

Check off the vocabulary words that you understand.

☐ rational exponent ☐ exponential form ☐ radical form

Rate how well you can *simplify expressions with rational exponents*.

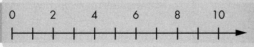

Need to review 0 2 4 6 8 10 Now I get it!

Lesson 6-4

6-5 Solving Square Root and Other Radical Equations

 Vocabulary

● **Review**

1. Circle the *equation* that is equivalent to $\sqrt{x + 1} = 5$.

| $\sqrt{x + 1} = 10$ | $\sqrt{x + 2} = 6$ | $\sqrt{x + 1} + 3 = 8$ |

2. Draw a line from each *equation* in Column A to its *solution* in Column B.

Column A	Column B
$3 + x = 5$	-10
$y - 4 = -6$	10
$2z = 20$	2
$\frac{w}{5} = -2$	-2

Circle the *radicand* in each expression.

3. $\sqrt{2x - 3}$ **4.** $7 - \sqrt{wz + 2}$ **5.** $\sqrt{y} + 7$

● **Vocabulary Builder**

reciprocal (noun) rih SIP ruh kul

Related Term: multiplicative inverse

Definition: Two numbers are **reciprocals** if their product is 1.

Main Idea: To write the **reciprocal** of a fraction, switch the numerator and the denominator.

Examples: 3 and $\frac{1}{3}$, $-\frac{4}{7}$ and $-\frac{7}{4}$, $\frac{1}{6}$ and 6

> **Reciprocals**
> $\frac{a}{b}$ and $\frac{b}{a}$
> where $a \neq 0$ and $b \neq 0$

● **Use Your Vocabulary**

Write T for *true* or F for *false.*

6. The *reciprocal* of -1 is itself.

7. A decimal has no *reciprocal.*

8. The reciprocal of a negative number is negative.

9. The only real number without a reciprocal is 0.

Solving a square root equation may require that you square each side of the equation. This can introduce extraneous solutions.

 Problem 1 **Solving a Square Root Equation**

Got It? What is the solution of $\sqrt{4x + 1} - 5 = 0$?

10. Circle the first step in solving the equation.

Isolate the square root.   Square each side.

11. Underline the correct word to complete each justification.

$\sqrt{4x + 1} = 5$ Isolate the square root / variable .

$4x + 1 = 25$ Take the square root / square of each side to remove the radical.

$4x = 24$ Subtract 1 to isolate the radical / variable term.

$x = 6$ Divide / Multiply by 4 to solve for x.

 Problem 2 **Solving Other Radical Equations**

Got It? What are the solutions of $2(x + 3)^{\frac{2}{3}} = 8$?

12. Complete each step to find the solution.

1 Isolate the radical term.

$$2(x + 3)^{\frac{2}{3}} = 8$$

$$(x + 3)^{\frac{2}{3}} = \boxed{}$$

$\downarrow$

2 Raise each side of the equation to the reciprocal power.

$$\left((x + 3)^{\frac{2}{3}}\right)^{\boxed{}} = 4$$

$\downarrow$

3 Solve for x.

$|x + 3| = \boxed{}$ Since the numerator of $\frac{2}{3}$ is even, $\left((x + 3)^{\frac{2}{3}}\right)^{\frac{3}{2}} = |x + 3|$.

$x + 3 = \pm \boxed{}$

$x = 5$ or $x = \boxed{}$

Lesson 6-5

Problem 4 Checking for Extraneous Solutions

Got It? What is the solution of $\sqrt{5x-1} + 3 = x$? Check your results.

13. Use the justifications at the right to complete each step.

$\sqrt{5x-1} + 3 = x$ Write the original equation.

$\sqrt{5x-1} = x - \boxed{}$ Isolate the radical.

$(\sqrt{5x-1})^2 = \boxed{}$ Square each side of the equation.

$5x - 1 = x^2 + \boxed{}\, x + \boxed{}$ Simplify.

$0 = x^2 - \boxed{}\, x + \boxed{}$ Combine like terms.

$0 = \left(x - \boxed{}\right)\left(x - \boxed{}\right)$ Factor.

$x = \boxed{}$ or $x = \boxed{}$ Use the Zero-Product Property.

14. Substitute each value into the original equation to check the solutions.

$\sqrt{5x-1} + 3 = x$ $\sqrt{5x-1} + 3 = x$

$\sqrt{5\left(\boxed{}\right) - 1} + 3 \stackrel{?}{=} 1$ $\sqrt{5\left(\boxed{}\right) - 1} + 3 \stackrel{?}{=} 10$

$\sqrt{\boxed{}} + 3 \stackrel{?}{=} 1$ $\sqrt{\boxed{}} + 3 \stackrel{?}{=} 10$

$\boxed{} + 3 \stackrel{?}{=} 1$ $\boxed{} + 3 \stackrel{?}{=} 10$

$\boxed{} \neq 1$ false $\boxed{} = 10$ ✓

15. The solution $\boxed{}$ is extraneous.

16. Multiple Choice What can cause an extraneous solution?

Ⓐ raising each side of the equation to an odd power

Ⓑ raising each side of the equation to an even power

Ⓒ adding the same number to each side of an equation

Ⓓ dividing each side of an equation by the same number

17. When should you check for extraneous solutions? Explain.

_____

_____

_____

 Problem 5 Solving an Equation With Two Radicals

Got It? What is the solution of $\sqrt{5x+4} - \sqrt{x} = 4$?

18. The equation has been solved below. Write the letter of the reason that justifies each step. Use the reasons in the box.

$$\sqrt{5x + 4} - \sqrt{x} = 4 \qquad \underline{\hspace{1cm}}$$

$$\sqrt{5x + 4} = \sqrt{x} + 4 \qquad \underline{\hspace{1cm}}$$

$$5x + 4 = (\sqrt{x} + 4)^2 \qquad \underline{\hspace{1cm}}$$

$$5x + 4 = x + 8\sqrt{x} + 16 \qquad \underline{\hspace{1cm}}$$

$$4x - 12 = 8\sqrt{x} \qquad \underline{\hspace{1cm}}$$

$$x - 3 = 2\sqrt{x} \qquad \underline{\hspace{1cm}}$$

$$(x - 3)^2 = 4x \qquad \underline{\hspace{1cm}}$$

$$x^2 - 6x + 9 = 4x \qquad \underline{\hspace{1cm}}$$

$$x^2 - 10x + 9 = 0 \qquad \underline{\hspace{1cm}}$$

$$(x - 9)(x + 1) \qquad \underline{\hspace{1cm}}$$

$$x = 9 \text{ or } x = -1 \qquad \underline{\hspace{1cm}}$$

A Addition Property of Equality
B Square each side.
C Division Property of Equality
D Factor
E Simplify.
F Original equation
G Zero Product Property

19. Only the solution $x = -1 \,/\, x = 9$ satisfies the original equation.

Lesson Check • Do you UNDERSTAND?

Vocabulary Which value, 12 or 3, is an extraneous solution of $x - 6 = \sqrt{3x}$?

20. The solution $x = 12$ satisfies / does not satisfy the original equation.

21. The solution $x = 3$ satisfies / does not satisfy the original equation.

22. The solution $x = 12 \,/\, x = 3$ is an extraneous solution of $x - 6 = \sqrt{3x}$.

Math Success

Check off the vocabulary words that you understand.

☐ radical equation   ☐ square root equation

Rate how well you can *solve square root and other radical equations.*

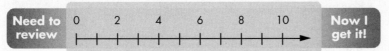

Lesson 6-5

Vocabulary

● Review

1. In *function notation,* gx / $g(x)$ / $x(g)$ is read *g of x.*

2. Circle the equation that shows a *function rule.*

$$x + 17y = -4.7 \qquad f(x) = 14x - 0.3 \qquad 15z(13t)$$

3. The function rule $f(t) = 1.83t$ represents the cost of a number of tons of wheat t.

The number of tons of wheat is the input / output .

The output is the cost of the wheat / number of tons of wheat .

● Vocabulary Builder

composite (adjective) **kum PAHZ it**

Related Words: composite function, composite number

Main Idea: Something that is **composite** is made up of more than one thing.

Math Usage: A **composite** function uses the output of one function as the input of a second function.

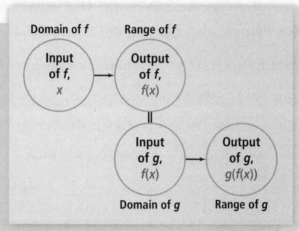

● Use Your Vocabulary

Complete each sentence with the correct form of the word *composite.*

composite   composition   compose

4. VERB The musician worked to __?__ a new piece of music.

5. ADJECTIVE A __?__ number has more than two factors.

6. NOUN The poster was a __?__ of photos and famous quotes.

Key Concept Function Operations

Addition	$(f + g)(x) = f(x) + g(x)$	**Subtraction**	$(f - g)(x) = f(x) - g(x)$
Multiplication	$(f \cdot g)(x) = f(x) \cdot g(x)$	**Division**	$\left(\dfrac{f}{g}\right)(x) = \dfrac{f(x)}{g(x)}, g(x) \neq 0$

The domains of the sum, difference, product, and quotient functions consist of the x-values that are in the domains of *both f* and *g*. Also, the domain of the quotient function does not contain any x-value for which $g(x) = 0$.

7. Let $f(x) = x^2 + 2$ and $g(x) = x - 6$. Complete the steps for finding $f(x) + g(x)$.

$$f(x) + g(x) = (x^2 + 2) + \boxed{} = x^2 + x - \boxed{}$$

Problem 1 Adding and Subtracting Functions

Got It? Let $f(x) = 2x^2 + 8$ and $g(x) = x - 3$. What are $f + g$ and $f - g$? What are their domains?

8. Circle $f + g$.

$2x^2 + x + 8$	$2x^2 + x + 5$	$x^2 + 5$	$x^2 + 8$

9. Circle $f - g$.

$2x^2 - x + 11$	$2x^2 - x + 5$	$x^2 + 5$	$x^2 + 11$

10. Write the domain of f.

11. Write the domain of g.

12. The domain of both $f + g$ and $f - g$ is _____.

Problem 2 Multiplying and Dividing Functions

Got It? Let $f(x) = 3x^2 - 11x - 4$ and $g(x) = 3x + 1$. What are $f \cdot g$ and $\dfrac{f}{g}$ and their domains?

13. Circle $f \cdot g$.

$3x^2 - 11x - 4 + 3x + 1$	$(3x^2 - 11x - 4)(3x + 1)$	$\dfrac{3x^2 - 11x - 4}{3x + 1}$

14. Circle $\dfrac{f}{g}$.

$\dfrac{3x + 1}{3x^2 - 11x - 4}$	$(3x^2 - 11x - 4)(3x + 1)$	$\dfrac{3x^2 - 11x - 4}{3x + 1}$

15. Simplify the product.

16. Simplify the quotient.

17. For what values of x does $g(x) = 0$?

Lesson 6-6

18. Write the domain of $f \cdot g$.

_____

19. Write the domain of $\frac{f}{g}$.

_____

Key Concept Composition of Functions

The composition of function g with function f is written $g \circ f$ and is defined as $(g \circ f)(x) = g(f(x))$. The domain of $g \circ f$ consists of the x-values in the domain of f for which $f(x)$ is in the domain of g.

$$(g \circ f)(x) = g(\underbrace{\underbrace{f(x)}_{1}}_{2})$$

1. Evaluate $f(x)$ first.

2. Then use $f(x)$ as the input for g.

Function composition is not commutative, since $f(g(x))$ does not always equal $g(f(x))$.

If $f(x) = x^2$ and $g(x) = x + 3$, find each composition.

20. $g \circ f = g(x^2) = \boxed{} + 3$

21. $f \circ g = f(x + 3) = (x + 3)^{\boxed{}} = x^2 + \boxed{} x + \boxed{}$

Problem 3 **Composing Functions**

Got It? Let $f(x) = x - 5$ and $g(x) = x^2$. What is $(f \circ g)(-3)$?

Method 1

22. Find $g(-3)$.

_____

23. Use $g(-3)$ as the input for $f(x)$.

$(f \circ g)(-3) = f(g(-3)) = f\left(\boxed{} \right) = \boxed{} = \boxed{}$

Method 2

24. Simplify $(f \circ g)(x) = f(g(x))$.

$f(g(x)) = f\left(\boxed{} \right)$

$\qquad = \boxed{} - 5$

25. Use the rule for $f(g(x))$ to find $f(g(-3))$.

$(f \circ g)(-3) = \boxed{} = \boxed{}$

Problem 4 **Using Composite Functions**

Got It? A store is offering a 15% discount on all items. Also, employees get a 20% employee discount. Write composite functions.
Model taking the 15% discount and then the 20% discount.
Model taking the 20% discount and then the 15% discount.

26. Let x be the price of an item. Write functions to model each discount.

$C(x)$ = cost using the storewide discount = $x - \boxed{}\; x = \boxed{}\; x$

$D(x)$ = cost using the employee discount = $x - \boxed{}\; x = \boxed{}\; x$

27. Draw a line from each composition to its rule.

$(D \circ C)(x)$ $0.85(0.8x)$

$(C \circ D)(x)$ $0.8(0.85x)$

28. Simplify each function.

$(D \circ C)(x) = \boxed{}$ $(C \circ D)(x) = \boxed{}$

29. If you were an employee, which discount would you take first? Why?

_____

_____

_____

Lesson Check • Do you UNDERSTAND?

Open-Ended Find two functions f and g such that $f(g(x)) = x$ for all real numbers x.

30. If $g(x) = x + 3$, write a function $f(x)$ to give $f(g(x)) = x$.

31. If $g(x) = 2x$, write a function $f(x)$ to give $f(g(x)) = x$.

32. Write a function $g(x)$. Then, find $f(x)$ such that $f(g(x)) = x$.

Math Success

Check off the vocabulary words that you understand.

☐ composite function   ☐ function operations

Rate how well you can *find the composition of two functions.*

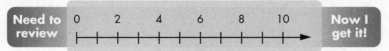

Need to review   0   2   4   6   8   10   Now I get it!

Vocabulary

● **Review**

1. Underline the correct term to complete each sentence.

The *domain* of a relation is the set of inputs, also called the x- / y- coordinates of the ordered pair.

The *range* of a relation is the set of outputs, also called the x- / y- coordinates of the ordered pair.

2. Use the relation {(4, 5), (6, 7), (12, 20), (8, 3), (2, 7)}. Write the domain and range of the relation.

Domain   **Range**

● **Vocabulary Builder**

inverse (noun) **in** VURS

Related Words: opposite, reverse

Math Usage: The **inverse** of a function is found by reversing the order of the elements in the ordered pairs.

Example: The **inverse** of the function {(1, 2), (2, 4), (3, 6)} is {(2, 1), (4, 2), (6, 3)}.

● **Use Your Vocabulary**

3. Complete the diagram below. Use relation *r* {(0, 1), (2, 3), (4, 1), (8, 3)}.

Relation *r*

Domain	Range

Inverse of Relation *r*

Domain	Range

Problem 1 Finding the Inverse of a Relation

Got It? What are the graphs of *t* and its inverse?

4. Complete the table of values for the inverse of relation *t*.

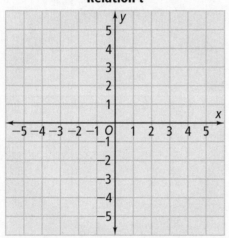

Relation t

x	y
0	−5
1	−4
2	−3
3	−3

Inverse of Relation t

x	y
−5	0
−4	

5. Plot the points from the Relation *t* table and from the Inverse of Relation *t* table.

Relation t

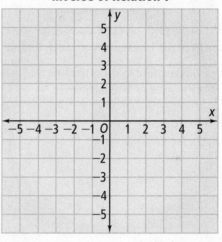

Inverse of Relation t

Problem 2 Finding an Equation for the Inverse

Got It? What is the inverse of $y = 2x + 8$?

6. Switch the *x* and *y* values in the function.

function $y = 2x + 8$

inverse $\boxed{} = 2 \boxed{} + 8$

Lesson 6-7

7. Solve the inverse equation for y.

 Problem 3 **Graphing a Relation and Its Inverse**

Got It? What are the graphs of $y = 2x + 8$ and its inverse?

8. Complete the table for $y = 2x + 8$.

x	−6	−4	−2	0
y				

9. Complete the table for the inverse of $y = 2x + 8$.

x	−4	0	4	8
y				

10. Plot and draw a line through the points from the $y = 2x + 8$ table.

11. On the same grid, plot and draw a line through the points from the inverse of $y = 2x + 8$ table.

12. Draw a dashed line to show the line that reflects the equation $y = 2x + 8$ to its inverse.

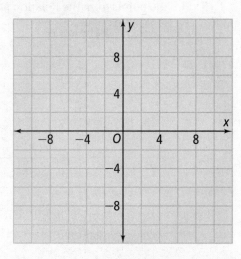

 Problem 5 **Finding the Inverse of a Formula**

Got It? The function $d = \dfrac{v^2}{19.6}$ relates the distance d, in meters, that an object has fallen to its velocity v, in meters per second. Find the inverse of this function. What is the velocity of the cliff diver in meters per second as he enters the water?

13. Solve the function for v.

24 meters

14. Let $d = 24$ meters. Write the value of the velocity v, to the nearest hundredth meter per second, of the diver as he enters the water.

Chapter 6

180

Key Concept   Composition of Inverse Functions

If f and f^{-1} are inverse functions, then $\left(f^{-1} \circ f\right)(x) = x$ and $\left(f \circ f^{-1}\right)(x) = x$ for x in the domains of f and f^{-1}, respectively.

Problem 6 **Composing Inverse Functions**

Got It? Let $g(x) = \frac{4}{x + 2}$. What is $g^{-1}(x)$?

15. Complete each step.

$$\boxed{} = \frac{4}{y + 2} \qquad \text{Write the inverse function.}$$

$$x\left(y + \boxed{}\right) = 4 \qquad \text{Multiply.}$$

$$(y + 2) = \frac{\boxed{}}{x} \qquad \text{Divide.}$$

$$y = \boxed{} \qquad \text{Subtract.}$$

16. So, $g^{-1}(x) = \boxed{}$.

Lesson Check • Do you UNDERSTAND?

Reasoning A function consists of the pairs $(2, 3)$, $(x, 4)$, and $(5, 6)$. What values, if any, may x *not* assume?

17. Each x-value in the domain of a function corresponds to

exactly one y-value / many y-values in the range.

18. What values, if any, may x not assume?

_____

Math Success

Check off the vocabulary words that you understand.

☐ inverse relation   ☐ inverse function   ☐ one-to-one function

Rate how well you can *find the inverse of a relation or function*.

| Need to review | 0 | 2 | 4 | 6 | 8 | 10 | Now I get it! |

Lesson 6-7

Graphing Radical Functions

Vocabulary

● Review

Write T if the figures show a *translation* or N if they do NOT show a translation.

1. _____

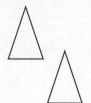

2. _____

3. _____

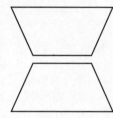

● Vocabulary Builder

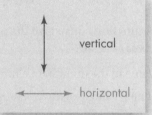

vertical (adjective) VUR **tih kul**

Related Word: horizontal

Main Idea: A **vertical** line is straight up and down.
A **vertical** shift moves something up or down.

Math Usage: A **vertical** translation moves the graph of a relation parallel to the *y*-axis.

● Use Your Vocabulary

Underline the correct word to complete each sentence.

4. A helicopter takes off vertically / horizontally .

5. A package on a flat conveyor belt moves vertically / horizontally .

6. Stepping side-to-side is a vertical / horizontal movement.

Key Concepts Families of Radical Functions

	Square Root	Radical
Parent function	$y = \sqrt{x}$	$y = \sqrt[n]{x}$
Reflection in *x*-axis	$y = -\sqrt{x}$	$y = -\sqrt[n]{x}$
Stretch $(a > 1)$, shrink $(0 < a < 1)$ by factor a	$y = a\sqrt{x}$	$y = a\sqrt[n]{x}$
Translation: horizontal by h, vertical by k	$y = \sqrt{x - h} + k$	$y = \sqrt[n]{x - h} + k$

Problem 1 Translating a Square Root Function Vertically

Got It? What are the graphs of $y = \sqrt{x} + 2$ and $y = \sqrt{x} - 3$?

7. The graph of $y = \sqrt{x} + 2$ is a   horizontal / vertical   translation of $y = \sqrt{x}$

   up / down / left / right   2 units.

8. What does the translation $y = \sqrt{x} - 3$ look like?

   _____

9. Draw the graph of the function $y = \sqrt{x}$.
   Then, use that graph to draw the graphs of
   $y = \sqrt{x} + 2$ and $y = \sqrt{x} - 3$ on the same grid.

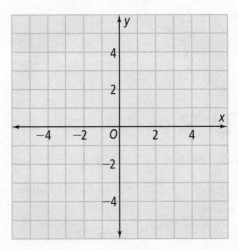

Problem 2 Translating a Square Root Function Horizontally

Got It? What are the graphs of $y = \sqrt{x - 3}$ and $y = \sqrt{x + 2}$?

10. The graph of $y = \sqrt{x - 3}$ is a   horizontal / vertical   translation of $y = \sqrt{x}$

    up / down / left / right   3 units.

11. What does the translation $y = \sqrt{x + 2}$ look like?

    _____

Lesson 6-8

12. Draw the graph of the function $y = \sqrt{x}$. Then, use that graph to draw the graphs of $y = \sqrt{x-3}$ and $y = \sqrt{x+2}$ on the same grid.

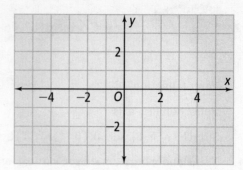

Problem 3 **Graphing a Square Root Function**

Got It? What is the graph of $y = 3\sqrt{x+2} - 4$?

13. Complete the table.

x	1	4	16
$\sqrt{x}$			
$3\sqrt{x}$			

14. Multiplying the y-coordinates of $y = \sqrt{x}$ by 3 shrinks / stretches the graph.

15. Explain how the graph of $y = 3\sqrt{x+2} - 4$ relates to the graph of $y = \sqrt{x}$.

Problem 5 **Graphing a Cube Root Function**

Got It? What is the graph of $y = 3 - \frac{1}{2}\sqrt[3]{x-2}$?

16. Write $y = 3 - \frac{1}{2}\sqrt[3]{x-2}$ in standard form.

Underline the correct numbers or words to complete each sentence.

17. The shift is 2 / 3 units left / right and 2 / 3 units up / down .

18. There is a shrink / stretch by a factor of $\frac{1}{2}$ / 2 and the result is / is not reflected.

19. Circle the graph of
$y = 3 - \frac{1}{2}\sqrt[3]{x-2}$.

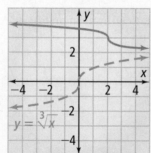
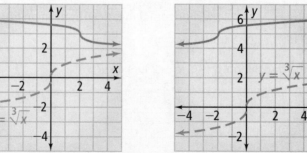

Problem 6 Rewriting a Radical Function

Got It? How can you rewrite $y = \sqrt[3]{8x + 32} - 2$ so you can graph it using transformations? Describe the graph.

20. Factor out the GCF of the radicand.

$$8x + 32 = \boxed{} \left(x + \boxed{} \right)$$

21. Complete the equation.

$$\sqrt[3]{8x + 32} - 2 = \boxed{} \sqrt[3]{x + 4} - \boxed{}$$

22. Underline the correct word to complete each phrase.

translated left / right by 4 units

stretched / shrunk by a factor of 2

translated up / down by 2 units

Lesson Check • Do you UNDERSTAND?

Error Analysis Your friend states that the graph of $g(x) = \sqrt{-x - 1}$ is a reflection of the graph of $f(x) = -\sqrt{x + 1}$ across the x-axis. Describe your friend's error.

23. The graph of the function $-f(x) \,/\, f(-x)$ is a reflection of $f(x)$ over the x-axis.

24. Write the expression that is equal to $-f(x)$.

25. Explain the error your friend made.

_____

_____

Math Success

Check off the vocabulary words that you understand.

☐ radical function   ☐ square root function

Rate how well you can *graph square root functions*.

| Need to review | 0 | 2 | 4 | 6 | 8 | 10 | Now I get it! |

Lesson 6-8

7-1 Exploring Exponential Models

Vocabulary

● Review

1. Cross out the expressions that are NOT *powers*.

$$2^4 \qquad 16x \qquad x^3 \qquad 6a + 7$$

2. Circle the *exponents* in the expressions below.

$$5^6 \qquad x^2y^4 \qquad -25a^{-4} \qquad \frac{4x^2 - 3y^{-4}}{z^2}$$

● Vocabulary Builder

exponential decay (noun) **ek spoh NEN shul dee KAY**

Related Word: decay (verb)

Definition: For the function $y = ab^x$, if $a > 0$ and $0 < b < 1$, the function represents **exponential decay**.

Math Usage: The equation $y = (0.98)^x$ represents **exponential decay**.

Main Idea: Something that decreases as time passes is **decaying**.

Example: A car loses about 15% of its value every year. Its value **decays exponentially**.

● Use Your Vocabulary

3. Circle the equations that represent *exponential decay*.

$$y = -(0.1)^x \qquad y = 2(0.3)^x \qquad y = \left(\frac{3}{4}\right)^x \qquad y = \left(\frac{7}{5}\right)^x$$

$$P = P_0(1.05)^n \qquad N = N_0(0.5)^{\frac{t}{9}} \qquad y = 105 \cdot 1.0001^x \qquad y = 28.0 \cdot 0.9999^n$$

4. Write numbers to make each equation represent *exponential decay*.

$$y = 3\left(\boxed{}\right)^x \qquad m = 0.02\left(\frac{\boxed{}}{2}\right)^n \qquad Q = Q_0\left(\frac{3}{\boxed{}}\right)^t$$

Problem 1 Graphing an Exponential Function

Got It? What is the graph of $y = 4^x$?

5. Complete the following table of values.

x	4^x	y
−3		
−2		
−1		
0		
1		
2		

6. Graph the points from your table. Then connect the points with a smooth curve.

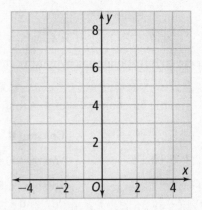

Summary Exponential Functions

For the function $y = ab^x$,
• if $a > 0$ and $b > 1$, the function represents *exponential growth*.
• if $a > 0$ and $0 < b < 1$, the function represents *exponential decay*.

In either case, the y-intercept is $(0, a)$, the domain is all real numbers, the asymptote is $y = 0$, and the range is $y > 0$.

7. Write **D** if the function represents *exponential decay*. Write **G** if it represents *exponential growth*.

_____ $y = 3(5^x)$ _____ $y = \frac{1}{2}(7^x)$ _____ $y = 35\left(\frac{1}{3}\right)^x$ _____ $y = (0.25)^x$

Problem 2 Identifying Exponential Growth and Decay

Got It? Identify $y = 3(4)^x$ as an example of exponential *growth* or *decay*. What is the y-intercept?

8. Compare $y = 3(4)^x$ to the function $y = ab^x$. Complete each equation.

$a = $ ▢ $b = $ ▢

Underline the correct word, expression, or phrase to complete each sentence.

9. The value of b is between 0 and 1 / greater than 1 .

10. So, the function represents exponential growth / decay .

11. The y-intercept is (0, 0) / (1, 0) / (0, 3) .

187

Lesson 7-1

Copyright © by Pearson Education, Inc. or its affiliates. All Rights Reserved.

Key Concept   Exponential Growth and Decay

You can model exponential growth or decay with this function.

Amount after t time periods   Rate of growth $(r > 0)$ or decay $(r < 0)$

$$A(t) = a(1 + r)^t$$

Initial amount   Number of time periods

For growth or decay to be exponential, a quantity changes by a fixed percentage each time period.

12. Draw a line from the function in Column A to the situation it models in Column B.

Column A	Column B
$B(m) = 300(1 - 0.02)^m$	You buy 50 mice. Every month, the population increases by 15%.
$P(m) = 50(1.15)^m$	You have 1 lb of dog food. Your dog eats a quarter of it the next day, and each day afterward the dog eats a quarter of what's left.
$S(t) = 8(1.05)^t$	You get a job paying $8 per hour. Every year, the salary increases by 5% to keep up with the cost of living.
$A(d) = 1(0.75)^d$	Your savings account holds $300. For all accounts under $1000, the bank charges a fee of 2% per month, drawn from the account.

Problem 3   Modeling Exponential Growth

Got It? Suppose you invest $500 in a savings account that pays 3.5% annual interest. How much will be in the account after five years?

13. An exponential growth model applies to this problem because the amount in the

bank <u>increases / decreases</u> by a fixed percentage of ___ % each year.

14. Complete the model.

$a = $ the initial amount invested $= $ ▢

$r = $ the rate of growth per year written as a decimal $= $ ▢

$A(t) = a(1 + r)^t = $ ▢ $\left(1 + \text{▢}\right)^t$

15. Evaluate the model for $t = 5$.

Problem 4 **Using Exponential Growth**

Got It? Suppose you invest $500 in a savings account that pays 3.5% annual interest. When will the account contain $650?

16. Complete the model.

$a =$ ⬚ = the initial amount invested

$r =$ ⬚

$A(t) = a(1 + r)^t =$ ⬚ $\left(\right)^t$

17. Use the TABLE feature on your calculator to complete the table. Use x for t and y for $A(t)$.

18. The account will contain $650 after ⬚ years.

x	y
4	
5	
6	
7	
8	

Lesson Check • **Do you UNDERSTAND?**

Vocabulary Explain how you can tell whether $y = ab^x$ represents exponential growth or exponential decay.

19. $y = 2(3)^x$ represents exponential growth. The value of b in this function is ⬚ .

20. $y = \left(\frac{1}{2}\right)^x$ represents exponential decay. The value of b in this function is ⬚ .

21. Now answer the question.

_____

_____

_____

Math Success

Check off the vocabulary words that you understand.

☐ exponential function   ☐ exponential growth   ☐ exponential decay

Rate how well you can *model exponential growth and decay*.

Need to review 0 2 4 6 8 10 Now I get it!

Lesson 7-1

Properties of Exponential Functions

Vocabulary

● Review

The dashed figure is the image of the solid figure. Identify each *transformation* as a *translation*, *reflection*, or *dilation*.

1.

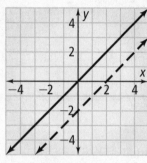

_____

2.

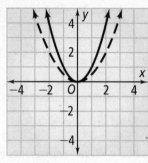

_____

3.

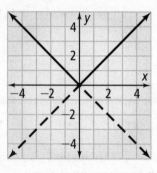

_____

● Vocabulary Builder

exponential growth (noun) ek spoh NEN shul grohth

Opposite: exponential decay

Definition: For the function $y = ab^x$, if $a > 0$ and $b > 1$, the function represents exponential growth.

Example: A savings account earns 3 percent interest annually. The amount in the account grows exponentially. The equation $y = 0.25(9)^x$ represents exponential growth.

● Use Your Vocabulary

4. Circle the functions that represent *exponential growth*.

$y = 2.5(0.75)^x$ $y = -5(1.02)^x$ $y = 0.8(2.7)^x$ $y = 6(9.3)^x$

5. Cross out the functions that do NOT represent *exponential growth*.

$y = 2(0.5)^x$ $y = 6(x - 9.3)^2$ $y = -(2)^x$ $y = 3(7)^x$

Problem 1 Graphing $y = ab^x$

Got It? How does the graph of $y = -0.5 \cdot 5^x$ compare to the graph of the parent function?

The graphs of $y = 5^x$ (solid) and $y = -0.5 \cdot 5^x$ (dashed) are shown at the right. Underline the correct words or value to complete each sentence.

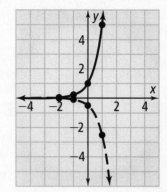

6. Graphing $y = -0.5 \cdot 5^x$ involves a reflection / translation of the parent function.

7. The domain of $y = -0.5 \cdot 5^x$ is / is not the same as the domain of the parent function.

8. The range of $y = -0.5 \cdot 5^x$ is / is not the same as the range of the parent function.

9. The y-intercept of $y = -0.5 \cdot 5^x$ is $(0, 1) / (0, -0.5)$.

10. Multiplying 5^x by 0.5 stretches / compresses the vertical scale.

Problem 2 Translating the Parent Function $y = b^x$

Got It? How does the graph of $y = 4^{(x+2)}$ compare to the graph of the parent function?

11. The graph of $y = 4^{(x+2)}$ is a horizontal / vertical translation of $y = 4^x$ two units to the left / right .

12. The graph at the right shows $y = 4^x$. Sketch the graph of $y = 4^{(x+2)}$ on the same set of axes.

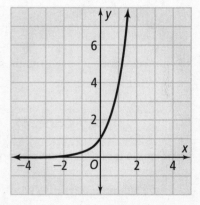

take note

Concept Summary Families of Exponential Functions

Parent Function	$y = b^x$
Stretch $\left(\lvert a \rvert > 1\right)$	
Compression (Shrink) $\left(0 < \lvert a \rvert < 1\right)$	$y = ab^x$
Reflection $(a < 0)$ in x-axis	
Translations (horizontal by h; vertical by k)	$y = b^{(x-h)} + k$
All transformations combined	$y = ab^{(x-h)} + k$

Lesson 7-2

13. Each dashed figure is a transformation of each solid figure. Label the transformation as a vertical *stretch*, vertical *compression*, *reflection*, or *translation*.

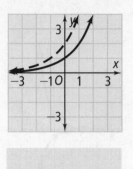 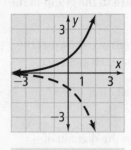 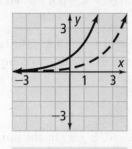 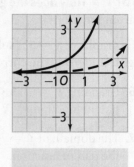

Problem 3 Using an Exponential Model

Got It? The initial temperature of a cup of coffee is 203 °F. An exponential model for the temperature y of the coffee after x minutes is $y = 134.5 \cdot 0.956^x + 68$. How long does it take for the coffee to reach a temperature of 100 °F?

14. Enter the function into your graphing calculator. Then complete the table.

x	31.6	31.7	31.8	31.9	32.0
y					

15. It takes about [ ] minutes to cool to 100 °F.

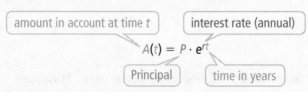

take note

Key Concept Continuously Compounded Interest

The formula for continuously compounded interest uses the number e:

amount in account at time t interest rate (annual)

$$A(t) = P \cdot e^{rt}$$

Principal   time in years

Problem 5 Continuously Compounded Interest

Got It? Suppose you won a contest at the start of 9th grade that deposited $3000 in an account that pays 5% annual interest compounded continuously. You start college 4 years later, and spend 4 years in college. About how much will be in the account after 4 years of college?

16. The money is earning interest over ⬚ years.

17. Use the justifications at the right to solve the problem.

$A = P \cdot e^{r \cdot t}$

$= \boxed{} \cdot e^{\left(\boxed{}\right)\left(\boxed{}\right)}$ Substitute values for P, r, and t.

$\approx \$ \boxed{}$ Use a calculator. Round to the nearest dollar.

Lesson Check • Do you UNDERSTAND?

Reasoning Is investing $2000 in an account that pays 5% annual interest compounded continuously the same as investing $1000 at 4% and $1000 at 6%, each compounded continuously? Explain.

18. Cross out the equation(s) that you could NOT use to solve this problem.

$A = 2000 \cdot e^{(0.05)t}$ $A = 1000 \cdot e^{(0.05)2t}$ $A = 1000 \cdot e^{(0.04)t}$

$A = 1000\left(e^{(0.05)t} + e^{(0.06)t}\right)$ $A = 1000 \cdot e^{(0.06)t}$

19. Use a calculator to complete the table. Round to the nearest dollar.

t	$2000 \cdot e^{0.5t}$	$1000 \cdot e^{0.4t}$	$1000 \cdot e^{0.6t}$	$1000 \cdot e^{0.4t} + 1000 \cdot e^{0.6t}$
1	$	$	$	$
3	$	$	$	$
5	$	$	$	$

20. Now answer the question.

_____

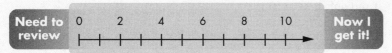

Math Success

Check off the vocabulary words that you understand.

☐ natural base exponential function   ☐ continuously compounded interest

Rate how well you can *graph exponential functions with base* e.

Need to review   0   2   4   6   8   10   Now I get it!

Lesson 7-2

Vocabulary

● Review

1. Circle the *base* in each *power*.

$$2^4 \qquad 52^2 \qquad 3x^5 \qquad (x-2)^3 \qquad 3^x$$

● Vocabulary Builder

---

logarithm (noun) LAWG uh rith um

Related Words: base, power, exponent

Definition: The **logarithm** base b of a positive number x is the exponent to which base b must be raised to get x.

Examples: Since $2^4 = 16$, the **logarithm** base 2 of 16 is 4.

Similarly, since $4^3 = 64$, the **logarithm** base 4 of 64 is 3.

Math Usage: A **logarithm** is written as $\log_b x$ and is read "log base b of x."

● Use Your Vocabulary

Write each *logarithm* in words. The first one is done for you.

Sample: $\log_2 16$ log base 2 of 16

2. $\log_3 4$ **3.** $\log_4 3$ **4.** $\log_x y$ **5.** $\log_y x$

_____   _____   _____   _____

---

take note

Key Concept   Logarithm

A **logarithm** base b of a positive number x satisfies the following definition.

$$\log_b x = y \text{ if and only if } b^y = x$$

6. Draw a line from each *logarithm* equation in Column A to its exponential equation in Column B.

Column A	Column B
$\log_2 16 = 4$	$10^3 = 1000$
$\log_3 9 = 2$	$b^y = x$
$\log_{10} 1000 - 3$	$3^2 = 9$
$\log_b x = y$	$2^4 = 16$

Problem 1 Writing Exponential Equations in Logarithmic Form

Got It? What is the logarithmic form of the equation $36 = 6^2$?

7. Use the definition of logarithm: If $x = b^y$, then $\log_b x = y$.

Since $36 = 6^{\boxed{}}$, $\log_{\boxed{}} 36 = \boxed{}$.

8. The logarithmic form of the equation is $\boxed{}$.

Problem 2 Evaluating a Logarithm

Got It? What is the value of $\log_5 125$?

9. Use the justifications at the right to complete the equations.

$x = \log_5 125$	Write the logarithm.
$125 = \boxed{}$	Use the definition of a logarithm to write an exponential equation.
$5^{\boxed{}} = \boxed{}$	Write 125 as a power of 5.
$\boxed{} = x$	Since the bases are the same, the exponents must be equal.
$\log_5 125 = \boxed{}$	Write the value of $\log_5 125$.

A **common logarithm** is a logarithm with base 10. You can write a common logarithm $\log_{10} x$ simply as $\log x$, without showing the 10.

Problem 3 Using a Logarithm Scale

Got It? In 1995, an earthquake in Mexico registered 8.0 on the Richter scale. In 2001, an earthquake of magnitude 6.8 shook Washington state. How many times more intense was the 1995 earthquake than the 2001 earthquake?

Use the formula $\log \frac{I_1}{I_2} = M_1 - M_2$ to compare the intensity levels of earthquakes, where I is the intensity level and M is the magnitude on the Richter scale.

10. Circle the equation that models the problem.

$$\log \frac{I_1}{I_2} = 2001 - 1995 \qquad \log \frac{I_1}{I_2} = 8.0 - 6.8 \qquad \log \frac{I_1}{I_2} = 10^{1.2} - 10^6$$

Lesson 7-3

11. Simplify the equation you circled in Exercise 10.

12. Circle the common logarithm that corresponds to the simplified equation.

$$\frac{I_1}{I_2} = 10^6 \qquad\qquad \frac{I_1}{I_2} = 10^{1.2} \qquad\qquad \frac{I_1}{I_2} = 10^{-4.8}$$

13. Use a calculator. The 1995 earthquake was about [   ] times more intense than the 2001 earthquake.

 Problem 4 Graphing a Logarithmic Function

Got It? What is the graph of $y = \log_4 x$? Describe the domain, range, y-intercept, and asymptotes.

14. The graph of $y = 4^x$ is at the right.

Circle the graph of its inverse $y = \log_4 x$.

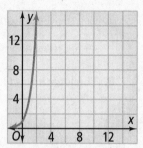

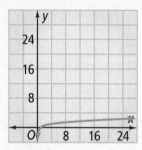 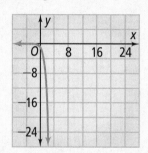

15. Draw a line from each item in Column A to a corresponding item in Column B.

Column A	Column B
Domain of $y = \log_4 x$	$x = 0$
Range of $y = \log_4 x$	$x > 0$
y-intercept of graph of $y = \log_4 x$	$y > 0$
Vertical asymptote(s) of $y = \log_4 x$	none
	all real numbers

take note

Concept Summary Families of Logarithmic Functions

Parent function	$y = \log_b x,\ b > 0,\ b \neq 1$
Stretch $(|a| > 1)$ Compression (shrink) $(0 < |a| < 1)$ Reflection $(a < 0)$ in x-axis	$y = a \log_b x$
Translations (horzontal by h; vertical by k)	$y = \log_b (x - h) + k$
All transformations together	$y = a \log_b (x - h) + k$

16. Circle each equation that is a *compression* of the parent function. Underline each equation that is a *reflection* of the parent function.

$$y = -3 \log_4 x \qquad y = 0.2 \log_8 x \qquad y = \log 3(x - 5) \qquad y = \frac{1}{5} \log_{10} x$$

 Problem 5 Translating $y = \log_b x$

Got It? How does the graph of $y = \log_b (x - 3) + 4$ compare to the graph of the parent function?

17. The graph at the right shows the parent function, $y = \log_2 x$. Underline the correct word or value to complete each sentence.

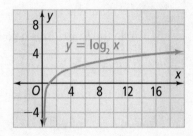

To graph $y = \log_2 (x - 3) + 4$, translate the graph of the parent

function 2 / 3 / 4 units left / right and 2 / 3 / 4 units up / down .

The domain becomes $x > -4 / 3$. The range does / does not change.

 Lesson Check • **Do you UNDERSTAND?**

Vocabulary Determine whether each logarithm is a common logarithm.

$\log_2 4$ $\qquad\qquad$ $\log 64$ $\qquad\qquad$ $\log_{10} 100$ $\qquad\qquad$ $\log_5 5$

18. Circle the base of each logarithm above.

Complete.

19. Common logarithms have a base of $\boxed{}$.

20. Logarithms without a base are assumed to have a base of $\boxed{}$.

21. Write **Y** for yes or **N** for no to indicate whether each logarithm is a common logarithm.

_____ $\log_2 4$ $\qquad$ _____ $\log 64$ $\qquad$ _____ $\log_{10} 100$ $\qquad$ _____ $\log_5 5$

Math Success

Check off the vocabulary words that you understand.

☐ logarithm $\qquad$ ☐ logarithmic function $\qquad$ ☐ common logarithm $\qquad$ ☐ logarithmic scale

Rate how well you can *use and graph logarithms*.

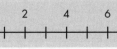

Need to review $\quad$ 0 $\quad$ 2 $\quad$ 4 $\quad$ 6 $\quad$ 8 $\quad$ 10 $\quad$ Now I get it!

Lesson 7-3

Vocabulary

Review

1. Circle the *logarithms* below.

| $\log_4 64$ | 3^9 | $\log(x^2 - 1)$ | $a \cdot b^{(x+1)}$ |

2. Circle the *base* of each logarithm

| $\log_2 32$ | $\log_7 49$ | $\log_{10} 57$ | $\log_5 125$ |

Write T for *true* or F for *false*.

_____ 3. If $\log_b x = y$, then $b^x = y$.

_____ 4. If $\log x = w$, then $10^w = x$.

_____ 5. If $3^2 = x$, then $\log_2 x = 3$.

Vocabulary Builder

formula (noun) FAWRM **yoo luh**

Other Word Forms: formulate (verb), formulaic (adjective)

Definition: A mathematical **formula** is an equation that you can use to solve a particular kind of problem.

Example: You can use the *quadratic* **formula** to solve quadratic equations. You can use the *distance* **formula** to find the distance between two points.

Use Your Vocabulary

6. Circle the slope *formula*.

| $A = \frac{1}{2}(b_1 + b_2)h$ | $A = Pe^{rt}$ | $P = 2l + 2w$ | $m = \dfrac{y_2 - y_1}{x_2 - x_1}$ |

Since $y = \log_a x$ if and only if $x = a^y$, logarithms and exponents have corresponding properties.

Properties Properties of Logarithms

For any positive numbers m, n, and b where $b \neq 1$, the following properties apply.

Product Property

$\log_b mn = \log_b m + \log_b n$

Quotient Property

$\log_b \frac{m}{n} = \log_b m - \log_b n$

Power Property

$\log_b m^n = n \log_b m$

Use the properties of logarithms to complete each equation.

7. $\log 20 = \log(5 \cdot 4) = \log 5 + \log \boxed{}$

8. $\log_5 (x^9) = \boxed{} \log_5 x$

9. $\log_2 24 - \log_2 3 = \log_2 \dfrac{\boxed{}}{\boxed{}} = \log_2 \boxed{}$

10. $\log_3(5x^4) = \log_3 \boxed{} + \log_3 x^4 = \log_3 \boxed{} + \boxed{} \log_3 x$

 Problem 1 Simplifying Logarithms

Got It? What is $2 \log_4 6 - \log_4 9$ written as a single logarithm? If possible, simplify the single logarithm.

11. Circle the property you can use to rewrite $2 \log_4 6$.

Product Property	Quotient Property	Power Property

12. Use the property you circled above to rewrite the first term of $2 \log_4 6 - \log_4 9$.

$2 \log_4 6 - \log_4 9 = \log_4 \boxed{} - \log_4 9$

13. Circle the property you can use to combine the last two terms in Exercise 12.

Product Property	Quotient Property	Power Property

14. Use the property you circled above to combine the two terms.

$\log_4 \boxed{} - \log_4 9 = \log_4 \dfrac{\boxed{}}{\boxed{}} = \log_4 \boxed{}$

15. Use the definition of logarithm to simplify the expression.

$\log_4 \boxed{} = \boxed{}$

 Problem 2 Expanding Logarithms

Got It? What is $\log_3 \frac{250}{37}$ expanded? Simplify your answer, if possible.

Lesson 7-4

16. Follow the steps to expand the logarithm.

$$\log_3 \frac{250}{37} = \log_3 \boxed{} - \log_3 \boxed{}$$ Use the Quotient Property of Logarithms.

$$= \log_3 2 + \log_3 \boxed{} - \log_3 \boxed{}$$ Use the Product Property of Logarithms.

$$= \log_3 2 + \log_3 \boxed{} - \log_3 \boxed{}$$ Write 125 as a power of 5.

$$= \log_3 2 + \boxed{} \log_3 5 - \log_3 \boxed{}$$ Use the Power Property of Logarithms.

Properties   Change of Base Formula

For any positive numbers m, b, and c, with $b \neq 1$ and $c \neq 1$, $\log_b m = \dfrac{\log_c m}{\log_c b}$.
Use the Change of Base Formula to complete each equation.

17. $\log_5 100 = \dfrac{\log 100}{\log \boxed{}}$

18. $\log_2 100 = \dfrac{\log_5 100}{\log_5 \boxed{}}$

19. $\log_{\boxed{}} 100 = \dfrac{\log_2 100}{\log_2 3}$

20. Reasoning The base implied in Exercise 17 is 2 / 5 / 10 / 100 .

Problem 3 **Using the Change of Base Formula**

Got It? What is the value of $\log_8 32$?

21. Circle the least common factor of 8 and 32.

2	4	8	32

22. Complete each equation.

Since $2^5 = 32$, $\log_2 32 = \boxed{}$.   Since $2^3 = 8$, $\log_2 8 = \boxed{}$.

23. $\log_8 32 = \dfrac{\log_2 \boxed{}}{\log \boxed{} \boxed{}} = \dfrac{\boxed{}}{\boxed{}}$

Got It? What is the value of $\log_4 18$?

24. Circle the calculator-ready form of $\log_4 18$.

$\dfrac{\log 4}{\log 18}$	$\dfrac{\log 9}{\log 2}$	$\dfrac{\log 9}{\log 4}$	$\dfrac{\log 18}{\log 4}$

25. The value of $\log_4 18$ is approximately $\boxed{}$.

Problem 4 **Using a Logarithmic Scale**

Got It? Chemistry The pH of a substance equals $-\log [H^+]$, where $[H^+]$ is
the concentration of hydrogen ions. Suppose the hydrogen ion concentration for
Substance A is twice that for Substance B. Which substance has a greater pH level?
What is the greater pH level minus the lesser pH level? Explain.

26. If $[\text{H}^+_b]$ is the concentration of hydrogen ions for Substance B, circle the pH of Substance B.

$$2\log[\text{H}^+_b] \qquad \log[-\text{H}^+_b] \qquad \log\tfrac{1}{2}[\text{H}^+_b] \qquad -\log[\text{H}^+_b]$$

27. Circle the expression for the concentration of hydrogen ions for Substance A.

$$[\text{H}^+_b] - 2 \qquad 2 \cdot [\text{H}^+_b] \qquad \frac{[\text{H}^+_b]}{2} \qquad \log[\text{H}^+_b]$$

28. Circle the expression for the pH of Substance A.

$$-\log[2 \cdot [\text{H}^+_b]] \qquad 2\log[-[\text{H}^+_b]] \qquad -\tfrac{1}{2}\log[\text{H}^+_b] \qquad -\log[\text{H}^+_b]$$

29. Use the Product Property of Logarithms to expand the expression you circled above.

$$\boxed{} = -\left(\log \boxed{} + \log[\text{H}^+_b]\right)$$

$$= - \boxed{} - \log[\text{H}^+_b]$$

$$(\text{pH of Substance A}) = - \boxed{} + (\text{pH of Substance B})$$

30. Circle the substance with the greater pH level.

$$\text{Substance A} \qquad\qquad \text{Substance B}$$

31. What is the difference between the pH levels? Explain how you know.

_____

_____

Lesson Check • Do you UNDERSTAND?

Reasoning If $\log x = 5$, what is the value of $\frac{1}{x}$?

32. Underline the correct expression to complete each sentence.

If $\log x = 5$, then $x = \boxed{10^5 \,/\, 5^{10}}$. Since $\frac{1}{x} = \boxed{x^0 \,/\, x^{-1}}$, I know $\frac{1}{x} = \boxed{10^{-5} \,/\, 5^{-10}}$.

Math Success

Check off the vocabulary words that you understand.

☐ logarithm ☐ Change of Base Formula

Rate how well you can _use the properties of logarithms_.

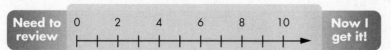

Need to review 0 2 4 6 8 10 Now I get it!

Lesson 7-4

Vocabulary

Review

1. Underline the *base* and circle the *exponent* in each expression.

$$3^7 \qquad 2x^2 \qquad (x + y)^2 \qquad 3 + 9^{(2x+7)}$$

2. Multiple Choice Which expression is read "five to the third *power*"?

Ⓐ 5^3 Ⓑ 5×3 Ⓒ $5x^3$ Ⓓ 3^5

Vocabulary Builder

isolate (verb) EYE soh layt

Other Word Forms: isolation (noun), isolated (adjective)

Definition: When you **isolate** something, you get it by itself.

Math Usage: To **isolate** a variable in an equation means to get the variable alone on one side of the equal sign.

Use Your Vocabulary

3. Draw a line from each equation in Column A to the operation(s) needed to *isolate* the variable in Column B.

Column A	Column B
$3b = 15$	Multiply both sides by 3. Then add 5 to both sides.
$4z + 9 = 81$	Divide both sides by 3.
$\frac{1}{3}(p - 5) = 2$	Subtract 9 from each side, then divide both sides by 4.

✓ **Problem 1** **Solving an Exponential Equation—Common Base**

Got It? What is the solution of $27^{3x} = 81$?

4. Circle the common base that you can use to rewrite 27 and 81.

$$2 \qquad 3 \qquad 6 \qquad 9$$

5. Rewrite 27 and 81 using the common base.

$$\left(\boxed{}^{\boxed{}} \right)^{3x} = \boxed{}^{\boxed{}}$$

6. If two numbers with the same base are equal, their exponents are

equal / not equal .

7. Solve for x.

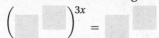**Problem 2** **Solving an Exponential Equation—Different Bases**

Got It? What is the solution of $5^{2x} = 130$?

8. The equation has been solved below. Write a justification for each step.

$$5^{2x} = 130$$

$$\log 5^{2x} = \log 130$$

$$2x \log 5 = \log 130$$

$$x = \frac{\log 130}{2 \log 5}$$

9. Use a calculator to determine the value of x to four decimal places.

$x \approx \boxed{}$

Problem 3 **Solving an Exponential Equation With a Graph or Table**

Got It? What is the solution of $7^{4x} = 800$?

10. Write the two equations you can graph on your graphing calculator to solve this equation.

$Y_1 = \boxed{}$ $Y_2 = \boxed{}$

11. Use a graphing calculator to find the point of intersection of the two equations. Write the approximate value of x.

$x \approx \boxed{}$

Lesson 7-5

Problem 4 Modeling With an Exponential Equation

Got It? Resource Management Wood is a sustainable, renewable, natural resource when you manage forests properly. Your lumber company has 1,200,000 trees. You plan to harvest 5% of the trees each year. How many years will it take to harvest half of the trees?

12. You are harvesting a fixed number / percentage of trees each year, so using a

    linear / exponential growth / exponential decay model is reasonable.

13. Use the phrases at the right to label each part of the formula.

| rate of decay |
| initial amount |
| amount after *n* periods |
| number of time periods |

_____   _____

$$T(n) = a(1 + r)^n$$

_____   _____

14. Use the information in the problem to write each amount.

    $a =$ _____ $r =$ _____ $T(n) =$ _____

15. Use your values for *a*, *r*, and *T(n)* to write an equation.

_____

16. Solve your equation for *n*, the approximate number of years it will take to harvest half the original trees.

Problem 5 Solving a Logarithmic Equation

Got It? What is the solution of log (3 − 2x) = −1?

17. Circle the equivalent exponential form of log (3 − 2x) = −1.

$$3 - 2x = (-1) \qquad 10^{(3-2x)} = 10^{-1} \qquad -\log(3 - 2x) = 1 \qquad 3 - 2x = 10^{-1}$$

18. Solve the exponential equation for *x*.

Got It? What is the solution of $\log 6 - \log 3x = -2$?

19. You can use the [Product / Quotient / Power] Property of Logarithms to write an equivalent equation with a single logarithm.

20. Write the single logarithm equation equivalent to $\log 6 - \log 3x = -2$.

21. Solve the single logarithm equation for x.

Lesson Check • Do you UNDERSTAND?

Error Analysis Describe and correct the error made in solving the equation.

22. If $\log_z x = \log_b y$, does $x = y$? Explain.

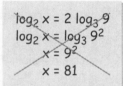

23. Complete the equation below.

$2 \log_3 9 = 2 \log_3 \boxed{}^2$

$ = \boxed{} \log_3 3$

$ = \boxed{}$

24. Correct the error and solve for x.

Math Success

Check off the vocabulary words that you understand.

☐ exponential equation　　　　☐ logarithmic equation

Rate how well you can *solve exponential and logarithmic equations.*

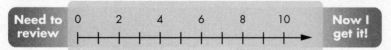

Lesson 7-5

Vocabulary

● **Review**

Write T for *true* or F for *false*.

_____ **1.** The function $y = \log_b x$, where $b > 0$ and $b \neq 1$ is called a *logarithmic function*.

_____ **2.** A *logarithmic* equation is an equation that contains only one *logarithm*.

_____ **3.** The *logarithm* of a power is the difference of the logarithm and the exponent.

● **Vocabulary Builder**

inverse function (noun) **IN vurs FUNGK shun**

Related Words: function, inverse, input, output

Definition: To find the **inverse function**, switch the order of the elements in the ordered pairs of the function.

Example: function, $f(x)$: {(1, 2), (3, 4)}; **inverse function**, $f^{-1}(x)$: {(2, 1), (4, 3)}

● **Use Your Vocabulary**

4. Complete the table of values for the inverse function, $f^{-1}(x)$, of the function $f(x)$.

$f(x) = x + 3$

x	−1	0	1	2
y	2	3	4	6

$f^{-1}(x) = x - 3$

x	2	3		6
y			1	

Key Concept Natural Logarithmic Function

If $y = e^x$, then $x = \log_e y = \ln y$. The natural logarithmic function is the inverse of $y = e^x$, so you can write it as $y = \ln x$.

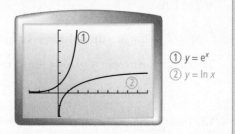

① $y = e^x$
② $y = \ln x$

5. If $y = e^5$, then $\ln y = $ ___ .

6. If $\ln b = 6$, then $b = e$ ___ .

Problem 1 Simplifying a Natural Logarithmic Expression

Got It? What is $\ln 7 + 2 \ln 5$ written as a single natural logarithm?

7. The expression is simplified below. Write a justification for each step.

$\ln 7 + 2 \ln 5$

$\ln 7 + \ln 5^2$

$\ln 7 + \ln 25$

$\ln (7 \cdot 25)$

$\ln 175$

Problem 2 Solving a Natural Logarithmic Equation

Got It? What are the solutions of $\ln x = 2$?

8. Complete: If $\ln x = 2$, then e ___ $= x$.

Got It? What are the solutions of $\ln (3x + 5)^2 = 4$? Check your answers.

9. The equation is solved below. Write a justification for each step.

$\ln (3x + 5)^2 = 4$

$(3x + 5)^2 = e^4$

$3x + 5 = \pm e^2$

$3x = -5 \pm e^2$

$x = (-5 \pm e^2) \div 3$

$x \approx 0.7964$ or $x \approx -4.1267$

Lesson 7-6

10. Check Substitute your values for x in $\ln (3x + 5)^2 = 4$. Use a calculator.

$$\ln \left(3 \cdot \boxed{} + 5\right)^2 \approx \boxed{} \qquad \ln \left(3 \cdot \boxed{} + 5\right)^2 \approx \boxed{}$$

Got It? What are the solutions of $\ln 2x + \ln 3 = 2$? Check your answers.

11. Circle the property of logarithms that justifies writing $\ln 2x + \ln 3$ as $\ln 6x$.

Power Property	Product Property	Quotient Property

12. Use the simplified equation to solve for x.

13. Check Substitute your value for x in $\ln 2x + \ln 3 = 2$. Use a calculator.

$$\ln 2 \cdot \boxed{} + \ln 3 \approx \boxed{}$$

Problem 3 Solving an Exponential Equation

Got It? What is the solution of $e^{x-2} = 12$? Check your answer.

14. Use the justifications at the right to solve the equation.

$$e^{x-2} = \boxed{} \qquad \text{Write the original equation.}$$

$$x - 2 = \boxed{} \qquad \text{Rewrite in logarithmic form.}$$

$$x = \boxed{} + 2 \qquad \text{Add 2 to each side.}$$

$$x \approx \boxed{} \qquad \text{Use a calculator.}$$

15. Check Substitute your value for x in $e^{x-2} = 12$. Use a calculator.

$$e^{\boxed{} - 2} \approx \boxed{}$$

Got It? What is the solution of $2e^{-x} = 20$? Check your answer.

16. Circle the first step in solving the equation. Underline the second step.

Divide each side of the equation by 2.	Use the Power Property.
Write in exponential form.	Write in logarithmic form.

17. Now solve the equation.

18. Check Substitute your value for x in $2e^{-x} = 20$. Use a calculator.

$$2e^{-\boxed{}} \approx \boxed{}$$

Problem 4 Using Natural Logarithms

Got It? Space A spacecraft can attain a stable orbit 300 km above Earth if it reaches a velocity of 7.7 km/s. The formula for a rocket's maximum velocity v in kilometers per second is $v = -0.0098t + c \ln R$. The booster rocket fires for t seconds and the velocity of the exhaust is c km/s. The ratio of the mass of the rocket filled with fuel to its mass without fuel is R.

Suppose a booster rocket for a spacecraft has a mass ratio of about 15, an exhaust velocity of 2.1 km/s, and a firing time of 30 s. Can the spacecraft achieve a stable orbit 300 km above Earth?

19. Identify the values for each variable.

$R = $ ☐ $c = $ ☐ $t = $ ☐

20. Complete the equation for finding the spacecraft's maximum velocity. Then use a calculator to simplify the equation.

$v = -0.0098 \cdot $ ☐ $ + \left($ ☐ $\ln$ ☐ $\right)$ km/s $\approx$ ☐ km/s

21. The spacecraft will / will not achieve a stable orbit 300 km above Earth. Explain.

_____

_____

Lesson Check • Do you UNDERSTAND?

Reasoning Can $\ln 5 + \log_2 10$ be written as a single logarithm? Explain your reasoning.

22. The $\ln 5 + \log_2 10$ can be written as $\ln 5 = \log_e$ ☐ $+ \log_2 10$.

23. Can you use the Product Property of Logarithms to combine the logarithms? Explain why or why not.

_____

24. $\ln 5 + \log_2 10$ can / cannot be written as a single logarithm.

Math Success

Check off the vocabulary words that you understand.

☐ function   ☐ logarithm   ☐ natural logarithmic function

Rate how well you can *write and solve equations with natural logarithms.*

| Need to review | 0 | 2 | 4 | 6 | 8 | 10 | Now I get it! |

Lesson 7-6

Vocabulary

● **Review**

1. Cross out the expressions that do NOT contain a *constant* term.

$6y + 5$	$x^2 + 3y$	$7y + \dfrac{-6}{x} + 2$	$x - 7y + z$

2. In the expression $7x^2 + 3x + 1$, what is the value of the *constant*? Circle your answer.

1	2	3	7

● **Vocabulary Builder**

inverse variation (noun) IN vurs vehr ee AY shun

> **inverse variation**
> $y = \dfrac{k}{x}$, $xy = k$, or $x = \dfrac{k}{y}$
> where $k \neq 0$

Definition: An **inverse variation** is a relationship between two quantities where one quantity increases as the other decreases by the same factor, k.

Main Idea: Two quantities vary *inversely* when one quantity increases as the other decreases proportionally.

Example: The time to complete a race decreases as average speed increases. This relationship between time and speed is an **inverse variation.**

Nonexample: As the force with which you throw a ball increases, the distance it travels also increases. The relationship between force and distance a ball is thrown is a *direct variation*, not an **inverse variation.**

● **Use Your Vocabulary**

Write T for *true* or F for *false*.

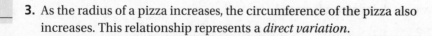

_____ **3.** As the radius of a pizza increases, the circumference of the pizza also increases. This relationship represents a *direct variation*.

_____ **4.** As the number of miles a car is driven increases, the number of gallons of gas in the car's tank decreases. This relationship represents an *inverse variation*.

_____ **5.** As the number of pages in a book increases, the weight of the book increases. This relationship represents an *inverse variation*.

In an *inverse variation*, the product of every x-value with its corresponding y-value is the same number. In a *direct variation*, the ratio of every y-value to its corresponding x-value is the same number.

 Problem 1 Identifying Direct and Inverse Variations

Got It? Is the relationship between the variables a *direct variation*, an *inverse variation*, or *neither*? Write function models for the direct and inverse variations.

x	y
0.2	8
0.5	20
1.0	40
1.5	60

6. Find the value of each expression.

xy	$\dfrac{y}{x}$
1.6	

7. Underline the correct word or words to complete each sentence.

The product of every x-value and its corresponding y-value is / is not constant.

The ratio of every y-value to its corresponding x-value is / is not constant.

The relationship between the variables represents a(n) direct / inverse variation.

8. Write a function to model the data.

$$\frac{y}{x} = \boxed{} \quad \text{or} \quad y = \boxed{} \cdot x$$

 Problem 2 Determining an Inverse Variation

Got It? Suppose x and y vary inversely, and $x = 8$ when $y = -7$. What is the function that models the inverse variation?

9. Circle the equation that represents the general form for inverse variation.

$$\frac{y}{x} = k \qquad\qquad xy = k \qquad\qquad \frac{y}{k} = x$$

10. Use the justifications at the right to determine the function.

$xy = k$	Write the general function form for inverse variation.
	Substitute for x and y.
	Solve for k.

11. The function $\boxed{}$ models the inverse variation.

211

Lesson 8-1

When one quantity varies with respect to two or more quantities, you have *combined variation*.
When one quantity varies directly with two or more quantities, you have *joint variation*.

Key Concepts Combined Variations

Combined Variation	Equation Form
z varies jointly with x and y.	$z = kxy$
z varies jointly with x and y and inversely with w.	$z = \dfrac{kxy}{w}$
z varies jointly with x and inversely with the product wy.	$z = \dfrac{kx}{wy}$

Identify the combined variation in each equation.

12. $p = ktn$

p varies jointly with

t and ____.

13. $m = \dfrac{ky}{xn}$

m varies jointly with

____ and inversely with

the product ____.

14. $v = \dfrac{krm}{z}$

v varies jointly with

____ and ____ and

inversely with ____.

 Problem 4 Using Combined Variation

Got It? The number of bags of mulch you need to mulch a planting area varies jointly with the area to be mulched a in square feet and the depth of the mulch d in feet. If you need 10 bags to mulch 120 ft^2 to a depth of 3 in., how many bags do you need to mulch 200 ft^2 to a depth of 4 in.?

15. If b is the number of bags of mulch you need, the function that represents the joint variation is $b = k \cdot$ ____ $\cdot$ ____.

16. Substitute the values you are given for a, b, and d into the function. Then solve for k.

17. Use the value of k to write a formula to find. the number of bags of mulch you need given the area and depth.

18. Use the equation you wrote in Exercise 17 to find the number of bags for an area of 200 ft^2 to a depth of 4 in.

19. You need ____ bags to mulch 200 ft^2 to a depth of 4 in.

Problem 5 Applying Combined Variation

Got It? How much potential energy would a 41-kg diver have standing on a 10-m diving platform?

20. Write the formula for potential energy.

21. Use the given data to find *PE*.

$g = 9.8$ $\quad m = \boxed{}$ $\quad h = \boxed{}$

$PE = gmh$ $\quad PE = 9.8 \cdot \boxed{} \cdot \boxed{}$ $\quad PE = \boxed{}$

The diver has $\boxed{}$ joules of potential energy.

Got It? An 80-kg diver stands on a 6-m diving platform. At what height should a 40-kg diver stand to have equal potential energy? Do you need to find the potential energy of either diver to solve this? Explain.

22. Write the formula for potential energy for each diver.

Diver 1: $PE = gmh = 9.8 \cdot \boxed{} \cdot \boxed{}$ Diver 2: $PE = gmh = 9.8 \cdot \boxed{} \cdot \boxed{}$

23. The potential energy of the divers needs to be equal. Substitute the value of PE for Diver 1 into the formula for Diver 2.

$9.8 \cdot \boxed{} \cdot \boxed{} = 9.8 \cdot \boxed{} \cdot h$

24. Solve for the height, *h*.

$\dfrac{9.8 \cdot \boxed{} \cdot \boxed{}}{9.8 \cdot \boxed{}}$ $\qquad h = \boxed{}$

The 40-kg diver should stand at $\boxed{}$ m.

25. Did you need to find the potential energy of either diver? yes no

Lesson Check • Do you UNDERSTAND?

Writing Describe how the variables in the equation $p = \dfrac{kqrt}{s}$ are related.

26. Circle the variable(s) that vary directly with p. Draw a box around the variable(s) that vary inversely with p.

	q	r	s	t

27. Describe how the variables in the given equation are related.

_____

Math Success

Check off the vocabulary words that you understand.

☐ inverse variation ☐ constant of variation ☐ combined variation ☐ joint variation

Rate how well you can *use direct, inverse, and joint variations.*

Need to review 0 2 4 6 8 10 Now I get it!

Vocabulary

Review

1. Place a ✓ in the box if the fractions are *reciprocals*. Place an ✗ in the box if they are NOT *reciprocals*.

| | $\frac{7}{8}$ and $\frac{8}{7}$ | | $\frac{1}{x}$ and $\frac{1}{2x}$ | | $\frac{1}{3x}$ and $3x$ |

2. The *reciprocal* of a positive number is positive.　　Yes / No

The *reciprocal* of a negative number is positive.　　Yes / No

A negative number has no *reciprocal*.　　Yes / No

The *reciprocal* of 0 is undefined.　　Yes / No

Vocabulary Builder

reciprocal function　(noun) rih SIP ruh kul FUNGK shun

Related Terms: reciprocal (noun), multiplicative inverse (noun), asymptote (noun), improper fraction (noun)

Main Idea: A reciprocal function is any function that contains a fraction with the independent variable in the denominator.

Examples: $y = \frac{1}{3x} + 1$, $f(x) = \frac{1}{x-2}$, $g(x) = \frac{5}{2x} - 8$

Nonexamples: $y = x - 2$, $f(x) = \frac{x}{2}$, $g(x) = \frac{x-1}{5}$, $h(x) = 8x + \frac{4x}{5}$

Use Your Vocabulary

Complete each equation with the given expressions to make a *reciprocal function*.

3. 5 and $3x$　　**4.** 7 and x　　**5.** $(x+1)$ and 2　　**6.** $(x-8)$ and 1

$y = \dfrac{6}{\boxed{}} + \boxed{}$　　$y = \dfrac{\boxed{}}{\boxed{}}$　　$f(x) = \dfrac{\boxed{}}{\boxed{}}$　　$f(x) = \dfrac{\boxed{}}{\boxed{}} - 3$

Got It? What is the graph of $y = \frac{12}{x}$? Identify the x- and y-intercepts and the asymptotes of the graph. Also, state the domain and range of the function.

7. Circle the graph that shows $y = \frac{12}{x}$.

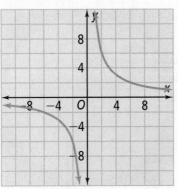 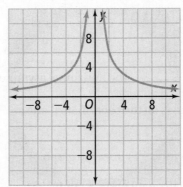 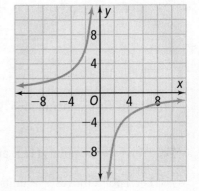

8. Underline the correct word or words to complete the sentences about the graph.

The value of x cannot be 0, so there is no x- / y-   intercept.

The value of y cannot be 0, so there is no x- / y-   intercept.

The x-axis is the   horizontal / vertical   asymptote.

The y-axis is the   horizontal / vertical   asymptote.

9. The domain is the set of all real numbers except $x = $ ▢ .

The range is the set of all real numbers except $y = $ ▢ .

Key Concepts   The Reciprocal Function Family

Parent function: $y = \frac{1}{x}, x \neq 0$

Stretches and compressions occur based on the value of a in $y = \frac{a}{x}, x \neq 0$.

When $\left\{ \begin{array}{l} |a| > 1, \\ 0 < |a| < 1, \\ a < 0, \end{array} \right\}$ the graph of $y = \frac{a}{x}$ $\left\{ \begin{array}{l} \text{stretches by a factor of } a. \\ \text{shrinks by a factor of } a. \\ \text{reflects across the } x\text{-axis.} \end{array} \right\}$

Combined
$y = \frac{a}{x - h} + k,$
where $x \neq h$

Translations occur based on the values of h and k in $y = \frac{1}{x - h} + k; x \neq h$.

The graph of $y = \frac{1}{x}$ $\left\{ \begin{array}{l} \text{shifts horizontally} \\ h \text{ units} \\ \text{shifts vertically} \\ k \text{ units} \end{array} \right\}$ and has a $\left\{ \begin{array}{l} \text{vertical asymptote} \\ \text{at } x = h. \\ \text{horizontal} \\ \text{asymptote at } y = k. \end{array} \right\}$

Lesson 8-2

Problem 3 Graphing a Translation

Got It? What is the graph of $y = \frac{1}{x-4} + 6$? Identify the domain and range.

10. Find the equations of the asymptotes. Then sketch the asymptotes on the graph.

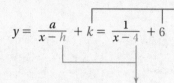

$$y = \frac{a}{x-h} + k = \frac{1}{x-4} + 6$$

The vertical asymptote is $x = \boxed{}$.   The horizontal asymptote is $y = \boxed{}$.

11. Graph the parent function, $y = \frac{1}{x}$, on the coordinate plane at the right.

12. Translate the points $(1, 1)$ and $(-1, -1)$ from the graph of $y = \frac{1}{x}$.

Each point moves $\boxed{}$ units to the right and $\boxed{}$ units up.

13. Draw the branches of $y = \frac{1}{x-4} + 6$ through the translated points.

14. Find the domain and range.

Domain: the set of all real numbers except $x = \boxed{}$

Range: the set of all real numbers except $y = \boxed{}$

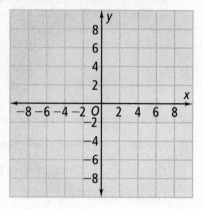

Problem 4 Writing the Equation of a Transformation

Got It? This graph of a function is a translation of the graph of $y = \frac{2}{x}$. What is an equation for the function?

15. Identify the asymptotes: $x = \boxed{}$ and $y = \boxed{}$

So $h = \boxed{}$ and $k = \boxed{}$.

16. Substitute the values of h and k into the general form of a translated reciprocal function.

$$y = \frac{a}{x-h} + k \longrightarrow y = \frac{2}{x - \boxed{}} + \boxed{}$$

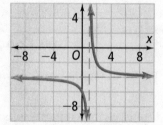

17. The simplified form of the equation is $y = \boxed{}$.

Problem 5 Using a Reciprocal Function

Got It? The junior class is renting a laser tag facility with a capacity of 325 people. The cost for the facility is $1200. The party must have 13 adult chaperones. If every student who attends shares the facility cost equally, what function models the cost per student C with respect to the number of students n who attend? What is the domain of the function? How many students must attend to make the cost per student no more than $7.50?

18. Complete the model.

Relate   C, cost per student   is $1200   divided by   n, the number of students who attend

Capacity — Number of chaperones

Write   ☐ = ☐ ÷ ☐   *or*   ☐ = ☐/☐

19. The domain of this function is ☐ $\leq n \leq$ ☐ .

20. Label the functions $y = 7.5$ and $y = \dfrac{1200}{x}$ in the graph at the right.

21. For the cost per student to be no more than $7.50,
☐ students must attend.

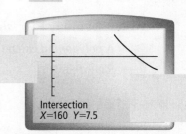

Intersection
X=160 Y=7.5

✓ Lesson Check • Do you UNDERSTAND?

Write an equation of the reflection of the graph $y = \frac{1}{x}$ across the x-axis.

22. Assume $y = \frac{a}{x}$ is a reflection across the x-axis of $y = \frac{1}{x}$. Circle the true statement.

   a must be a fraction between 0 and 1.   *a* must be negative.

23. Complete the equation with values of your choosing so the graph is a reflection of $y = \frac{1}{x}$ across the x-axis. Place a zero in any box you choose to leave blank.

$$y = \frac{\boxed{}}{x - \boxed{}} + \boxed{}$$

✓ Math Success

Check off the vocabulary words that you understand.

☐ reciprocal function   ☐ asymptote   ☐ translation

Rate how well you can *graph translations of reciprocal functions*.

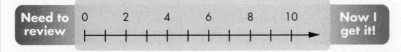

Need to review 0 2 4 6 8 10 Now I get it!

Lesson 8-2

Vocabulary

● **Review**

1. Write T for *true* or F for *false*.

☐ A *polynomial* can be named
___ by its degree.

☐ A *polynomial* with one term
___ is called a binomial.

● **Vocabulary Builder**

discontinuous (noun) dis kun TIN yoo us

Math Usage: When graphed, a discontinuous function contains gaps.

Related Words: continuous (adjective), point of discontinuity (noun)

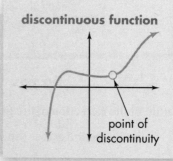

● **Use Your Vocabulary**

Write C if the graph is *continuous* or D if it is *discontinuous*.

2. ___

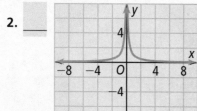

3. ___

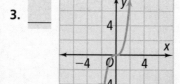

4. ___

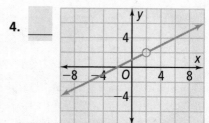

Key Concept   Point of Discontinuity

If a is a real number for which the denominator of a rational function $f(x)$ is zero, then a is not in the domain of $f(x)$. The graph of $f(x)$ is not continuous at $x = a$ and the function has a **point of discontinuity** at $x = a$.

A point of discontinuity is **removable** if the function can be redefined at that point to make the function continuous, as happens when there are common factors in the numerator and the denominator. A point of discontinuity is **non-removable** if the function cannot be redefined at that point.

Problem 1 Finding Points of Discontinuity

Got It? What are the domain and points of discontinuity of the rational function $y = \frac{1}{x^2 - 16}$? Are the points of discontinuity *removable* or *non-removable*? What are the *x*- and *y*-intercepts of the rational function?

5. The function is undefined where ⬚ = 0.

The domain is the set of all real numbers except $x = $ ⬚ and $x = $ ⬚.

6. *Removable* discontinuities happen when there are common factors in the numerator and the denominator of a rational function. Underline the correct word to complete each sentence.

The function can / cannot be redefined at the points of discontinuity.

The points of discontinuity are removable / non-removable .

7. The *x*-intercept of any function occurs where $y = $ ⬚.

For a rational function, that happens only when the numerator is ⬚.

8. How do you know there is no *x*-intercept for the function? Explain.

_____

_____

_____

9. To find the *y*-intercept, let $x = 0$.

$$ y = \frac{1}{\left(\;⬚\;\right)^2 - 16} = ⬚ $$

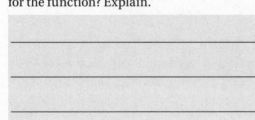

---

take note

Key Concepts   Vertical and Horizontal Asymptotes of Rational Functions

The graph of a rational function has a *vertical asymptote* at each real zero of the expression in the *denominator* if the numerator and denominator have no common factors.

If the numerator and denominator do have common factors, then the rational function still has a *vertical asymptote* at that zero as long as the degree of the common factor in the denominator is greater than the degree of the common factor in the numerator.

To find the *horizontal asymptote* of the graph of a rational function, compare the degree of the numerator *m* to the degree of the denominator *n*.

If...	then the graph has...
$m < n$	horizontal asymptote $y = 0$
$m > n$	no horizontal asymptote
$m = n$	horizontal asymptote $y = \frac{a}{b}$, where a is the coefficient of the highest-degree term in the numerator and b is the coefficient of the highest-degree term in the denominator.

Lesson 8-3

Determine the point(s) of discontinuity, vertical asymptote(s), and horizontal asymptote of the graph of the rational function.

$$y = \frac{x + 4}{(x - 2)(x + 3)}$$

10. Use the justifications at the right to find the points of discontinuity.

$\left(x - \boxed{}\right)\left(x + \boxed{}\right) = 0$ Set the expression in the denominator equal to 0 to find where the function is undefined.

$\boxed{} = 0$ and $\boxed{} = 0$ Set each factored expression equal to 0.

$x = \boxed{}$ and $x = \boxed{}$ Solve for x.

11. Write T for *true* or F for *false*.

_____ The numerator and denominator have common factors.

_____ There are vertical asymptotes at the points of discontinuity.

12. The degree of the numerator, m, is $\boxed{}$.

The expanded denominator is $x^2 + \boxed{} - 6$.

The degree of the denominator, n, is $\boxed{}$.

13. Circle the correct inequality.

$m > n$ $m = n$ $m < n$

14. The equation of the horizontal asymptote is $\boxed{}$.

✓ **Problem 4** Graphing Rational Functions

Got It? What is the graph of the rational function $y = \frac{x + 3}{x^2 - 6x + 5}$?

Step 1 Find the horizontal asymptote, if it exists.

15. Identify the degree of each.

numerator   denominator

$m = \boxed{}$ $n = \boxed{}$

16. Compare. Write $<$, $>$, or $=$.

$m \boxed{} n$

17. horizontal asymptote

$y = \boxed{}$

Step 2 Find the vertical asymptote(s).

18. Set the denominator equal to zero. Solve for x.

$x^2 - 6x + 5 = \boxed{}$

$\left(\boxed{}\right)\left(\boxed{}\right) = \boxed{}$

19. Vertical Asymptotes

$x = \boxed{}$ and $x = \boxed{}$

Step 3 Find the x-intercept(s).

20. Set the numerator equal to zero.

$x + 3 = 0$ when $x = \boxed{}$

Step 4 Find the y-intercept(s).

21. Let $x = 0$ and solve for y.

Step 5 Summarize by graphing the function.

22. Circle the graph that shows

$$y = \frac{x + 3}{x^2 - 6x + 5}$$

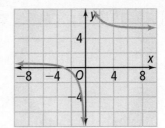 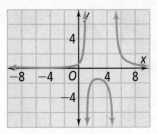

 Problem 5 Using a Rational Function

Got It? You have a 10% orange juice drink for mixing with 100% pure orange juice to make a juice drink that is 40% orange juice. The function $y = \frac{(2)(1.0) + x(0.1)}{2 + x}$ gives the amount x, in gallons, of the 10% drink that you must mix with pure orange juice to make a drink that has concentration y of orange juice. How much of the 10% drink must you add to 2 gallons of pure orange juice for a drink that is 40% orange juice?

23. Substitute for y and solve for x. (*Hint:* Use 0.4 for 40%.)

24. You should add ☐ gallons of the 10% drink to get a 40% drink.

 Lesson Check • **Do you UNDERSTAND?**

What do the **Y1** values for **X** = −3 and **X** = 1 tell you about the rational function?

25. Underline the correct word to complete each sentence.

The **Y1** values for **X** = −3 and **X** = 1 are defined / undefined .

The domain / range is all real numbers except $x = -3$ and $x = 1$.

The asymptotes / intercepts occur at $x = -3$ and $x = 1$.

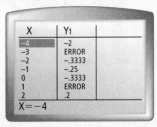

 Math Success

Check off the vocabulary words that you understand.

☐ rational function ☐ continuous ☐ discontinuous ☐ point of discontinuity

Rate how well you can *graph rational functions*.

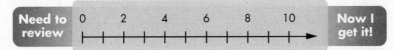

Lesson 8-3

Vocabulary

● Review

1. Circle the fractions that are in *simplest form*.

$$\frac{2}{6} \qquad \frac{3}{5} \qquad \frac{6}{9} \qquad \frac{5}{11} \qquad \frac{7}{12}$$

2. Match each fraction in Column A with its *simplest form* in Column B.

Column A	Column B
$\frac{36}{54}$	$\frac{16}{27}$
$\frac{16}{27}$	$\frac{3}{4}$
$\frac{48}{64}$	$\frac{2}{3}$

● Vocabulary Builder

rational expression (noun) RASH **un ul ek** SPRESH **un**

Definition: A **rational expression** is the quotient of two polynomials.

Main Idea: Just as fractions can be simplified (reduced to simplest form), multiplied, and divided, **rational expressions** may also be simplified, multiplied, and divided.

Examples: $\dfrac{x}{x + 5}$ $\qquad \dfrac{x^2 - 4}{x^2 + 4x + 4}$ $\qquad \dfrac{-3x^4y^3z^2}{9x^6yz}$

● Use Your Vocabulary

Is each expression a *rational expression*? Circle *Yes* or *No*. Explain your reasoning.

3. $\dfrac{\sqrt{6x - 8}}{3x - 4}$

Yes / No

4. $\dfrac{4x}{x^2 - 5}$

Yes / No

5. $\dfrac{3x^{-2}}{x + 4}$

Yes / No

Problem 1 Simplifying a Rational Expression

Got It? What is the rational expression $\frac{24x^3y^2}{-6x^2y^3}$ in simplest form? State any restrictions on the variables.

6. Complete the reasoning model below.

Think	Write
First I find the greatest common factor so I can factor it out of the numerator and denominator.	$\dfrac{24x^3y^2}{-6x^2y^3} = \dfrac{6x^2y^2 \cdot \boxed{}}{6x^2y^2 \cdot \boxed{}}$
Then I divide out the common factor and simplify.	$= \dfrac{\cancel{6x^2y^2} \cdot \boxed{}}{\cancel{6x^2y^2} \cdot \boxed{}}$ $= \dfrac{\boxed{}}{\boxed{}}$
The denominator of the original fraction cannot be equal to 0.	So $x \neq \boxed{}$ and $y \neq \boxed{}$.

Got It? What is the rational expression $\frac{x^2 + 2x - 8}{x^2 - 5x + 6}$ in simplest form? State any restrictions on the variables.

7. Complete the steps to simplify the rational expressions.

$\dfrac{x^2 + 2x - 8}{x^2 - 5x + 6} = \dfrac{\left(\boxed{}\right) \cdot (x - 2)}{\left(\boxed{}\right) \cdot (x - 2)}$ Factor the numerator and the denominator.

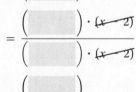

$= \dfrac{\left(\boxed{}\right) \cdot \cancel{(x - 2)}}{\left(\boxed{}\right) \cdot \cancel{(x - 2)}}$ Divide out the common factor.

$= \dfrac{\left(\boxed{}\right)}{\left(\boxed{}\right)}$ Simplify.

8. The denominator of the original expression cannot equal 0. Complete the steps to find any restrictions on x.

$\boxed{} - 5x + \boxed{} \neq 0$

$(x - 2) \cdot \boxed{} \neq 0$

$x - 2 \neq \boxed{}$ and $\boxed{} \neq \boxed{}$

$x \neq \boxed{}$ and $x \neq \boxed{}$

Lesson 8-4

Got It? What is the rational expression $\frac{12 - 4x}{x^2 - 9}$ in simplest form? State any restrictions on the variables.

9. Is the expression $4(3 - x)$ equivalent to $-4(x - 3)$? Explain.

_____

_____

10. Now simplify $\frac{12 - 4x}{x^2 - 9}$. State any restrictions on the variable.

Problem 2 Multiplying Rational Expressions

Got It? What is the product $\frac{2x - 8}{x^2 - 16} \cdot \frac{x^2 + 5x + 4}{x^2 + 8x + 16}$ in simplest form? State any restrictions on the variable.

11. The product is found below. Write a justification for each step.

$$\frac{2x - 8}{x^2 - 16} \cdot \frac{x^2 + 5x + 4}{x^2 + 8x + 16} = \frac{2(x - 4)}{(x - 4)(x + 4)} \cdot \frac{(x + 4)(x + 1)}{(x + 4)(x + 4)}$$

_____

$$= \frac{2\cancel{(x - 4)}}{\cancel{(x - 4)}(x + 4)} \cdot \frac{\cancel{(x + 4)}(x + 1)}{\cancel{(x + 4)}(x + 4)}$$

_____

$$= \frac{2(x + 1)}{(x + 4)(x + 4)}$$

_____

$$= \frac{2(x + 1)}{(x + 4)^2}, x \neq -4 \text{ or } 4$$

_____

Problem 3 Dividing Rational Expressions

Got It? What is the quotient $\frac{x^2 + 5x + 4}{x^2 + x - 12} \div \frac{x^2 - 1}{2x^2 - 6x}$ in simplest form? State any restrictions on the variable.

12. What is the rule for dividing by a fraction?

_____

_____

13. Find the quotient $\dfrac{x^2 + 5x + 4}{x^2 + x - 12} \div \dfrac{x^2 - 1}{2x^2 - 6x}$. State any restrictions on the variable.

Lesson Check • Do you UNDERSTAND?

Reasoning The width of the rectangle at the right is $\dfrac{a + 10}{3a + 24}$. Write an expression for the length of the rectangle.

$\boxed{\dfrac{2a + 20}{3a + 15} \quad w}$

ℓ

14. Circle the equation below that you can use to find the length of a rectangle.

$$\ell = A - w \qquad \ell = \dfrac{w}{A} \qquad \ell = Aw \qquad \ell = \dfrac{A}{w}$$

15. Write and simplify the expression for the length of the rectangle.

16. The length and width must both be greater than 0. Therefore, a must be restricted so that $a < -10$ or $\boxed{a > -8 \,/\, a > -5 \,/\, a < 5}$.

Math Success

Check off the vocabulary words that you understand.

☐ rational expression ☐ simplest form

Rate how well you can *simplify, multiply, and divide rational expressions.*

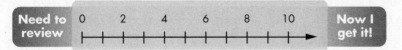

Vocabulary

● **Review**

Write the *least common multiple* of each pair of numbers.

1. 4 and 5

2. 6 and 12

3. 9 and 15

Write the *least common multiple* of each pair of expressions.

4. $2x$ and $7x$

5. $(x + 2)$ and $(x + 3)$

6. $8(x + 5)$ and $12(x + 5)^2$

7. What is the difference between the greatest common factor and *least common multiple* of two or more factors?

_____

_____

_____

● **Vocabulary Builder**

complex (adjective) KAHM **pleks**

Math Usage: A **complex** fraction is a rational expression that has at least one fraction in its numerator or denominator or both.

Examples:  $\dfrac{\frac{1}{3}}{7}, \dfrac{8}{\frac{x}{4}}, \dfrac{\frac{2x}{3} - \frac{1}{5}}{\frac{x+2}{5} + \frac{3x}{4}}$

● **Use Your Vocabulary**

Write T for *true* or F for *false*.

8. The fraction $\dfrac{\frac{1}{3}}{\frac{2}{5}}$ is a complex fraction.

9. The fraction $\dfrac{a + b}{3a - 1}$ is a complex fraction.

Problem 2 Adding Rational Expressions

Got It? What is the sum $\dfrac{x+1}{x-1} + \dfrac{-2}{x^2-x}$ in simplest form? State any restrictions on the variable.

10. Factor the denominators.

$$\frac{x+1}{x-1} + \frac{-2}{x^2-x} = \frac{x+1}{\boxed{}} + \frac{-2}{\boxed{} \cdot \left(\boxed{}\right)}$$

11. Circle the least common denominator (LCD).

x	$x-1$	$x(x-1)$	$x(x-1)^2$

12. Use the justifications at the right to complete each step to add the expressions.

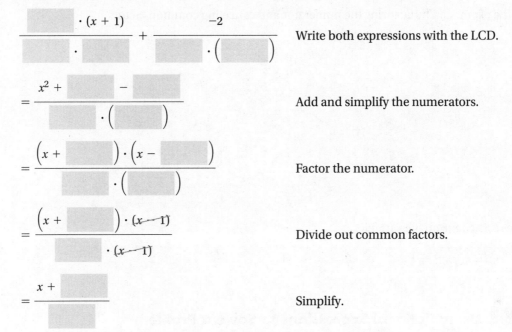

$$\frac{\boxed{} \cdot (x+1)}{\boxed{} \cdot \boxed{}} + \frac{-2}{\boxed{} \cdot \left(\boxed{}\right)}$$ Write both expressions with the LCD.

$$= \frac{x^2 + \boxed{} - \boxed{}}{\boxed{} \cdot \left(\boxed{}\right)}$$ Add and simplify the numerators.

$$= \frac{\left(x + \boxed{}\right) \cdot \left(x - \boxed{}\right)}{\boxed{} \cdot \left(\boxed{}\right)}$$ Factor the numerator.

$$= \frac{\left(x + \boxed{}\right) \cdot (x-1)}{\boxed{} \cdot (x-1)}$$ Divide out common factors.

$$= \frac{x + \boxed{}}{\boxed{}}$$ Simplify.

13. Use the factored denominators you wrote in Exercise 10 to determine any restrictions on the variable.

$$x \neq \boxed{} \text{ and } x \neq \boxed{}$$

Problem 3 Subtracting Rational Expressions

Got It? What is the difference $\dfrac{x+3}{x-2} - \dfrac{6x-7}{x^2-3x+2}$ in simplest form? State any restrictions on the variable.

14. Circle the first step in finding the sum or difference of two rational expressions.

Subtract the numerators.   Factor the denominators.   Rewrite both expressions with the LCD.

Lesson 8-5

15. Find the difference $\dfrac{x + 3}{x - 2} - \dfrac{6x - 7}{x^2 - 3x + 2}$.

16. Simplify the expression by factoring the numerator and canceling common factors.

17. Circle the restrictions on the variable.

$$-2 \qquad -1 \qquad 0 \qquad 1 \qquad \frac{7}{6} \qquad 2$$

✓ **Problem 5** **Using Rational Expressions to Solve a Problem**

Got It? A woman drives an SUV that gets 10 mi/gal (mpg). Her husband drives a hybrid that gets 60 mpg. Every week, they travel the same number of miles. They want to improve their combined mpg. They have three options on how they can improve it. Which of the three options will give the best combined mpg?

Option 1 They can tune the SUV to increase its mileage and keep the hybrid as it is. This gives a combined 18.6 mpg.

Option 2 They can buy a new hybrid that gets 80 mpg and keep the SUV as it is. This gives a combined 17.8 mpg.

Option 3 They can buy a new hybrid that will get double the mileage of the present hybrid and keep the SUV as it is.

18. You can find the combined mpg by using the rational expression

$$\dfrac{\text{SUV miles} + \underline{\hspace{3cm}}}{\text{SUV gallons} + \underline{\hspace{3cm}}}.$$

19. Let $x =$ the number of miles driven each week. The complex fraction is simplified below. Write a justification for each step.

$$\frac{x + x}{\frac{x}{10} + \frac{x}{120}}$$

$$= \frac{2x}{\frac{12x}{120} + \frac{x}{120}}$$

$$= \frac{2x}{\frac{13x}{120}}$$

$$= 2x \cdot \frac{120}{13x}$$

$$= \frac{240}{13}$$

20. The combined gas mileage for Option 3 is about ⬚ mpg.

21. Of the three options, the husband and wife should choose Option ⬚ because it will give the best combined gas mileage.

Lesson Check • Do you UNDERSTAND?

Error Analysis Describe and correct the error made in simplifying the complex fraction.

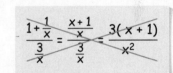

$$\frac{1 + \frac{1}{x}}{\frac{3}{x}} = \frac{\frac{x+1}{x}}{\frac{3}{x}} = \frac{3(x+1)}{x^2}$$

22. Did the student add correctly in the numerator?   Yes / No

23. What error did the student make in simplifying the complex fraction?

24. Now simplify the complex fraction correctly.

Math Success

Check off the vocabulary words that you understand.

☐ complex fraction   ☐ least common denominator (LCD)

Rate how well you can *add and subtract rational expressions.*

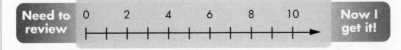

Need to review   0   2   4   6   8   10   Now I get it!

Lesson 8-5

8-6 Solving Rational Equations

Vocabulary

● Review

1. Circle the phrase that best describes a *rational expression*.

| an expression that contains a variable | an expression that is a quotient of two polynomials | an expression that is a difference of two polynomials |

2. Circle the *rational expressions* below.

$$\frac{2}{5} \qquad \frac{\sqrt{x}+3}{\sqrt{x}-2} \qquad \frac{x^{-3}+x-1}{x^{-1}+4} \qquad \frac{x^2+5x-2}{x+8} \qquad \frac{x+3}{x^2-9}$$

● Vocabulary Builder

extraneous (adjective) **ek STRAY nee us**

Definition: Something is **extraneous** if it does not belong to the matter under consideration or is not pertinent to the situation.

Math Usage: An **extraneous** solution is a solution to a simplified (or derived) form of the equation that does not satisfy the original equation.

● Use Your Vocabulary

3. A possible *extraneous* solution may be any value that makes a numerator / denominator in the original equation equal to 0.

4. Draw a line from each rational equation in Column A to a possible value of an *extraneous* solution to that equation in Column B.

Column A	Column B
$\dfrac{3}{x-2} = 4$	0
$\dfrac{1}{2x} + \dfrac{x-2}{2x-6} = 8$	$\dfrac{2}{5}$
$\dfrac{2x+5}{5x-2} = -1$	3
$\dfrac{5}{3+x} + \dfrac{5}{3-x} = 10$	2

Problem 1 Solving a Rational Equation

Got It? What are the solutions of the rational equation $\frac{x-1}{x+2} = \frac{x^2+2x-3}{x+2}$?

5. Use a computer algebra system to solve.

Step 1 Add Calculator page in a new document.

Step 2 Choose Menu, Algebra, Solve.

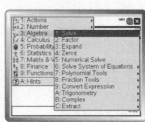

Step 3 Enter the equation, followed by a comma and x. Then press enter.

$x = \boxed{}$

6. Check for extraneous solutions. Substitute the value of x into the original equation.

$$\frac{\boxed{} - 1}{\boxed{} + 2} \stackrel{?}{=} \frac{\boxed{}^2 + 2 \cdot \boxed{} - 3}{\boxed{} + 2}$$

$$\frac{\boxed{}}{\boxed{}} = \frac{\boxed{}}{\boxed{}}$$

7. Is this value of x an extraneous solution? yes no

8. The solution is $x = \boxed{}$.

Problem 2 Using Rational Equations

Got It? You ride your bike to the store, 4 mi away, to pick up things for dinner. When there is no wind, you ride at 10 mi/h. Today your trip to the store and back took 1 hour. What was the speed of the wind today?

9. Circle what the variable x represents in this problem.

| speed of the wind | amount of time to get to the store | speed at which you ride your bike |

10. Complete the table to organize the information from the problem.

Trip	Rate	Distance
To the Store	$10 + x$	4
Back Home		

Lesson 8-6

11. Circle the equation that correctly relates rate, distance, and time.

$$t = \frac{d}{r} \qquad\qquad t = rd \qquad\qquad t = \frac{r}{d}$$

12. Use the relationship to complete the expressions for time in the table.

Trip	Rate	Time	Distance
To the Store	$10 + x$	$\dfrac{4}{10 + \boxed{}}$	4
Back Home	$\boxed{}$	$\dfrac{\boxed{}}{\boxed{} - \boxed{}}$	$\boxed{}$

13. The total time for the trip to the store and back was $\boxed{}$.

14. Complete. Use $+$ or $-$ and $=$.

$$\frac{4}{10 + x} \;\boxed{}\; \frac{4}{10 - x} \;\boxed{}\; 1$$

15. Circle the LCD for this equation.

$$10 \qquad 10 + x \qquad 10 - x \qquad (10 + x)(10 - x)$$

16. Now solve the equation.

 17. The speed of the wind was about $\boxed{}$ mph.

Problem 3 Using a Graphing Calculator to Solve a Rational Equation

Got It? What are the solutions of the rational equation $\frac{x + 2}{1 - 2x} = 5$? Use a graphing calculator to solve.

18. Describe the procedure for using a graphing calculator to solve a rational equation.

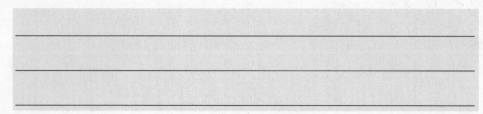

19. The graphing calculator screen shows the intersection of $y = 5$ and $y = \frac{x + 2}{1 - 2x}$. Check the solution in the original equation. Round the solution to the nearest hundredth.

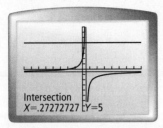

Intersection
X=.27272727 Y=5

 Lesson Check • **Do you UNDERSTAND?**

Error Analysis Describe and correct the error made in solving the equation.

20. Circle the type of error the student made.

added the fractions incorrectly	solved the proportion incorrectly	the solution obtained is extraneous

21. Solve the equation correctly.

$$\frac{5}{x} + \frac{9}{7} = \frac{28}{x}$$

$$\frac{14}{x + 7} = \frac{28}{x}$$

$$14x = 28(x + 7)$$

$$14x = 28x + 196$$

$$-196 = 14x$$

$$-14 = x$$

Math Success

Check off the vocabulary words that you understand.

☐ rational equation   ☐ extraneous

Rate how well you can *solve rational equations*.

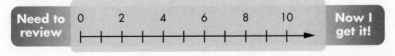

Need to review   0   2   4   6   8   10   Now I get it!

Lesson 8-6

 Vocabulary

● **Review**

Write the next *term* for each number or letter pattern.

1. $\frac{1}{2}, \frac{1}{4}, \frac{1}{8},$ ▢

2. $Y, W, U, S,$ ▢

3. $5, 15, 25,$ ▢

● **Vocabulary Builder**

sequence (noun) SEE **kwuns**

Definition: A **sequence** is an ordered arrangement.

Math Usage: A **sequence** is an ordered list of numbers. Each number is a *term* of the sequence.

What It Means: A **sequence** is a set of numbers that follow a certain pattern, or *rule*.

Example: 0, 10, 20, 30, 40, 50, 60, 70, . . . is a **sequence**. Each number is found by adding 10 to the previous number.

sequence

$$6, 10, 14, 18, 22, \ldots$$
$$\uparrow \quad \uparrow \quad \uparrow \quad \uparrow \quad \uparrow$$
$$a_1, \ a_2, \ a_3, \ a_4, \ a_5, \ \ldots$$

● **Use Your Vocabulary**

Draw a line from each *sequence* in Column A to its pattern or rule in Column B.

Column A	Column B
4. 100, 85, 70, 55, 40, . . .	even numbers
5. a, b, c, d, e, f, g, h, i, . . .	odd numbers
6. 1, 3, 5, 7, 9, 11, 13, . . .	subtract 15
7. 2, 4, 6, 8, 10, 12, 14, . . .	alphabetical order

An **explicit formula** describes the *n*th term of a sequence using the number *n*.

 Problem 1 Generating a Sequence Using an Explicit Formula

Got It? A sequence has an explicit formula $a_n = 12n + 3$. What is term a_{12} in the sequence?

8. Complete the reasoning model below.

Think	Write
I write the formula.	
Next, I substitute ▢ for *n*.	$a_{12} = 12 \cdot \boxed{} + 3$
I simplify.	$a_{12} = \boxed{}$

A **recursive definition** for a sequence contains two parts: (1) an initial condition, which is the value of the first term; and (2) a recursive formula, which relates each term to the next term.

Problem 2 Writing a Recursive Definition for a Sequence

Got It? What is a recursive definition for the sequence? (*Hint:* Look for simple addition or multiplication patterns to relate consecutive terms.)

1, 2, 6, 24, 120, 720, . . .

9. To check for an addition pattern, subtract consecutive terms. Complete each equation.

$a_2 - a_1 = \boxed{} - 1 = \boxed{}$

$a_3 - a_2 = \boxed{} - 2 = \boxed{}$

$a_4 - a_3 = 24 - \boxed{} = \boxed{}$

$a_5 - a_4 = 120 - \boxed{} = \boxed{}$

$a_6 - a_5 = 720 - \boxed{} = \boxed{}$

10. To check for a multiplication pattern, divide consecutive terms. Complete each equation.

$a_2 \div a_1 = \boxed{} \div 1 = \boxed{}$

$a_3 \div a_2 = \boxed{} \div 2 = \boxed{}$

$a_4 \div a_3 = 24 \div \boxed{} = \boxed{}$

$a_5 \div a_4 = 120 \div \boxed{} = \boxed{}$

$a_6 \div a_5 = 720 \div \boxed{} = \boxed{}$

11. Underline the correct number and word to complete the sentence.

Exercise 9 / 10 shows a simple addition / multiplication pattern.

12. Circle the operation you can use to write the recursive formula.

addition	multiplication

Lesson 9-1

13. Write the recursive definition for the sequence.

State the initial condition: $a_1 = $ ▢

Write the recursive formula using the operation you circled in Exercise 12: $a_n = $ ▢

 Problem 3 Writing an Explicit Formula for a Sequence

Got It? What is an explicit formula for the sequence 0, 3, 8, 15, 24, . . . ? What is the 20th term?

14. Find what happens from one term to the next. Complete each equation.

$a_2 = $ ▢ $= 1 \cdot $ ▢

$a_3 = 8 = 2 \cdot $ ▢

$a_4 = 15 = $ ▢ $\cdot 5$

$a_5 = 24 = $ ▢ $\cdot 6$

15. Cross out the statement that is NOT correct.

The nth term is the product of one less than n and one more than n.	The nth term is the product of n and one less than n.

16. Complete the explicit formula.

$a_n = \left(n - \boxed{} \right)\left(\boxed{} \right)$

17. Use the formula from Exercise 16 to find the 20th term.

 Problem 4 Using Formulas to Find Terms of a Sequence

Got It? Finance Pierre began the year with an unpaid balance of $300 on his credit card. Because he had not read the credit card agreement, he did not realize that the company charged 1.8% interest each month on his unpaid balance in addition to a $29 penalty in any month he might fail to make a minimum payment. Pierre ignored his credit card bill for many months. After how many months will the balance reach $1,000?

18. Step 1 Write the recursive definition.

Initial condition: $a_0 = $ ▢ (Use a_0 so that a_1 represents the balance after 1 month.)

Recursive formula: $a_n = 1.018 \cdot a_{n-1} + $ ▢ for $n \geq 1$

19. Step 2 Use a calculator.

| In the **MODE** menu, change the digit display from **FLOAT** to 2. | Enter 300 in the home screen. | Enter the recursive formula **1.018ANS + 29.** | Press **ENTER** for the balance after each month. |

Explain how to find the number of months it will take to reach $1000.

_____

_____

20. It will take [   ] months for Pierre's balance to reach $1000.

Lesson Check • Do you UNDERSTAND?

Error Analysis A student writes that $a_n = 3n + 1$ is an explicit formula for the sequence 1, 4, 7, 10, . . . Explain the student's error and write a correct explicit formula for the sequence.

21. Write the first four terms of the explicit formula $a_n = 3n + 1$.

[   ] , [   ] , [   ] , [   ]

22. Explain the student's error.

_____

_____

23. Find and write a correct explicit formula for the sequence.

Math Success

Check off the vocabulary words that you understand.

☐ sequence   ☐ term   ☐ explicit formula   ☐ recursive formula

Rate how well you can *write recursive definitions and explicit formulas.*

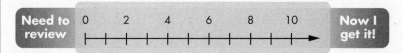

Need to review   0   2   4   6   8   10   Now I get it!

Lesson 9-1

Arithmetic Sequences

Vocabulary

● Review

1. Cross out the expressions that do NOT show a *difference*.

25 + 6	18 − 3	7 · 8	60 ÷ 12

Find each difference.

2. $27 - 10 =$

3. $100 - 40 =$

4. $15y - 7y =$

5. $110g - 27g =$

● Vocabulary Builder

arithmetic mean   (noun)   **ar ith** MET **ik meen**

Related Words: average (noun), mean (noun)

Definition: The **arithmetic mean** of a set of values is the value obtained by calculating the sum of the set and dividing that sum by the number of values in the set.

Example: The **arithmetic mean** of 8, 4, and 12 is $\frac{8 + 4 + 12}{3}$, or 8. The **arithmetic mean**, or average, of two numbers x and y is $\frac{x + y}{2}$.

● Use Your Vocabulary

Write T for *true* or F for *false*.

6. The *arithmetic mean* of 3 and 5 is 4.

7. The *arithmetic mean* of 12, 24, 36, and 48 is 24.

8. The *arithmetic mean* of 3, 5, 7, and 9 is 6.

9. To find the *arithmetic mean* of 10, 15, 20, 25, and 30, divide the sum by   .

Find each quotient.

10. $\frac{6 + 9 + 6}{3} =$

11. $\frac{5 + 7}{2} =$

12. $\frac{2.3 + 2.5}{2} =$

13. $\frac{9 + 7 + 8 + 8}{4} =$

An **arithmetic sequence** is a sequence in which the difference between consecutive terms is constant. This difference is the **common difference**.

Key Concept Arithmetic Sequence

An **arithmetic sequence** with starting value a and common difference d is a sequence of the form

$$a, a + d, a + 2d, a + 3d, \ldots.$$

A *Recursive Definition* for this sequence has two parts.

$a_1 = a$ initial condition

$a_{n+1} = a_n + d$, for $n \geq 1$ recursive formula

An *Explicit Definition* for this sequence is a single formula.

$a_n = a + (n - 1)d$, for $n \geq 1$

14. If $a = 2$ and $d = 4$, use the expression $a, a + d, a + 2d, a + 3d$ to write the first four terms of a sequence.

first term: $a =$ ▢

second term: $a + d = 2 + 4 =$ ▢

third term: $2 + 2d = 2 + 2(4) =$ ▢

fourth term: $a + 3d = 2 + 3(4) =$ ▢

15. The first four terms of the sequence are ▢ , ▢ , ▢ , ▢ .

Problem 1 Identifying Arithmetic Sequences

Got It? Is the sequence 2, 4, 8, 16, . . . an arithmetic sequence?

16. Find each difference.

$4 - 2 =$ ▢ $8 - 4 =$ ▢ $16 - 8 =$ ▢

17. Underline the correct word(s) to complete each sentence.

In an arithmetic sequence, the difference between consecutive

terms is / is not the same.

In the sequence 2, 4, 8, 16, . . . , the difference is / is not the same.

The sequence 2, 4, 8, 16, . . . is / is not an arithmetic sequence.

Problem 2 Analyzing Arithmetic Sequences

Got It? What is the 46th term of the arithmetic sequence that begins 3, 5, 7, . . . ?

18. Circle the value of the first term a and underline the common difference d.

| 2 | 3 | 5 | 7 | 12 |

Lesson 9-2

19. Use the justifications below to complete the steps.

$$a_n = a + (n - 1)d \qquad \text{Use the explicit formula.}$$

$$a_{46} = \boxed{} + (46 - 1) \cdot \boxed{} \qquad \text{Substitute.}$$

$$= \boxed{} \qquad \text{Simplify.}$$

20. The 46th term is $\boxed{}$.

 Problem 3 Using the Arithmetic Mean

Got It? The 9th and 11th terms of an arithmetic sequence are 132 and 98. What is the 10th term?

21. Use the information from the problem to complete the diagram.

arithmetic mean of
$\boxed{}$ and $\boxed{}$

term number ... 9 10 11 ...

term ... $\boxed{}$ x $\boxed{}$ ...

arithmetic mean of
$\boxed{}$ and $\boxed{}$

22. Calculate the arithmetic mean.

$$x = \frac{\boxed{} + \boxed{}}{2} = \frac{\boxed{}}{2} = \boxed{}$$

23. The 10th term of the sequence is $\boxed{}$.

Got It? **Reasoning** If you know the 5th and 6th terms of an arithmetic sequence, how can you find the 7th term using the arithmetic mean?

24. Underline the correct numbers to complete the sentence.

The 5th / 6th / 7th term of an arithmetic sequence is the arithmetic mean of the

5th / 6th / 7th and the 5th / 6th / 7th terms.

25. Circle the equation you can use to find the 7th term of the sequence if you know the 5th and 6th terms.

$$\frac{\text{5th term} + \text{6th term}}{2} = \text{7th term} \qquad \frac{\text{5th term} + \text{7th term}}{2} = \text{6th term} \qquad \frac{\text{6th term} + \text{7th term}}{2} = \text{5th term}$$

 Problem 4 Using an Explicit Formula for an Arithmetic Sequence

Got It? The numbers of seats in the first 16 rows in a curved section of an arena form an arithmetic sequence. If there are 20 seats in Row 1 and 23 seats in Row 2, how many seats are in Row 16?

26. When finding a common difference, you add / subtract consecutive terms.

27. Use 20 and 23 to find the common difference. $d = 23 - 20 = \boxed{}$

28. Use the information in the problem to complete the formula.

$$a_n = a + (n - 1)d$$

$$a_{16} = \boxed{} + \left(\boxed{} - 1 \right) \cdot \boxed{}$$

29. Simplify.

$$a_{16} = \boxed{} + \boxed{} \cdot \boxed{}$$

$$a_{16} = \boxed{}$$

30. There are $\boxed{}$ seats in Row 16.

Lesson Check • Do you know HOW?

Find the tenth term of the arithmetic sequence 2, 8, 14, 20, . . .

31. Find the common difference.

32. Write a formula for the sequence.

33. Use the formula to find the tenth term of the sequence.

Find the missing term of the arithmetic sequence . . . 25, ■, 53, . . .

34. Find the arithmetic mean.

35. The missing term of the arithmetic sequence is $\boxed{}$.

Math Success

Check off the vocabulary words that you understand.

☐ arithmetic sequence ☐ common difference ☐ arithmetic mean

Rate how well you can *define, identify, and apply arithmetic sequences.*

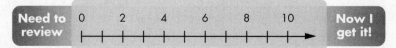

Lesson 9-2

9-3   Geometric Sequences

Vocabulary

● Review

1. Cross out the *ratio* that is NOT equal to the others.

| 8:2 | $\frac{2}{1}$ | 2 to 4 | 4 to 2 |

● Vocabulary Builder

geometric mean   (noun)   jee uh MEH trik meen

Definition: The **geometric mean** of two positive numbers x and y is $\sqrt{xy}$.

Example: The **geometric mean** of 36 and 9 is $\sqrt{36 \cdot 9} = 18$.

Math Usage: In the geometric sequence 4, 8, ▦, 32, . . . , the geometric mean is one possible value that will complete the sequence.

● Use Your Vocabulary

Circle the expression that shows how to determine the *geometric mean* of each pair of numbers.

2. 9 and 16

| $9 + 16$ | $16 - 9$ | $\sqrt{9 \cdot 16}$ | $\sqrt{9 + 16}$ |

3. 25 and 4

| $25 - 4$ | $25 + 4$ | $\sqrt{25 - 4}$ | $\sqrt{25 \cdot 4}$ |

Find the *geometric mean* of each pair of numbers.

4. 100 and 49

$$\sqrt{100 \cdot \boxed{}} = \sqrt{100} \cdot \sqrt{\boxed{}} = 10 \cdot \boxed{} = \boxed{}$$

5. 72 and 8

$$\sqrt{\boxed{} \cdot \boxed{}} = \sqrt{\boxed{}} \cdot \sqrt{\boxed{}} = \sqrt{\boxed{}} = \boxed{}$$

Key Concept   Geometric Sequence

A **geometric sequence** with a starting value a and a **common ratio** r is a sequence of the form $a, ar, ar^2, ar^3, \ldots$

A *Recursive Definition* for the sequence has two parts: 1) initial condition: $a_1 = a$; and 2) recursive formula: $a_{n+1} = a_n \cdot r$. An *Explicit Definition* for this sequence is a single formula: $a_n = a \cdot r^{n-1}$.

Problem 1   Identifying Geometric Sequences

Got It? Is the sequence 2, 4, 8, 16, . . . geometric? If it is, what are a_1 and r?

6. Circle the first step you would take to find the common ratio.

| Find the ratio between the first and third terms. | Find the ratio between consecutive terms. |

7. Circle the common ratio.

| $\frac{1}{2}$ | 2 | 4 | There is no common ratio. |

8. Write **T** for *true* or **F** for *false*.

_____ The sequence is a geometric sequence.

9. The value of a_1 is ____ . The value of r is ____ .

Problem 2   Analyzing Geometric Sequences

Got It? What is the 2nd term of the geometric sequence 3, ■, 12, . . . ?

10. Underline the correct number or word to complete each sentence.

The first term a_1 is 3 / 12 .

The number 12 is the 3rd / 4th term of the sequence.

11. Use the justifications at the right to find the common ratio r.

$a_n = $ ⬚   Write the general form of the explicit formula.

$a_3 = $ ⬚   Substitute ⬚ for a_1 and ⬚ for n.

⬚ $= 3r^2$ Substitute ⬚ for a_3.

⬚ $= r^2$ Divide.

⬚ $= r$ Take the square root of each side.

12. To find the second term, begin with $a_1 = $ ⬚ and multiply by $r = $ ⬚ .

The second term is ⬚ .

Lesson 9-3

Problem 3 Using a Geometric Sequence

Got It? Physics When a ball bounces, the heights of consecutive bounces form a geometric sequence.

The first bounce of the ball is 100 cm high. The common ratio of the sequence is $r = \frac{7}{10}$. To find the height of the 20th bounce, would you use the *recursive* or the *explicit* formula? Explain.

13. Multiple Choice Which equation is the explicit formula for the geometric sequence of the ball bounces?

Ⓐ $a_n = 100 \cdot \left(\frac{7}{10}\right)^n$

Ⓒ $a_n = 100 \cdot \left(\frac{7}{10}\right)^{n-1}$

Ⓑ $a_n = 81 \cdot \left(\frac{7}{10}\right)^n$

Ⓓ $a_n = 81 \cdot \left(\frac{7}{10}\right)^{n-1}$

14. Write a recursive formula for the geometric sequence of the ball bounces.

$a_1 = $ ⬚ $; a_n = $ ⬚

15. Explain whether you would use the *recursive* or the *explicit* formula to find the height of the 20th bounce.

Problem 4 Using the Geometric Mean

Got It? The 9th and 11th terms of a geometric sequence are 45 and 80. What are possible values for the 10th term?

16. You use the geometric mean to find the possible values for the 10th term. Circle the expression that gives the geometric mean of two positive numbers x and y.

$\sqrt{x^2 y}$ $\qquad$ $\sqrt{x + y}$ $\qquad$ $\sqrt{xy}$

17. Find the geometric mean of 45 and 80.

18. The value of the 10th term is either ⬚ or ⬚.

Lesson Check • **Do you know HOW?**

Determine whether the sequence 5, 10, 15, . . . is geometric. If it is, find the common ratio.

19. The ratio between the second term and the first term is ⬜ .

The ratio between the third term and the second term is ⬜ .

20. Underline the correct word(s) to complete the sentence.

Because the ratios between consecutive terms are / are not equal, the sequence

is / is not geometric.

Lesson Check • **Do you UNDERSTAND?**

Error Analysis To find the third term of the geometric sequence 5, ▦, ▦, ▦, 80, your friend says that there are two possible answers—the geometric mean of 5 and 80, and its opposite. Explain your friend's error.

21. Explain how to use the geometric mean to find a missing term in a geometric sequence.

_____

_____

_____

22. Explain your friend's error.

_____

_____

_____

Math Success

Check off the vocabulary words that you understand.

☐ geometric sequence   ☐ common ratio   ☐ geometric mean

Rate how well you can *write the explicit formula of a geometric sequence*.

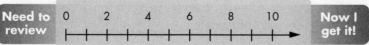

Lesson 9-3

Arithmetic Series

Vocabulary

Review

1. Cross out the expressions that do NOT show a *sum*.

| 42 − 12 | 27 + 6 | 17 · 18 | 160 ÷ 10 |

2. What is the *sum* of 2, 5, 8, 11, and 14?

Vocabulary Builder

series (noun) SEER eez

Definition: A series is a number of objects that happen in order or one after another.

Math Usage: A **series** is the sum of the terms of a sequence. A finite **series** has a first term and a last term. An infinite **series** continues without end.

Related Words: serial (adjective), serialize (verb), serialization (noun)

> Sequence
> 4, 8, 12, 16, 20
>
> Series
> 4 + 8 + 12 + 16 + 20 = 60

Use Your Vocabulary

Write I for an infinite series. Write F for a finite series.

3. 10 + 20 + 30 + 40

4. 3 + 9 + 12 + 15 + 18 + . . .

5. 1 + 6 + 36 + 216 + . . .

Complete each statement with the correct word from the list.

serialization   serialize   serial   series

6. United States one-dollar bills have __?__ numbers.

7. The sum 4 + 16 + 64 is a __?__ .

8. The process of ordering in computer programming is called __?__ .

9. The writer will __?__ her novel by publishing the chapters separately.

Property Sum of a Finite Arithmetic Series

The sum S_n of a finite arithmetic series $a_1 + a_2 + a_3 + \cdots + a_n$ is $S_n = \frac{n}{2}(a_1 + a_n)$, where a_1 is the first term, a_n is the nth term, and n is the number of terms.

Problem 1 Finding the Sum of a Finite Arithmetic Series

Got It? What is the sum of the finite arithmetic series
$4 + 9 + 14 + 19 + 24 + \cdots + 99$?

10. Complete the reasoning model below.

Think	Write
I need to identify the first and last terms and the common difference.	first term (a_1) = ☐ last term (a_n) = ☐ common difference = ☐
I need to determine how many terms there are in the series.	$99 - 4 = 95$ $n = (95 \div \text{common difference}) + 1 = $ ☐
Next, I substitute into the formula and simplify.	$S_n = \frac{n}{2}(a_1 + a_n)$ $S_{20} = \frac{20}{2}\left(\boxed{} + \boxed{}\right)$ $S_{20} = $ ☐

11. The sum of the finite series $4 + 9 + 14 + 19 + 24 + \cdots + 99$ is ☐ .

Problem 2 Using the Sum of a Finite Arithmetic Series

Got It? A company pays a \$5000 bonus if a new salesperson makes 10 sales in the first week and then improves by one sale per week each week thereafter. One salesperson qualified for this bonus with the minimum number of sales. How many sales did the salesperson make in week 50? In all 50 weeks?

12. Circle the first week's sales (a_1) and underline the common difference (d).

1	2	5	8	10

13. Use the justifications at the right to find the sales in Week 50.

$a_n = a_1 + (n - 1)d$ Use the explicit formula.

$a_{50} = \boxed{} + (50 - 1) \cdot \boxed{}$ Substitute.

$= \boxed{}$ Simplify.

Lesson 9-4

14. Complete the steps to find the total sales for all 50 weeks.

$$S_n = \frac{n}{2}(a_1 + a_n)$$

$$S_{50} = \frac{50}{2}\left(\boxed{} + \boxed{}\right)$$

$$S_{50} = 25 \cdot \boxed{}$$

$$S_{50} = \boxed{}$$

15. The total sales for all 50 weeks is $\boxed{}$.

 Problem 3 Writing a Series in Summation Notation

Got It? What is summation notation for the series
$-5 + 2 + 9 + 16 + \cdots + 261 + 268$?

16. The first term is $a_1 = \boxed{}$.

17. The common difference is $d = \boxed{}$.

18. Use the explicit formula for an arithmetic sequence. Substitute and simplify.

19. The explicit formula for the nth term is $a_n = \boxed{}$.

20. Complete the steps to find the value of n for the last term.

$a_n = 7n - 12$		Use the explicit formula from Exercise 19.
$\boxed{} = 7n - 12$		Substitute.
$\boxed{} = 7n$		Add.
$\boxed{} = n$		Simplify.

21. **Multiple Choice** Which is the summation notation for the series
$-5 + 2 + 9 + 16 + \cdots + 261 + 268$?

Ⓐ $\displaystyle\sum_{n=1}^{50} 7n - 12$ Ⓑ $\displaystyle\sum_{n=1}^{40} 7n - 12$ Ⓒ $\displaystyle\sum_{n=-5}^{40} 7n - 12$ Ⓓ $\displaystyle\sum_{n=-5}^{50} 5n - 10$

 Problem 4 Finding the Sum of a Series

Got It? What is the sum of the finite series $\displaystyle\sum_{n=1}^{40}(3n - 8)$?

22. Circle the first step in finding the sum.

Find the first and last terms.	Use the summation formula for a finite arithmetic series.

23. Complete the steps for finding the sum of the series.

$a_1 = 3(1) - 8 = $ ▢ $a_{40} = 3\left(\boxed{}\right) - 8 = $ ▢

Use the formula for a finite arithmetic series.

$$S_n = \frac{n}{2}(a_1 + a_n)$$

$$S_{40} = \frac{40}{2}\left(\boxed{} + \boxed{}\right)$$

$$S_{40} = \boxed{}$$

24. The sum of the series is ▢ .

Lesson Check • Do you UNDERSTAND?

Error Analysis A student writes the arithmetic series 3, 8, 13, . . . , 43 in summation notation as $\sum_{n=3}^{8}(3 + 5n)$. Describe and correct the error.

25. Use the explicit formula for a_n for an arithmetic sequence.

26. Use the last term to find the total number of terms.

27. Write the correct summation notation and explain the student's error.

_____

_____

_____

_____

Math Success

Check off the vocabulary words that you understand.

☐ series   ☐ finite series   ☐ infinite series   ☐ arithmetic series   ☐ limits

Rate how well you can _work with arithmetic series._

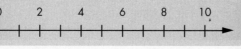

Need to review   0   2   4   6   8   10   Now I get it!

Vocabulary

● **Review**

1. Circle the *infinite* series.

| 3, 9, 27, . . . | 5 + 9 + 13 + 17 + . . . | 4 + 16 + 64 + 256 | 7, 13, 20, 28, . . . |

2. Cross out the sequence that is not an *infinite* sequence.

| 5, 8, 12, 17, . . . | 100, 120, 135, 150 | 7, 13, 20, 28, . . . |

● **Vocabulary Builder**

converge (verb) **con VURJ**

diverge (verb) **dy VURJ**

Related Words: convergent (adjective), convergence (noun), divergent (adjective), divergence (noun)

Definitions: To **converge** means to come or join together. To **diverge** means to draw away or come apart.

Math Usage: An infinite series **converges** when it has a sum and **diverges** otherwise.

● **Use Your Vocabulary**

Write T for *true* or F for *false*.

3. A *divergent* infinite series does not have a sum.

4. If two rivers *converge*, they do not meet.

5. An infinite series that has a sum is *convergent*.

6. When two lines *diverge*, they move away from each other.

7. When two people share the same ideas, they are said to have a *divergence* of minds.

Key Concept   Sum of a Finite Geometric Series

The sum S_n of a finite geometric series $a_1 + a_1r + a_1r^2 + \cdots + a_1r^{n-1}$ is

$$S_n = \frac{a_1(1 - r^n)}{1 - r},$$

where a_1 is the first term, r is the common ratio, and n is the number of terms.

Problem 1   Finding the Sums of Finite Geometric Series

Got It? What is the sum of the finite geometric series?

$$-15 + 30 - 60 + 120 - 240 + 480$$

8. The first term, a_1, is ▭.

9. The common ratio, r, is $\dfrac{}{}$ = ▭.

10. Count the number of terms. The value of n is ▭.

11. Complete the steps to find the sum of the series.

$$S_n = \frac{a_1(1 - r^n)}{1 - r}$$ Use the sum formula.

$$S_6 = \frac{\boxed{}\left(1 - \boxed{}\right)}{1 - \boxed{}}$$ Substitute values for a_1, r, and n.

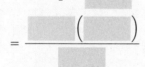

$$= \frac{\boxed{}\left(\boxed{}\right)}{\boxed{}}$$ Simplify.

$$= \boxed{}$$

Problem 2   Using the Geometric Series Formula

Got It? To save money for a vacation, you set aside $100. For each month thereafter, you plan to set aside 10% more than the previous month. How much money will you save in 12 months?

12. The first term of this geometric series is $a_1 =$ ▭.

13. The number of terms is $n =$ ▭.

14. $r = \dfrac{\text{amount of previous month} + 10\%}{\text{amount of previous month}} = \dfrac{110}{\boxed{}} =$ ▭

Lesson 9-5

15. Follow the steps to find the amount you will save in 12 months.

1 Write the sum formula.

$S_n =$

2 Substitute the values into the sum formula.

$S_{12} =$

3 Use a calculator to find the sum.

$S_{12} \approx$

Key Concept Infinite Geometric Series

An infinite geometric series with first term a_1, and common ratio $|r| < 1$ has a finite sum S.

$$S = \frac{a_1}{1 - r}$$

An infinite geometric series with $|r| \geq 1$ does not have a finite sum. An infinite series that has a sum is said to *converge* to that sum. When an infinite series does not converge to a sum, the series *diverges*.

Problem 3 **Analyzing Infinite Geometric Series**

Got It? Does the infinite series $\frac{1}{2} + \frac{3}{4} + \frac{9}{8} + \dots$ *converge* or *diverge*? If it converges, what is the sum?

16. Find the common ratio r.

$r = \dfrac{}{} = \boxed{}$

17. The geometric series converges / diverges because

$|r|$ is equal to / less than / greater than 1.

Lesson Check • **Do you UNDERSTAND?**

Error Analysis A classmate uses the formula for the sum of an infinite geometric series to evaluate $1 + 1.1 + 1.21 + 1.331 + \dots$ and gets -10. What error did your classmate make?

18. Find the common ratio.

Chapter 9

252

19. Underline the correct word or expression to complete each sentence.

Because $|r| < 1 / |r| \geq 1$, the series converges / diverges .

The series has a sum of -10 / no sum .

Lesson Check • Do you UNDERSTAND?

Writing Explain how you can determine whether an infinite geometric series has a sum.

20. Determine $|r|$ for the infinite geometric series $\sum_{n=1}^{\infty} \left(\frac{1}{5}\right)^n$.

21. Does the infinite series $\sum_{n=1}^{\infty} \left(\frac{1}{5}\right)^n$ have a sum? Explain.

_____

_____

22. Explain how you can determine whether an infinite geometric series has a sum.

_____

_____

_____

Math Success

Check off the vocabulary words that you understand.

☐ geometric series   ☐ converge   ☐ diverge

Rate how well you can *find the sum of a geometric series.*

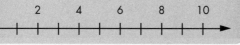

Need to review   0   2   4   6   8   10   Now I get it!

Lesson 9-5

10-1 Exploring Conic Sections

Vocabulary

● Review

1. Multiple Choice Which equation gives the graph of a *parabola*?

Ⓐ $y = 3x + 7$

Ⓒ $y = 3x^3 + 6x^2 - 4x - 1$

Ⓑ $y = -5x^2 + 8$

Ⓓ $y = x^4 - 2x^3 - x^2 - x$

2. Cross out the equations whose graphs are NOT *parabolas*.

$y = -2x + 6$ $y = \frac{3}{4}x^2 + \frac{5}{8}$ $y = 9x^3 + x^2$ $y = 3x^2 - 6x + 9$

● Vocabulary Builder

cone (noun) **kohn**	
conic (noun) **KAHN ik**	

cone   **double cone**

Definition: A **cone** is a three-dimensional shape whose base is a circle and whose sides taper to a point. A *double* **cone** is made up of two cones that meet at their points. A **conic** is the intersection of a plane and a cone.

Examples: A circle is a **conic** because it is the intersection of a horizontal plane and a **double cone**. An ellipse is a **conic** because it is the intersection of a plane and a **double cone** where the plane is neither horizontal nor vertical.

● Use Your Vocabulary

Write T for *true* and F for *false*.

_____ **3.** A *cone* is a three-dimensional shape whose sides taper to a point.

_____ **4.** A *cone* is the intersection of a plane and a conic.

_____ **5.** An ellipse is formed by the intersection of a double *cone* and a plane that is neither horizontal nor vertical.

Key Concept Conic Sections

A **conic section** is a curve you get by intersecting a plane and a double cone. By changing the inclination of the plane, you can get a circle, a parabola, an ellipse, or a hyperbola.

 Problem 1 Graphing a Circle

Got It? What is the graph of $x^2 + y^2 = 9$? What are its lines of symmetry? What are the domain and range?

6. Complete the table of values.

x	−3	−2.4	−1.8	−1.2	0	1.2	1.8	2.4	3
y		±1.8	±	±2.75	±3	±	±2.4	±	

7. Plot the points and connect them with a smooth curve.

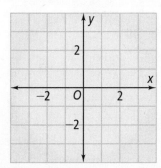

8. The graph is a circle with a radius of ☐.

Every line through the center / x-axis is a line of symmetry.

9. The domain is the set of real numbers x with ☐ ≤ x ≤ 3. The range is the set of real numbers y with ☐ ≤ y ≤ ☐.

 Problem 2 Graphing an Ellipse

Got It? What is the graph of $2x^2 + y^2 = 18$? What are its lines of symmetry? What are the domain and range?

10. Cross out the table of values that does NOT match the graph of the ellipse.

x	−3	−1	0	1	3
y	0	±4	±4.2	±4	0

x	−3	−1	0	1	3
y	0	±3.3	±4	±3.3	0

Lesson 10-1

11. Graph the equation

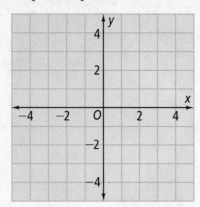

12. The graph is an ellipse. The lines of symmetry are the _____ and the _____.

The domain is

_____ .

The range is

_____ .

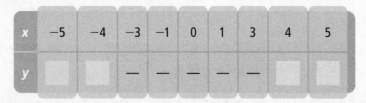

Problem 3 Graphing a Hyperbola

Got It? Graph $x^2 - y^2 = 16$. What are its lines of symmetry? What are the domain and range?

13. Complete the table of values.

x	−5	−4	−3	−1	0	1	3	4	5
y			—	—	—	—	—		

14. Graph the equation.

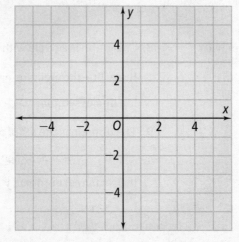

15. The graph is a hyperbola with two branches. Write the lines of symmetry.

_____   _____

16. Write the domain and range of the equation.

Domain: _____

Range: _____

Problem 4 Identifying Graphs of Conic Sections

Got It? What are the center and intercepts of the conic section? What are the domain and range?

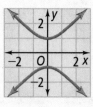

17. Circle the center of the hyperbola. Underline the intercepts.

$(0, -1)$ $(0, 0)$

          $(1, 1)$ $(0, 1)$

18. The domain is the set of _____.

The range is the set of real numbers y with _____ or _____.

Lesson Check • **Do you UNDERSTAND?**

Compare and Contrast How is the domain of an ellipse different from the domain of a hyperbola?

19. Circle the expression that could represent the domain of an ellipse. Underline the expression that could represent the domain of a hyperbola.

set of real numbers x with $x \leq -5$ or $x \geq 5$ set of real numbers x with $-7 \leq x \leq 7$

20. Explain how the domain of an ellipse is different from the domain of a hyperbola.

_____

_____

_____

_____

_____

Math Success

Check off the vocabulary words that you understand.

☐ cone   ☐ conic section   ☐ circle   ☐ ellipse   ☐ hyperbola

Rate how well you can *graph and identify conic sections*.

Need to review   0   2   4   6   8   10   Now I get it!

Lesson 10-1

Parabolas

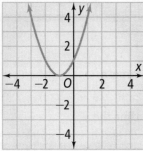

Vocabulary

● Review

Identify the coordinates of the *vertex* of each graph.

1.

2.

● Vocabulary Builder

focus (noun) FOH **kus**

Math Usage: A focus is a fixed point in a plane that, when combined with a fixed line called a **directrix**, identifies a conic section.

Example: For a parabola, a point is a focus if $d_1 \div d_2 = d_3 \div d_4$ for any points on the curve.

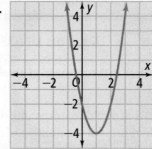

● Use Your Vocabulary

Use the figure at the right for Exercises 3–5.

3. Use a centimeter ruler to measure d_1, d_2, d_3, and d_4 to the nearest millimeter.

d_1 d_2 d_3 d_4

    mm   mm   mm   mm

4. Find each quotient.

$d_1 \div d_2 =$ $d_3 \div d_4 =$

5. Point F is / is not a focus of the parabola.

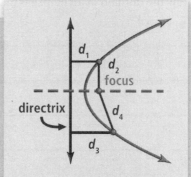

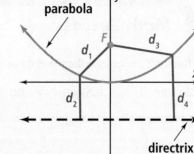

take note

Key Concept Parabola

A parabola is the set of all points in a plane that are the same distance from the **directrix** and the **focus of the parabola.**

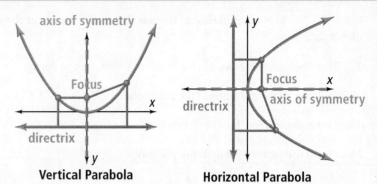

Vertical Parabola   **Horizontal Parabola**

6. The **focus** is a point located on the directrix / axis of symmetry .

A *vertical parabola* with vertex $(0, 0)$ has equation $y = ax^2$. The coefficient $a = \frac{1}{4c}$ determines both the focus $(0, c)$ and the directrix $y = -c$.

A *horizontal parabola* with vertex $(0, 0)$ has equation $x = ay^2$. The coefficient $a = \frac{1}{4c}$ determines both the focus $(c, 0)$ and the directrix $x = -c$.

7. Solve $a = \frac{1}{4c}$ for c.

Use your answer to Exercise 7 to complete Exercises 8 and 9.

8. Parabola $y = 2x^2$ $a = 2$ $c = \boxed{}$ focus $\left(\boxed{}, 0\right)$ directrix $y = -c = -\boxed{}$

9. Parabola $x = -\frac{1}{6}y^2$ $a = \boxed{}$ $c = \boxed{}$ focus $\left(\boxed{}, 0\right)$ directrix $x = -c = \boxed{}$

10. Which exercise describes a horizontal parabola, Exercise 8 or Exercise 9?   Exercise 8 / Exercise 9

✓ **Problem 1** **Parabolas With Equation $y = ax^2$**

Got It? What is an equation of the parabola with vertex $(0, 0)$ and focus $(0, -1.5)$?

11. The focus is above / below / right of / left of the vertex.

12. This is a vertical / horizontal parabola.

13. The focus is $(c, 0) / (0, c)$, so $c = \boxed{}$, and $\frac{1}{4c} = \dfrac{1}{\boxed{}}$.

14. Circle the general form of the parabola.

$$y = \frac{1}{4c}x^2 \qquad\qquad x = \frac{1}{4c}y^2$$

15. Substitute the value of c and simplify.

16. The equation of the parabola is $\boxed{}$.

259

Problem 2 Parabolas With Equation $x = ay^2$

Got It? What is an equation of the parabola with vertex at the origin and directrix $x = -\frac{5}{2}$?

17. The directrix is above / below / left of / right of the vertex.

18. This is a vertical / horizontal parabola.

19. The equation for the directrix is $x = -c$, so $c =$ ⬚ .

20. Circle the general form of the parabola.

$$y = \frac{1}{4c}x^2 \qquad\qquad x = \frac{1}{4c}y^2$$

21. Substitute the value of c and simplify.

22. The equation of the parabola is ⬚ .

 note

Key Concept   Transformations of a Parabola

Parabola	Vertex	Focus	Directrix	Equation
Vertical	(h, k)	$(h, k + c)$	$y = k - c$	$y = \frac{1}{4c}(x - h)^2 + k$
Horizontal	(h, k)	$(h + c, k)$	$x = h - c$	$x = \frac{1}{4c}(y - k)^2 + h$

23. Write the vertex of a vertical parabola whose equation is $y = 3(x - 7)^2 + 5$.

$$\left(\boxed{} , \boxed{} \right)$$

Problem 4 Analyzing a Parabola

Got It? What are the vertex, focus, and directrix of the parabola with equation $y = x^2 + 8x + 18$?

24. Use the justifications at the right to complete the steps below.

$\left(\frac{1}{2} \cdot 8\right)^2 =$ ⬚   Find the value of $\left(\frac{1}{2}b\right)^2$ to complete the square.

$y = \left(x^2 + 8x + \boxed{}\right) + 18 - \boxed{}$ Add the value inside the parentheses and subtract it outside the parentheses.

$= \left(x + \boxed{}\right)\left(x + \boxed{}\right) + 2$ Factor inside the parentheses.

$= \left(x + \boxed{}\right)^2 + \boxed{}$ Write in vertex form.

$h = \boxed{}$ and $k = \boxed{}$ Identify h and k.

25. Use the vertex form of the equation. Circle the value of the coefficient *a*.

−4	1	2	4	8	16	18

26. Use $a = \frac{1}{4c}$ and the value from Exercise 25 to find the value of *c*.

27. Use the values of *h*, *k*, and *c* to identify the vertex, focus and directrix of the parabola.

Vertex: (h, k) is $\left(\underline{\quad\quad} , \underline{\quad\quad} \right)$ **Focus:** $(h, k + c)$ is $\left(\underline{\quad\quad} , \underline{\quad\quad} \right)$

 Directrix: $y = k - c$, so $y = \underline{\quad\quad}$

Lesson Check • Do you know HOW?

Write an equation of a parabola with vertex (3, 2) and focus (4, 2).

28. The focus is above / below / left of / right of the vertex.

29. The parabola is vertical / horizontal .

30. Circle the value of *h*. Underline the value of *k*.

−4	−3	−2	2	3	4

31. The focus is at $(h + c, k)$. Find the value of *c*.

32. Circle the equation of the parabola.

$$x = \tfrac{1}{4}(y - 2)^2 + 3 \qquad x = (y - 2)^2 + 4 \qquad y = \tfrac{1}{4}(x - 2)^2 + 3 \qquad y = (x - 2)^2 + 4$$

Math Success

Check off the vocabulary words that you understand.

☐ parabola ☐ focus ☐ directrix ☐ vertex

Rate how well you can *graph and write equations of parabolas*.

Need to review 0 2 4 6 8 10 Now I get it!

Lesson 10-2

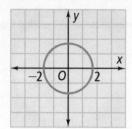

Vocabulary

● **Review**

1. Cross out the graph that is NOT the graph of a *circle*.

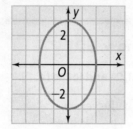 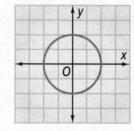

● **Vocabulary Builder**

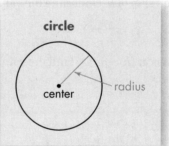

radius (noun) RAY **dee us**

Plural: radii

Definition: A **radius** is a line segment that connects the center of a circle to any point on the circle.

circle

center — radius

● **Use Your Vocabulary**

2. Is line segment *AB* a *radius* of circle *C*? Explain how you know.

_____

_____

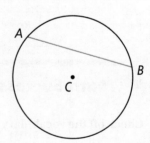

3. Draw a *radius* in circle *P*. Label the radius *r*.

Key Concept Standard Form of an Equation of a Circle

The **standard form of an equation of a circle** with center (h, k) and radius r is
$(x - h)^2 + (y - k)^2 = r^2$.

Problem 1 Writing an Equation of a Circle

Got It? What is an equation of the circle with center $(5, -2)$ and radius 8? Check your answer.

4. Identify the values of h, k, and r.

$$h = \boxed{} \qquad\qquad k = \boxed{} \qquad\qquad r = \boxed{}$$

5. Complete the steps for writing the equation of the circle.

$(x - h)^2 + (y - k)^2 = r^2$	Use the standard form.
$\left(x - \boxed{}\right)^2 + \left(y - \left(\boxed{}\right)\right)^2 = \boxed{}^2$	Substitute for h, k, and r.
$\left(x - \boxed{}\right)^2 + \left(y + \boxed{}\right)^2 = 64$	Simplify.

6. To check your work, first solve the equation for y.

7. Use your graphing calculator to graph the two equations you got for y on the same screen. How does the graph on your screen compare with a circle with a center at $(5, -2)$ and radius 8?

Problem 2 Using Translations to Write an Equation

Got It? What is an equation for the graph of $x^2 + y^2 = 1$ translated 5 units left and 3 units down?

8. Use the information in the problem to identify the values of h, k, and r in the standard form of the equation.

$$(x - h)^2 + (y - k)^2 = r^2, \text{ so } \left(x - \boxed{}\right)^2 + \left(y - \boxed{}\right)^2 = \boxed{}^2$$

Lesson 10-3

9. Simplify the equation.

$$\left(x + \boxed{}\right)^2 + \left(y + \boxed{}\right)^2 = \boxed{}$$

Key Concept   Transforming a Circle

You can use parameter r to stretch or shrink the unit circle $x^2 + y^2 = 1$ to the circle $x^2 + y^2 = r^2$ with radius r.

You can use parameters h and k to translate the circle $x^2 + y^2 = r^2$ with center $(0, 0)$ to the circle $(x - h)^2 + (y - k)^2 = r^2$ with center (h, k).

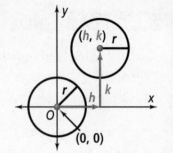

10. The unit circle $x^2 + y^2 = 1$ can be translated / stretched / shrunk to the circle $x^2 + y^2 = 5^2$.

Problem 3   Using a Graph to Write an Equation

Got It? What is the equation of a circle for a circular irrigation field that has radius 12 and has center $(7, -10)$?

11. Cross out the equation that is NOT the standard form of the equation of a circle with center $(7, -10)$ and radius 12.

$$(x - 7)^2 + (y - (-10))^2 = 12^2 \qquad (x - (-7))^2 + (y - 10)^2 = 12^2$$

12. Write the equation for the circle in simplified form.

Problem 5   Graphing a Circle Using Center and Radius

Got It? What is the graph of $(x - 4)^2 + (y + 2)^2 = 49$?

13. Multiple Choice Which equation is the standard form of the equation $(x - 4)^2 + (y + 2)^2 = 49$?

- Ⓐ $(x + 4)^2 + (y - 2)^2 = 49$
- Ⓒ $(x - 4)^2 + (y - (-2))^2 = 49$
- Ⓑ $(x - 4)^2 + (y - 2)^2 = 49$
- Ⓓ $(x - (-4))^2 + (y - (-2))^2 = 49$

14. Identify the values of h, k, and r.

$$h = \boxed{} \qquad k = \boxed{} \qquad r = \boxed{}$$

15. The center of the circle is $\left(\boxed{}\,,\,\boxed{}\right)$ and the radius is $\boxed{}$.

16. Plot the center of the circle on the coordinate grid. Then draw the circle.

Error Analysis A student claims that the circle $(x + 7)^2 + (y - 7)^2 = 8$ is a translation of the circle $x^2 + y^2 = 8$, 7 units right and 7 units down. What is the student's mistake?

17. Circle the standard form of the equation $(x + 7)^2 + (y - 7)^2 = 8$.

$$(x - (-7))^2 + (y - 7)^2 = 8 \qquad (x - 7)^2 + (y - (-7))^2 = 8$$

18. The center of the circle with equation $(x + 7)^2 + (y - 7)^2 = 8$

is   .

19. The center of the circle is translated to the right / left of the origin and up / down from the origin.

20. Explain the student's error.

_____

_____

_____

✓ **Math Success**

Check off the vocabulary words that you understand.

☐ circle   ☐ center of a circle   ☐ radius   ☐ standard form of the equation of a circle

Rate how well you can *write and graph the equation of a circle*.

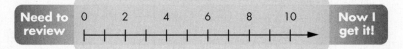

 **10-4** Ellipses

Vocabulary

● **Review**

Identify the *axis of symmetry* in each figure.

1.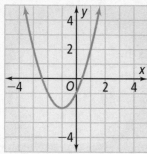

2.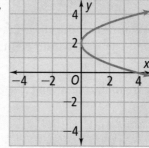

● **Vocabulary Builder**

ellipse (noun) eh LIPS

Related Word: conic section (noun)

Definition: An **ellipse** is a closed, symmetric curve shaped like an oval. The sum of the distances of any point on an ellipse from two fixed points (foci) remains constant no matter where the point is on the curve.

Main Idea: An **ellipse** is formed by intersecting a *cone* with a plane that is neither parallel nor perpendicular to the axis of the cone.

● **Use Your Vocabulary**

3. Circle the graph of an *ellipse*.

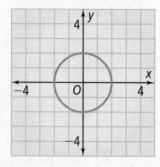 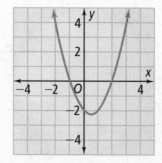 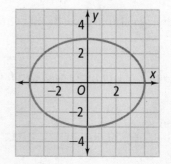

Key Concept Properties of Ellipses with Center (0, 0)

	Horizontal Ellipses	Vertical Ellipses
Standard Equation	$\frac{x^2}{a^2} + \frac{y^2}{b^2} = 1$, $a > b > 0$	$\frac{x^2}{b^2} + \frac{y^2}{a^2} = 1$, $a > b > 0$
Major Axis	horizontal	vertical
Vertices	$(\pm a, 0)$	$(0, \pm a)$
Co-vertices	$(0, \pm b)$	$(\pm b, 0)$
Foci	$(\pm c, 0)$ on x-axis	$(0, \pm c)$ on y-axis

4. Underline the correct word to complete the sentence.

An ellipse with equation $\frac{x^2}{36} + \frac{y^2}{49} = 1$ is a horizontal / vertical ellipse.

Problem 1 Writing an Equation of an Ellipse

Got It? What is the equation in standard form of an ellipse centered at the origin with a vertex at (0, 5) and a co-vertex at (2, 0)?

5. The major axis is horizontal / vertical .

6. The vertex is at (0, 5), so $a = $ ▢ and $a^2 = $ ▢ .

7. The co-vertex is at (2, 0), so $b = $ ▢ and $b^2 = $ ▢ .

8. Use the values for a^2 and b^2 to complete the equation.

$$y = \frac{x^2}{\boxed{}} + \frac{y^2}{\boxed{}} = 1$$

Problem 2 Finding the Foci of an Ellipse

Got It? What are the coordinates of the foci of the ellipse with the equation $36x^2 + 100y^2 = 3600$? Graph the ellipse.

9. Divide both sides of the equation by 36 / 100 / 3600 to write it in standard form.

10. Write the equation $36x^2 + 100y^2 = 3600$ in standard form.

11. Circle the value of a^2 and underline the value of b^2.

10	36	64	100

12. The major axis of the ellipse is horizontal / vertical .

13. Use your values of a and b and the equation $c^2 = a^2 - b^2$ to find the value of c.

14. The foci are located at the point $(\pm c, 0)$. Write the foci as ordered pairs.

[   ] and [   ]

15. Plot the points for the vertices, co-vertices, and foci. Then draw the ellipse.

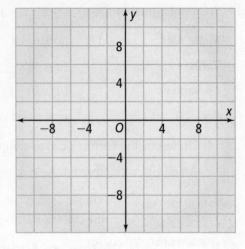

 Problem 3 Using the Foci of an Ellipse

Got It? How far apart are the foci of an ellipse with a major axis of 26 ft and a minor axis of 10 ft?

16. Circle the equation that you can use to solve for the length of the major axis. Underline the equation that you can use to find the length of the minor axis.

$$2a = 26 \qquad 2a = 10 \qquad 2b = 26 \qquad 2b = 10$$

17. Solve for a and b.

18. Multiple Choice Which equation can you use to find the value of c?

Ⓐ $c = \sqrt{13^2 - 5^2}$ Ⓑ $c = \sqrt{13^2 + 5^2}$

Ⓒ $c = \sqrt{26^2 - 10^2}$ Ⓓ $c = \sqrt{26^2 + 10^2}$

19. The foci are $2c =$ [   ] feet apart.

 Problem 4 Using the Foci of an Ellipse

Got It? What is the standard form equation of an ellipse with foci at $(0, \pm\sqrt{17})$ and co-vertices at $(\pm 6, 0)$?

20. The foci are on the x-axis / y-axis , so the ellipse is horizontal / vertical .

21. Write the value of c.

22. Write the value of b.

23. Use your values for c and b and the equation $c^2 = a^2 - b^2$ to find the value of a^2.

24. Write the standard form of the ellipse.

Lesson Check • Do you UNDERSTAND?

Error Analysis A student claims that an equation of the ellipse shown is $\frac{x^2}{41} + \frac{y^2}{29} = 1$. Describe the student's error. What is the correct equation in standard form of the ellipse?

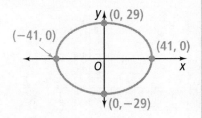

25. Identify the values of a and b in the ellipse shown.

$a =$ _____ and $b =$ _____

26. Use your values for a and b and the general form for the equation of a horizontal ellipse to write the equation of the ellipse shown.

General Form: $\frac{x^2}{a^2} + \frac{y^2}{b^2} = 1$

27. Explain the student's error.

_____

Math Success

Check off the vocabulary words that you understand.

☐ ellipse ☐ focus ☐ center ☐ vertex ☐ co-vertex

☐ major axis ☐ minor axis

Rate how well you can *write and graph equations of an ellipse*.

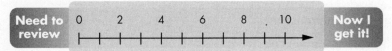

Need to review 0 2 4 6 8 10 Now I get it!

Lesson 10-4

Vocabulary

● Review

Write the equation of the vertical and horizontal *asymptotes* in each graph.

1.

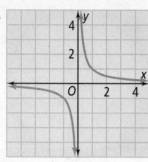

2.

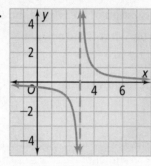

3.

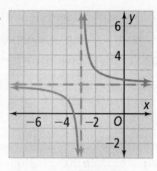

Vertical: ☐

Horizontal: ☐

Vertical: ☐

Horizontal: ☐

Vertical: ☐

Horizontal: ☐

● Vocabulary Builder

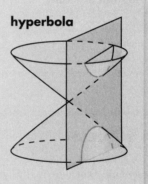

hyperbola

hyperbola (noun) **hy PUR buh luh**

Definition: When a plane, parallel to the axis of a *double cone*, slices the double cone, a *conic section* called a **hyperbola** is formed.

Main Idea: A **hyperbola** has two foci, two vertices, and two curves.

● Use Your Vocabulary

Write T for *true* or F for *false*.

____ **4.** The graph of a hyperbola consists of only one curve.

____ **5.** A hyperbola is *not* a conic section.

____ **6.** A hyperbola has two vertices and two foci.

Key Concept Properties of Hyperbolas with Centers (0, 0)

Horizontal Hyperbola

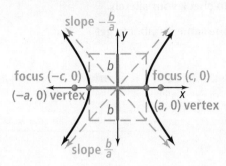

Equation: $\dfrac{x^2}{a^2} - \dfrac{y^2}{b^2} = 1$

Transverse axis: Horizontal

Vertices $(\pm a, 0)$

Foci: $(\pm c, 0)$, where $c^2 = a^2 + b^2$

Asymptotes: $y = \pm \dfrac{b}{a}x$

Vertical Hyperbola

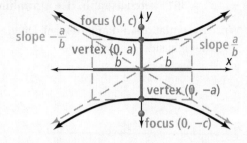

Equation: $\dfrac{y^2}{a^2} - \dfrac{x^2}{b^2} = 1$

Transverse axis: Vertical

Vertices $(0, \pm a)$

Foci: $(0, \pm c)$, where $c^2 = a^2 + b^2$

Asymptotes: $y = \pm \dfrac{a}{b}x$

Problem 1 Writing and Graphing the Equation of a Hyperbola

Got It? What is the standard-form equation of the hyperbola with the vertices $(0, \pm 4)$ and foci $(0, \pm 5)$?

7. The vertices are $(0, \pm 4)$, so $a = \boxed{}$.

8. The foci are $(0, \pm 5)$. Then $c = \boxed{}$.

9. Use the values you found for a and c and $c^2 = a^2 + b^2$ to find b.

10. The vertices and foci are on the x-axis / y-axis .

11. The transverse axis of the hyperbola is horizontal / vertical .

12. Complete the steps to find the standard form of the equation of the hyperbola.

$\dfrac{y^2}{a^2} - \dfrac{x^2}{b^2} = 1$ Write the standard form.

$\dfrac{y^2}{\boxed{}} - \dfrac{x^2}{\boxed{}} = 1$ Substitute values for a and b.

$\dfrac{y^2}{\boxed{}} - \dfrac{x^2}{\boxed{}} = 1$ Simplify.

Lesson 10-5

Got It? What are the vertices, foci, and asymptotes of the hyperbola with equation $9x^2 - 4y^2 = 36$? Sketch a graph. Use a graphing calculator to check your sketch.

13. Write the equation in standard form. Divide each side by the same number to get 1 on the right side.

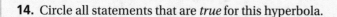

14. Circle all statements that are *true* for this hyperbola.

The transverse axis is horizontal.	The transverse axis is vertical.
The vertices are on the *y*-axis.	The vertices are on the *x*-axis.
The foci are on the *y*-axis.	The foci are on the *x*-axis.

15. Use the standard form of the equation to identify the values of a^2, a, b^2, and b.

$a^2 = $ _____ $a = $ _____ $b^2 = $ _____ $b = $ _____

16. Use the values you found for a and b and $c^2 = a^2 + b^2$ to find c^2 and c.

$c^2 = $ _____ $c = $ _____

17. The vertices are ($\pm$ _____, 0) and the foci are ($\pm$ _____, 0).

The slopes of the asymptotes are $m = \pm\frac{b}{a}$, so $m = \pm$ _____.

The equations of the asymptote are $y = \pm$ _____ x.

18. Plot the vertices and foci. Draw dashed lines for the asymptotes. Then sketch a graph the hyperbola.

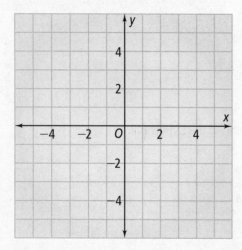

19. Solve the equation for y.

20. Use your graphing calculator to graph the two equations you found in Exercise 19 on the same screen. Compare the graph on your screen to your sketch.

_____

_____

Lesson Check • Do you UNDERSTAND?

Error Analysis Your friend says that a graph must be a vertical hyperbola because the greater denominator is under the y^2 term. What error did your friend make?

21. Circle the equation that represents a vertical hyperbola. Underline the equation that represents a horizontal hyperbola

$$\frac{y^2}{36} - \frac{x^2}{9} = 1 \qquad\qquad \frac{x^2}{9} - \frac{y^2}{36} = 1$$

22. Name one way the two equations differ.

_____

_____

_____

Math Success

Check off the vocabulary words that you understand.

☐ hyperbola ☐ focus of the hyperbola ☐ vertex ☐ transverse axis

Rate how well you can _graph a hyperbola_.

Need to review 0 2 4 6 8 10 Now I get it!

Lesson 10-5

Vocabulary

● Review

Identify each *transformation* as a reflection, rotation, or dilation.

1.

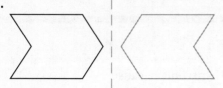

2.

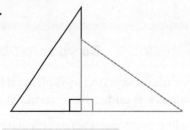

● Vocabulary Builder

analyze (verb) AN uh lyz

Related Word: analysis (noun)

Definition: To **analyze** something means you look at it in great detail to understand it better.

Example: If you **analyze** the equation $y = 3x + 8$, you find that it is the equation of a line with a slope of 3 and an intercept at (0, 8).

● Use Your Vocabulary

Analyze each equation. Complete each statement with the correct number from the list. Use each number once.

   2   5   6   9

3. The slope of the equation $y = 5x + 6$ is __?__ .

4. The slope of the equation $y = 2x - 6$ is __?__ .

5. The equation $y = 5x + 9$ has an intercept at (0, __?__).

6. The equation $y = 9x + 6$ has an intercept at (0, __?__).

Summary   Translating Horizontal and Vertical Ellipses

Horizontal Ellipse	Center (0, 0)	Center (h, k)
Standard-Form Equation	$\dfrac{x^2}{a^2} + \dfrac{y^2}{b^2} = 1$	$\dfrac{(x - h)^2}{a^2} + \dfrac{(y - k)^2}{b^2} = 1$
Vertices	$(\pm a, 0)$	$(h \pm a, k)$
Co-vertices	$(0, \pm b)$	$(h, k \pm b)$
Foci	$(\pm c, 0)$	$(h \pm c, k)$
a, b, c relationship	$c^2 = a^2 - b^2$	$c^2 = a^2 - b^2$

Vertical Ellipse	Center (0, 0)	Center (h, k)
Standard-Form Equation	$\dfrac{x^2}{b^2} + \dfrac{y^2}{a^2} = 1$	$\dfrac{(x - h)^2}{b^2} + \dfrac{(y - k)^2}{a^2} = 1$
Vertices	$(0, \pm a)$	$(h, k \pm a)$
Co-vertices	$(\pm b, 0)$	$(h \pm b, k)$
Foci	$(0, \pm c)$	$(h, k \pm c)$
a, b, c relationship	$c^2 = a^2 - b^2$	$c^2 = a^2 - b^2$

Problem 1   Writing an Equation of a Translated Ellipse

Got It? What is the standard-form equation of an ellipse with vertices (2, 3) and (22, 3), and one focus at (6, 3)? Sketch the ellipse.

7. Graph the vertices on the coordinate grid. Locate and graph the point halfway between the vertices.

8. Calculate the distance, a, from the center to (2, 3).

   $a = $, so $a^2 = $.

9. Calculate the distance, c, from the center to the focus.

   $c = $, so $c^2 = $.

10. Use $c^2 = a^2 - b^2$ to determine the value of b^2.

    $b^2 = $

11. Write the location of the co-vertices.

    $\left(12, \right)$ and $\left(12, \right)$.

12. Graph the co-vertices and foci on the coordinate grid. Draw an ellipse through the vertices and co-vertices.

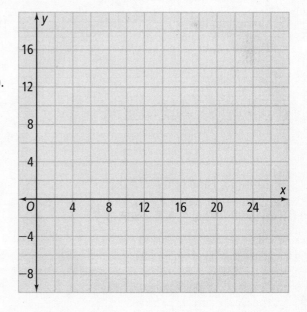

Lesson 10-6

13. Circle the equation of the ellipse.

$$\frac{(x-12)^2}{100} + \frac{(y-3)^2}{64} = 1 \qquad \frac{(x-12)^2}{64} + \frac{(y-3)^2}{100} = 1 \qquad \frac{(x-3)^2}{100} + \frac{(y-12)^2}{64} = 1$$

Summary Translating Horizontal and Vertical Hyperbolas

	Horizontal Hyperbola		Vertical Hyperbola	
	Center $(0,0)$	Center (h,k)	Center $(0,0)$	Center (h,k)
Standard-Form Equation	$\dfrac{x^2}{a^2} - \dfrac{y^2}{b^2} = 1$	$\dfrac{(x-h)^2}{a^2} - \dfrac{(y-k)^2}{b^2} = 1$	$\dfrac{y^2}{a^2} - \dfrac{x^2}{b^2} = 1$	$\dfrac{(y-k)^2}{a^2} - \dfrac{(x-h)^2}{b^2} = 1$
Vertices	$(\pm a, 0)$	$(h \pm a, k)$	$(0, \pm a)$	$(h, k \pm a)$
Foci	$(\pm c, 0)$	$(h \pm c, k)$	$(0, \pm c)$	$(h, k \pm c)$
Asymptotes	$y = \pm\dfrac{b}{a}x$	$y - k = \pm\dfrac{b}{a}(x - h)$	$y = \pm\dfrac{a}{b}x$	$y - k = \pm\dfrac{a}{b}(x - h)$
a, b, c relationship	$c^2 = a^2 + b^2$	$c^2 = a^2 + b^2$	$c^2 = a^2 + b^2$	$c^2 = a^2 + b^2$

Problem 2 Analyzing a Hyperbola From Its Equation

Got It? What are the center, vertices, foci, and asymptotes of the hyperbola with equation $\dfrac{(x-2)^2}{36} - \dfrac{(y+2)^2}{64} = 1$? Sketch the graph.

14. Use the general form of a horizontal hyperbola. Write the values of h, k, a, and b.

$h =$ ☐ $k =$ ☐ $a =$ ☐ $b =$ ☐

15. Complete.

Center (h, k)

$\left(\boxed{}, \boxed{} \right)$

Vertices $(h \pm a, k)$

$\left(8, \boxed{} \right)$ and $\left(\boxed{}, \boxed{} \right)$

Foci $(h \pm c, k)$

$\left(12, \boxed{} \right)$ and $\left(\boxed{}, \boxed{} \right)$

Asymptotes $y - k = \pm\dfrac{b}{a}(x - h)$

$y + 2 = \pm\dfrac{\boxed{}}{\boxed{}}(x - 2)$

16. Sketch the graph.

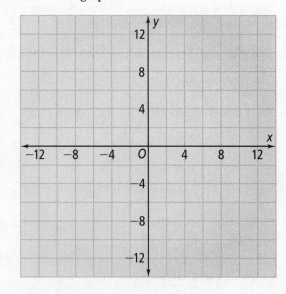

Problem 4 Modeling With a Conic Section

Got It? Navigation A lighthouse is on an island 8 miles from the shore. A boat sails around the island, deliberately following a path that always keeps it 3 times as far from the shoreline as it is from the lighthouse. What is an equation of the conic section describing the boat's path?

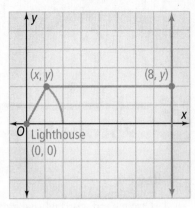

17. Label the diagram with the words *shore* and *boat*.

18. Circle the distance from the boat to the lighthouse.

$$\sqrt{x^2 - y^2} \qquad \sqrt{x^2 + y^2}$$

19. Circle the distance from the boat to the shore.

$$8 - x \qquad y - 8$$

20. Complete the model.

| **Relate** | 3 times the distance from the boat to lighthouse | is | the distance from boat to shore |

| **Write** | ⬚ | = | ⬚ |

Lesson Check • Do you UNDERSTAND?

Vocabulary Which of the conic sections have more than one focus: circle, parabola, ellipse, hyperbola?

21. Draw a line from each conic section in Column A to the number of foci in Column B.

Column A	Column B
circle	0
parabola	1
ellipse	2
hyperbola	

22. Circle the conic sections that have more than one focus.

circle   parabola

ellipse   hyperbola

Math Success

Check off the vocabulary words that you understand.

☐ ellipse   ☐ hyperbola   ☐ translation

Rate how well you can *translate conic sections.*

Need to review 0 2 4 6 8 10 Now I get it!

Lesson 10-6

Vocabulary

● **Review**

1. Circle each word whose meaning is similar to that of *fundamental*.

| basic | essential | extra | necessary | secondary | unimportant |

● **Vocabulary Builder**

set of numbers 5, 7, 11, 8

permutation 11, 7, 8, 5

permutation (noun) **pur myoo TAY shun**

Related Word: combination (noun)

Definition: A **permutation** is an arrangement of items in a particular order.

Main Idea: When you put a set of objects in a certain order, you make a **permutation**.

● **Use Your Vocabulary**

2. Write a *permutation* of each set.

⊃, ∩, ⊂, ∪   A, W, 6, 7, 2, E, V   y, o, U, R

3. Write all possible *permutations* of the numbers 5, 9, and 8.

4. There are ⬚ *permutations* of the numbers 5, 9, and 8.

Problem 1 **Using the Fundamental Counting Principle**

Got It? In 1966, one type of Maryland license plate had two letters followed by four digits. How many of this type of plate were possible?

5. Multiple Choice Which set of letters and digits gives a possible 1966 Maryland license plate?

ⓐ TV 432   ⓑ RC 2301   ⓒ KPH 621   ⓓ OMNQ 23

6. There are [ ] possible letters for each letter in the license plate.

There are [ ] possible digits for each digit.

7. Use the Fundamental Counting Principle to find the number of possible license plates. Complete the expression.

26 · [ ] · [ ] · [ ] · [ ]

8. Circle the number of possible 1966 Maryland license plates.

| 26,000 | 45,697,600 | 6,760,000 |

Using *factorial* notation, you can write 3 · 2 · 1 as 3!, read "three factorial." For any positive integer *n*, **n factorial** is $n! = n(n - 1) \cdot \ldots \cdot 3 \cdot 2 \cdot 1$. The zero factorial is $0! = 1$.

 Problem 2 **Finding the Number of Permutations of *n* Items**

Got It? In how many ways can you arrange 8 shirts on hangers in a closet?

9. Complete the model below.

number of ways to arrange the

Relate	1st shirt	2nd shirt	3rd shirt	4th shirt	5th shirt	6th shirt	7th shirt	8th shirt
Write	8	7	[ ]	[ ]	[ ]	[ ]	[ ]	[ ]

10. The total number of permutations is

8! = 8 · [ ] · 6 · [ ] · 4 · [ ] · 2 · 1 = [ ]

take note

Key Concept Number of Permutations

The number of permutations of *n* items of a set arranged *r* items at a time is

$$_nP_r = \frac{n!}{(n - r)!} \text{ for } 0 \le r \le n.$$

Example: $_{10}P_4 = \frac{10!}{6!} = 5040$

11. Why can't *r* be greater than *n*?

_____

_____

_____

Lesson 11-1

Problem 3 Finding $_nP_r$

Got It? In how many ways can 15 runners finish first, second, and third?

12. Use the permutation formula. Circle the value of n, the number of runners in the set. Underline the value of r, the number of runners arranged at a time.

| 1 | 2 | 3 | 15 |

13. Use the justifications at the right to find the number of ways in which 15 runners can finish first, second, and third.

$$_nP_r = \frac{n!}{(n-r)!}$$ Write the formula.

$$= \frac{\boxed{}!}{\left(\boxed{} - \boxed{}\right)!}$$ Substitute n and r.

$$= \frac{\boxed{}!}{\boxed{}!} = \boxed{}$$ Simplify.

take note

Key Concept Number of Combinations

The number of combinations of n items of a set chosen r items at a time is

$$_nC_r = \frac{n!}{r!(n-r)!} \text{ for } 0 \le r \le n$$

Example: $_5C_3 = \frac{5!}{3!(5-3)!} = \frac{5!}{3! \cdot 2!} = \frac{120}{6 \cdot 2} = 10$

14. Which is greater, $_5C_3$ or $_5P_3$? Explain.

Problem 4 Finding $_nC_r$

Got It? What is the value of $_8C_3$?

15. Cross out the equations that do NOT give the correct formula for $_8C_3$.

$$_8C_3 = \frac{8!}{3!(8-3)!} \qquad _8C_3 = 8! \qquad _8C_3 = \frac{8!}{(8-3)!}$$

16. Simplify the remaining equation from Exercise 15.

Problem 5 Identifying Whether Order Is Important

Got It? A chemistry teacher has a class work in groups to draw the molecular structure of water. Each group submits one drawing. There are eight groups. The teacher selects the four drawings that earn the highest grades. In how many ways can he select and arrange the four drawings from left to right on the wall?

17. Circle the formula you will use to solve this problem.

$$_nC_r = \frac{n!}{r!(n-r)!} \qquad\qquad _nP_r = \frac{n!}{(n-r)!}$$

18. Identify each value.

$n =$ ____ $r =$ ____

19. In how many different ways can the teacher select and arrange the drawings?

 Lesson Check • **Do you UNDERSTAND?**

Reasoning Use the definition of permutation to show why 0! should equal 1.

20. Circle the equation that shows the Fundamental Counting Principle and the Permutation Formula for n items arranged n at a time.

$$0! = \frac{n!}{(n-0)!} \qquad n! = \frac{n!}{(n-n)!} \qquad n! = \frac{n!}{(n-0)!}$$

21. Simplify the equation you chose in Exercise 20.

22. Underline the correct expressions to complete the sentence.

For $\frac{n!}{0!}$ to equal $0! \,/\, n!$, 0! must equal $0 \,/\, 1$.

 Math Success

Check off the vocabulary words that you understand.

☐ Fundamental Counting Principle   ☐ permutation   ☐ n factorial   ☐ combination

Rate how well you can *find permutations and combinations*.

Need to review   0   2   4   6   8   10   Now I get it!

Vocabulary

● Review

1. Draw a line from each *experiment* in Column A to a corresponding set of possible outcomes in Column B.

Column A

Toss a coin.

Roll a six-sided number cube.

Draw a ball at random from a box holding 1 green, 1 red, and 1 blue ball.

Column B

G, R, B

heads or tails

1, 2, 3, 4, 5, 6

● Vocabulary Builder

theoretical probability (noun)

thee uh RET ih kul prah buh BIL uh tee

probability

$$P(\text{event}) = \frac{\text{number of times the event occurs}}{\text{number of trials}}$$

Definition: The **theoretical probability** of an event is the ratio of the number of ways that the event can occur to the total number of equally likely outcomes in the sample space.

Example: A student rolls a six-sided number cube. The **theoretical probability** that the student rolls an even number is

$$P(\text{even}) = \frac{\text{number of ways to roll an even number}}{\text{number of possible outcomes}} = \frac{3}{6}$$

● Use Your Vocabulary

2. Write T for *true* or F for *false*.

_____ *Theoretical probability* is the sum of the number of ways an event can occur and the number of possible outcomes.

_____ The ratio of the number of ways for an event to occur to the total number of possible outcomes is the *theoretical probability*.

Problem 1 **Finding Experimental Probability**

Got It? A softball player got a hit in 20 of her last 50 times at bat. What is the experimental probability that she will get a hit in her next at bat?

3. Use the words in the box at the right to complete the ratio. Then substitute and simplify.

$$P(\text{hit}) = \frac{\rule{3cm}{0.4pt}}{\rule{3cm}{0.4pt}}$$

number of times at bat

number of hits

$$= \frac{}{} = \boxed{} = \boxed{}\%$$

 Problem 3 **Finding Theoretical Probabilities**

Got It? What is the theoretical probability of getting a sum that is an odd number on one roll of two fair number cubes?

4. The table shows the possible sums for one roll of two number cubes. Circle the favorable outcomes.

5. There are ☐ favorable outcomes.

6. Complete and simplify the ratio.

$$P(\text{odd number}) = \frac{}{36} = \frac{}{}$$

	1	2	3	4	5	6
1	2	3	4	5	6	7
2	3	4	5	6	7	8
3	4	5	6	7	8	9
4	5	6	7	8	9	10
5	6	7	8	9	10	11
6	7	8	9	10	11	12

Problem 4 **Finding Probability Using Combinatorics**

Got It? What is the theoretical probability of being dealt all four 7's in a 5-card hand?

7. Complete the reasoning model below.

Think	Write
First, I find the number of combinations of four 7's from four 7's.	$_4C_4 = \dfrac{4!}{\boxed{}!\left(4 - \boxed{}\right)!} = \boxed{}$
A five-card hand with four 7's has one non-7 card. I find the number of combinations of one non-7 from 48 remaining cards.	$_{48}C_{\boxed{}} = \dfrac{48!}{\boxed{}!\left(48 - \boxed{}\right)!} = \dfrac{48!}{\boxed{}!} = \boxed{}$
I multiply to find the number of 5-card hands with four 7's.	$_4C_4 \cdot {_{48}}C_{\boxed{}} = \boxed{} \cdot \boxed{} = \boxed{}$

Lesson 11-2

8. Find the total number of possible 5-card hands.

$$_{52}C\,\boxed{} = \frac{52!}{\boxed{}!\left(52 - \boxed{}\right)!} = \frac{52!}{\boxed{}!\left(\boxed{}\right)!} = \boxed{}$$

9. Use your answers to Exercises 7 and 8 to write the probability.

$$P(\text{hand with four 7's}) = \frac{\text{5-card hands with four 7's}}{\boxed{}}$$

10. Substitute and simplify.

$$P(\text{hand with four 7's}) = \frac{\boxed{}}{\boxed{}} = \frac{\boxed{}}{\boxed{}}$$

Problem 5 **Finding Geometric Probability**

Got It? Suppose a batter's strike zone is 15 in. by 20 in. and his high-inside strike zone is 3 in. by 5 in. What is the probability that a baseball thrown at random within the strike zone will be a high-inside strike?

11. Find the area of the batter's strike zone.

$$A(\text{strike zone}) = 15 \cdot \boxed{} = \boxed{} \text{ in.}^2$$

12. Find the area of the batter's high-inside strike zone.

$$A(\text{high-inside}) = 3 \cdot \boxed{} = \boxed{} \text{ in.}^2$$

13. Complete the equation to solve the problem. Round your final answer to two decimal places.

$$P(\text{high-inside strike}) = \frac{\text{area of high-inside strike zone}}{\boxed{}} = \frac{\boxed{}}{\boxed{}} \approx \boxed{}$$

14. The probability that a baseball thrown at random within the strike zone will be a

high-inside strike is $\boxed{}$ %.

Lesson Check • **Do you know HOW?**

Find $P(3)$ when rolling a fair number cube.

15. Complete.

$$P(3) = \frac{\text{number of ways you can roll 3}}{\text{number of possible outcomes}} = \frac{\boxed{}}{\boxed{}}$$

Find $P(2 \text{ or } 4)$ when rolling a fair number cube.

16. Complete.

$$P(2 \text{ or } 4) = \frac{\text{number of ways you can roll 2 or 4}}{\text{number of possible outcomes}} = \frac{\boxed{}}{\boxed{}}, \text{ or } \frac{\boxed{}}{\boxed{}}$$

Lesson Check • Do you UNDERSTAND?

Reasoning Why is a simulation better the more times you perform it?

17. Using your graphing calculator, enter randInt (1, 2, 5). This will generate a list of 5 outcomes of 1 or 2. Let 1 represent a tossed coin landing heads-up and let 2 represent a tossed coin landing tails-up. Record your results in the table.

18. Repeat the experiment two more times with 10 and 20 in place of the 5. Record the results.

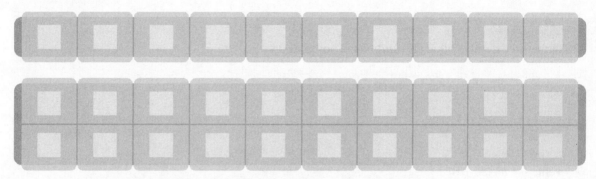

19. Find the experimental probability of landing on heads for each experiment above.

$$P(\text{heads}) = \frac{}{5} = \qquad P(\text{heads}) = \frac{}{10} = \qquad P(\text{heads}) = \frac{}{20} = $$

20. Explain why a simulation is better the more times you perform it.

Math Success

Check off the vocabulary words that you understand.

☐ experimental probability ☐ simulation ☐ theoretical probability

Rate how well you can *determine the probability of events.*

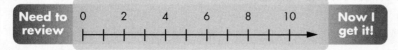

Lesson 11-2

Vocabulary

● Review

1. Cross out all numbers that are NOT *multiples* of 8.

| 48 | 74 | 405 | 136 |

2. Write three numbers that are *multiples* of both 2 and 9.

● Vocabulary Builder

> **event** (noun) **ee VENT**
>
> **Math Usage:** An **event** is one or more outcomes from the set of all possible outcomes of an experiment.
>
> **Example:** Roll a number cube. The set of all possible outcomes is {1, 2, 3, 4, 5, 6}. The set of outcomes resulting in the **event** that an even number is rolled is the set {2, 4, 6}.

● Use Your Vocabulary

Write a possible *event* for each experiment.

3. A basket has 5 red balls and 3 blue balls. You pick one ball without looking.

4. You roll a number cube one time.

Problem 1 Classifying Events

Got It? You select a coin at random from your pocket. You replace the coin and select again. Are your selections independent events? Explain.

5. Circle the true statement.

| Selecting the first coin affects the possible outcomes of picking the second coin, because you replace the coin. | Selecting the first coin does not affect the possible outcomes of picking the second coin, because you replace the coin. |

6. The two selections are independent / dependent .

Key Concept Probability of Compound Events

Probability of A and B   If A and B are independent events, then $P(A \text{ and } B) = P(A) \cdot P(B)$.

Probability of A or B   If A and B are *not* mutually exclusive, then $P(A \text{ or } B) = P(A) + P(B) - P(A \text{ and } B)$.

If A and B are mutually exclusive, then $P(A \text{ or } B) = P(A) + P(B)$.

Events A and B are independent and mutually exclusive. $P(A) = \frac{3}{5}$ and $P(B) = \frac{4}{9}$.
Write T for *true* or F for *false*.

7. $P(A \text{ and } B) = \frac{4}{15}$

8. $P(A \text{ or } B) = \frac{3}{5} + \frac{4}{9} - \frac{4}{15}$

Problem 2 Finding the Probability of Independent Events

Got It? At a picnic there are 10 diet drinks and 5 regular drinks. There are also 8 bags of fat-free chips and 12 bags of regular chips. If you grab a drink and a bag of chips without looking, what is the probability that you get a regular drink and regular chips?

9. Define each event.

Event $A =$ You pick a regular drink.   Event $B = $ _____

10. Complete each equation.

$$P(A) = \frac{}{\text{total number of drinks}} = \frac{}{15}$$

$$P(B) = \frac{}{\text{total number of bags of chips}} = \frac{}{}$$

11. Use the justifications at the right to find the probability.

$P(A \text{ and } B) = P(A) \cdot P(B)$ Multiply to find the probability of independent events.

$= \boxed{} \cdot \boxed{}$ Substitute.

$= \boxed{}$, or $\boxed{}$ Simplify.

Lesson 11-3

Problem 3 Mutually Exclusive Events

Got It? You roll a standard number cube. Are the events rolling an even number and rolling a prime number mutually exclusive? Explain.

12. The numbers on the number cube are listed below. Circle the even numbers. Underline the prime numbers.

	1	2	3	4	5	6

13. Are the events mutually exclusive? Explain.

_____

_____

_____

 Problem 4 Finding Probability for Mutually Exclusive Events

Got It? **Languages** At your high school, a student can take one foreign language each term. About 37% of the students take Spanish. About 15% of the students take French. About 9% of the students take Mandarin Chinese. What is the probability that a student chosen at random is taking Spanish, French, or Mandarin Chinese?

14. Are the events of a student taking Spanish, taking French, or taking Mandarin Chinese mutually exclusive? Explain.

_____

_____

_____

15. Circle the formula you would use to find the probability.

$$P(A \text{ or } B \text{ or } C) = P(A) \cdot P(B) \cdot P(C) \qquad P(A \text{ or } B \text{ or } C) = P(A) + P(B) + P(C)$$

16. Find the probability that a student is taking Spanish, French, or Mandarin Chinese.

Problem 5 Finding Probability

Got It? Suppose you reach into the dish at the right and select a token at random. What is the probability that the token is square or red (R)?

17. Complete.

number of tokens in the dish	number of square tokens	number of red (R) tokens	number of tokens that are square and red (R)
	3		

18. Use your answers to Exercise 17 to find each probability.

| P(square token) | P(red (R) token) | P(square and red (R) token) |

$$\frac{3}{\boxed{}}$$ $$\frac{}{}$$ $$\frac{}{}$$

19. Find the probability that the token you select is square or red (R).

 Lesson Check • **Do you UNDERSTAND?**

Error Analysis The weather forecast for the weekend is a 30% chance of rain on Saturday and a 70% chance of rain on Sunday. Your friend says that means there is a 100% chance of rain this weekend. What error did your friend make?

20. Which formula should you use to find the chance of rain for this weekend? Circle your answer.

$$P(A \text{ or } B) = P(A) + P(B) - P(A \text{ and } B) \qquad P(A \text{ and } B) = P(A) \cdot P(B)$$

21. Explain your friend's error.

_____

_____

_____

Math Success

Check off the vocabulary words that you understand.

☐ event   ☐ independent events   ☐ mutually exclusive events

Rate how well you can *find probabilities of multiple events.*

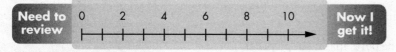

Lesson 11-3

Vocabulary

● Review

1. Multiple Choice A basket has 7 plain, 8 wheat, 2 raisin, and 3 blueberry bagels. What is the *probability* of selecting a plain bagel without looking?

   (A) $\frac{3}{20}$ (B) $\frac{7}{20}$ (C) $\frac{1}{10}$ (D) $\frac{2}{5}$

2. A pencil machine contains 15 blue, 16 red, 18 green, and 26 purple pencils. The machine randomly dispenses a pencil when one is purchased. Keisha buys a pencil. Circle the *probability* that the pencil she buys is red.

$\frac{1}{16}$	$\frac{4}{25}$	$\frac{16}{75}$	$\frac{59}{75}$	16

● Vocabulary Builder

conditional (adjective) kun DISH un ul

Related Words: conditions (adjective), conditionally (adjective), conditioned (adjective), conditioning (noun or adjective)

Definition: A **conditional** statement is a sentence stating that the probability of one event depends on the occurrence of another event.

● Use Your Vocabulary

Complete each statement with the correct word from the list. Use each word only once.

   conditioning   conditions   conditioned   condition

3. The _?_ in the classroom made concentration difficult.

           _____

4. The track and field athletes were having spring _?_ .

           _____

5. Matthew had a heart _?_ that made participating in physical activities difficult.

           _____

6. The dog was _?_ to ring the bells on the door when he wanted to go outside.

           _____

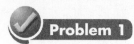 **Problem 1** Finding Conditional Probability

Student Genders

	Males (in thousands)	Females (in thousands)
Two-year colleges	1866	2462
Four-year colleges	4324	5517
Graduate schools	1349	1954

Source: U.S. Census Bureau

Got It? The table shows the number of students of each gender at two-year and four-year colleges and graduate schools in 2005. What is $P(\text{four-year} \mid \text{male})$?

7. Find the total number of male students.

1866 + _____ + _____ = _____

8. Complete the steps to solve the problem. Round your answer to the nearest hundredth.

$P(\text{four-year} \mid \text{male}) = \dfrac{\text{number of males attending four–year colleges}}{\text{total number of male students}}$

$= \dfrac{}{} \approx $

Got It? **Reasoning** Without calculating, given a student is enrolled in a four-year college, is it more likely for the student to be male or female? Explain.

9. There are _____ male students enrolled in four-year colleges.

10. There are _____ female students enrolled in four-year colleges.

11. Is it more likely for a four-year college student to be male or female? Explain.

_____

_____

 Problem 2 Conditional Probability in Statistics

Got It? Americans recycle increasing amounts through municipal waste collection. The table shows the collection data for 2007. What is the probability that a sample of recycled waste is plastic?

Municipal Waste Collected (millions of tons)

Material	Recycled	Not Recycled
Paper	45.2	37.8
Metal	7.2	13.6
Glass	3.2	10.4
Plastic	2.1	28.6
Other	21.7	46.3

Source: U.S. Environmental Protection Agency

12. Find the total number of tons (in millions) of recycled waste.

13. Circle the amount of recycled waste that is plastic.

| 2.1 | 3.2 | 7.2 | 21.7 | 45.2 |

14. Complete.

$P(\text{plastic} \mid \text{recycled}) = \dfrac{\text{plastic}}{} = \dfrac{}{} \approx $

Lesson 11-4

15. The probability that a sample of recycled waste is plastic is about [ ] %.

Key Concept   **Conditional Probability**

For any two events A and B, with $P(A) \neq 0$, $P(B \mid A) = \dfrac{P(A \text{ and } B)}{P(A)}$.

 Problem 3   **Using the Conditional Probability Formula**

Got It? **Market Research** Researchers asked shampoo users whether they apply shampoo directly to the head, or indirectly using a hand. What is the probability that a respondent applies shampoo directly to the head, given that the respondent is female?

Applying Shampoo

	Directly Onto Head	Into Hand First
Male	2	18
Female	6	24

16. Determine each probability.

$$P(\text{female}) = \frac{30}{} \qquad P(\text{female and directly to head}) = \frac{}{}$$

17. Circle the form the conditional probability formula will have.

$$P(\text{directly} \mid \text{female}) = \frac{P(\text{female})}{P(\text{female and directly to head})} \qquad P(\text{directly} \mid \text{female}) = \frac{P(\text{female and directly to head})}{P(\text{female})}$$

18. Use your answers to Exercises 16 and 17 to find the probability that a female respondent applies shampoo directly onto her head.

19. The probability that a female respondent applies shampoo directly onto her head is [ ] .

 Problem 4   **Using a Tree Diagram**

Got It? **Education** A school system compiled the following information from a survey it sent to people who were juniors 10 years earlier.

- 85% of the students graduated from high school.

- Of the students who graduated from high school, 90% are happy with their present jobs.

- Of the students who did not graduate from high school, 60% are happy with their present jobs.

What is the probability that a student from the junior class 10 years ago did not graduate and is happy with his or her present job?

20. In the tree diagram at the right, G = graduated, NG = not graduated, H = happy with present job, and NH = not happy with present job. Use the numbers in the shaded box to complete the tree diagram below. Use each number once.

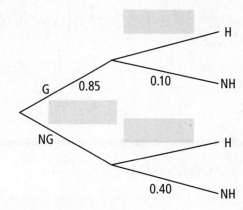

0.90
0.60
0.15

G   0.85   0.10   NH

H

NG   H   0.40   NH

21. Highlight the path on the tree diagram that shows the probability that a person who did not graduate is happy with his or her present job.

22. Calculate the probability.

$$P(\text{NG and H}) = P(\text{NG}) \cdot P(\text{H} \mid \text{NG}) = \underline{\hspace{1.5cm}} \cdot \underline{\hspace{1.5cm}} = \underline{\hspace{1.5cm}}$$

Lesson Check • Do you know HOW?

The probability that a car has two doors, given that it is red, is 0.6. The probability that a car has two doors *and* is red is 0.2. What is the probability that a car is red?

23. Circle the equation you will use to solve this problem.

$$0.6 = \frac{0.2}{P(\text{red})} \qquad 0.2 = \frac{0.6}{P(\text{red})} \qquad P(\text{red}) = 0.2 \cdot 0.6$$

24. Solve the equation you circled in Exercise 23.

25. The probability that a car is red is $\underline{\hspace{1cm}}$ %.

Math Success

Check off the vocabulary words that you understand.

☐ conditional probability

Rate how well you can *determine conditional probability*.

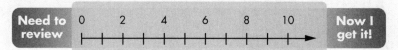

Need to review   0   2   4   6   8   10   Now I get it!

Lesson 11-4

11-5 Probability Models

Vocabulary

● **Review**

1. Circle the type of *probability* that is equal to the ratio of the number of times an *event* occurs divided by the number of *trials*.

> theoretical probability   experimental probability   geometric probability

2. Fill in the blanks to complete the sentence.

The possible values of *probabilities* are real numbers between ⬚ and ⬚, inclusive.

● **Vocabulary Builder**

Probability model (noun) prä-bə-BI-lə-tē

Related Words: outcome, fair decision, simulation, equally likely

Definition: A **probability model** is a model used to assign probabilities to outcomes of a chance process. A simulation is an example of a probability model.

Example: One student will be selected at random from four volunteers for class representative. You can use a spinner divided into four equal sections to predict the chances of each student being selected.

● **Use Your Vocabulary**

3. Fill in the blanks to complete the sentence.

If a sample space has *n* equally likely outcomes and an event *A* occurs in *m* of these

outcomes, then the _____ of event *A* is

$P(A) = \dfrac{⬚}{⬚}$.

4. Circle the spinner that has equally likely outcomes.

 **Problem 1** Making a Fair Decision

Got It? Two siblings are trying to decide who has to mow the lawn this weekend. They decide to race, and the winner does not have to mow the lawn. Is the result a fair decision?

5. Circle all the things you do not know about the siblings.

   age   gender   weight

6. Underline the correct word to complete the sentence.

   It is very likely / unlikely the two siblings have the same speed when running a race.

7. Do the siblings have an equal chance of winning the race? Explain.

   _____

   _____

8. Underline the correct word to complete the sentence.

   The result is a(n) fair / unfair decision.

Problem 2 Using Random Numbers

Got It? A teacher wants to organize 10 students into two teams for a math game. The teacher assigns each student a number between 0 and 9. He uses the second line of digits from the random number table below to select the teams. He alternates the assigned team as each student is chosen. Which numbers will be used to create team 1?

Random Number Table						
87494	39707	20525	95704	48361	27556	34599
14164	15888	24997	82392	08525	47551	37304
61249	08241	16243	18371	03349	91759	53613
67868	56747	73521	05975	40411	49493	70904

9. Circle the second row of digits in the table. Rewrite the numbers in the second row as a list of single digits. Starting with the first number on the left, circle each digit from 0 to 1 the first time it is shown. Put an X through any duplicates.

   ①④X 6 4 1 5

10. Alternate the circled numbers between team 1 and team 2 to fill in the blanks.

    Numbers for Team 1   Number for Team 2

    ☐ ☐ ☐ ☐ ☐   ☐ ☐ ☐ ☐ ☐

Lesson 11-5

Problem 3 Modeling with a Simulation

Got It? Suppose that you are playing a board game for which you must roll a 6 on a number cube before you are able to move your game piece from start. Describe a simulation you can use to predict the number of times you would expect to have to roll the number cube before you can move from start.

Know

You know you must roll a ▢ on a number cube before you can move your game piece from ▢.

Need

You need to find a probability model that generates ▢ equally-likely events.

Plan

You can use a spinner with ▢ equal sections to simulate the number of times you have to roll the number cube before you can move from start.

11. **Step 1** The results of 5 trials are shown in the table. Complete the table to show the number of spins until the spinner lands on 6 for each trial.

12. **Step 2** The number of spins until ▢ occurs for 20 more trials are shown below.

3, 8, 2, 11, 4, 4, 2, 6, 4, 7, 8, 2, 11, 3, 3, 1, 5, 1, 4, 12

13. **Step 3** Use the results from Steps 1 and 2 to find the average number of rolls until a 6.

$$\frac{\boxed{}}{25} = \boxed{}$$

14. On the average, you will need to roll ▢ time until you can start the game.

Spins Until You Can Start Game Simulation

Trial	Individual Spin Results	Spins until 6
1	5, 1, 6	
2	5, 6	
3	3, 3, 6	
4	3, 3, 3, 1, 5, 3, 2, 2, 6	
5	1, 6	

 Problem 4 Using Probability to Analyze Decisions

Got It? A pharmaceutical company is testing the effectiveness of a new drug for asthma patients. The results of a test are shown in the contingency table below. Should the company produce and distribute the new drug?

	Reported improvements	Did not report improvements	Totals
Received the drug	23	27	50
Received the placebo	19	31	50
Totals	42	58	100

15. What is the probability a volunteer reported noticeable improvement in symptoms given the volunteer received the test drug?

$P(\text{improvement} \mid \text{drug}) = \dfrac{\text{number of volunteers who improved}}{\text{number of volunteers who received the drug}} = \dfrac{}{} = \boxed{}$

16. What is the probability a volunteer received the placebo given the volunteer did not report a noticeable improvement in symptoms?

$P(\text{placebo} \mid \text{no improvement}) = \dfrac{}{} \approx \boxed{}$

17. The results are around 50-50. The company should/should not produce this new drug.

Lesson Check • Do you UNDERSTAND?

A classmate conducted a simulation to predict how many boxes of cereal he would need to buy to get all 5 prizes. After one trial of the simulation, he concluded that he would need to buy 7 boxes of cereal to get all 5 prizes. Do you agree with your classmate's conclusion? Explain.

18. Circle the correct answer for each question. In a simulation to predict how many boxes of cereal you would need to buy to get all 5 prizes, what is the least possible number of boxes you would need to buy?

4	5	6	7	10	15	undetermined

what is the greatest possible number of boxes you would need to buy?

4	5	6	7	10	15	undetermined

19. After one trial, you get all 5 prizes when you buy 7 boxes of cereal. Does that mean that you will get all 5 prizes with the next 7 boxes you buy? Explain.

20. Do you agree with your classmate's conclusion? Explain.

Math Success

Check off the vocabulary words that you understand.

☐ probability model   ☐ fair decision   ☐ simulation   ☐ two-way frequency table

Rate how well you can use *probability models to assign probabilities of a chance process.*

Need to review   0   2   4   6   8   10   Now I get it!

Lesson 11-5

Vocabulary

● Review

1. Find the *median* of the set of numbers.

1, 5, 7, 9, 3, 12, 7, 6

● Vocabulary Builder

quartile (noun) KWAWR tyl

Related Words: interquartile range, median

Definition: A **quartile** is one of three numbers, Q_1, Q_2, Q_3, that divide an ordered data set into four parts. Each part includes the same number of data values.

quartiles

| 8 | 11 | 14 | 21 | 25 | 30 | 31 |

Q_1 Q_2 Q_3

Example: The **quartiles** of the data set 1, 2, 3, 6, 6, 8, 10 are $Q_1 = 2$, $Q_2 = 6$, and $Q_3 = 8$. The second **quartile**, $Q_2 = 6$, is also the median of the data set.

● Use Your Vocabulary

2. Write T for *true* or F for *false*.

_____ You must order a data set before finding the *quartiles*.

_____ Every data set of numbers has four *quartiles*.

_____ The number Q_2 represents the first *quartile*.

_____ *Quartiles* divide an ordered data set into three parts.

Key Concepts Measures of Central Tendency

Measure	Definition	Example, using 1, 2, 3, 3, 4, 5, 5, 9
Mean	sum of the data values / number of data values	$\dfrac{1 + 2 + 3 + 3 + 4 + 5 + 5 + 9}{8} = 4$
Median	For a data set listed in order: The middle values for an odd number of data values; the mean of the two middle values for an even number of data values	For 1, 2, 3, 3, 4, 5, 5, 9 the middle values are 3 and 4. The median is the mean $\dfrac{3 + 4}{2} = 3.5$.
Mode	the most frequently occurring value(s)	Two modes: In 1, 2, 3, 3, 4, 5, 5, 9 both 3 and 5 occur twice.

3. Since the data set 18, 21, 25, 16, 14, 29, 35 has an even /odd number of

values, the median is 16 / 21 / 23 .

Problem 2 Identifying an Outlier

Got It? Suppose the values 56, 65, 73, 59, 98, 65, 59 are the number of customers in a small restaurant each night in one week. Would you discard the outlier? Explain.

4. Next to each reason below, write D if it is a reason for *discarding* the outlier. Write K if it is reason for *keeping* the outlier.

_____ 98 is very different from the other data values and will skew the mean.

_____ 98 could represent the number of customers on a Friday or Saturday night.

_____ The numbers could be used to determine how much food to order for the restaurant.

_____ 98 might represent an inaccurate count since it is so different from the other data values.

_____ The numbers could be used to decide whether there is a consistent need for a larger restaurant.

Problem 3 Comparing Data Sets

Got It? **Temperature** The table shows average monthly water temperatures for two locations on the Gulf of Mexico. How can you compare the 12 water temperatures from Dauphin Island with the 12 water temperatures from Grand Isle?

Gulf of Mexico Eastern Coast Water Temperatures (°F)

Location	J	F	M	A	M	J	J	A	S	O	N	D
Dauphin Island, Alabama	51	53	60	70	75	82	84	84	80	72	62	56
Grand Isle, Louisiana	61	61	64	70	77	83	85	85	83	77	70	65

Source: National Oceanographic Data Canter

Lesson 11-6

5. Find the sum of temperatures for each location.

Dauphin Island

=

Grand Isle

=

6. Find the mean temperature for each location.

Dauphin Island $\dfrac{}{12} = $ **Grand Isle** $\dfrac{}{} = $

7. Find the mode(s), minimum value, maximum value, and range.

	Mode(s)	Minimum	Maximum	Range
Dauphin Island				___ − ___ = ___
Grand Isle				___ − ___ = ___

8. Use the ordered temperatures below. Circle the middle two temperatures for each location. Draw a box around the middle two temperatures in the lower half of the data set. Underline the middle two temperatures in the upper half of the data set.

Dauphin Island

51, 53, 56, 60, 62, 70, 72, 75, 80, 82, 84, 84

Grand Isle

61, 61, 64, 65, 70, 70, 77, 77, 83, 83, 85, 85

9. Use your answers to Exercise 8 to complete the table.

	Median	Quartile 1	Quartile 3	Interquartile Range
Dauphin Island	$\dfrac{+}{2}$ =	$\dfrac{+}{2}$ =	$\dfrac{+}{2}$ =	$Q_3 - Q_1$ = ___ − ___ = ___
Grand Isle	$\dfrac{+}{2}$ =	$\dfrac{+}{2}$ =	$\dfrac{+}{2}$ =	$Q_3 - Q_1$ = ___ − ___ = ___

A **percentile** is a number from 0 to 100 that you can associate with a value x from a data set. If x is at the 63rd percentile, then 63% of the data are less than or equal to x.

10. If 71% of the data in a set are less than or equal to 269, then 269 is at the

70th / 71st / 72nd percentile of the data set.

Problem 5 Finding Percentiles

Got It? Testing Here is an ordered list of midterm test scores for a Spanish class. What value is at the 55th percentile?

41	54	61	65	67	73	74
77	77	77	79	80	82	88
89	93	97	98	98	100	

11. Multiply to find how many values fall at or below the 55th percentile.

Relate   number of test scores   times   percentile   =   number of values at or below indicated percentile

Write   ☐   •   ☐   =   ☐

12. ☐ values fall at or below ☐, the value at the 55th percentile.

Lesson Check • Do you UNDERSTAND?

Error Analysis A student found the median of the data set below. Explain the student's error. What is the median?

Score	80	85	90	95
Frequency	6	4	10	1

~~Median: $\dfrac{85 + 90}{2} = \dfrac{175}{2} = 87.5$~~

13. There are ☐ data values in the data set.

14. What error did the student make?

_____

_____

15. Find the median.

Math Success

Check off the vocabulary words that you understand.

☐ mean   ☐ median   ☐ mode

Rate how well you can *find the mean, median and mode.*

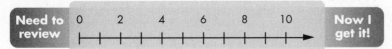

Need to review   0   2   4   6   8   10   Now I get it!

Lesson 11-6

Vocabulary

● Review

1. A softball pitcher threw softballs at speeds of 55 mph, 42 mph, 62 mph, and 52 mph. Explain how you can find the *mean* speed of the softballs thrown.

● Vocabulary Builder

variance (noun) VEHR ee uns

Related Words: vary (verb), variable (noun), various (adjective)

Definition: **Variance** is a difference between what is expected and what actually occurs.

Math Usage: The **variance** is a measure of spread, calculated as the average of the square of the difference between each number and the mean of a data set.

● Use Your Vocabulary

Complete each sentence with the correct form of the word *variance*.

variance	variable	vary	various

2. Use a __?__ such as *x* to stand for an unknown amount in an equation.

3. There are __?__ ways to answer that question.

4. The exact wording of students' answers may __?__, but all the answers should cover the key ideas.

5. By comparing the __?__ of two data sets, you can see how spread out the data is around the mean.

Key Concepts Variance and Standard Deviation

- Find the mean, $\bar{x}$, of the n values in the data set.

- Find the difference, $x_i - \bar{x}$, between each value x_i and the mean.

- Square each difference, $(x_i - \bar{x})^2$.

- Find the average (mean) of these squares. This is the variance.

$$\sigma^2 = \frac{\sum(x - \bar{x})^2}{n}$$

- Take the square root of the variance. This is the standard deviation.

$$\sigma = \sqrt{\frac{\sum(x - \bar{x})^2}{n}}$$

Problem 1 Finding Variance and Standard Deviation

Got It? What are the mean, variance, and standard deviation of these values?

52 63 65 77 80 82

6. Find the mean of the values. Round your answer to the nearest whole number.

7. Complete the table at the right.

8. Find the sum of the squares of the differences.

x	$\bar{x}$	$x - \bar{x}$	$(x - \bar{x})^2$
52		−18	324
63		−7	
65			
77			
80			
82			

9. Use the formula for variance.

$$\sigma^2 = \frac{\sum(x - \bar{x})^2}{n} = \frac{\quad}{6}$$

$$= \boxed{}$$

10. Use the formula for standard deviation.

$$\sigma = \sqrt{\sigma^2} = \sqrt{\quad}$$

$$= \boxed{}$$

Lesson 11-7

Problem 2 Using a Calculator to Find Standard Deviation

Got It? Meteorology The table below displays the number of hurricanes in the Atlantic Ocean from 1992 to 2006. What are the mean and standard deviation?

Year	1	2	3	4	5	6	7	8	9	10	11	12	13	14	15
Number	4	4	3	11	10	3	10	8	8	9	4	7	9	14	5

SOURCE: National Hurricane Center

11. Enter the data from the table into your graphing calculator. In the STAT CALC menu, select 1-VAR STAT. Circle the graphing calculator screen that shows the statistics.

1-Var Stats
$\bar{x}$=7.266666667
Σx=109
Σx^2=947
Sx=3.326659987
σx=3.213858878
↓n=15

1-Var Stats
$\bar{x}$=8
Σx=120
Σx^2=1240
Sx=4.472135955
σx=4.320493799
↓n=15

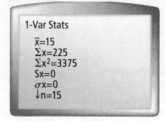

1-Var Stats
$\bar{x}$=15
Σx=225
Σx^2=3375
Sx=0
σx=0
↓n=15

12. The mean is approximately [ ] and the standard deviation is approximately [ ].

Problem 3 Using Standard Deviation to Describe Data

Got It? Meteorology Use the Atlantic Ocean hurricane data from Problem 2. Within how many standard deviations of the mean do all of the values fall?

13. Draw an ✗ for each data value from Problem 2 on the number line. The data value for year 12 has been placed for you.

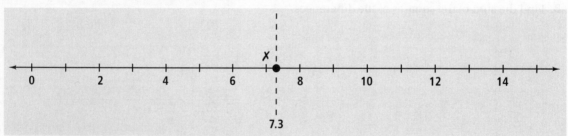

7.3

14. Use the number line in Exercise 13. The mean is drawn for you. Determine the standard deviations above and below the mean and mark them on the number line.

1 standard deviation above
mean + standard deviation

= 7.3 + 3.2 = [ ]

2 standard deviations above
mean + 2 · standard deviation

= 7.3 + 2 · [ ] = [ ]

1 standard deviation below
mean − standard deviation

= 7.3 − [ ] = [ ]

2 standard deviations below
mean − 2 · standard deviation

= 7.3 − 2 · [ ] = [ ]

15. Underline the correct numbers to complete the sentence.

All of the data values fall within 1 / 2 / 3 standard deviations of the mean.

Lesson Check • Do you UNDERSTAND?

Compare and Contrast Three data sets each have a mean of 70. Set A has a standard deviation of 10. Set B has a standard deviation of 5. Set C has a standard deviation of 20. Compare and contrast these three sets.

16. The mean is plotted on each number line below. For each data set, draw lines to show two standard deviations above and below the mean.

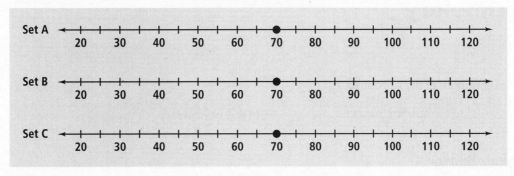

17. Write 1, 2, or 3 to put Set A, Set B, and Set C in order from most spread out to least spread out.

　　Set A　　　　　　　Set B　　　　　　　Set C

18. How are the three data sets the same?

_____

_____

19. How are the three data sets different?

_____

_____

_____

Math Success

Check off the vocabulary words that you understand.

☐ measure of variation　　　☐ variance　　　☐ standard deviation

Rate how well you can *find the standard deviation and variance of a set of data.*

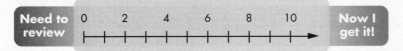

Vocabulary

● **Review**

1. Circle the definition of the word *survey*.

to examine or inspect	to rely or lean on

● **Vocabulary Builder**

bias (noun) BY us

Related Words: biased (adjective), unbiased (adjective)

Definition: Bias is an influence on someone or something in an unfair way.

Main Idea: Bias means supporting one side of an issue or a situation.

Math Usage: A **bias** is a systematic error introduced by the sampling method of a survey.

● **Use Your Vocabulary**

Complete each sentence with the correct form of the word *bias*.

   bias   unbiased   biased

2. The news report about the mayor tried to be fair and ___?___.

3. Survey questions should be free from ___?___.

4. A judge should not be ___?___ when presiding over court cases.

5. A newspaper article had the headline "Apex Company's Prices Unfair." Do you expect this article to be *biased* or *unbiased*? Explain.

Key Concepts   Sampling Types and Methods

Convenience sample	Choose any members of the population who are conveniently and readily available.
Random sample	All members of the population are equally likely to be chosen.
Self-selected sample	Choose any members of the population who volunteer for the sample.
Systematic sample	Order the population in some way, then select from it at regular intervals.

 Problem 1 Analyzing Sampling Methods

Got It? To survey the eating habits of the community, employees of a local television station interview people visiting a food court in the mall. What sampling method are they using? Does the sample have bias? Explain.

6. Circle the sampling method used.

convenience	random	self-selected	systematic

7. Does the sampling method have a bias? Explain.

_____

_____

Got It? **Reasoning** A poll of every person in a population is a *census*. What is a situation that requires a census instead of a sample?

8. Cross out the situation that does NOT require a census.

You need to know the sizes of members of the band to order uniforms.	You need to know whether students of a school prefer chicken or hamburger to plan school meals.

9. **Open-Ended** Write your own example of a situation that requires a census instead of a sample.

_____

_____

Key Concept   Study Methods

In an **observational study**, you measure or observe members of a sample in such a way that they are not affected by the study.

In a **controlled experiment**, you divide the sample into two groups. You impose a treatment on one group but not on the other "control" group. Then you compare the effect on the treated group to the control group.

In a **survey**, you ask every member of the sample a set of questions.

Lesson 11-8

A poorly designed study can result in unreliable statistics. An observational study does not influence behavior, but it is difficult to avoid experimenter bias in the collection of the data. An experiment allows for control over the factors that may impact results, but may be difficult and costly to conduct.

Problem 2 Analyzing Study Methods

Got It? A pharmaceuticals company asks for volunteers to test a new drug to treat high blood pressure. Half of the volunteers will be given the drug, and half will be given a placebo. The researcher will monitor the blood pressure of each volunteer. Which type of study method is the researcher using? Should the sample statistics be used to make a general conclusion about the effectiveness of the drug in the larger population?

12. For each situation, circle whether the group being observed is affected by the study or not affected by the study. Then tell whether it is an *observational study* (O) or a *controlled experiment* (E).

_____ A student randomly sorts 20 volunteers for a study into two groups. Over 6 weeks, one group runs on a treadmill 30 minutes each school day and the other group does not run. Each volunteer's weight is recorded each school day.

Affected
Not Affected

_____ A laboratory technician records the diameter of 3 different bacterial colonies every 4 hours for 3 days.

Affected
Not Affected

_____ A field biologist records the type and number of each bird he observes from one location, every Friday for 12 months.

Affected
Not Affected

_____ A pharmaceuticals company asks for volunteers to test a new drug to treat high blood pressure. Half of the volunteers will be given the drug, and half will be given a placebo. The researcher will monitor the blood pressure of each volunteer.

Affected
Not Affected

13. For the last scenario in Example 12, circle the factors that need to be considered to be able to make a general conclusion about the effectiveness of the drug.

| age | gender | overall health | number of study participants |

14. Suppose a study for a pharmaceutical company includes 500 participants of a variety of ages, 350 of which are female. After accounting for overall health, they find that the drug has a significant effect over 50% of the time. Should the sample statistics be used to make a general conclusion about the effectiveness of the drug in the larger population?

_____

_____

_____

_____

Problem 3 Designing a Survey

Got It? What sampling method could you use to find the percent of residents in your neighborhood who recognize the governor of your state by name? What is an example of a survey question that is likely to yield information that has no bias?

14. What kind of sampling will give the least bias? Explain.

_____

_____

_____

15. **Open-Ended** Write an example of a survey question that is likely to have no bias.

_____

_____

_____

Lesson Check • Do you UNDERSTAND?

Reasoning Would a large or small sample tend to give a better estimate of how the total population feels about a topic? Explain.

16. You want to know whether people like or dislike the new park in town. Which sample, 2 people or 200 people from the town, would give you a better idea of how the entire town feels about the new park?

_____

_____

17. Underline the correct words to complete the sentence.

A large / small sample tends to give a better estimate of how a total population feels about a topic

because that way the population is better represented / overrepresented / underrepresented .

Math Success

Check off the vocabulary words that you understand.

☐ controlled experiment ☐ study ☐ survey ☐ bias

Rate how well you can *analyze survey questions for bias.*

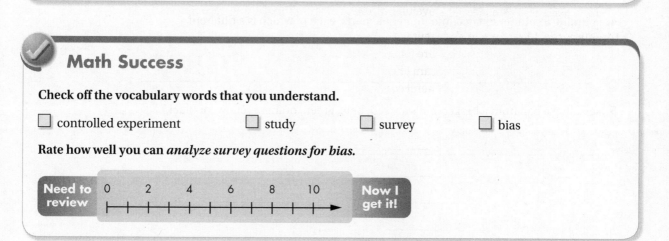

Lesson 11-8

Vocabulary

● Review

1. Circle the *binomial* expressions.

$6a$	$7x^2 + 3x$	$8x + 4y + 3$	$2y + 1$

2. Write the *binomials* that are factors of $x^2 + x - 12$.

● Vocabulary Builder

outcome (noun) OUT kum

Definition: An **outcome** is the final product or the end result.

Example: If you toss a coin, the two **outcomes** of the event are tossing heads or tails.

● Use Your Vocabulary

List the *outcomes* of each event.

3. rolling a six-sided number cube

4. spinning a spinner divided into four equal parts, each of which is a different color—red, blue, green, or purple

5. selecting a ball from a basket (balls are red, blue, green, orange, yellow, or black)

Key Concept Binomial Probability

Suppose you have n repeated independent trials, each with a probability of success p and a probability of failure q (with $p + q = 1$). Then, the **binomial probability** of x successes in n trials can be found by the following formula.

$$P(x) = {}_nC_x\,p^x q^{n-x}$$

6. Why must $p + q = 1$?

_____

_____

_____

Problem 1 Using a Formula to Find Probabilities

Got It? **Merchandising** As part of a promotion, a store is giving away scratch-off cards. Each card has a 40% chance of awarding a prize. Suppose you had five cards. What is the probability that the number of cards that reveal a prize is 0? 1? 2? 3? 5?

7. Use the information from the problem and the formula $P(x) = {}_nC_x\,p^x q^{n-x}$. Identify the value of each variable.

$n =$ ☐ $p =$ ☐ $q =$ ☐

8. If no card is a winner, the value of x is ☐.

9. Determine the probability $P(0)$.

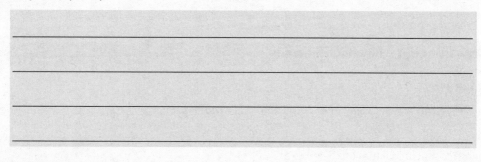

$$P(x) = {}_nC_x\,p^x q^{n-x}$$

$$P(0) = {}_5C\,\square \;\cdot\;(0.4)^{\square}\;\cdot\;\left(\square\right)^5$$

$$= 1 \cdot \square \cdot \square$$

$$= \square \;\approx\; \square$$

10. Determine each probability.

1 card

2 cards

3 cards

5 cards

Lesson 11-9

11. The probability that no card reveals a prize is [ ] %.

The probability that exactly 1 card reveals a prize is [ ] %.

The probability that exactly 2 cards reveal a prize is [ ] %.

The probability that exactly 3 cards reveal a prize is [ ] %.

The probability that exactly 5 cards reveal a prize is [ ] %.

take note

Key Concept   Binomial Theorem

For every positive integer n,

$$(a + b)^n = {}_nC_0 a^n + {}_nC_1 a^{n-1}b + {}_nC_2 a^{n-2}b^2 + \ldots + {}_nC_{n-1}ab^{n-1} + {}_nC_n b^n$$

Problem 2   Expanding Binomials

Got It? What is the binomial expansion of $(3x + y)^4$?

12. Use the Binomial Theorem. Identify each value.

$a = 3x$ $\qquad$ $b = $ [ ] $\qquad$ $n = $ [ ]

13. Expand the binomial.

$$(3x + y)^4 = {}_4C_0(3x)^4 + {}_4C_1(3x)\,\boxed{}\,y + {}_4C_2(3x)\,\boxed{}\,y^2 + {}_4C_3(3x)\,\boxed{}\,y^3 + {}_4C_4 y^4$$

$$= \boxed{} \cdot (3x)^4 + \boxed{} \cdot (3x)^3 y + \boxed{} \cdot (3x)^2 y^2 + \boxed{} \cdot (3x)y^3 + \boxed{} \cdot y^4$$

$$= 81x^4 + \boxed{}\,x^3 y + \boxed{}\,x^2 y^2 + \boxed{}\,xy^3 + y^4$$

Problem 3   Applying Binomial Probability

Got It? A multiple choice quiz has five questions. Each question has four answer choices. If you guess every answer, what is the probability of getting at least three correct?

14. Each question has four answer choices. The probability of guessing an answer correctly is $p = $ [ ].

15. The probability of guessing an answer incorrectly is $q = $ [ ].

16. Circle the value of n, the number of questions on the test.

1	2	3	4	5

17. Circle the statement that corresponds to the phrase "getting at least three correct."

answering 4 or 5 correctly	answering 3, 4, or 5 correctly
answering only 3 correctly	

18. Evaluate the binomial probabilities.

Relate | probability of getting at least 3 correct | is | probability of getting 3 correct | plus | probability of getting 4 correct | plus | probability of getting 5 correct

Write P(at least 3 correct) $= {}_5C_3\left(\right)^2\left(\right)^3 + {}_5C_4\left(\right)\left(\right)^4 + \left(\right)^5$

$= + + $

$= $

19. The probability of getting at least three questions correct by guessing is about %.

Lesson Check • Do you UNDERSTAND?

Vocabulary Explain how flipping a coin 10 times meets all of the conditions for a binomial experiment.

20. Circle the two true statements about 10 coin tosses.

> Each toss has two possible outcomes.
>
> Every toss has equal probability of success.
>
> In 10 tosses, 5 outcomes will be heads and 5 will be tails.
>
> The probability of the outcome tails increases as the number of tosses increases.

21. Underline the correct words to complete the sentence.

In a binomial experiment, each trial must have 1 / 2 / *n* possible outcomes, and

the probability of a success must be constant / varying throughout the trials.

Math Success

Check off the vocabulary words that you understand.

☐ binomial experiment   ☐ binomial probability   ☐ Binomial Theorem

Rate how well you can *find binomial probabilities.*

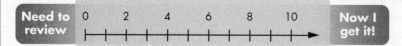

Vocabulary

● **Review**

1. Cross out the phrase that is NOT the definition of *distribute*.

to collect or gather   to give or hand out

● **Vocabulary Builder**

discrete (noun) **dih SKREET**

Related Word: continuous (adjective)

Definition: Something that is **discrete** is separate or distinct from something else.

Example: Roll a number cube once. There are six **discrete** outcomes for this experiment: 1, 2, 3, 4, 5, 6.

Non-example: A person's body temperature is *not* **discrete.** It can take on any value in a certain interval.

● **Use Your Vocabulary**

Write D if the experiment has *discrete* outcomes. Write N if it does *not* have *discrete* outcomes.

_____ **2.** Toss a coin once.

_____ **3.** Weigh a package.

_____ **4.** Count the number of pages in a newspaper.

_____ **5.** Count the number of miles a person jogs.

_____ **6.** Pick a number from 1 to 1000.

_____ **7.** Find the grams of sugar in an apple.

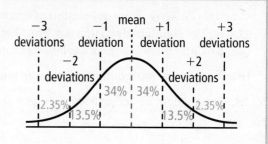

Key Concept Normal Distribution

In a normal distribution,

- 68% of data fall within one standard deviation.

- 95% of data fall within two standard deviations.

- 99.7% of data fall within three standard deviations.

A normal distribution has a symmetric bell shape centered on the mean.

8. If babies' weights are normally distributed around a mean weight, ___ % of the

weights should fall within one standard deviation *above* the mean.

Problem 1 Analyzing Normally Distributed Data

Got It? Zoology The bar graph gives the weights of a population of female brown bears. The red curve shows how the weights are normally distributed about the mean, 115 kg. Approximately what percent of female brown bears weigh less than 120 kg?

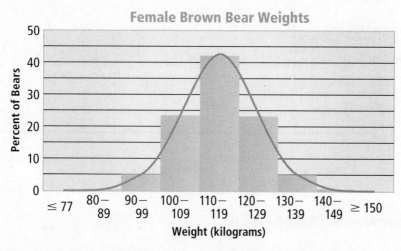

Female Brown Bear Weights

9. Circle all intervals on the graph above that are less than 120 kg.

10. Estimate the percent for each interval.

11. Add the percents.

12. About ___ % of the female brown bears weigh less than 120 kg.

Lesson 11-10

Got It? Zoology For a population of female European eels, the mean body length is
21.1 in. The standard deviation is 4.7 in. Sketch a normal curve showing eel lengths at
one, two, and three standard deviations from the mean.

Use the information from the problem to find each length.

13. one standard deviation from the mean

mean − 1 deviation = 21.1 − [____] = [____]   mean + 1 deviation = 21.1 + [____] = [____]

14. two standard deviations from the mean

mean − 2 deviations = 21.1 − 2 [____] = [____]   mean + 2 deviations = 21.1 + 2 [____] = [____]

15. three standard deviations from the mean

mean − 3 deviations = [_____]

mean + 3 deviations = [_____]

16. Sketch a normal curve
showing the eel lengths
at one, two, and three
standard deviations.

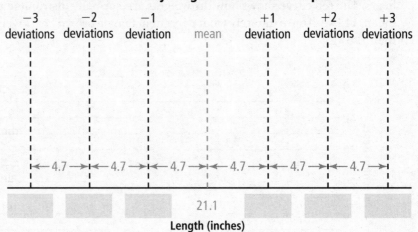

Distribution of Body Lengths for Female European Eels

Length (inches)

 Problem 3 Analyzing a Normal Distribution

Got It? The scores on the Algebra 2 final are approximately normally distributed
with a mean of 150 and a standard deviation of 15. What percentage of the students
who took the test scored above 180?

Use the normal curve at the right for Exercises 17–19.

17. Use the information from the
problem to label the mean and
the standard deviations.

18. Label each standard deviation
section with its percentage.

19. Shade the portion of the
graph that corresponds to
the percentage of students
with scores above 180.

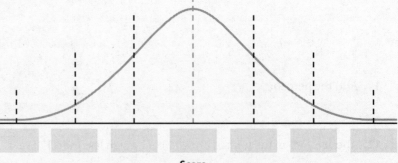

Score

20. About _____ % of the students who took the test scored above 180.

Reasoning What is the effect on a normal distribution if the mean increases by 10? If the standard deviation increases by 10?

Use the following statement for Exercises 21 and 22. Write T for *true* or F for *false*.

A population is normally distributed with a mean of 34 and a standard deviation of 6.

21. Suppose the mean increases by 10.

_____ The new mean is 44.

_____ The new standard deviation is 16.

_____ Each interval shifts 10 units to the right.

22. Suppose the standard deviation increases by 10.

_____ The new mean is 44.

_____ The new standard deviation is 16.

_____ The width of each interval increases to 16.

Underline the correct word or number to complete each sentence about a normal distribution.

23. If the mean increases by 10, the bell curve shifts 10 units to the right / left .

24. If the mean increases by 10, each standard deviation shifts 10 units to the right / left .

25. If the standard deviation increases by 10, each interval becomes narrower / wider by 10 units.

Math Success

Check off the vocabulary words that you understand.

☐ discrete ☐ continuous ☐ normal distribution

Rate how well you can *solve problems involving the normal distribution.*

| Need to review | 0 | 2 | 4 | 6 | 8 | 10 | Now I get it! |

12-1 Adding and Subtracting Matrices

Vocabulary

● Review

1. Circle the words whose meaning is similar to that of *corresponding*.

different	equivalent	intersecting
matching	related	similar

● Vocabulary Builder

matrix (noun) MAY triks

Related Word: matrices (plural)

Definition: A **matrix** is a rectangular array of numbers written within brackets. A **matrix** with m horizontal rows and n vertical columns is an $m \times n$ **matrix**.

a 2 x 3 **matrix**

$$\begin{bmatrix} -5 & 3 & 1 \\ 7 & 12 & -4 \end{bmatrix}$$

● Use Your Vocabulary

Write T for *true* or F for *false*.

_____ **2.** The *matrix* $\begin{bmatrix} 4 & -2 \\ 0 & 7 \end{bmatrix}$ has two horizontal rows and two vertical columns.

_____ **3.** The *matrix* $\begin{bmatrix} 25 & 3 \\ -2 & -18 \\ 4 & 13 \end{bmatrix}$ is a 3 × 2 *matrix*.

4. Write an example of a 4 × 3 *matrix*.

5. Write an example of a *matrix* with one column.

Key Concept   Matrix Addition and Subtraction

To add matrices A and B with the same dimensions, add *corresponding* elements. Similarly, to subtract matrices A and B with the same dimensions, subtract *corresponding* elements. *Corresponding* elements are elements in the same position in each matrix.

$$A = \begin{bmatrix} a_{11} & a_{12} \\ a_{21} & a_{22} \end{bmatrix} \qquad\qquad B = \begin{bmatrix} b_{11} & b_{12} \\ b_{21} & b_{22} \end{bmatrix}$$

$$A + B = \begin{bmatrix} a_{11} + b_{11} & a_{12} + b_{12} \\ a_{21} + b_{21} & a_{22} + b_{22} \end{bmatrix} \qquad A - B = \begin{bmatrix} a_{11} - b_{11} & a_{12} - b_{12} \\ a_{21} - b_{21} & a_{22} - b_{22} \end{bmatrix}$$

Problem 1   Adding and Subtracting Matrices

Got It? Given $A = \begin{bmatrix} -12 & 24 \\ -3 & 5 \\ -1 & 10 \end{bmatrix}$ and $B = \begin{bmatrix} -3 & 1 \\ 2 & -4 \\ -1 & 5 \end{bmatrix}$, what is $A + B$?

6. Use the justifications at the right to add the matrices.

$$A + B = \begin{bmatrix} -12 & \\ & \\ & \end{bmatrix} + \begin{bmatrix} & \\ & \\ & \end{bmatrix}$$ Write the original matrices.

$$= \begin{bmatrix} -12 + (-3) & 24 + \\ -3 + & 5 + \left(\right) \\ & \end{bmatrix}$$ Add corresponding elements.

$$= \begin{bmatrix} -15 & \\ & \\ & \end{bmatrix}$$ Simplify.

Problem 2   Solving a Matrix Equation

Got It? If $B = \begin{bmatrix} 1 & 6 & -1 \\ 2 & 6 & 1 \\ -1 & -2 & 4 \end{bmatrix}$, $C = \begin{bmatrix} 2 & 0 & 0 \\ -1 & -3 & 6 \\ 2 & 3 & -1 \end{bmatrix}$, and $A - B = C$, what is A?

7. To solve the equation $A - B = C$ for A, you add B to / subtract B from both sides of the equation.

8. Solve the equation $A - B = C$ for A. Write your answer below.

$A = $

Lesson 12-1

9. Use your answer from Exercise 8 and the values of B and C to find matrix A.

For $m \times n$ matrices, the additive identity matrix is the zero matrix, O, with all elements zero. The *opposite*, or *additive inverse*, of an $m \times n$ matrix A is $-A$, where each element is the opposite of the corresponding element of A.

 Problem 3 **Using Identity and Opposite Matrices**

Got It? What is the sum $\begin{bmatrix} 14 & 5 \\ 0 & -2 \end{bmatrix} + \begin{bmatrix} -14 & -5 \\ 0 & 2 \end{bmatrix}$?

10. Multiple Choice Which matrix is equal to $\begin{bmatrix} 14 & 5 \\ 0 & -2 \end{bmatrix} + \begin{bmatrix} -14 & -5 \\ 0 & 2 \end{bmatrix}$?

Ⓐ $\begin{bmatrix} 14 & 5 \\ 0 & -2 \end{bmatrix}$ Ⓑ $\begin{bmatrix} 28 & 10 \\ 0 & -4 \end{bmatrix}$ Ⓒ $\begin{bmatrix} 1 & 0 \\ 0 & 1 \end{bmatrix}$ Ⓓ $\begin{bmatrix} 0 & 0 \\ 0 & 0 \end{bmatrix}$

Got It? What is the sum $\begin{bmatrix} 0 & 0 & 0 \\ 0 & 0 & 0 \end{bmatrix} + \begin{bmatrix} -1 & 10 & -5 \\ 0 & 2 & -3 \end{bmatrix}$?

11. The matrix $\begin{bmatrix} 0 & 0 & 0 \\ 0 & 0 & 0 \end{bmatrix}$ is the additive inverse / zero matrix.

12. The sum of the two matrices is $\begin{bmatrix} \end{bmatrix}$.

 Problem 4 **Finding Unknown Matrix Values**

Got It? What values of x and y make the following equation true?

$$\begin{bmatrix} x + 3 & -2 \\ y - 1 & x + 1 \end{bmatrix} = \begin{bmatrix} 9 & -2 \\ 2y + 5 & 7 \end{bmatrix}$$

13. Equal matrices have the same / different dimensions and equal / unequal corresponding elements.

14. Explain how you can solve for the values of x and y.

_____

_____

15. Complete the steps to solve for y.

$$2y + 5 = y - 1$$ Corresponding elements are equal.

$$2y - \boxed{} = -1 - \boxed{}$$ Group like terms on the same side.

$$y = \boxed{}$$ Simplify.

16. Solve for x.

17. The values of x and y that make the equation true are $x = \boxed{}$ and $y = \boxed{}$.

Lesson Check • Do you UNDERSTAND?

Vocabulary Are the two matrices equal? Explain.

$$\begin{bmatrix} \frac{1}{2} & \frac{3}{8} \\ 0.2 & \sqrt[3]{27} \end{bmatrix} \text{ and } \begin{bmatrix} 0.5 & 0.375 \\ \frac{1}{5} & 3 \end{bmatrix}$$

18. Circle the items that you must check to be sure the two matrices are equal.

corresponding elements	additive inverses
number of columns	number of rows

19. Are the two matrices equal? Explain how you know.

Math Success

Check off the vocabulary words that you understand.

☐ matrix   ☐ corresponding elements   ☐ matrix equation   ☐ zero matrix

Rate how well you can *add and subtract matrices and solve matrix equations.*

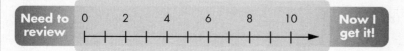

Need to review   0   2   4   6   8   10   Now I get it!

Lesson 12-1

12-2 Matrix Multiplication

Vocabulary

● Review

1. Circle the expression that does NOT show *multiplication*.

$4 \cdot 8$ $12 + 5$ $18(20)$ 9×9

2. *Multiplication* can be thought of as repeated addition / division or the inverse of addition / division .

● Vocabulary Builder

scalar (noun, adjective) SKAY lur

Math Usage: **Scalar** multiplication is an operation that multiplies a matrix A by a scalar c.

Example: The **scalar** in the multiplication $4\begin{bmatrix} -1 & 2 \\ -3 & 7 \end{bmatrix}$ is the real number factor 4.

● Use Your Vocabulary

Circle the *scalar* in each multiplication.

3. $6\begin{bmatrix} 1 & -2 \\ 0 & 3 \end{bmatrix}$ **4.** $\dfrac{1}{2}\begin{bmatrix} 0 & 3 \\ 6 & 8 \end{bmatrix}$ **5.** $-2\begin{bmatrix} 7 & -3 \\ 2 & 9 \end{bmatrix}$

take note

Key Concept Scalar Multiplication

To multiply a matrix by a **scalar** c, multiply each element of the matrix by c.

$$A = \begin{bmatrix} a_{11} & a_{12} & a_{13} \\ a_{21} & a_{22} & a_{23} \end{bmatrix} \qquad cA = \begin{bmatrix} ca_{11} & ca_{12} & ca_{13} \\ ca_{21} & ca_{22} & ca_{23} \end{bmatrix}$$

6. Complete the scalar multiplication.

$$3\begin{bmatrix} 8 & a & 12 \\ b & -20 & c \end{bmatrix} = \begin{bmatrix} 24 & (a) & \\ & & \end{bmatrix}$$

Problem 1 Using Scalar Products

Got It? If $A = \begin{bmatrix} 2 & 8 & -3 \\ -1 & 5 & 2 \end{bmatrix}$ and $B = \begin{bmatrix} -1 & 0 & 5 \\ 0 & 3 & -2 \end{bmatrix}$, what is $3A - 2B$?

7. First, multiply each matrix by its scalar.

$3A = 3\begin{bmatrix} 2 & 8 & -3 \\ -1 & 5 & 2 \end{bmatrix}$ $\qquad$ $2B = 2\begin{bmatrix} -1 & 0 & 5 \\ 0 & 3 & -2 \end{bmatrix}$

$= \begin{bmatrix} & & \\ & & \end{bmatrix}$ $\qquad$ $= \begin{bmatrix} & & \\ & & \end{bmatrix}$

8. Then, subtract the resulting matrices.

$3A - 2B = \begin{bmatrix} - & - & - \\ - & - & - \end{bmatrix} = \begin{bmatrix} & & \\ & & \end{bmatrix}$

Problem 2 Solving a Matrix Equation With Scalars

Got It? What is the solution of $3X - 2\begin{bmatrix} -1 & 5 \\ 7 & 0 \end{bmatrix} = \begin{bmatrix} 17 & -13 \\ -7 & 0 \end{bmatrix}$?

9. To isolate $3X$, would you first subtract $\begin{bmatrix} -1 & 5 \\ 7 & 0 \end{bmatrix}$ from each side of the equation? Explain why or why not.

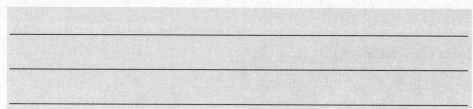

10. Complete the steps to solve for X.

$3X - 2\begin{bmatrix} -1 & 5 \\ 7 & 0 \end{bmatrix} = \begin{bmatrix} 17 & -13 \\ -7 & 0 \end{bmatrix}$ $\qquad$ Write the original equation.

$3X - \begin{bmatrix} & \\ & 0 \end{bmatrix} = \begin{bmatrix} 17 & -13 \\ -7 & 0 \end{bmatrix}$ $\qquad$ Multiply by the scalar 2.

$3X = \begin{bmatrix} & \\ & \end{bmatrix}$ $\qquad$ Add the same matrix to both sides.

$X = \begin{bmatrix} & \\ & 0 \end{bmatrix}$ $\qquad$ Divide each side by 3 and simplify.

Lesson 12-2

Key Concept Matrix Multiplication

To find element c_{ij} of the product matrix AB, multiply each element of the ith row of A by the corresponding element in the jth column of B. Then add the products.

$$AB = \begin{bmatrix} a_{11} & a_{12} \\ a_{21} & a_{22} \end{bmatrix} \begin{bmatrix} b_{11} & b_{12} \\ b_{21} & b_{22} \end{bmatrix} = \begin{bmatrix} a_{11}b_{11} + a_{12}b_{21} & a_{11}b_{12} + a_{12}b_{22} \\ a_{21}b_{11} + a_{22}b_{21} & a_{21}b_{12} + a_{22}b_{22} \end{bmatrix}$$

Problem 4 Applying Matrix Multiplication

Got It? There are three ways to score in a basketball game: three-point field goals, two-point field goals, and one-point free throws. In 1994, suppose a high school player scored 36 two-point field goals and 28 free throws. In 2006, suppose a high school player scored 7 three-point field goals, 21 two-point field goals, and 18 free throws. Using matrix multiplication, how many points did each player score?

11. Complete the steps to find how many points each player scored.

1 Enter the information into matrices. Let S be the matrix for the two players. Let P be the matrix for the points.

$$S = \begin{bmatrix} 0 & 36 & 28 \\ \boxed{} & \boxed{} & \boxed{} \end{bmatrix} \qquad P = \begin{bmatrix} 3 \\ 2 \\ \boxed{} \end{bmatrix}$$

2 Multiply the matrices to find the product matrix SP.

$$SP = \begin{bmatrix} (0 \cdot 3) + (36 \cdot 2) + \left(28 \cdot \boxed{}\right) \\ \left(\boxed{} \cdot 3\right) + \left(\boxed{} \cdot 2\right) + \left(\boxed{} \cdot 1\right) \end{bmatrix} = \begin{bmatrix} 100 \\ \boxed{} \end{bmatrix}$$

3 Interpret the product matrix SP.

The player in 1994 scored _____ points.

The player in 2006 scored _____ points.

Property Dimensions of a Product Matrix

If A is an $m \times n$ matrix and B is an $n \times p$ matrix, then the product matrix AB is an $m \times p$ matrix.

Product matrix AB is a 3×4 matrix.

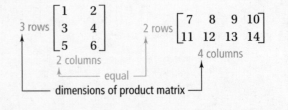

Problem 5 Determining Whether Product Matrices Exist

Got It? If $A = \begin{bmatrix} 1 & 4 \\ -3 & 5 \end{bmatrix}$ and $B = [-1 \quad 1]$, does the product AB exist?

12. Write the dimensions of each matrix.

$A = 2 \times \boxed{}$ $\qquad\qquad$ $B = 1 \times \boxed{}$

Underline the correct word(s) to complete each sentence.

13. For the product AB to exist, the number of columns / rows in A must equal the number of columns / rows in B.

14. The product AB exists / does not exist .

Lesson Check • **Do you UNDERSTAND?**

Error Analysis Your friend says there is a right order and a wrong order when multiplying A (a 2 × 4 matrix) and B (a 3 × 6 matrix). Explain your friend's error.

Underline the correct numbers to complete each sentence.

15. There are 2 / 3 / 4 / 6 columns in A and 2 / 3 / 4 / 6 rows in B.

The matrix product AB exists / does not exist .

16. There are 2 / 3 / 4 / 6 columns in B and 2 / 3 / 4 / 6 rows in A.

The matrix product BA exists / does not exist .

17. Explain your friend's error.

_____

_____

_____

Math Success

Check off the vocabulary words that you understand.

☐ scalar $\qquad\qquad$ ☐ scalar multiplication $\qquad\qquad$ ☐ matrix multiplication

Rate how well you can *multiply matrices*.

Need to review $\quad$ 0 $\quad$ 2 $\quad$ 4 $\quad$ 6 $\quad$ 8 $\quad$ 10 $\quad$ Now I get it!

Vocabulary

● Review

1. Circle the multiplicative *inverse* of −6.

$$6 \qquad \frac{1}{6} \qquad -\frac{1}{6} \qquad -6$$

2. Show how you know that 4 and −4 are additive *inverses.*

3. Write the additive *inverse* of each number.

13   0.2 $\frac{1}{6}$ −10

● Vocabulary Builder

determinant (noun) **dee TUR mih nunt**

Definition: A **determinant** is a number associated with a square matrix having real-number elements. For a matrix A, the **determinant** of A is written as det A.

What It Means: You find the value of the **determinant** of a 2 × 2 matrix by finding the difference of the products of the two diagonals of the matrix.

> **determinant** of a 2 x 2 matrix
>
> $$A = \begin{bmatrix} a & b \\ c & d \end{bmatrix}$$
>
> det $A = ad - bc$

● Use Your Vocabulary

Write T for *true* or F for *false.*

4. You can find the *determinant* of a 4 × 7 matrix.

5. You find the *determinant* of a 2 × 2 matrix by subtracting the products of the two diagonals.

6. The matrix $F = \begin{bmatrix} 4 & -2 & 0 & 5 \\ 7 & 4 & -1 & 3 \end{bmatrix}$ does not have a *determinant.*

Key Concepts   Identity and Multiplicative Inverse Matrices

For an $n \times n$ matrix, the **multiplicative identity matrix** is an $n \times n$ matrix I, or I_n, with 1's along the main diagonal and 0's elsewhere.

$$I_2 = \begin{bmatrix} 1 & 0 \\ 0 & 1 \end{bmatrix}, I_3 = \begin{bmatrix} 1 & 0 & 0 \\ 0 & 1 & 0 \\ 0 & 0 & 1 \end{bmatrix}, \text{ and so forth.}$$

If A and B are square matrices and $AB = BA = I$, then B is the **multiplicative inverse matrix** of A, written A^{-1}.

Problem 1   Determining Whether Matrices Are Inverses

Got It? Are $A = \begin{bmatrix} 1 & 1 \\ 5 & 4 \end{bmatrix}$ and $B = \begin{bmatrix} -4 & 1 \\ 5 & -1 \end{bmatrix}$ inverses?

7. Find each product.

$AB =$

$BA =$

8. Matrices A and B are / are not inverses.

Key Concept   Area of a Triangle

The area of a triangle with vertices (x_1, y_1), (x_2, y_2), and (x_3, y_3) is

$$\text{Area} = \tfrac{1}{2} \left| \det A \right|, \text{ where } A = \begin{bmatrix} x_1 & y_1 & 1 \\ x_2 & y_2 & 1 \\ x_3 & y_3 & 1 \end{bmatrix}$$

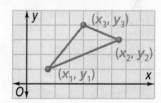

Problem 3   Finding the Area of a Polygon

Got It? What is the area of the triangle with vertices $(1, 3)$, $(-3, 0)$, and $(5, 0)$?

9. Write the vertices of the triangle in matrix form.

$$A = \begin{bmatrix} 1 & & \\ & & \\ & & \end{bmatrix}$$

10. Use your graphing calculator to find $\tfrac{1}{2} \left| \det A \right|$.

$\det A =$ ____, so $\tfrac{1}{2} \left| \det A \right| =$ ____

11. The area of the triangle is ____ units^2.

Lesson 12-3

Key Concept   Inverse of a 2 × 2 Matrix

Let $A = \begin{bmatrix} a & b \\ c & d \end{bmatrix}$.

If det $A = 0$, then A is a **singular matrix** and has no inverse.

If det $A \neq 0$, then the inverse of A, written A^{-1}, is

$$A^{-1} = \frac{1}{\det A}\begin{bmatrix} d & -b \\ -c & a \end{bmatrix} = \frac{1}{ad - bc}\begin{bmatrix} d & -b \\ -c & a \end{bmatrix}.$$

Problem 5   Encoding and Decoding With Matrices

Got It? How can you use matrix multiplication and the coding matrix $\begin{bmatrix} 4 & 8 \\ -2 & 4 \end{bmatrix}$ to encode the credit card account number from this credit card?

12. Complete the steps below.

1 Write the coding matrix. $C = \begin{bmatrix} \ \ \end{bmatrix}$

2 Write the credit card numbers in an information matrix with two equal rows.

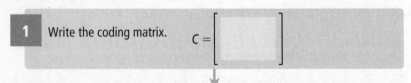

3 Multiply the coding matrix C by the information matrix A.

4 Write the coded account number.

Got It? How can you use the inverse of the coding matrix to recover the credit card number?

13. Find the determinant of $C = \begin{bmatrix} 4 & 8 \\ -2 & 4 \end{bmatrix}$.

det $C = ad - bc = \left(4 \cdot \boxed{}\right) - \left(\boxed{} \cdot 8\right) = \boxed{}$

14. Since det $C \neq 0$, matrix C has an inverse. Complete the steps to find C^{-1}.

$$C^{-1} = \frac{1}{\det C}\begin{bmatrix} d & -b \\ -c & a \end{bmatrix} = \frac{1}{\square}\begin{bmatrix} 4 & \square \\ \square & \square \end{bmatrix}$$

$$= \begin{bmatrix} \frac{4}{32} & \square \\ \square & \square \end{bmatrix} = \begin{bmatrix} \frac{1}{8} & \square \\ \square & \square \end{bmatrix}$$

15. Use your graphing calculator to find the product $C^{-1}CA$. Describe the product.

16. Explain how you can use the inverse matrix C^{-1} to recover the credit card number.

Lesson Check • Do you UNDERSTAND?

Error Analysis What mistake did the student make when finding the determinant of $\begin{bmatrix} 2 & 5 \\ -3 & 1 \end{bmatrix}$?

$$\det\begin{bmatrix} 2 & 5 \\ -3 & 1 \end{bmatrix} = (2)(1) + (-3)(5) = 2 - 15 = -13$$

17. Find the determinant of $\begin{bmatrix} 2 & 5 \\ -3 & 1 \end{bmatrix}$.

18. Explain the student's error.

Math Success

Check off the vocabulary words that you understand.

☐ multiplicative identity matrix   ☐ multiplicative inverse matrix   ☐ determinant

Rate how well you can *find the determinant of a square matrix*.

Need to review   0   2   4   6   8   10   Now I get it!

Lesson 12-3

12-4 Inverse Matrices and Systems

Vocabulary

Review

1. Cross out the expression that does NOT contain a *variable*.

$$4y \qquad w + 7 \qquad \frac{2a}{3} \qquad 121 \div 11$$

2. Circle the *variable(s)* in each expression.

$$8 - t \qquad 9(a + 2b) \qquad w + 2y + z \qquad \frac{y^2 + 2y + 1}{y - 3}$$

Vocabulary Builder

matrix equation (noun) MAY triks ee KWAY zhun

Definition: A **matrix equation** is an equation that contains a variable matrix.

Math Usage: You can use the **matrix equation** $AX = B$ to solve a system of equations. The system of equations $\begin{cases} 3x + 4y = 11 \\ 2x - 3y = 12 \end{cases}$ becomes the matrix equation $\begin{bmatrix} 3 & 4 \\ 2 & -3 \end{bmatrix}\begin{bmatrix} x \\ y \end{bmatrix} = \begin{bmatrix} 11 \\ 12 \end{bmatrix}$.

Examples: If $\begin{bmatrix} 4 & 2 \\ 5 & 8 \end{bmatrix} + X = \begin{bmatrix} 5 & 3 \\ 6 & 10 \end{bmatrix}$, then $X = \begin{bmatrix} 1 & 1 \\ 1 & 2 \end{bmatrix}$.

If $\begin{bmatrix} 1 & 2 \\ 3 & 4 \end{bmatrix} W = \begin{bmatrix} -4 \\ -6 \end{bmatrix}$, then $W = \begin{bmatrix} 2 \\ -3 \end{bmatrix}$.

Use Your Vocabulary

Circle the variable matrix in each *matrix equation*.

3. $\begin{bmatrix} 5 & -1 \\ 2 & -1 \end{bmatrix}\begin{bmatrix} x \\ y \end{bmatrix} = \begin{bmatrix} 8 \\ 5 \end{bmatrix}$

4. $\begin{bmatrix} 1 & -2 & 3 \\ -1 & 3 & 1 \\ 2 & 5 & 8 \end{bmatrix}\begin{bmatrix} x \\ y \\ z \end{bmatrix} = \begin{bmatrix} 12 \\ -4 \\ 8 \end{bmatrix}$

5. $\begin{bmatrix} 3 & 6 \\ 2 & 1 \end{bmatrix} X = \begin{bmatrix} 9 \\ 3 \end{bmatrix}$

 **Problem 1** Solving Matrix Equations Using an Inverse Matrix

Got It? What is the solution of the matrix equation $\begin{bmatrix} 4 & 3 \\ 2 & 2 \end{bmatrix} X = \begin{bmatrix} -5 \\ 2 \end{bmatrix}$?

6. Circle the inverse of $\begin{bmatrix} 4 & 3 \\ 2 & 2 \end{bmatrix}$.

$$\begin{bmatrix} 4 & 3 \\ 2 & 2 \end{bmatrix} \qquad \begin{bmatrix} 2 & -3 \\ -2 & 4 \end{bmatrix} \qquad \begin{bmatrix} 1 & -\frac{3}{2} \\ -1 & 2 \end{bmatrix} \qquad \frac{1}{4(2) - 3(2)}$$

7. Use the justifications at the right to solve the matrix equation.

$$\begin{bmatrix} 4 & 3 \\ 2 & 2 \end{bmatrix} X = \begin{bmatrix} -5 \\ 2 \end{bmatrix}$$ Write the original equation.

$$\begin{bmatrix} \square & \square \\ \square & \square \end{bmatrix}\begin{bmatrix} 4 & 3 \\ 2 & 2 \end{bmatrix} X = \begin{bmatrix} \square & \square \\ \square & \square \end{bmatrix}\begin{bmatrix} -5 \\ 2 \end{bmatrix}$$ Multiply each side by the inverse matrix.

$$\begin{bmatrix} 1 & 0 \\ 0 & 1 \end{bmatrix} X = \begin{bmatrix} (\square)(\square) + (\square)(\square) \\ (\square)(\square) + (\square)(\square) \end{bmatrix}$$ Multiply.

$$X = \begin{bmatrix} \square \\ \square \end{bmatrix}$$ Simplify.

 Problem 2 Writing a System as a Matrix Equation

Got It? What is the matrix equation that corresponds to the system $\begin{cases} 3x - 7y = 8 \\ 5x + y = -2 \end{cases}$?

8. Draw a line from each type of matrix in Column A to a corresponding matrix in Column B.

Column A

coefficient matrix, A

variable matrix, X

constant matrix, B

Column B

$$\begin{bmatrix} 8 \\ -2 \end{bmatrix}$$

$$\begin{bmatrix} 3 & -7 \\ 5 & 1 \end{bmatrix}$$

$$\begin{bmatrix} x \\ y \end{bmatrix}$$

9. Write the matrix equation $AX = B$.

Lesson 12-4

Problem 3 Solving a System of Two Equations

Got It? What is the solution of the system of equations $\begin{cases} 9x + 2y = 3 \\ 3x + y = -6 \end{cases}$?
Solve using matrices.

10. Circle the expression you can use to determine A^{-1}.

$$\frac{1}{(9)(3) - (1)(2)}\begin{bmatrix} 1 & -2 \\ -3 & 9 \end{bmatrix} \qquad \frac{1}{(9)(1) - (3)(2)}\begin{bmatrix} 1 & -2 \\ -3 & 9 \end{bmatrix} \qquad \frac{1}{(9)(1) - (3)(2)}\begin{bmatrix} 9 & 2 \\ 3 & 1 \end{bmatrix}$$

11. Complete the reasoning model at the right.

Think	Write
Write the system as a matrix equation.	$\begin{bmatrix} 9 & 2 \\ 3 & 1 \end{bmatrix}\begin{bmatrix} x \\ y \end{bmatrix} = \begin{bmatrix} \\ \end{bmatrix}$
Determine A^{-1}.	$A^{-1} = \dfrac{1}{}\begin{bmatrix} 1 & -2 \\ -3 & 9 \end{bmatrix} = \begin{bmatrix} & \\ & \end{bmatrix}$
Multiply each side of the matrix equation by A^{-1} on the left.	$\begin{bmatrix} & \\ & \end{bmatrix}\begin{bmatrix} 9 & 2 \\ 3 & 1 \end{bmatrix}\begin{bmatrix} x \\ y \end{bmatrix} = \begin{bmatrix} & \\ & \end{bmatrix}\begin{bmatrix} \\ \end{bmatrix}$
Solve for $\begin{bmatrix} x \\ y \end{bmatrix}$.	$\begin{bmatrix} 1 & 0 \\ 0 & 1 \end{bmatrix}\begin{bmatrix} x \\ y \end{bmatrix} = \begin{bmatrix} \\ \end{bmatrix}$ $\begin{bmatrix} x \\ y \end{bmatrix} = \begin{bmatrix} \\ \end{bmatrix}$

12. The solution is $x = \boxed{}$ and $y = \boxed{}$.

 Problem 4 Solving a System of Three Equations

Got It? Your friend plans to exercise for 40 min every other day. She wants to burn 460 calories during each session. If she only runs and jogs, how many minutes of each exercise type should she do?

Calories Burned

Running (8 mi/h)	Jogging (5 mi/h)	Walking (3.5 mi/h)
12.5 cal/min	7.5 cal/min	3.5 cal/min

13. Define the variables.

Let x = minutes spent exercising by running.

Let y = minutes spent exercising by running / jogging .

Let z = minutes spent exercising by walking / running .

14. Write a system of equations to solve the problem.

$$\begin{cases} 12.5x + \boxed{}y + \boxed{}z = \boxed{} \\ x + \boxed{}y + z = \boxed{} \\ z = \boxed{} \end{cases}$$

15. Write the system as a matrix equation.

$$\begin{bmatrix} 12.5 & \boxed{} & \boxed{} \\ 1 & \boxed{} & \boxed{} \\ \boxed{} & \boxed{} & \boxed{} \end{bmatrix} \begin{bmatrix} x \\ y \\ z \end{bmatrix} = \begin{bmatrix} \boxed{} \\ \boxed{} \\ \boxed{} \end{bmatrix}$$

16. Use your graphing calculator to solve for the variable matrix.

$$\begin{bmatrix} x \\ y \\ z \end{bmatrix} = \begin{bmatrix} \boxed{} \\ \boxed{} \\ \boxed{} \end{bmatrix}$$

17. Your friend should run for $\boxed{}$ min, jog for $\boxed{}$ min, and walk for $\boxed{}$ min.

Lesson Check • Do you UNDERSTAND?

Reasoning Explain how to write the matrix equation $\begin{bmatrix} -2 & 3 \\ 4 & 1 \end{bmatrix}\begin{bmatrix} p \\ q \end{bmatrix} = \begin{bmatrix} 2 \\ -5 \end{bmatrix}$ as a system of linear equations.

18. Circle the system of equations that corresponds to the matrix equation.

$$\begin{cases} 3p - 2q = 2 \\ 4p + q = -5 \end{cases} \qquad \begin{cases} 3p - 2q = 2 \\ p + 4q = -5 \end{cases} \qquad \begin{cases} -2p + 3q = 2 \\ 4p + q = -5 \end{cases}$$

19. Explain how the system of equations you circled can be derived from the matrix equation.

_____

_____

_____

Math Success

Check off the vocabulary words that you understand.

☐ coefficient matrix   ☐ variable matrix   ☐ constant matrix   ☐ matrix equation

Rate how well you can *solve systems of equations using inverse matrices.*

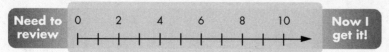

Lesson 12-4

Geometric Transformations

Vocabulary

● Review

1. Draw a line from each *transformation* in Column A to its description in Column B.

Column A	Column B
dilation	moving a figure by turning it around a fixed point
rotation	moving a figure by sliding it
reflection	enlarging or reducing a figure
translation	moving a figure by flipping it

● Vocabulary Builder

image (noun) **IM ij**

Related Word: preimage (noun)

Definition: An **image** is a figure obtained by a *transformation* of the original image, called the *preimage*.

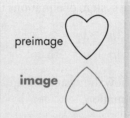

preimage

image

● Use Your Vocabulary

Circle the *image* after a rotation of 90° clockwise.

2.

3.

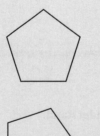

4.

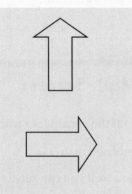

Problem 1 Translating a Figure

Got It? **Reasoning** How would you translate the kite image $A'B'C'D'$ back to the kite preimage $ABCD$?

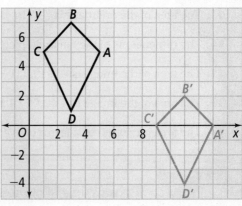

5. Each matrix represents one of the kites. Each column represents the coordinates of a vertex. Circle the matrix that represents the vertices of the kite image $A'B'C'D'$. Underline the matrix that represents the vertices of the kite preimage $ABCD$.

$$\begin{bmatrix} 13 & 11 & 9 & 11 \\ 0 & 2 & 0 & -4 \end{bmatrix} \begin{matrix} \longleftarrow x\text{-coordinates} \longrightarrow \\ \longleftarrow y\text{-coordinates} \longrightarrow \end{matrix} \begin{bmatrix} 5 & 3 & 1 & 3 \\ 5 & 7 & 5 & 1 \end{bmatrix}$$

6. Use the matrix of the kite image $A'B'C'D'$. To get the matrix

   of the kite preimage $ABCD$, you add 8 to /subtract 8 from each x-coordinate

   and you add 5 to /subtract 5 from each y-coordinate.

7. Cross out the matrix that is NOT the translation matrix for going from the kite image $A'B'C'D'$ to the kite preimage $ABCD$.

$$\begin{bmatrix} -8 & -8 & -8 & -8 \\ 5 & 5 & 5 & 5 \end{bmatrix} \qquad \begin{bmatrix} 8 & 8 & 8 & 8 \\ -5 & -5 & -5 & -5 \end{bmatrix}$$

Problem 2 Dilating a Figure

Got It? You are to enlarge a picture by the factor 2. The preimage is 5 in. by 3 in. Write a matrix of coordinates of the preimage vertices. Make one vertex (0, 0).

8. Let each unit on the grid represent 1 in. Draw the preimage on the coordinate grid.

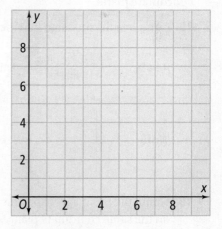

9. Write the matrix of coordinates of the preimage vertices.

$$\begin{bmatrix} 0 & & & \\ 0 & & & \end{bmatrix}$$

Got It? What are the coordinates of the vertices of the image? Show the multiplication that you used for the dilation.

10. Circle the factor by which you are to enlarge the picture.

   1   2   3   4

11. Use scalar multiplication to find the matrix of the coordinates of the image.

12. The vertices of the image are _____ , _____ , _____ , _____ .

Lesson 12-5

Got It? Reasoning You enlarged the picture by the factor 2. By what factor did you increase its area?

13. The area of the preimage is [ ] in.².

14. The dimensions of the enlarged picture are [ ] in. by [ ] in.

15. The area of the image is [ ] in.².

16. The area of the image is 1 / 2 / 3 / 4 times the area of the preimage.

17. The area increased by a factor of [ ].

Properties   Rotation and Reflection Matrices for the Coordinate Plane

Rotation	90° counterclockwise	180°	270° counterclockwise	360°
	$\begin{bmatrix} 0 & -1 \\ 1 & 0 \end{bmatrix}$	$\begin{bmatrix} -1 & 0 \\ 0 & -1 \end{bmatrix}$	$\begin{bmatrix} 0 & 1 \\ -1 & 0 \end{bmatrix}$	$\begin{bmatrix} 1 & 0 \\ 0 & 1 \end{bmatrix}$
Reflection	across x-axis	across y-axis	across $y = x$	across $y = -x$
	$\begin{bmatrix} 1 & 0 \\ 0 & -1 \end{bmatrix}$	$\begin{bmatrix} -1 & 0 \\ 0 & 1 \end{bmatrix}$	$\begin{bmatrix} 0 & 1 \\ 1 & 0 \end{bmatrix}$	$\begin{bmatrix} 0 & -1 \\ -1 & 0 \end{bmatrix}$

 Problem 3 Rotating a Figure

Got It? Rotate the triangle with vertices $D(-3, 0)$, $E(-4, 4)$, and $F(1, 1)$ 270°. What are the vertices of the image? Graph the preimage and the image in the same coordinate plane.

18. Complete the model to find the coordinates of the image.

Relate   [270° rotation matrix] times [preimage coordinates] is [image coordinates]

Write

$$\begin{bmatrix} \boxed{} & \boxed{} \\ \boxed{} & \boxed{} \end{bmatrix} \cdot \begin{bmatrix} -3 & \boxed{} \\ \boxed{} & 4 \end{bmatrix} = \begin{bmatrix} 0 & \boxed{} \\ \boxed{} & 4 \end{bmatrix}$$

19. Graph the preimage. Label the vertices. Graph and label the image on the same coordinate plane.

20. The coordinates of the image are $D'($ [ ] , [ ] $)$, $E'($ [ ] , [ ] $)$,

and $F'($ [ ] , [ ] $)$.

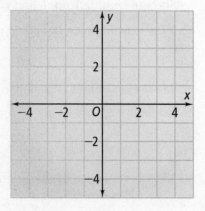

Problem 4 **Reflecting a Figure**

Got It? Reflect the quadrilateral with vertices
E(1, 1), *F*(3, 1), *G*(6, 4) and *H*(1, 3) across the *x*-axis.
What are the vertices of the image? Graph the preimage
and the image in the same coordinate plane.

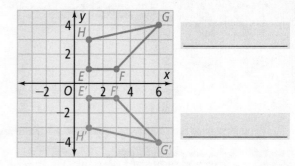

21. The image and the preimage are graphed in the
coordinate plane at the right. Label each figure
image or *preimage*.

22. Circle the expression that gives the coordinates of the image.

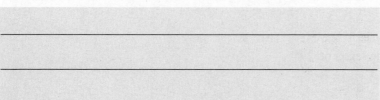

23. The vertices of the image are *E*′ _____ , *F*′ _____ , *G*′ _____ , *H*′ _____ .

 Lesson Check • **Do you UNDERSTAND?**

Writing Describe two ways that the point (3, 7) can be transformed to the
point (7, 3).

24. Graph the points at (3, 7) and (7, 3) on the coordinate plane.

25. Circle two matrix expressions that will transform the
point (3, 7) to the point (7, 3).

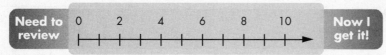

26. Explain two ways that you can transform (3, 7) to (7, 3).

_____

_____

_____

Math Success

Check off the vocabulary words that you understand.

☐ image   ☐ preimage   ☐ translation   ☐ dilation   ☐ rotation   ☐ reflection

Rate how well you can *transform geometric figures using matrix operations.*

Need to review 0 2 4 6 8 10 Now I get it!

Lesson 12-5

12-6 Vectors

Vocabulary

● Review

1. Circle the word(s) whose meaning is similar to that of *length*.

| distance | area | speed |

2. The area of a rectangle is 42 ft². Its width is 6 ft, so its *length* is [   ] ft.

● Vocabulary Builder

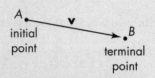

vector (noun) **VEK tur**

Definition: A **vector** is a quantity, such as velocity, that has both *length* (magnitude) and direction.

What It Means: You can think of a **vector** as a directed line segment with initial and terminal points and an arrow to show its direction.

In Symbols: A **vector** can be represented by $\mathbf{v} = \overrightarrow{AB}$.

● Use Your Vocabulary

Write T for *true* or F for *false*.

_____ **3.** A *vector* is a directed line segment.

_____ **4.** A *vector* has only size.

_____ **5.** A *vector* has an initial point and a terminal point.

Problem 1 **Representing a Vector**

Got It? What are the component forms of the two vectors shown here?

6. Complete to move the initial points R and T to the origin.

$$R: \left(-1 + \boxed{}, \; 4 - \boxed{}\right) \rightarrow (0, 0)$$

$$T: \left(2 - \boxed{}, \; 1 - \boxed{}\right) \rightarrow (0, 0)$$

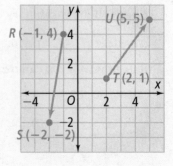

7. Move the terminal points S and U the same way you moved the initial points.

$$S: \left(-2 + \boxed{}, -2 - \boxed{}\right) \rightarrow \left(\boxed{}, \boxed{}\right)$$

$$U: \left(5 - \boxed{}, 5 - \boxed{}\right) \rightarrow \left(\boxed{}, \boxed{}\right)$$

8. Use the new terminal points for S and U to write the component forms of the two vectors.

$$\overrightarrow{RS} = \left\langle \boxed{}, \boxed{} \right\rangle \qquad\qquad \overrightarrow{TU} = \left\langle \boxed{}, \boxed{} \right\rangle$$

Problem 2 Rotating a Vector

Got It? Rotate the vector $v = \langle -3, 5 \rangle$ by 270°. What is the component form of the resulting vector?

9. Complete the reasoning model below.

Think	Write
I need to write the vector in matrix form.	$\begin{bmatrix} \boxed{} \\ \boxed{} \end{bmatrix}$
Next, I need to multiply the vector in matrix form by the 270° rotation matrix.	$\begin{bmatrix} 0 & 1 \\ -1 & 0 \end{bmatrix} \begin{bmatrix} \boxed{} \\ \boxed{} \end{bmatrix} = \begin{bmatrix} \boxed{} \\ \boxed{} \end{bmatrix}$

10. The resulting vector is $\left\langle \boxed{}, \boxed{} \right\rangle$.

take note

Properties Operations With Vectors

Given $v = \langle v_1, v_2 \rangle$, $w = \langle w_1, w_2 \rangle$, and any real number k:

$$v + w = \langle v_1 + w_1, v_2 + w_2 \rangle$$

$$v - w = \langle v_1 - w_1, v_2 - w_2 \rangle$$

$$kv = \langle kv_1, kv_2 \rangle$$

Note that
$w + (v - w) = v$
and $(v - w) + w = v$.

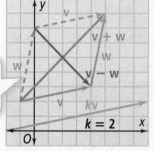

Suppose $v = \langle 5, 1 \rangle$, $w = \langle 1, 5 \rangle$, and $k = 2$.
Find each vector.

11. $v + w = \left\langle 5 + \boxed{}, 1 + \boxed{} \right\rangle$ **12.** $v - w = \left\langle 5 - \boxed{}, 1 - \boxed{} \right\rangle$ **13.** $kv = \left\langle \boxed{}(5), \boxed{}(1) \right\rangle$

$\quad = \left\langle \boxed{}, \boxed{} \right\rangle$ $= \left\langle \boxed{}, \boxed{} \right\rangle$ $= \left\langle \boxed{}, \boxed{} \right\rangle$

Lesson 12-6

Problem 3 Adding and Subtracting Vectors

Got It? Let $u = \langle -2, 3 \rangle$ and $v = \langle 5, -2 \rangle$. What is $|u - v|$, rounded to the nearest hundredth?

14. Label vectors **u** and **v** on the coordinate plane.

15. Starting from the origin, draw and label the vector $-v$. The component form of $-v$ is $\left\langle , \right\rangle$.

16. Starting from the tip of vector **u**, draw and label a copy of vector $-v$.

17. Draw and label vector $u - v$.

18. Circle the component form of $u - v$.

$\langle -3, -1 \rangle$ $\langle 3, 1 \rangle$ $\langle -7, 5 \rangle$

19. Circle the expression that you can use to determine $|u - v|$.

$\sqrt{(-3)^2 + (-1)^2}$ $\sqrt{(-7)^2 + (5)^2}$ $\sqrt{(3)^2 + (1)^2}$ $\sqrt{(7)^2 + (2)^2}$

20. To the nearest hundredth, $|u - v| = $ _____ .

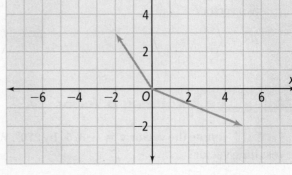

 Problem 4 Scalar Multiplication

Got It? Given $u = \langle -2, 4 \rangle$, what is the graph of the vector $-u$?

21. Complete.

$u = \langle -2, 4 \rangle$

$-u = \langle -2, 4 \rangle = \left\langle , \right\rangle$

22. Draw and label the graph of $-u$ on the coordinate grid.

Got It? Given $u = \langle -2, 4 \rangle$, what is the graph of the vector $\frac{1}{2}u$?

23. **Multiple Choice** What is the component form of the vector $\frac{1}{2}u$?

Ⓐ $\langle -2, 2 \rangle$ Ⓑ $\langle 1, 2 \rangle$ Ⓒ $\langle -1, 2 \rangle$ Ⓓ $\langle -4, 8 \rangle$

24. Draw and label the graph of $\frac{1}{2}u$ on the coordinate grid.

✓ **Problem 5** Finding Dot Products

Got It? If $v \cdot w = 0$, the two vectors v and w are *normal vectors*, or perpendicular to each other. Are the vectors $\langle -2, 6 \rangle$ and $\langle -9, -18 \rangle$ normal?

25. Complete the dot product.

$\langle -2, 6 \rangle \cdot \langle -9, -18 \rangle = (-2)\Big(\Big) + (6)\Big(\Big)$

$= + = $

26. The vectors are / are not normal.

Got It? Are the vectors $\left\langle 3, \frac{5}{6} \right\rangle$ and $\left\langle -\frac{10}{9}, 4 \right\rangle$ normal?

27. Circle the expression that shows the dot product.

$$(3)\left(\frac{5}{6}\right) + \left(-\frac{10}{9}\right)(4) \qquad (3)(4) + \left(-\frac{10}{9}\right)\left(\frac{5}{6}\right) \qquad (3)\left(-\frac{9}{10}\right) + \left(\frac{6}{5}\right)(4) \qquad (3)\left(-\frac{10}{9}\right) + \left(\frac{5}{6}\right)(4)$$

28. Simplify the dot product.

29. The vectors are /are not normal.

 Lesson Check • **Do you UNDERSTAND?**

Vocabulary Which of the following vectors has the greatest magnitude? Explain.

$$\mathbf{a} = \langle 3, 4 \rangle \qquad\qquad \mathbf{b} = \langle -4, 3 \rangle \qquad\qquad \mathbf{c} = \langle 4, -3 \rangle$$

30. How can you determine the magnitude of a vector?

_____

_____

31. Square the components of each vector and add them together. What do you notice?

_____

_____

32. Which vector has the greatest magnitude?

_____

_____

Math Success

Check off the vocabulary words that you understand.

☐ vector ☐ magnitude ☐ initial point ☐ terminal point ☐ dot product ☐ normal vectors

Rate how well you can *solve problems involving vectors*.

Lesson 12-6

13-1 Exploring Periodic Data

Vocabulary

● Review

1. Circle the equation that shows a *function* rule.

$$f(x) = 2x + 8 \qquad 0 = x^2 + 2x + 4 \qquad f(x) - 5$$

2. Write an example of a quadratic *function*.

● Vocabulary Builder

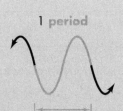

period   (noun) PEER ee ud

Related Words: periodic (adjective), amplitude (noun), cycle (noun), interval (noun)

Math Usage: The **period** of a function is the horizontal length of one cycle. A *periodic function* is a function that repeats a pattern of *y*-values at regular intervals. The *amplitude* of a periodic function measures the amount of variation in the function values.

● Use Your Vocabulary

3. Draw a line from each word in Column A to the *period* of time it describes in Column B.

Column A	Column B
year	100 years
month	28, 29, 30, or 31 days
decade	365 days
week	10 years
century	7 days

Problem 1   Identifying Cycles and Periods

Got It? Analyze the periodic function. Identify the cycle in two different ways. What is the period of the function?

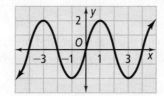

4. Circle the graph whose gray tracing represents one cycle of the function.

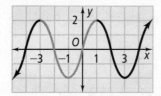 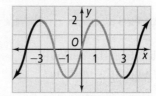

5. Circle the beginning *x*-value of the period you circled in Exercise 4. Underline the ending *x*-value.

−3	−1	0	1	4

6. The period of the function is ⬚ − ⬚ = ⬚.

Got It? Analyze the periodic function. Identify the cycle in two different ways. What is the period of the function?

7. Use the art at the right. Trace one cycle of the function. The beginning of the cycle is marked for you.

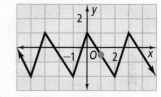

8. Identify the beginning and ending *x*-values of the cycle.

    beginning *x*-value   ending *x*-value

    ⬚   ⬚

9. The period of the function is ⬚ − ⬚ = ⬚.

Problem 2   Identifying Periodic Functions

Got It? Is the function periodic? If it is, what is its period?

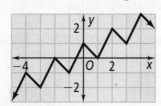

10. Cross out the phrase that does NOT give the definition of a periodic function.

a function that repeats a pattern of *y*-values at regular intervals	a function that repeats a pattern of *x*-values at regular intervals

Lesson 13-1

11. Is the function periodic? Explain.

_____

_____

The **midline** is the horizontal line midway between the maximum and minimum values of a periodic function. The **amplitude** is half the difference between the maximum and minimum values of the function.

amplitude $= \frac{1}{2}$(maximum value $-$ minimum value)

Problem 3 Finding Amplitude and Midline of a Periodic Function

Got It? What is the amplitude of the periodic function? What is the equation of the midline?

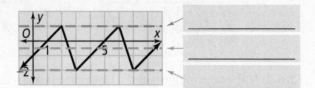

12. Use the words *maximum*, *minimum*, and *midline* to label the graph.

13. The maximum value is [ ]. The minimum value is [ ].

14. Complete the model to find the amplitude.

$$\underline{\hspace{3cm}} = \frac{1}{2}\left(\underline{\hspace{4cm}} - \underline{\hspace{4cm}}\right)$$

$$= \frac{1}{2}\left([\ ] - [\ ]\right)$$

$$= [\ ]$$

15. Complete the model to find the equation of the midline.

$$y = \frac{1}{2}\left(\underline{\hspace{3cm}} + \underline{\hspace{3cm}}\right)$$

$$= \frac{1}{2}\left([\ ] + [\ ]\right)$$

$$= [\ ]$$

The equation of the midline is [ ] = [ ].

Problem 4 Using a Periodic Function to Solve a Problem

Got It? Sound Waves Sound is produced by periodic changes in air pressure called sound waves. What are the period, amplitude and the equation of the midline of the bottom graph in the digital wave display?

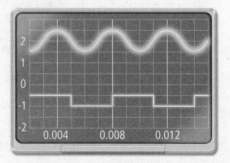

16. Complete the problem-solving model below.

Know	Need	Plan

17. What is the period of the rigid bottom graph? Explain.

_____

18. Find the amplitude and the equation of the midline of the rigid bottom graph.

amplitude $= \frac{1}{2}\left(\boxed{} - \left(\boxed{}\right)\right)$ $\qquad$ $\boxed{} = \frac{1}{2}\left(-0.5 + \boxed{}\right)$

$\qquad\qquad = \frac{1}{2}\left(\boxed{}\right) = \boxed{}$ $\qquad\qquad = \boxed{}\left(\boxed{}\right)$

$\qquad\qquad\qquad\qquad\qquad\qquad\qquad\qquad\qquad = \boxed{}$

Lesson Check • Do you UNDERSTAND?

Reasoning Suppose f is a periodic function. The period of f is 5 and $f(1) = 2$. What are $f(6)$ and $f(11)$? Explain.

19. Underline the correct word or phrase to complete each sentence.

In a periodic function, the x-values / y-values repeat at regular intervals.

A function with a period of 5 repeats every five x-values / y-values.

20. Complete.

$\qquad\qquad 6 - 1 = \boxed{} \qquad\qquad 11 - 6 = \boxed{}$

$f(1) = 2 \qquad\qquad f(6) = \boxed{} \qquad\qquad f(11) = \boxed{}$

Math Success

Check off the vocabulary words that you understand.

☐ periodic function ☐ cycle ☐ period ☐ amplitude

Rate how well you can *find the period and amplitude of a periodic function.*

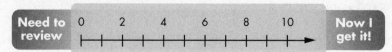

Lesson 13-1

Vocabulary

● **Review**

1. Circle the equation for a *circle* centered at the origin.

$$\frac{x^2}{36} + \frac{y^2}{49} = 1 \qquad x^2 - y^2 = 49 \qquad x^2 + y^2 = 6^2 \qquad \frac{x^2}{36} - \frac{y^2}{49} = 1$$

● **Vocabulary Builder**

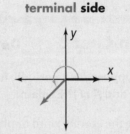

terminal **side**

terminal (adjective) TUR **muh nul**

Related Words: terminate (verb), termination (noun), terminated (verb)

Definition: Terminal means situated at or forming the end of something.

Math Usage: An angle in standard position is formed by rotating a ray from the *x*-axis about its endpoint. The final position of the ray is the **terminal side** of the angle. Two angles in standard position are *coterminal* angles if they have the same **terminal side**.

● **Use Your Vocabulary**

2. Complete each statement with the correct word from the list.

terminated   coterminal   terminal   termination

The ringing of the bell __?__ the game.

Two angles that share a *terminal* side are __?__ angles.

The last monthly payment on a mortgage is the __?__ payment.

Jess paid a fee for early __?__ to end a cell phone contract early.

Problem 1 Measuring Angles in Standard Position

Got It? What is the measure of the angle shown?

3. Underline the correct word or expression to complete the sentence.

   The angle is a counterclockwise / clockwise rotation that goes

   90° / 45° beyond a straight angle.

4. Circle the measure of the angle shown.

   | 45° | 180° | 225° | 245° |

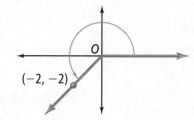

Problem 2 Sketching Angles in Standard Position

Got It? What is a sketch of an 85° angle in standard position?

Underline the correct word(s) to complete each sentence.

5. In standard position, the initial side of the angle lies along the positive

   x-axis / y-axis .

6. The angle will lie in Quadrant I / Quadrant II / Quadrants I and II .

7. Use the coordinate plane at the right. Sketch an angle with a measure of 85° in standard position.

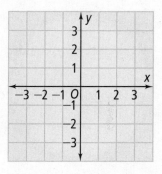

 Problem 3 Identifying Coterminal Angles

Got It? Which of the following angles is *not* coterminal with the other three?

| 45° | 405° | −315° | 315° |

8. The measure of coterminal angles differ by a multiple of 360°. Complete each equation.

   45° − 405° = [ ]   45° − (−315°) = [ ]   45° − 315° = [ ]

9. The angles of 45°, [ ], and [ ] are coterminal with each other.

10. The angle that is not coterminal with the others measures [ ]°.

The **unit circle** has a radius of 1 unit and its center at the origin of the coordinate plane.

take note

Key Concepts Cosine and Sine of an Angle

Suppose an angle in standard position has measure θ. The **cosine of θ** (cos θ) is the x-coordinate of the point at which the terminal side of the angle intersects the unit circle. The **sine of θ** (sin θ) is the y-coordinate.

Use the unit circle at the right for Exercises 11 and 12.

11. The coordinates of point P are ([ ] , [ ]).

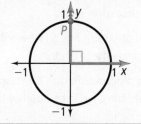

Lesson 13-2

12. Circle the cosine of *P*. Underline the sine of *P*.

$$-1 \qquad -\frac{1}{2} \qquad 0 \qquad \frac{1}{2} \qquad 1$$

Finding Cosines and Sines of Angles

Got It? What are cos θ and sin θ for θ = −90°, θ = 360°, and θ = 540°?

13. Draw a line from each angle in Column A to a corresponding sketch in Column B.

Column A	Column B
θ = −90°	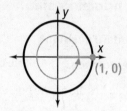
θ = 360°	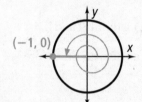
θ = 540°	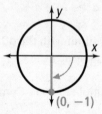

14. Use your work from Exercise 13 to complete the equations.

cos −90° = ☐   cos 360° = ☐   cos 540° = ☐

sin −90° = ☐   sin 360° = ☐   sin 540° = ☐

Problem 5 Finding Exact Values of Cosine and Sine

Got It? What are the cosine and sine of −45°?

15. On the unit circle to the right draw an angle in standard position with measure −45°.

16. Label the point *P*(*x, y*) where the terminal side of the angle intersects the unit circle.

17. Draw a perpendicular line segment from *P* to the *x*-axis. You should have a right triangle with hypotenuse 1.

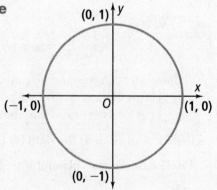

18. Underline the correct word or expression to complete each sentence.

Point *P* is in the first / fourth quadrant.

The sign of *x* will be positive / negative . The sign of *y* will be positive / negative .

The triangle is a 45°-45°-90° / 30°-60°-90° triangle.

The lengths of the legs of the triangle are $\frac{\sqrt{2}}{2}$ / $\frac{1}{2}$ times the hypotenuse.

19. Complete each equation.

$x = \cos(-45°)$ = length of leg = ⬜ $y = \sin(-45°)$ = −(length of leg) = ⬜

Lesson Check • Do you UNDERSTAND?

Error Analysis On a test, a student wrote that the measure of an angle coterminal to a 50° angle is 310°. Describe and correct the student's error.

20. On the coordinate plane at the right, draw a 50° angle and a 310° angle in standard position.

21. Describe the student's error.

_____

_____

_____

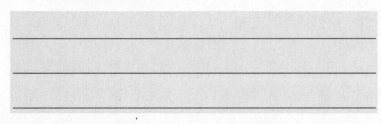

22. Correct the student's error.

_____

_____

Math Success

Check off the vocabulary words that you understand.

☐ standard position   ☐ terminal side   ☐ coterminal angles   ☐ cosine of θ   ☐ sine of θ

Rate how well you can *find the cosine and sine of special angles.*

Need to review   0   2   4   6   8   10   Now I get it!

Lesson 13-2

Radian Measure

Vocabulary

● Review

1. What is the measure of each *central angle*?

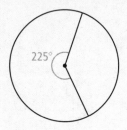

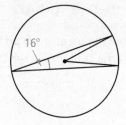

[____] degrees   [____] degrees

● Vocabulary Builder

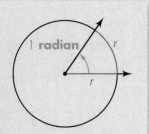

---

radian   (noun) **RAY dee un**

Definition: A **radian** is the measure of a central angle
that intercepts an arc with length equal to the radius
of the circle.

Math Usage: **Radians** measure the amount of rotation from
the initial side to the terminal side of an angle. An angle
with a full-circle rotation measures 2π **radians**.

● Use Your Vocabulary

2. Write T for *true* or F for *false*.

[____]   *Radians* are like degrees in that they measure an amount of rotation.

[____]   A *radian* is always 30 degrees.

[____]   An angle with a full-circle rotation is 2π *radians*.

[____]   An angle with an angle measure of 180 degrees is π *radians*.

Key Concept Converting Between Radians and Degrees

To convert degrees to radians, multiply by $\frac{\pi \text{ radians}}{180°}$.

To convert radians to degrees, multiply by $\frac{180°}{\pi \text{ radians}}$.

3. Circle the expression you would use for each conversion.

127° to radians		4π radians to degrees	
$\frac{\pi \text{ radians}}{180°}$	$\frac{180°}{\pi \text{ radians}}$	$\frac{\pi \text{ radians}}{180°}$	$\frac{180°}{\pi \text{ radians}}$

Problem 1 **Using Dimensional Analysis**

Got It? What is the degree measure of an angle of $\frac{\pi}{2}$ radians?

4. Write the expression you will use for the conversion.

$$\frac{\pi}{2} \cdot \underline{\hspace{2cm}}$$

5. Now simplify the conversion.

Problem 2 **Finding Cosine and Sine of a Radian Measure**

Got It? What are the exact values of $\cos\left(\frac{7\pi}{6} \text{ radians}\right)$ and $\sin\left(\frac{7\pi}{6} \text{ radians}\right)$?

6. The graph shows an angle of $\frac{7\pi}{6}$ radians. Circle the measure of the angle in degrees.

90°	150°	210°	270°

7. Use the values $\frac{1}{2}$, $\frac{\sqrt{3}}{2}$, 1, and 30° to label the graph. Use each value once.

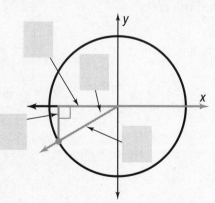

8. Complete.

$$\cos\left(\frac{7\pi}{6} \text{ radians}\right) = \boxed{} \qquad \sin\left(\frac{7\pi}{6} \text{ radians}\right) = \boxed{}$$

Lesson 13-3

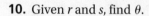

Key Concept   Length of an Intercepted Arc

For a circle of radius *r* and a central angle of measure θ (in radians), the length *s* of the intercepted arc is $s = r\theta$.

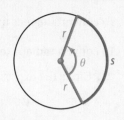

Circle the operation you would use to solve each problem.

9. Given *r* and θ, find *s*.

| Multiply *r* and θ. | Divide *r* by θ. | Divide θ by *r*. |

10. Given *r* and *s*, find θ.

| Multiply *r* and *s*. | Divide *r* by *s*. | Divide *s* by *r*. |

 Problem 3   Finding the Length of an Arc

Got It? Use the circle at the right. What is the length of *b* to the nearest tenth?

11. The arc length is found below. Write a justification for each step.

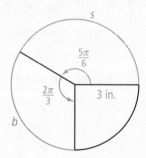

$b = r\theta$

$= 3 \cdot \dfrac{2\pi}{3}$

$= 2\pi$

≈ 6.3

Problem 4   Using Radian Measure to Solve a Problem

Got It? Weather Satellite A weather satellite is in a circular orbit 3600 km above Earth's surface and completes one orbit every 4 h. How far does the satellite travel in 1 h?

12. If the satellite completes an orbit every 4 hours, it completes

_____ of an orbit in one hour.

13. Use the justifications at the right to find the distance the satellite travels in 1 h.

$\theta = \frac{1}{4} \cdot 2\pi =$ [ ]   Find the angle the satellite travels in 1 h.

$s = r\theta$ Use the arc length formula.

$= \left(6400 + \right) \cdot $ Substitute.

$= \cdot $ Add.

$\approx $ Simplify. Round to the nearest whole number.

14. The satellite travels about [ ] km in 1 h.

Lesson Check • Do you UNDERSTAND?

Reasoning A certain baker believes that a perfect slice of pie has a central angle of 1 radian. How many "perfect" slices can he get out of one pie?

15. Convert 1 radian to degrees.

16. There are [ ]° in one whole pie.

17. How many "perfect" slices can the baker get out of a pie? Explain.

_____

_____

_____

Math Success

Check off the vocabulary words that you understand.

☐ central angle   ☐ intercepted arc   ☐ radian

Rate how well you can *use radian measure for angles.*

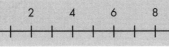

Need to review   0   2   4   6   8   10   Now I get it!

The Sine Function

Vocabulary

● Review

1. Circle the graph that shows a *periodic function*.

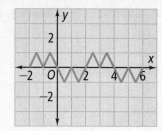

● Vocabulary Builder

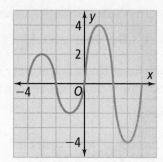

$$\sin \theta = y\text{-coordinate} = \frac{\sqrt{3}}{2}$$

sine (noun) **syn**

Related Words: sine function (noun), sine curve (noun), cosine (noun)

Definition: If the terminal side of an angle θ in standard position intersects the unit circle at the point (x, y), then the **sine** of θ is the y-coordinate of the point (x, y).

In Symbols: $\sin \theta$

● Use Your Vocabulary

2. Circle the sine of each angle θ.

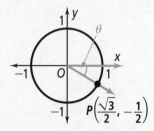

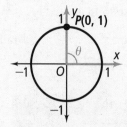

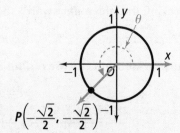

-1	$-\dfrac{1}{2}$	$\dfrac{\sqrt{3}}{2}$	1

-1	0	1

-1	$-\dfrac{\sqrt{2}}{2}$	$\dfrac{\sqrt{2}}{2}$	1

Problem 1 Estimating Sine Values Graphically

Got It? What is a reasonable estimate for the value sin 3 from the graph? Check your estimate with a calculator.

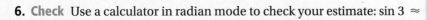

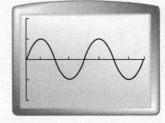

$y = \sin\theta$

3. Circle the θ-value that is closest to $\theta = 3$.

0	$\frac{\pi}{2}$	π

4. The value of $y = \sin\theta$ at your chosen θ-value is ⬚.

5. Circle the best estimate of sin 3.

0	0.01	0.1	1	$\frac{\pi}{3}$	$\frac{\pi}{2}$

6. Check Use a calculator in radian mode to check your estimate: sin 3 ≈ ⬚.

The graph of the sine function is called a **sine curve**.

Problem 2 Finding the Period of a Sine Curve

Got It? How many cycles occur in the graph? What is the period of the cycle?

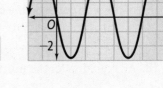

Xmin = 0
Xmax = 4π
Xscl = $\pi/2$
Ymin = -2
Ymax = 2
Yscl = 1

7. Circle each cycle in the graph. There are ⬚ cycles.

8. To find the period of one cycle, divide the length of the interval by the number of cycles. Cross out the expressions that do NOT give the period.

$2\pi \div 2$	$4\pi \div 2$	$4\pi \div 4$

9. The period is ⬚.

Problem 3 Finding the Amplitude of a Sine Curve

Got It? The equation of the graph is of the form $y = a \sin x$. What is the amplitude of the sine curve? What is the value of a?

10. Underline the correct words to complete each sentence.

The amplitude of a periodic function is the difference / half the difference

of the maximum and the minimum values.

Because the first cycle begins below the x-axis, the value of a in the sine

curve at the right is positive / negative .

11. Use the graph at the right. Find the amplitude of the sine curve.

12. The amplitude is ⬚, and the value of a is ⬚.

355

Lesson 13-4

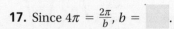

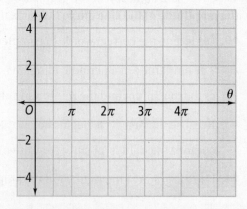# Concept Summary   Properties of Sine Functions

Suppose $y = a \sin b\theta$, with $a \neq 0$, and θ in radians.

- $|a|$ is the amplitude of the function.
- b is the number of cycles in the interval from 0 to 2π.
- $\frac{2\pi}{b}$ is the period of the function.

13. Identify the amplitude, number of cycles, and period of $y = -\sin\frac{1}{2}\theta$.

amplitude = ☐   number of cycles = ☐   period = ☐

Sketching a Graph

Got It? What is the graph of one cycle of a sine curve with amplitude 3, period 4π, and $a > 0$? Use the form $y = a \sin b\theta$. What is an equation with $a > 0$ for the sine curve?

14. Underline the correct word or number to complete each sentence.

The amplitude is 3, so the maximum is $-4 / -3 / 0 / 3 / 4$ and the minimum is $-4 / -3 / 0 / 3 / 4$.

Since $a > 0$, the maximum value occurs before / after the minimum value.

15. Complete the table.

16. Use the ordered pairs from the table to graph one cycle of the sine curve on the coordinate plane.

17. Since $4\pi = \frac{2\pi}{b}$, $b =$ ☐.

18. An equation for the function is $y =$ ☐ $\sin$ ☐ θ.

Got It? What is the graph of one cycle of the sine function $y = 1.5 \sin 2\theta$?

19. Write the value of each variable or expression.

$a = \boxed{}$ $b = \boxed{}$ $\dfrac{2\pi}{b} = \dfrac{2\pi}{\boxed{}} = \boxed{}$

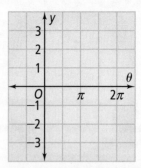

20. One cycle runs from 0 to $\dfrac{\pi}{4} \,/\, \dfrac{\pi}{2} \,/\, \pi \,/\, 2\pi$.

21. Graph one cycle of $y = 1.5 \sin 2\theta$ on the coordinate plane.

 Lesson Check • **Do you UNDERSTAND?**

Error Analysis A student drew this graph for the function $y = -3 \sin \pi\theta$. Describe and correct the student's error.

22. Cross out the statements that do NOT describe the graph of $y = -3 \sin \pi\theta$.

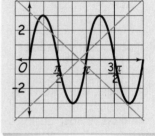

$a > 0$	The period is 2.	The amplitude is -3.
$a < 0$	The period is 2π.	The amplitude is 3.

23. Describe the student's error.

_____

24. Circle the graph of $y = -3 \sin \pi\theta$.

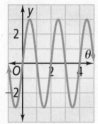   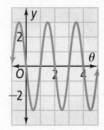   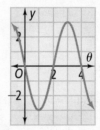

 Math Success

Check off the vocabulary words that you understand.

☐ sine function   ☐ sine curve   ☐ periodic function   ☐ amplitude

Rate how well you can *graph a sine function.*

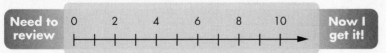

Lesson 13-4

13-5   The Cosine Function

Vocabulary

● Review

Write the *amplitude* of each sine function.

1. $y = 4 \sin 2\theta$

2. $y = -3 \sin \frac{\theta}{2}$

3. $y = -0.6 \sin \theta$

● Vocabulary Builder

cosine (noun) KOH syn	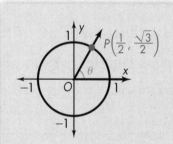
Related Words: cosine function (noun), sine (noun)	
Definition: If the terminal side of an angle θ in standard position intersects the unit circle at the point (x, y), then the **cosine** of θ is the x-coordinate of the point (x, y).	
In Symbols: $\cos \theta$	

$\cos \theta = x\text{-coordinate} = \frac{1}{2}$

● Use Your Vocabulary

4. Circle the cosine of each angle θ.

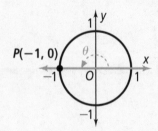

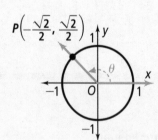

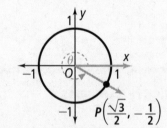

-1	0	1

-1	$-\frac{\sqrt{2}}{2}$	$\frac{\sqrt{2}}{2}$	0

-1	$-\frac{1}{2}$	$\frac{\sqrt{3}}{2}$	1

Problem 1 Interpreting a Graph

Got It? Use the graph. What are the domain, period, range, and amplitude of the sine function? Where do the maximum and minimum values occur? Where do the zeros occur?

5. Draw a line from each part of the sine function in Column A to a corresponding expression in Column B.

Column A	Column B
domain	$-1 \leq y \leq 1$
period	1
range	2π
amplitude	all real numbers

6. The maximum value is ▢. The minimum value is ▢.

7. Circle the phrase that best describes the zeros of the graph.

multiples of $\frac{\pi}{2}$ multiples of π multiples of 2π

---

take note

Concept Summary   Properties of Cosine Functions

Suppose $y = a \cos b\theta$, with $a \neq 0$, $b > 0$, and θ in radians.

- $|a|$ is the amplitude of the function.
- b is the number of cycles in the interval from 0 to 2π.
- $\frac{2\pi}{b}$ is the period of the function.

8. Identify the amplitude, number of cycles in the interval from 0 to 2π, and period of $y = 2 \cos \theta$.

amplitude = ▢   number of cycles = ▢   period = ▢

Problem 2 Sketching the Graph of a Cosine Function

Got It? Sketch one cycle of $y = 2 \cos \frac{\theta}{3}$.

9. Write T for *true* or F for *false*.

_____ The amplitude of the graph is 2.

_____ The value of b is 3.

_____ The period is 6π.

10. Follow the steps to graph the function.

    Step 1 Mark one period on the horizontal axis.

    Step 2 Divide the period into four equal sections.

    Step 3 Plot the zeros of the function.

    Step 4 Plot the minimums and maximums of the function.

    Step 5 Sketch the curve.

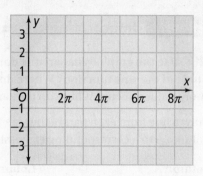

Problem 3 **Modeling With a Cosine Function**

Got It? Oceanography The water level along a support pillar for a pier varies 70 inches between low tide at 8:40 A.M. and high tide at 2:55 P.M. What is a cosine function that models the variation in inches above and below the average water level as a function of the number of hours since 8:40 A.M.?

11. Complete the reasoning model below.

Think	Write
First, I need to find the difference between the times of high tide and low tide.	2:55 P.M. − 8:40 A.M. is ▢ hours and ▢ minutes, or $6\frac{1}{4}$ hours.
Next, I should find the amplitude.	amplitude $= \frac{1}{2}\left(\ \boxed{}\ \right) = \boxed{}$
I can use the amplitude and reasoning to find the value of *a*.	At time 0, the tide is 35 inches below / above the average water level. The curve follows the *min-zero-max-zero-min* / *max-zero-min-zero-max* pattern. The value of *a* is −35 / 35 .
The cycle is halfway complete after $6\frac{1}{4}$ hours.	The full period is ▢ hours.
I solve for *b* by setting $\frac{2\pi}{b}$ equal to the length of a full period.	$\frac{2\pi}{b} = \boxed{}$ $2\pi = \boxed{}$ $4\pi = \boxed{}$ $\boxed{} = b$

12. A cosine function that models the water level variation is

    $y = \boxed{}\ \cos\ \boxed{}\ t.$

Problem 4 Solving a Cosine Equation

Got It? What are all the solutions to the equation $3 \cos 2t = -2$ in the interval from 0 to 2π?

13. Circle the pair of functions to graph.

$y = 3 \cos 2t$	$y = 3 \cos 2t$	$y = 3 \cos 2t$
$y = -2$	$y = 2$	$y = 2\pi$

14. Graph the functions on a graphing calculator. Use the ZTrig window. Circle the graph that matches your calculator screen. For each screen, Xmin $= -2\pi$, Xmax $= 2\pi$, Xscl $= \frac{\pi}{2}$, Ymin $= -4$, Ymax $= 4$, and Yscl $= 1$.

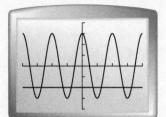 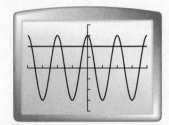 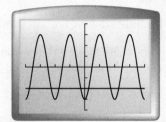

 Lesson Check • Do you UNDERSTAND?

For what values of θ is y positive for $y = \cos \theta$?

15. Cos θ is the x-coordinate / y-coordinate of the point P where the terminal side of angle θ intersects the unit circle.

16. Circle all that apply.

$\cos \theta = 0$ when $\theta = $ $0 / \frac{\pi}{4} / \frac{\pi}{2} / \frac{3\pi}{4} / \pi / \frac{5\pi}{4} / \frac{3\pi}{2} / \frac{7\pi}{4} / 2\pi$

17. Circle the intervals in which $\cos \theta$ is positive. Draw a square around the intervals in which $\cos \theta$ is negative.

$0 < \theta < \frac{\pi}{2}$ $0 < \theta < \pi$ $\frac{\pi}{2} < \theta < \pi$ $\frac{\pi}{2} < \theta < \frac{3\pi}{2}$ $\pi < \theta < 2\pi$ $\frac{3\pi}{2} < \theta < 2\pi$

 Math Success

Check off the vocabulary words that you understand.

☐ cosine   ☐ cosine function   ☐ periodic function   ☐ period

Rate how well you can *graph a cosine function*.

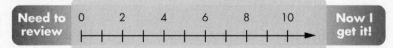

Need to review 0 2 4 6 8 10 Now I get it!

Lesson 13-5

13-6 The Tangent Function

Vocabulary

Review

1. Underline the correct word or expression to complete each statement.

The *unit circle* has a radius of one unit / ten units on the coordinate plane.

The *unit circle* has a center at $(1, 0)$ / $(0, 0)$.

Vocabulary Builder

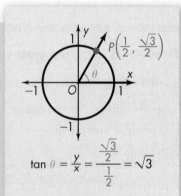

tangent (noun) TAN junt

Related Words: cosine (noun), sine (noun), tangent function (noun)

Definition: If the terminal side of an angle θ in standard position intersects the unit circle at the point (x, y) then the **tangent** of θ is the ratio of the y-coordinate to the x-coordinate, $\frac{y}{x}$.

In Symbols: $\tan \theta$

$$\tan \theta = \frac{y}{x} = \frac{\frac{\sqrt{3}}{2}}{\frac{1}{2}} = \sqrt{3}$$

Use Your Vocabulary

Determine the value of tan θ.

2.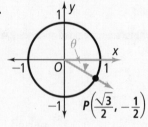

$$\tan \theta = \frac{-\frac{1}{2}}{\frac{\sqrt{3}}{2}} = \boxed{}$$

3.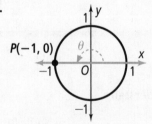

$$\tan \theta = \frac{\boxed{}}{-1} = \boxed{}$$

4.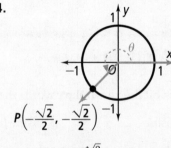

$$\tan \theta = \frac{-\frac{\sqrt{2}}{2}}{\boxed{}} = \boxed{}$$

Problem 1 **Finding Tangents Geometrically**

Got It? What is the value of $\tan \frac{\pi}{2}$? Do not use a calculator.

5. Draw the angle $\frac{\pi}{2}$ in standard position on the unit circle.

6. Plot a point at the intersection of the unit circle and the terminal side of the angle. The coordinates of the point are $\left(\boxed{} , \boxed{} \right)$.

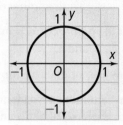

7. Use your answer from Exercise 6 to find the value of $\tan \frac{\pi}{2}$.

$$\tan \frac{\pi}{2} = \frac{y}{x} = \frac{\boxed{}}{\boxed{}}$$

8. The value of $\tan \frac{\pi}{2}$ is $1 \,/\, 0 \,/\, \text{undefined}$.

take note

Concept Summary **Properties of Tangent Functions**

Suppose $y = a \tan b\theta$, with $a \neq 0$, $b > 0$ and θ in radians.

- $\frac{\pi}{b}$ is the period of the function.
- One cycle occurs in the interval from $-\frac{\pi}{2b}$ to $\frac{\pi}{2b}$.
- There are vertical asymptotes at each end of the cycle.

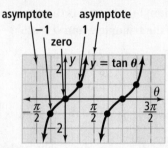

You can use asymptotes and three points to sketch one cyle of a tangent curve. Use the pattern *asymptote-($-a$)-zero-(a)-asymptote* to sketch one cycle of a tangent curve.

9. In the graph at the right, the interval of one cycle is $-\frac{\pi}{2}$ to $0 \,/\, \frac{\pi}{2} \,/\, \pi \,/\, \frac{3\pi}{2}$.

Problem 2 **Graphing a Tangent Function**

Got It? Sketch two cycles of the graph of $y = \tan 3\theta, 0 \leq \theta \leq \frac{2\pi}{3}$.

10. Circle the value of a. Underline the value of b.

1	2	3	6

11. The period of the function is $\frac{\pi}{b} = \dfrac{\pi}{\boxed{}}$.

12. One cycle of the graph goes from $-\frac{\pi}{2b}$ to $\frac{\pi}{2b}$, or $-\dfrac{\pi}{\boxed{}}$ to $\dfrac{\pi}{\boxed{}}$.

13. Use the pattern *asymptote-($-a$)-zero-(a)-asymptote*. Identify each x-value.

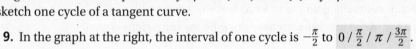

asymptote	$-a$	zero	a	asymptote
$-\dfrac{\pi}{\boxed{}}$	$-\dfrac{\pi}{12}$	0	$\boxed{}$	$\dfrac{\pi}{\boxed{}}$

Lesson 13-6

Use the coordinate plane at the right and your answers to Exercise 13 for Exercises 14–17.

14. Draw three asymptotes, the two from Exercise 13 and another one.

15. Plot the points corresponding to $-a$, 0, and a.

16. Draw a smooth curve through the points.

17. Draw another curve identical to the one from Exercise 16 between the remaining two asymptotes.

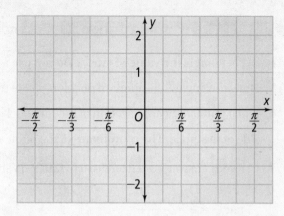

 Problem 3 **Using the Tangent Function to Solve Problems**

Got It? **Design** An architect is designing the front facade of a building to include a triangle, as shown in the figure. The function $y = 100 \tan \theta$ models the height of the triangle, where θ is the angle indicated. What is the height of the triangle when $\theta = 25°$?

18. Use your calculator.

$y = 100 \tan$ ⬚ ° = ⬚

19. The height of the triangle is about ⬚ ft when $\theta = 25°$.

Got It? **Reasoning** The architect wants the triangle to be at least one story tall. The average height of a story is 14 ft. What must the measure of θ be for the height of the triangle to be at least 14 ft?

20. The graphing calculator screens below show the function and the associated table. Circle the line on the table that shows the measure of θ for a triangle height of at least 14 ft.

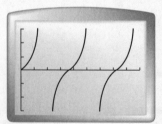

Xmin = 0
Xmax = 470
Xscl = 50
Ymin = −300
Ymax = 300
Yscl = 90

X	Y₁	
8	14.054	
9	15.838	
10	17.633	
11	19.438	
12	21.256	
13	23.087	
14	24.933	

X=12

21. Explain how to use the TABLE feature to find the measure of θ.

_____

_____

_____

_____

22. The measure of θ must be at least ⬚ .

Lesson Check • Do you UNDERSTAND?

Writing Explain how you can write a tangent function that has the same period as $y = \text{an } 4\theta$.

23. Circle the expression that gives the period of the sine function $y = \sin b\theta$.

$$\frac{1}{b} \qquad\qquad \frac{\pi}{b} \qquad\qquad \frac{2\pi}{b} \qquad\qquad \frac{3\pi}{b}$$

24. The period of $y = \sin 4\theta$ is ☐.

25. The general form of the equation of the tangent function is $y = a \tan b\theta$.

You need the value of the variable a / b to determine the period of the tangent function.

26. Circle the expression that gives the period of the tangent function.

$$\frac{\pi}{2b} \qquad\qquad -\frac{\pi}{2b} \qquad\qquad \frac{\pi}{b}$$

27. Set your answer from Exercise 26 equal to your answer from Exercise 24.

Then solve for the variable ☐.

28. Write a tangent function that has the same period as $y = 4 \sin \theta$.

Math Success

Check off the vocabulary words that you understand.

☐ tangent   ☐ tangent function   ☐ period

Rate how well you can *graph a tangent function*.

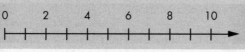

Lesson 13-6

13-7 Translating Sine and Cosine Functions

Vocabulary

● Review

1. Cross out each transformation that is NOT a *translation*.

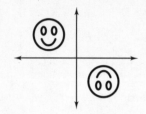 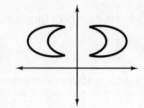 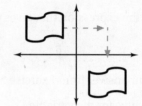

● Vocabulary Builder

phase shift (noun) **fayz shift**

Math Usage: A **phase shift** of a sine or cosine function is a horizontal translation of the graph.

● Use Your Vocabulary

2. Circle the graph that shows a *phase shift* of the function $y = \sin \theta$.

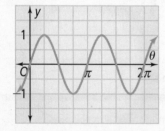 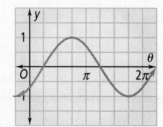 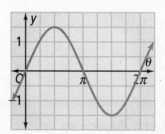

✓ **Problem 3** Graphing a Combined Translation

Got It? Use the graph at the right of the parent function $y = \cos x$.
What is the graph of $y = \cos(x - 2) + 5$ in the interval $0 \leq x \leq 2\pi$?

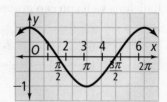

3. Identify each value.

$a =$ ☐ $b =$ ☐ $h =$ ☐ $k =$ ☐

4. Draw the graph on the coordinate plane at the right. Use the graph of $y = \cos x$ as a guide.

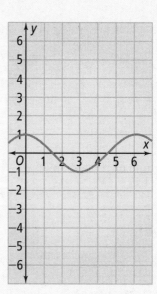

Concept Summary Families of Sine and Cosine Functions

Parent Function	Transformed Function
$y = \sin x$	$y = a \sin b(x - h) + k$
$y = \cos x$	$y = a \cos b(x - h) + k$

- $|a| =$ amplitude (vertical stretch or shrink)
- $\dfrac{2\pi}{b} =$ period (when x is in radians and $b > 0$)
- $h =$ phase shift
- $k =$ vertical shift ($y = k$ is the midline)

5. Circle the value of k for the function $y = 3 \sin 2(x - \pi) + 5$.

-5	$-\pi$	2	3	π	5

Problem 4 Graphing a Translation of $y = \sin 2x$

Got It? What is the graph of the translation $y = -3 \sin 2\left(x - \frac{\pi}{3}\right) - \frac{3}{2}$ in the interval from 0 to 2π?

6. Identify each value.

$a =$ ☐ $b =$ ☐ $h =$ ☐ $k =$ ☐

7. Circle each phrase that describes the graph of $y = -3 \sin 2\left(x - \frac{\pi}{3}\right) - \frac{3}{2}$.

translated $\frac{3}{2}$ units up	translated $\frac{\pi}{3}$ units left	reflected over the y-axis	stretched by a factor of 2
translated $\frac{3}{2}$ units down	translated $\frac{\pi}{3}$ units right	reflected over the x-axis	stretched by a factor of 3

Lesson 13-7

8. Circle the graph of $y = \sin 2x$ in the interval from 0 to 2π.

 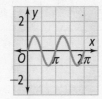

9. Circle the graph of $y = -3 \sin 2\left(x - \frac{\pi}{3}\right) - \frac{3}{2}$ in the interval from 0 to 2π.

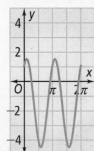 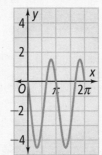 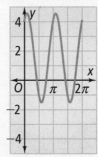

Problem 5 **Writing Translations**

Got It? What is an equation that models $y = \cos x$, $\frac{\pi}{2}$ units up?

10. The general form of the transformed function is $y = a \cos b(x - h) + k$.
Circle the quantity that will be affected by a move of $\frac{\pi}{2}$ units up.

$$a \qquad\qquad b \qquad\qquad h \qquad\qquad k$$

11. An equation of a translation is $y =$ [_____].

Problem 6 **Writing a Trigonometric Equation to Model a Situation**

Got It? **Temperature Cycles** The model $y = 22 \cos \frac{2\pi}{365}(x - 198) + 55$ models
the average daily temperature in your town x days after the start of the calendar year
$(0 \le x \le 365)$. Use the model to find the average temperature 150 days into the year.

12. Underline the correct word or words to complete the sentence.

The variable x represents the number of days / temperature in the equation.

13. Use the justifications at the right to find the average temperature.

$$y = \boxed{} \cos \frac{2\pi}{365}\left(x - \boxed{}\right) + \boxed{} \qquad \text{Write the original equation.}$$

$$= \boxed{} \cos \frac{2\pi}{365}\left(\boxed{} - \boxed{}\right) + \boxed{} \qquad \text{Substitute the value of } x \text{ into the equation.}$$

$$= \boxed{} \cos \frac{2\pi}{365}\left(\boxed{}\right) + \boxed{} \qquad \text{Simplify.}$$

$$= \boxed{}\left(\boxed{}\right) + \boxed{} \qquad \text{Evaluate cosine.}$$

$$\approx \boxed{} \qquad \text{Simplify.}$$

Lesson Check • Do you kow HOW?

Describe any phase shift or vertical shift in the graph of $y = 4\cos(x - 2) + 9$.

14. Identify each value.

$a =$ ☐ $b =$ ☐ $h =$ ☐ $k =$ ☐

15. Circle the variable that has an effect on the phase shift. Underline the variable that has an effect on the vertical shift.

a	b	h	k

16. Underline the correct numbers to complete the sentence.

The graph has a phase shift of $-9 \,/\, -2 \,/\, 1 \,/\, 2 \,/\, 4 \,/\, 9$ and a vertical shift

of $-9 \,/\, -2 \,/\, 1 \,/\, 2 \,/\, 4 \,/\, 9$.

Lesson Check • Do you UNDERSTAND?

Error Analysis Two students disagree on the translation for $y = \cos 3\left(x + \frac{\pi}{6}\right)$.
Amberly says it is $\frac{\pi}{2}$ units left of $y = \cos 3x$. Scott says that it is $\frac{\pi}{6}$ units left of
$y = \cos 3x$. Is either student correct? Describe any errors made by each student.

17. Write T for *true* or F for *false*.

_____ $y = \cos 3\left(x + \frac{\pi}{6}\right)$ is equivalent to $y = \cos\left(3x + \frac{\pi}{2}\right)$.

_____ The general form of the equation of the function includes $(x + h)$.

18. Is either student correct? Describe any errors made by each student.

_____

_____

_____

Math Success

Check off the vocabulary words that you understand.

☐ phase shift   ☐ translation   ☐ trigonometric functions

Rate how well you can *graph and write equations of translations of trigonometric functions*.

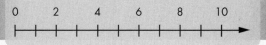

Reciprocal Trigonometric Functions

Vocabulary

● Review

1. Write T for *true* or F for *false*.

_____ The *reciprocal* of a negative number is negative.

_____ The *reciprocal* of a whole number is a fraction.

_____ The *reciprocal* of 0 is 1.

● Vocabulary Builder

secant (noun) SEEK **unt**

Related Words: cosecant, cosine, cotangent

Definition: The **secant** of an angle is the reciprocal of the cosine of the angle.

In Symbols: sec θ

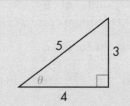

$\cos \theta = \frac{4}{5}$, so **sec** $\theta = \frac{5}{4}$

● Use Your Vocabulary

2. The cosine of an angle in a right triangle is the ratio of the length of adjacent side to the length of the hypotenuse. Find the *secant* of each angle marked θ.

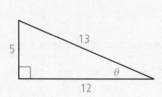

sec θ = ☐   sec θ = ☐   sec θ = ☐

Definition Cosecant, Secant, and Cotangent Functions

The *cosecant* (csc), *secant* (sec), and *cotangent* (cot) functions are defined using reciprocals. Their domains do not include the real numbers θ that make a denominator zero.

$$\csc \theta = \frac{1}{\sin \theta} \qquad \sec \theta = \frac{1}{\cos \theta} \qquad \cot \theta = \frac{1}{\tan \theta}$$

3. The tangent of an angle θ is $\sqrt{3}$. Circle the cotangent of the same angle.

$$\frac{\sqrt{3}}{3} \qquad\qquad \frac{\sqrt{3}}{2} \qquad\qquad \sqrt{3} \qquad\qquad 3$$

Problem 1 Finding Values Geometrically

Got It? What is the exact value of $\csc \frac{\pi}{3}$? Do not use a calculator.

4. Circle the graph that shows the angle $\frac{\pi}{3}$ radians.

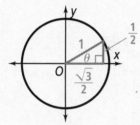 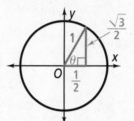 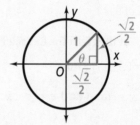 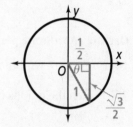

5. Use the graph you circled in Exercise 4 to write the sine of the angle.

$$\sin \frac{\pi}{3} = \underline{\qquad\qquad}$$

6. Use the definition of cosecant.

$$\csc \frac{\pi}{3} = \frac{1}{\sin \frac{\pi}{3}} = \frac{1}{\underline{\quad\quad}}$$

7. Circle the exact value of $\csc \frac{\pi}{3}$.

$$1 \qquad \frac{\sqrt{3}}{2} \qquad \frac{2\sqrt{3}}{3} \qquad \sqrt{3}$$

Got It? What is the exact value of $\cot\left(-\frac{5\pi}{4}\right)$? Do not use a calculator.

8. Use the unit circle at the right. Draw the angle $-\frac{5\pi}{4}$ radians.

9. Circle the coordinates of the point on the unit circle corresponding to $-\frac{5\pi}{4}$ radians.

$$\left(\frac{\sqrt{2}}{2}, \frac{\sqrt{2}}{2}\right) \qquad \left(-\frac{\sqrt{2}}{2}, \frac{\sqrt{2}}{2}\right) \qquad \left(-\frac{\sqrt{2}}{2}, -\frac{\sqrt{2}}{2}\right) \qquad \left(\frac{\sqrt{2}}{2}, -\frac{\sqrt{2}}{2}\right)$$

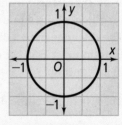

10. Use the definition of cotangent.

$$\cot\left(-\frac{5\pi}{4}\right) = \frac{1}{\underline{\quad\quad}\left(-\frac{5\pi}{4}\right)}$$

11. Find the exact value of $\cot\left(-\frac{5\pi}{4}\right)$.

$$\underline{\qquad\qquad}$$

Lesson 13-8

Got It? What are the graphs of $y = \tan x$ and $y = \cot x$ in the interval from 0 to 2π?

12. Make a table of values for both $\tan x$ and $\cot x$. Place an ✗ in the box if the value is undefined.

x	0	$\frac{\pi}{4}$	$\frac{\pi}{2}$	$\frac{3\pi}{4}$	π	$\frac{5\pi}{4}$	$\frac{3\pi}{2}$	$\frac{7\pi}{4}$	2π
tan x									
cot x									

13. Circle the boxes in Exercise 12 that show where the asymptotes for each graph are located.

The asymptotes for the tangent graph are at

☐ and ☐ .

The asymptotes for the cotangent graph are at

☐ , ☐ , and ☐ .

Use the coordinate plane at the right for Exercises 14 and 15.

14. Draw the asymptotes for the graphs.

15. Sketch the graphs of $y = \tan x$ and $y = \cot x$.

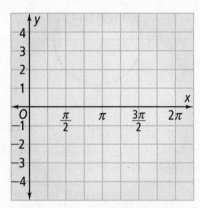

Got It? A restaurant is near the top of a tower. A diner looks down on an object along a line of sight that makes an angle of θ with the tower. The distance in feet of an object from the observer is modeled by the function $d = 553 \sec \theta$. How far away are objects sighted at angles of 50° and 80°?

16. Use the reciprocal rule.

$$\sec \theta = \frac{1}{\boxed{}}$$

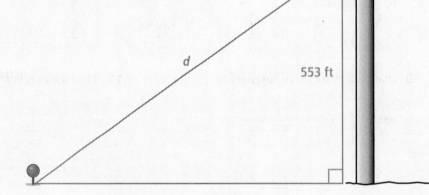

17. Use the TABLE screen below. Circle the rows that correspond to 50° and 80°.

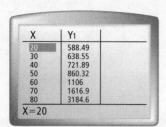

X	Y1
20	588.49
30	638.55
40	721.89
50	860.32
60	1106
70	1616.9
80	3184.6

X=20

18. An object sighted at 50° is about _____ ft away. An object sighted at 80° is about _____ ft away.

Lesson Check • Do you UNDERSTAND?

Reasoning Explain why the graph of $y = 5 \sec \theta$ has no zeros.

19. Multiple Choice How does the graph of $y = 5 \sec \theta$ differ from the graph of the parent function $y = \sec \theta$?

Ⓐ The period is shorter by a factor of 5. Ⓑ The graph is stretched vertically by a factor of 5.

Ⓒ The graph moves 5 units to the left. Ⓓ The graph moves 5 units up.

20. Circle the number of zeros in the graph $y = \sec \theta$.

0	1	2	3

21. Why does the graph of $y = 5 \sec \theta$ have no zeros?

_____

_____

_____

Math Success

Check off the vocabulary words that you understand.

☐ cosecant ☐ secant ☐ cotangent

Rate how well you can *graph and evaluate reciprocal trigonometric functions.*

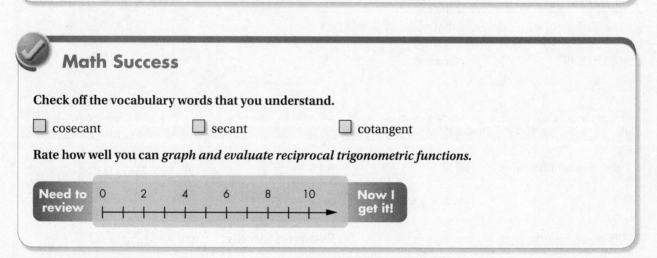

Lesson 13-8

Vocabulary

Review

1. Use the *identity properties* to make each equation true.

$3 + \boxed{} = 3$ $\qquad$ $-8\left(\boxed{}\right) = -8$ $\qquad$ $5 + \boxed{} + 17 = 17$ $\qquad$ $7x\left(\boxed{}\right) = x$

Vocabulary Builder

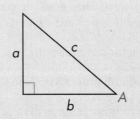

trigonometry (noun) **trig uh NAHM uh tree**

Main Idea: **Trigonometry** relates the measures of angles of a triangle to the lengths of its sides.

Related Words: cosecant, secant, cosine, sine, cotangent, tangent, trigonometric

$$\sin A = \frac{a}{c}$$
$$\cos A = \frac{b}{c}$$
$$\tan A = \frac{a}{b}$$

Use Your Vocabulary

2. Use the triangle at the right. Draw a line from the *trigonometric* expression in Column A to the corresponding ratio in Column B.

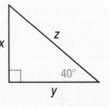

Column A	Column B
sin 40°	$\frac{x}{y}$
cos 40°	$\frac{x}{z}$
tan 40°	$\frac{y}{z}$

---

take note

Key Concept Basic Identities

Reciprocal Identities	$\csc \theta = \dfrac{1}{\sin \theta}$	$\sec \theta = \dfrac{1}{\cos \theta}$	$\tan \theta = \dfrac{1}{\cot \theta}$
	$\sin \theta = \dfrac{1}{\csc \theta}$	$\cos \theta = \dfrac{1}{\sec \theta}$	$\cot \theta = \dfrac{1}{\tan \theta}$
Tangent Identity	$\tan \theta = \dfrac{\sin \theta}{\cos \theta}$	**Cotangent Identity**	$\cot \theta = \dfrac{\cos \theta}{\sin \theta}$

Rewrite each function as a fraction using basic identities.

3. $\cos 58° = \dfrac{1}{}$

4. $\cot 129° = \dfrac{}{\sin 129°}$

5. $\tan \dfrac{\pi}{4} = \dfrac{1}{}$

The *domain of validity* of an identity is the set of values of the variable for which all expressions in the equation are defined.

Problem 2 Verifying an Identity Using Basic Identities

Got It? **Verify the identity $\dfrac{\csc \theta}{\sec \theta} = \cot \theta$. What is the domain of validity?**

6. Use basic identities and the justifications at the right to verify the identity.

$\dfrac{\csc \theta}{\sec \theta} = \dfrac{\dfrac{1}{\sin \theta}}{\dfrac{1}{}}$ Rewrite the left side using reciprocal identities.

$= \dfrac{1}{\sin \theta} \cdot \dfrac{}{}$ Rewrite fraction division as multiplication.

$= \dfrac{}{}$ Multiply.

$= \cot \theta$ Simplify.

7. Underline the correct words to complete each sentence.

The domain / range of $\cot \theta$ excludes multiples of π.

The domain / range of $\sec \theta$ excludes all odd / even multiples of $\frac{\pi}{2}$.

The domain / range of $\csc \theta$ excludes all odd / even multiples of $\frac{\pi}{2}$.

8. The domain of validity is the set of all real numbers except all multiples of $\boxed{}$.

Key Concept Pythagorean Identities

$$\cos^2 \theta + \sin^2 \theta = 1 \qquad\qquad 1 + \tan^2 \theta = \sec^2 \theta \qquad\qquad 1 + \cot^2 \theta = \csc^2 \theta$$

Complete.

9. $\sec^2 \theta - 1 = \boxed{}$

10. $\csc^2 \theta - \cot^2 \theta = \boxed{}$

Lesson 14-1

Problem 3 Verifying a Pythagorean Identity

Got It? Verify the third Pythagorean identity, $1 + \cot^2 \theta = \csc^2 \theta$.

11. The identity is verified below. Write a justification for each step.

$$1 + \cot^2 \theta = 1 + \frac{\cos^2 \theta}{\sin^2 \theta}$$

$$= \frac{\sin^2 \theta}{\sin^2 \theta} + \frac{\cos^2 \theta}{\sin^2 \theta}$$

$$= \frac{\sin^2 \theta + \cos^2 \theta}{\sin^2 \theta}$$

$$= \frac{1}{\sin^2 \theta}$$

$$= \csc^2 \theta$$

Got It? **Reasoning** Explain why the domain of validity is not the same for all three Pythagorean identities.

12. Draw a line from each expression in Column A to its domain of validity in Column B.

Column A	Column B
$\cos^2 \theta + \sin^2 \theta$	real numbers except odd multiples of $\frac{\pi}{2}$
$1 + \tan^2 \theta$	real numbers except multiples of π
$1 + \cot^2 \theta$	real numbers except multiples of $\frac{\pi}{2}$
	all real numbers

Problem 4 Verifying an Identity

Got It? Verify the identity $\sec^2 \theta - \sec^2 \theta \cos^2 \theta = \tan^2 \theta$.

13. Use the justifications at the right to verify the identity.

$$\sec^2 \theta - \sec^2 \theta \cos^2 \theta = \sec^2 \theta - \left(\frac{1}{\boxed{}} \right) \cos^2 \theta \qquad \text{Definition of secant}$$

$$= \sec^2 \theta - \boxed{} \qquad \text{Simplify.}$$

$$= \boxed{} - 1 \qquad \text{Pythagorean identity}$$

$$= \boxed{} \qquad \text{Simplify.}$$

Problem 5 Simplifying an Expression

Got It? What is a simplified trigonometric expression for sec θ cot θ?

14. Complete the reasoning model below to simplify the expression.

Think	Write
Write the original expression.	sec θ cot θ
Rewrite sec θ and cot θ using sin θ and cos θ.	$= \left(\right)\left(\right)$
Simplify.	$= \dfrac{}{\sin \theta}$
Use a reciprocal identity.	$=$

Lesson Check • Do you UNDERSTAND?

Error Analysis A student simplified the expression $2 - \cos^2 \theta$ to $1 - \sin^2 \theta$. What error did the student make? What is the correct simplified expression?

15. The expression is simplified below. Write a justification for each step.

$2 - \cos^2 \theta = 2 - (1 - \sin^2 \theta)$

$\qquad = 2 - 1 + \sin^2 \theta$

$\qquad = 1 + \sin^2 \theta$

16. What error did the student make?

 ## Math Success

Check off the vocabulary words that you understand.

☐ trigonometric identity

Rate how well you can *verify trigonometric identities*.

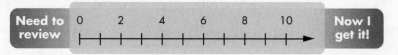

Lesson 14-1

Vocabulary

● Review

1. Draw a line from each item in Column A to its additive *inverse* in Column B.

Column A	Column B
5	0
−9	−y
0	9
y	−5

● Vocabulary Builder

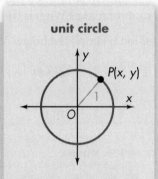

unit circle

unit circle (noun) YOO nit SUR kul

Definition: A **unit circle** is a circle with radius 1 centered at (0, 0) on the coordinate plane.

Main Idea: For any point (x, y) on the **unit circle**, a right triangle can be formed with a hypotenuse of length 1 and side lengths x and y. Using the definition of sine and cosine, $x = \cos \theta$, and $y = \sin \theta$.

● Use Your Vocabulary

Use a calculator and the *unit circle* to find each value. Round to the nearest tenth.

2. $x \approx$ _____ , $y \approx$ _____

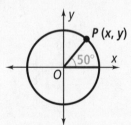

3. $x \approx$ _____ , $y \approx$ _____

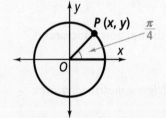

Key Concept Inverses of Three Trigonometric Functions

Function	Domain	Range	Inverse Function	Domain	Range
$y = \cos\theta$	$0 \leq \theta \leq \pi$	$-1 \leq y \leq 1$	$\theta = \cos^{-1}x$	$-1 \leq x \leq 1$	$0 \leq \theta \leq \pi$
$y = \sin\theta$	$-\frac{\pi}{2} \leq \theta \leq \frac{\pi}{2}$	$-1 \leq y \leq 1$	$\theta = \sin^{-1}x$	$-1 \leq x \leq 1$	$-\frac{\pi}{2} \leq \theta \leq \frac{\pi}{2}$
$y = \tan\theta$	$-\frac{\pi}{2} \leq \theta \leq \frac{\pi}{2}$	y is any real number	$\theta = \tan^{-1}x$	x is any real number	$-\frac{\pi}{2} \leq \theta \leq \frac{\pi}{2}$

4. How are the domains given above of trigonometric functions different from those of inverse trigonometric functions?

_____

_____

5. What is the range of the inverse function $y = \sin^{-1}(x)$ in degrees?

$\frac{\pi}{2}$ radians = ⬚°, so the range is ⬚° $\leq \theta \leq$ ⬚°.

 Problem 1 **Using the Unit Circle**

Got It? Use a unit circle. What is the value of the inverse function $\cos^{-1}\left(-\frac{1}{2}\right)$ in degrees?

6. Follow the steps below to find the value in degrees.

Step 1 Use the unit circle at the right. Mark each point on the unit circle that has an x-coordinate of $\left(-\frac{1}{2}\right)$.

Step 2 Draw two right triangles using the points you marked in Step 1 and the origin.

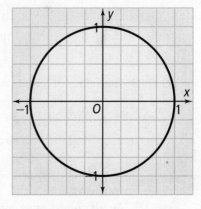

7. Circle the type of right triangle you drew.

30-60-90	45-45-90

8. Use the unit circle and the triangles. Label the angle in standard position with its measure.

9. The value of the inverse function $\cos^{-1}\left(-\frac{1}{2}\right)$ is 30° / 60° / 120° .

 Problem 2 **Using a Calculator to Find the Inverse of Sine**

Got It? What are the radian measures of all angles whose sine is 0.44?

10. Use a calculator. Circle the radian measure with a sine value closest to 0.44.

0.43	0.46	26.1	28.2

Lesson 14-2

11. Circle the two quadrants in which an angle with a positive sine value falls.

| I | II | III | IV |

12. Complete to identify the solutions between 0 and 2π.

0.46 and $\pi -$ ☐ $\approx$ ☐

13. The radian measures of all angles whose sine is 0.44 are ☐ $+ 2\pi n$

and ☐ $+ 2\pi n$.

 Problem 5 **Solving by Factoring**

Got It? What are the values for θ that satisfy the equation $\sin \theta \cos \theta - \cos \theta = 0$ for $0 \le \theta \le 2\pi$?

14. Circle the common factor of $\sin \theta \cos \theta$ and $\cos \theta$.

| $\sin \theta$ | $\cos \theta$ | $\sin^2 \theta$ | $\cos^2 \theta$ |

15. Factor $\sin \theta \cos \theta - \cos \theta = 0$.

16. Set each factor from Exercise 15 equal to 0 and simplify.

17. Circle the values of θ that satisfy both equations in Exercise 16.

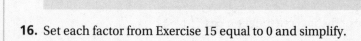

| 0 | $\dfrac{\pi}{2}$ | π | $\dfrac{3\pi}{2}$ | 2π |

Problem 6 **Using the Inverse of a Trigonometric Function**

Got It? An air conditioner cools a home when the temperature outside is above 26°C. During the summer, you can model the outside temperature in degrees Celsius using the function $f(t) = 24 - 8 \cos \frac{\pi}{12} t$, where t is the number of hours past midnight. During what hours is the air conditioner cooling the home?

18. Use the justifications at the right to find t when $f(t) = 26$.

$$\boxed{} = 24 - 8 \cos \frac{\pi}{12}t \qquad \text{Substitute 26 for } f(t).$$

$$\boxed{} = \cos \frac{\pi}{12}t \qquad \text{Subtract 24 and divide by } -8.$$

$$\cos^{-1} \boxed{} = \frac{\pi}{12}t \qquad \text{Use inverse cosine.}$$

$$\boxed{} \cos^{-1} \boxed{} = t \qquad \text{Isolate the variable.}$$

$$t = \boxed{} \qquad \text{Evaluate.}$$

19. The air conditioner goes on about $\boxed{}$ hours after midnight, or $\boxed{}$ A.M.

It goes off about $\boxed{}$ hours before midnight, or $\boxed{}$ P.M.

Lesson Check • Do you UNDERSTAND?

Error Analysis A student solved the equation $\sin^2 \theta = \frac{1}{2} \sin \theta$, $0 \le \theta < 2\pi$, as shown. What error did the student make?

$$\sin^2 \theta = \frac{1}{2} \sin \theta$$
$$\sin \theta = \frac{1}{2}$$
$$\theta = \frac{\pi}{6} \text{ and } \frac{5\pi}{6}$$

20. Use the justifications at the right to solve for $\sin \theta$.

$$\sin^2 \theta - \frac{1}{2} \sin \theta = \boxed{} \qquad \text{Subtract } \sin \theta \text{ from both sides of the equation.}$$

$$\left(\boxed{} \right)\left(\sin \theta - \frac{1}{2} \right) = 0 \qquad \text{Factor.}$$

$$\sin \theta = 0 \text{ or } \sin \theta = \boxed{} \qquad \text{Use the zero product property of equality.}$$

21. The values $\boxed{}$, $\frac{\pi}{6}$, $\frac{5\pi}{6}$, $\boxed{}$, and $\boxed{}$ are solutions.

22. What error did the student make?

_____

_____

Math Success

Check off the vocabulary words that you understand.

☐ inverse trigonometric functions   ☐ trigonometric equations

Rate how well you can *work with trigonometric functions and equations.*

Need to review   0   2   4   6   8   10   Now I get it!

Lesson 14-2

Right Triangles and Trigonometric Ratios

Vocabulary

● Review

Express each *ratio* as a fraction in simplest form.

1. 7 red marbles out of 30 marbles

2. 1 state out of 50 United States

3. 2 cups of pretzels to 8 cups of party mix

4. 15 girls to a class of 25 students

● Vocabulary Builder

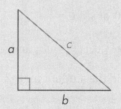

right triangle

Sides *a* and *b* are the legs.
Side *c* is the hypotenuse.

right triangle   (noun) **ryt TRY ang gul**

Related Words: hypotenuse, leg

Definition: A **right triangle** is a triangle with exactly one right angle.

● Use Your Vocabulary

5. Circle the hypotenuse of each *right triangle* below.

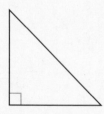

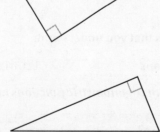

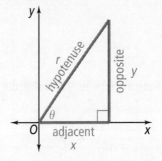

Key Concept   Trigonometric Ratios for a Right Triangle

If θ is an acute angle of a right triangle, x is the length of the adjacent leg (ADJ), y is the length of the opposite leg (OPP), and r is the length of the hypotenuse (HYP), then the trigonometric ratios of θ are as follows.

$$\sin \theta = \frac{y}{r} = \frac{\text{OPP}}{\text{HYP}} \qquad \csc \theta = \frac{r}{y} = \frac{\text{HYP}}{\text{OPP}}$$

$$\cos \theta = \frac{x}{r} = \frac{\text{ADJ}}{\text{HYP}} \qquad \sec \theta = \frac{r}{x} = \frac{\text{HYP}}{\text{ADJ}}$$

$$\tan \theta = \frac{y}{x} = \frac{\text{OPP}}{\text{ADJ}} \qquad \cot \theta = \frac{x}{y} = \frac{\text{ADJ}}{\text{OPP}}$$

6. Use $\triangle PQR$ at the right to write each ratio.

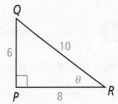

$$\sin \theta = \underline{\quad\quad} \qquad \cos \theta = \underline{\quad\quad} \qquad \tan \theta = \underline{\quad\quad}$$

Problem 2   Finding Distance

Got It? The large glass pyramid at the Louvre in Paris has a square base. The angle formed by each face and the ground is 49.7°. What is the distance from the center of a side of the base to the top along the lateral face?

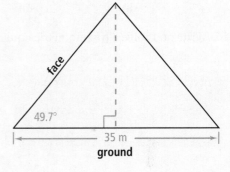

7. Underline the correct word to complete each sentence.

Let x equal the length of a leg / the hypotenuse of the right triangle.

The length of the vertical / horizontal leg of the right triangle is 17.5 ft.

You can use the sine / cosine function to find the length of the missing side.

8. Write and solve a trigonometric equation to find the missing length.

Problem 3   Finding Trigonometric Ratios

Got It? In $\triangle DEF$, $\angle D$ is a right angle and $\tan E = \frac{3}{4}$. What are $\sin E$ and $\sec F$?

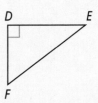

9. Use the triangle at the right. Circle the side that is $3n$ units long. Underline the side that is $4n$ units long.

$$\overline{DE} \qquad\qquad \overline{EF} \qquad\qquad \overline{DF}$$

Lesson 14-3

10. Use the Pythagorean Theorem to find the length of the third side.

11. Complete each ratio. Then simplify to find sin *E* and sec *F*.

$$\sin E = \frac{\boxed{}}{\text{HYP}} = \boxed{} \qquad \sec F = \frac{\boxed{}}{\text{ADJ}} = \boxed{}$$

Problem 5 **Finding an Angle Measure**

Got It? **What is $m\angle A$? Use a trigonometric ratio.**

12. In relation to $\angle A$, circle the two sides whose lengths are given in the triangle at the right.

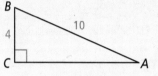

| opposite | adjacent | hypotenuse |

13. Circle the trigonometric function you can use to find $m\angle A$.

| sine | cosine | tangent |

14. Write and solve a trigonometric equation to find $m\angle A$.

Problem 6 **Using the Inverse of a Trigonometric Function**

Got It? **Construction** An entrance to a building is not wheelchair-accessible. The entrance is 6 ft above ground level and 30 ft from the roadway. The maximum angle that a wheelchair ramp can make with the ground is 4.8° for the slope to meet the regulation of 1 in. of rise for every 1 ft of run. How long must the ramp be?

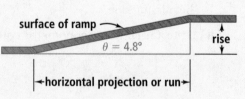

15. Circle the equation you can use to find the length of the ramp.

$$\sin 4.8° = \frac{6}{x} \qquad \sin 4.8° = \frac{x}{6} \qquad \cos 4.8° = \frac{6}{x} \qquad \cos 4.8° = \frac{x}{6} \qquad \tan 4.8° = \frac{6}{x}$$

16. Use the equation you circled in Exercise 15 to find the length of the ramp.

Lesson Check • Do you UNDERSTAND?

Writing In a right triangle, the length of the shortest side is 8.4 m, and the length of the hypotenuse is 12.9 m. Show and describe how you can find the acute angle measures.

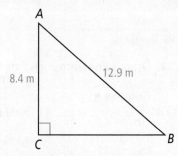

17. To find $m\angle B$, I can use inverse sine / inverse cosine / inverse tangent .

18. Describe how you can find the measure of the other acute angle in the triangle.

_____

_____

_____

19. Find the acute angle measures.

Math Success

Check off the vocabulary words that you understand.

☐ trigonometric ratios

Rate how well you can *find side lengths and angle measures in a right triangle.*

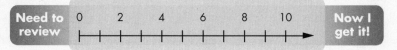

Need to review 0 2 4 6 8 10 Now I get it!

Vocabulary

● **Review**

1. Draw a line from each figure in Column A to the formula for its *area* in Column B.

Column A	Column B
circle	$A = bh$
trapezoid	$A = \left(\frac{1}{2}\right)bh$
rectangle	$A = h\left(\frac{b_1 + b_2}{2}\right)$
triangle	$A = \pi r^2$

● **Vocabulary Builder**

Law of Sines   (noun)   **law uv synz**

Related Words: angle measure, side length, sine, triangle

Main Idea: If you know two angle measures and a side length of a triangle, you can use the **Law of Sines** to find the lengths of the other sides. If you know two side lengths and the measure of the angle opposite one of them, you can use the **Law of Sines** to find the measure of the other angles of the triangle.

Math Usage: In $\triangle ABC$, $\frac{\sin A}{a} = \frac{\sin B}{b} = \frac{\sin C}{c}$.

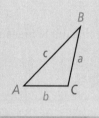

● **Use Your Vocabulary**

2. Use the triangle at the right to complete the extended proportion of the *Law of Sines*.

$$\frac{\sin \boxed{}}{f} = \frac{\sin G}{\boxed{}} = \frac{\boxed{}}{17}$$

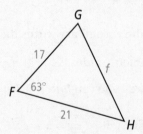

Formula Area of a Triangle

Any $\triangle ABC$ with side lengths a, b, and c has area

$$\frac{1}{2}bc\sin A = \frac{1}{2}ac\sin B = \frac{1}{2}ab\sin C.$$

Problem 1 Finding the Area of a Triangle

Got It? A triangle has two sides 12 in. and 15 in. long. The measure of the angle between the sides is 24°. What is the area of the triangle?

3. Use $\frac{1}{2}bc\sin A$. If b is 12 in., then c is _____ in., and A is _____°.

4. Use the formula to find the area.

5. The area of the triangle is about _____ in.^{2}.

Theorem Law of Sines

In any triangle, the ratio of the sine of each angle to its opposite side is constant. In particular, for $\triangle ABC$, labeled as shown,

$$\frac{\sin A}{a} = \frac{\sin B}{b} = \frac{\sin C}{c}.$$

6. Write T for *true* or F for *false*.

_____ In an equiangular triangle, the values of a, b, and c must always be equal.

_____ If $\angle A$ has the greatest measure in $\triangle ABC$, then $a < b$ and $a < c$.

Problem 2 Finding a Side of a Triangle

Got It? In $\triangle KLM$, $m\angle K = 120°$, $m\angle M = 50°$, and $ML = 35$ yd. What is KL?

7. Use the information in the problem to label the triangle.

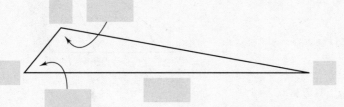

Lesson 14-4

8. Use the Law of Sines and the justifications at the right to find KL.

$$\frac{\sin K}{\boxed{}} = \frac{\boxed{}}{KL}$$ Write a proportion.

$$\frac{\sin \boxed{}}{35} = \frac{\sin \boxed{}}{KL}$$ Substitute.

$$KL = \frac{35 \sin \boxed{}}{\sin \boxed{}}$$ Solve for KL.

$$KL \approx \boxed{}$$ Simplify.

Problem 3 Finding an Angle of a Triangle

Got It? In $\triangle PQR$, $m\angle R = 97.5°$, $r = 80$, and $p = 75$. What is $m\angle P$?

9. Complete the proportion.

$$\frac{\sin \boxed{}}{r} = \frac{\sin P}{\boxed{}}$$

10. Use the justifications at the right to find $m\angle P$.

$$\frac{\sin 97.5°}{\boxed{}} = \frac{\sin P}{\boxed{}}$$ Substitute.

$$\frac{\sin 97.5°}{\boxed{}} = \sin P$$ Isolate the sine term.

$$\sin^{-1}\left(\frac{\sin 97.5°}{\boxed{}}\right) = P$$ Apply the inverse sine function.

$$\boxed{} \approx P$$ Simplify.

Problem 4 Using the Law of Sines to Solve a Problem

Got It? A landscaper sights the top of a tree at a 68° angle. She then moves an additional 70 ft directly away from the tree and sights the top at a 43° angle. How tall is the tree to the nearest tenth of a foot?

11. Use the information in the problem to label the diagram.

12. Using supplementary angles, $m\angle ABD$ is $180 - \boxed{}$, or $\boxed{}°$.

13. Using the Triangle-Sum Theorem, $m\angle ADB$ is $\boxed{}°$.

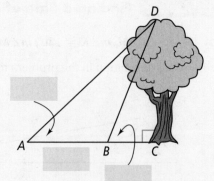

14. The Law of Sines was used to find BD. Write a justification for each step.

$$\frac{\sin A}{BD} = \frac{\sin D}{AB}$$

_____

$$\frac{\sin 43}{BD} = \frac{\sin 25}{70}$$

_____

$$BD = \frac{70 \sin 43}{\sin 25} \approx 113.0$$

_____

15. Substitute known values into $\sin \theta = \frac{\text{opposite}}{\text{hypotenuse}}$ to find CD.

$$\sin \boxed{} = \frac{CD}{\boxed{}}$$

$$CD = \boxed{} \sin \boxed{} = \boxed{}$$

16. To the nearest tenth of a foot, the tree is $\boxed{}$ feet tall.

Lesson Check • Do you UNDERSTAND?

Error Analysis Suppose you used the Law of Sines and wrote $a = \frac{3 \sin 22°}{\sin 45°}$. Is that the same equation as $a = 3 \sin \left(\frac{22}{45}\right)°$? Explain.

17. Find the value of each expression to the nearest ten-thousandth.

$\sin 22°$	$\sin 45°$	$\dfrac{\sin 22°}{\sin 45°}$	$\sin \left(\dfrac{22}{45}\right)°$

18. Is $\sin \left(\frac{22}{45}\right)°$ equal to $\frac{\sin 22°}{\sin 45°}$? Explain.

_____

_____

Math Success

Check off the vocabulary words that you understand.

☐ Law of Sines   ☐ area of a triangle

Rate how well you can *use the Law of Sines*.

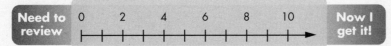

Need to review   0   2   4   6   8   10   Now I get it!

Lesson 14-4

14-5 The Law of Cosines

 Vocabulary

Review

1. Classify each *angle* measure as *acute*, *right*, or *obtuse*.

135° _____   17° _____   90° _____

76° _____   164° _____   94° _____

2. Classify each triangle described below as *acute*, *right*, or *obtuse*.

A triangle with one *acute angle* is acute / obtuse / right / any of these .

A triangle with one *right angle* is acute / obtuse / right / any of these .

A triangle with one *obtuse angle* is acute / obtuse / right / any of these .

Vocabulary Builder

Law of Cosines (noun) law uv KOH synz

Related Words: triangle, side length, angle measure, sine

Main Idea: The **Law of Cosines** relates the length of a side of a triangle to the measure of the opposite angle.

Math Usage: In $\triangle ABC$, $a^2 = b^2 + c^2 - 2bc \cos A$. Similarly, $b^2 = a^2 + c^2 - 2ac \cos B$, and $c^2 = a^2 + b^2 - 2ab \cos C$.

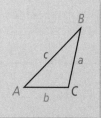

Use Your Vocabulary

3. Use the triangle at the right and the *Law of Cosines* to complete the equation.

$a^2 = \boxed{}^2 + \boxed{}^2 - 2(17)\left(\boxed{}\right) \cos \boxed{}$

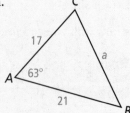

Theorem Law of Cosines

In $\triangle ABC$, let a, b, and c represent the lengths of the sides opposite $\angle A$, $\angle B$, and $\angle C$, respectively.

- $a^2 = b^2 + c^2 - 2bc \cos A$
- $b^2 = a^2 + c^2 - 2ac \cos B$
- $c^2 = a^2 + b^2 - 2ab \cos C$

4. To find the length of a side of a triangle using the Law of Cosines, what information must you know?

_____

_____

_____

 Problem 1 Using the Law of Cosines to Solve a Problem

Got It? The lengths of two sides of a triangle are 8 and 10, and the measure of the angle between them is 40°. What is the approximate length of the third side?

5. Let $b = 8$, $c = 10$, and $m\angle A = 40°$. Use the justifications at the right to find a.

$a^2 = b^2 + c^2 - 2bc \cos A$ Write the Law of Cosines.

$a^2 = \boxed{}^2 + \boxed{}^2 - 2\left(\boxed{}\right)\left(\boxed{}\right) \cos \boxed{}°$ Substitute.

$a^2 = \boxed{} - \boxed{}\left(\cos \boxed{}\right)$ Simplify powers.

$a^2 \approx \boxed{}$ Evaluate and simplify.

$a \approx \boxed{}$ Take the square root.

6. The length of the third side is about $\boxed{}$.

 Problem 2 Finding an Angle Measure

Got It? The lengths of the sides of a triangle are 10, 14, and 15. What is the measure of the angle opposite the longest side?

7. Let $a = 15$. Circle the equation you can use to find the measure of the angle opposite side a.

$a^2 = b^2 + c^2 - 2bc \cos A$ $b^2 = a^2 + c^2 - 2ac \cos B$

$c^2 = a^2 + b^2 - 2ab \cos C$

Lesson 14-5

8. Use the information in the problem to solve the equation you chose in Exercise 7.

9. The measure of the angle opposite the longest side is about ⬚°.

Problem 3 **Finding an Angle Measure**

Got It? In $\triangle RST$, $s = 41$, $t = 53$, and $m\angle R = 126°$. What is $m\angle T$?

10. Use the information in the problem to label the triangle below.

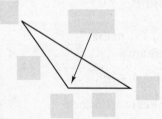

11. The Law of Cosines was used to find the length of r. Write a justification for each step.

$r^2 = s^2 + t^2 - 2st \cos R$

$r^2 = 41^2 + 53^2 - 2(41)(53) \cos 126°$

$r^2 = 1681 + 2809 - 4346 \cos 126°$

$r^2 = 4490 - 4346 \cos 126°$

$r^2 \approx 7044.51$

$r \approx 83.9$

12. Now use $t^2 = r^2 + s^2 - 2rs \cos T$ and your answer from Exercise 11 to find $m\angle T$.

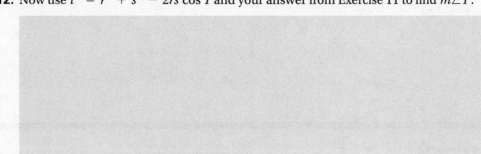

Lesson Check • Do you UNDERSTAND?

Writing Explain how you choose between the Law of Sines and the Law of Cosines when finding the measure of a missing angle or side.

13. Write **C** if you would use the Law of Cosines to find a missing measure in a triangle or **S** if you would use the Law of Sines.

_____ The lengths of two sides and the measure of the included angle are given. Find the length of the third side.

_____ The lengths of three sides are given. Find the measure of one angle.

_____ The measures of two angles and the length of the included side are given. Find the length of another side.

14. Explain how to choose between the Law of Sines and the Law of Cosines in solving a triangle.

_____

_____

_____

_____

Math Success

Check off the vocabulary words that you understand.

☐ Law of Cosines   ☐ Law of Sines   ☐ trigonometry

Rate how well you can *use the Law of Cosines*.

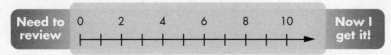

Lesson 14-5

Angle Identities

Vocabulary

● Review

1. Circle the inequality that completes the definition of a *negative* number. A number x is *negative* if __?__ .

$$x < 0 \qquad x > 0 \qquad x = 0 \qquad x \geq 0$$

Underline the correct word to complete each sentence.

2. The product of a positive number and a *negative* number is positive / negative .

3. The sum of two *negative* numbers is always positive / negative .

● Vocabulary Builder

verify (verb) VEHR **uh fy**

Definition: To **verify** is to prove or confirm.

Math Usage: You use identities to **verify** trigonometric statements.

Examples: Please **verify** that the doors are closed and the lights are off. The company could not **verify** the employee's address.

● Use Your Vocabulary

Complete each statement with the correct form of the word *verify*.

verify   verified   verifying

4. The students were __?__ the results of their experiment.

_____

5. The chemistry students __?__ their hypothesis by conducting an experiment.

_____

6. You must __?__ that all the arrangements have been made.

_____

Properties Angle Identities

Negative Angle Identities	$\sin(-\theta) = -\sin\theta$	$\cos(-\theta) = \cos\theta$	$\tan(-\theta) = -\tan\theta$
Cofunction Identities	$\sin\left(\frac{\pi}{2} - \theta\right) = \cos\theta$	$\cos\left(\frac{\pi}{2} - \theta\right) = \sin\theta$	$\tan\left(\frac{\pi}{2} - \theta\right) = \cot\theta$

7. Use the negative angle identities and the cofunction identities. Circle an expression equivalent to $\cos(-30°)$.

$\cos(30°)$	$\tan(-30°)$	$-\cos 30°$	$\sin(-30°)$

Problem 2 Deriving a Cofunction Identity

Got It? How can you use the definitions of the trigonometric ratios for a right triangle to derive the cofunction identity for $\sec(90° - A)$?

8. Use the triangle and the justifications at the right to solve the equation.

$\sec(90° - A) = \sec\left(\boxed{}\right)$ A and B are complementary.

$= \dfrac{\boxed{}}{a}$ Definition of secant in a right triangle

$= \boxed{}\ A$ Definition of cosecant in a right triangle

Properties Angle Difference Identities

$$\sin(A - B) = \sin A \cos B - \cos A \sin B \qquad \cos(A - B) = \cos A \cos B + \sin A \sin B$$

$$\tan(A - B) = \frac{\tan A - \tan B}{1 + \tan A \tan B}$$

9. Use the justifications at the right to derive the sine negative angle identity from the sine angle difference identity.

$\sin\left(\boxed{} - B\right) = \sin\boxed{}\cos B - \cos\boxed{}\sin B$ Substitute 0 for A.

$\sin(-B) = \boxed{}\cos B - \boxed{}\sin B$ Evaluate sine and cosine.

$\sin(-B) = \boxed{}$ Simplify.

Problem 4 Using an Angle Difference Identity

Got It? What is the exact value of $\sin 15°$?

10. Circle the pair of angles whose difference is $15°$.

$A = 60°, B = 30°$	$A = 45°, B = 30°$	$A = 90°, B = 45°$

Lesson 14-6

11. Cross out the formula that you would NOT use to find the exact value of sin 15°.

$$\cos(A - B) = \cos A \cos B + \sin A \sin B \qquad \sin(A - B) = \sin A \cos B - \cos A \sin B$$

12. Substitute the pair of angles from Exercise 10 into the difference formula you did *not* cross out in Exercise 11. Then solve for the value of sin 15°.

Problem 5 Deriving a Sum Identity

Got It? How can you derive an identity for sin (A + B)? Use the difference identity for sin (A − B).

13. Use the justifications at the right to derive the sine angle sum identity.

$\sin (A + B) = \sin (A - (-B))$ Substitute −(−B) for B.

$\qquad = \sin A \cos \boxed{} - \cos A \sin \boxed{}$ Use the sine angle difference identity.

$\qquad = \sin A \boxed{} - \cos A \boxed{}$ Use negative angle identities.

$\qquad = \boxed{} + \boxed{}$ Simplify.

---

take note

Properties Angle Sum Identities

$$\sin (A + B) = \sin A \cos B + \cos A \sin B \qquad \cos (A + B) = \cos A \cos B - \sin A \sin B$$

$$\tan (A + B) = \frac{\tan A + \tan B}{1 - \tan A \tan B}$$

14. To find the exact value of sin 75°, I can write 75° as $\boxed{}° + \boxed{}°$.

Problem 6 Using an Angle Sum Identity

Got It? What is the exact value of tan 105°?

15. Circle the first step in finding the exact value of tan 105°. Underline the second step.

Substitute the values of two angles into the equation $\tan (A + B) = \frac{\tan A + \tan B}{1 - \tan A \tan B}$.

Write 105° as the sum of two angles.

16. $105° = 60° + \boxed{}°$

---

17. Use the tangent angle sum identity to find the exact value of tan 105°.

Lesson Check • Do you UNDERSTAND?

Error Analysis A question on a test asked, "Between 0 and 2π, the equation $-\cos\theta = \cos\theta$ has how many solutions?" A student divided each side by $\cos\theta$ to get $-1 = 1$ and concluded that there are no solutions. What mistake did the student make?

18. Use the functions $y = \sin\theta$, $y = -\sin\theta$, $y = \cos\theta$, and $y = -\cos\theta$ to label each graph.

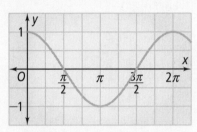 $y =$

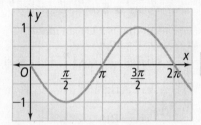 $y =$

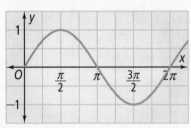 $y =$

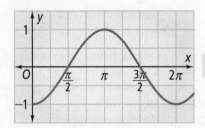 $y =$

19. $\cos\theta = -\cos\theta$ only when $\cos\theta = \boxed{0 / \frac{\sqrt{2}}{2} / 1}$ or when $\theta = \boxed{}$ or $\theta = \boxed{}$.

20. Explain the mistake the student made.

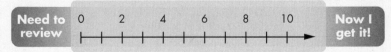

Math Success

Check off the vocabulary words that you understand.

☐ verify   ☐ negative angle identity   ☐ cofunction angle identity

Rate how well you can *use angle identities*.

| Need to review | 0 | 2 | 4 | 6 | 8 | 10 | Now I get it! |

Lesson 14-6

14-7 Double-Angle and Half-Angle Identities

Vocabulary

● **Review**

1. Circle the equation that gives the *Pythagorean identity*.

$$\sin^2\theta - \cos^2\theta = 1 \qquad \sin^2\theta + \cos^2\theta = 1 \qquad \tan^2\theta + \cos^2\theta = 1$$

2. Cross out the equation that is NOT an *identity*.

$$\sin(-\theta) = \sin\theta \qquad \cos\left(\frac{\pi}{2} - \theta\right) = \sin\theta \qquad \tan(-\theta) = -\tan\theta$$

● **Vocabulary Builder**

formula (noun) FAWRM **yoo luh**

Definition: A **formula** is an equation that uses numbers and letters to represent a relationship between two or more quantities.

Example: The quadratic **formula** is $x = \frac{-b \pm \sqrt{b^2 - 4ac}}{2a}$.

● **Use Your Vocabulary**

3. Circle the *formula* for the Pythagorean Theorem.

$$a + b = c \qquad a^2 + b^2 = c^2 \qquad |a + b| = |c| \qquad |a| + |b| \ge |c|$$

take note

Properties   Double-Angle Identities

$$\cos 2\theta = \cos^2\theta - \sin^2\theta \qquad \cos 2\theta = 2\cos^2\theta - 1 \qquad \cos 2\theta = 1 - 2\sin^2\theta$$

$$\sin 2\theta = 2\sin\theta\cos\theta \qquad \tan 2\theta = \frac{2\tan\theta}{1 - \tan^2\theta}$$

4. Cross out all the θ values for which you could NOT use double-angle identities to find the exact value of sine, cosine, or tangent.

| 15° | 20° | 30° | 45° | 55° | 60° | 75° | 90° | 100° |

Problem 2 Using a Double-Angle Identity

Got It? What is the exact value of sin 120°? Use a double-angle identity.

5. Circle the double-angle identity you can use to find the exact value of sin 120°.

$$\sin(2 \cdot 60°) = 2\sin 60° \cos 60° \qquad \sin(2 \cdot 60°) = 2\cos^2 60° - 1$$

6. **Multiple Choice** Which is the exact value of sin 120°?

Ⓐ $\frac{1}{2}$ Ⓑ $-\frac{\sqrt{3}}{2}$ Ⓒ $\frac{\sqrt{3}}{2}$ Ⓓ $-\frac{1}{2}$

Problem 3 Verifying an Identity

Got It? Verify the identity $2\cos 2\theta = 4\cos^2 \theta - 2$.

7. Circle the double-angle identity that you can use to verify that
$2\cos 2\theta = 4\cos^2 \theta - 2$.

$$\cos 2\theta = \cos^2 \theta - \sin^2 \theta \qquad \cos 2\theta = 2\cos^2 \theta - 1 \qquad \cos 2\theta = 1 - \sin^2 \theta$$

8. Verify the identity using the equation you circled in Exercise 7.

---

take note

Properties Half-Angle Identities

$$\sin \frac{A}{2} = \pm\sqrt{\frac{1 - \cos A}{2}} \qquad \cos \frac{A}{2} = \pm\sqrt{\frac{1 + \cos A}{2}} \qquad \tan \frac{A}{2} = \pm\sqrt{\frac{1 - \cos A}{1 + \cos A}}$$

The positive or negative sign for each function depends on the quadrant in which $\frac{A}{2}$ lies.

---

9. For which values of $\frac{A}{2}$ is $\tan \frac{A}{2}$ positive? Explain.

Lesson 14-7

Got It? What is the exact value of sin 150°? Use half-angle identities.

10. Use the justifications at the right to find sin 150°.

$$\sin 150 = \sin \dfrac{\boxed{}}{2}$$ Rewrite 150 as a fraction with denominator 2.

$$= \pm\sqrt{\dfrac{1 - \cos \boxed{}}{2}}$$ Use a half-angle identity.

$$= \pm\sqrt{\dfrac{1 - \boxed{}}{2}}$$ Evaluate the cosine.

$$= \pm \boxed{}$$ Simplify.

11. 150° is in Quadrant $\boxed{}$, so sin 150 is positive / negative .

12. The exact value of sin 150° is $\boxed{}$.

Got It? Given $\sin \theta = -\dfrac{24}{25}$ and $180° < \theta < 270°$, what is the exact value of $\cos \dfrac{\theta}{2}$?

13. Complete the reasoning model below to find cos θ.

Think	Write
Write the Pythagorean identity.	$\boxed{} + \cos^2 \theta = 1$
Substitute for sin θ.	$\boxed{} + \cos^2 \theta = 1$
Now I can solve for cos θ. The square root is negative because θ is in Quadrant $\boxed{}$.	$\cos^2 \theta = 1 - \dfrac{\boxed{}}{625}$ $\cos^2 \theta = \dfrac{\boxed{}}{625}$ $\cos \theta = \dfrac{\boxed{}}{25}$

14. Since $180° < \theta < 270°$, $90° < \dfrac{\theta}{2} < \boxed{}$.

Therefore, $\dfrac{\theta}{2}$ is in Quadrant $\boxed{}$, and $\cos \dfrac{\theta}{2}$ is negative / positive .

15. The cosine half-angle identity was used to find $\cos\frac{\theta}{2}$. Write a justification for each step.

$$\cos\frac{\theta}{2} = \pm\sqrt{\frac{1 + \cos\theta}{2}}$$

$$= -\sqrt{\frac{1 + \left(-\frac{7}{25}\right)}{2}}$$

$$= -\sqrt{\frac{\frac{18}{25}}{2}}$$

$$= -\sqrt{\frac{9}{25}}$$

$$= -\frac{3}{5}$$

Lesson Check • Do you UNDERSTAND?

Express 2 sin 2A cos 2A as a single-term trigonometric expression.

16. Write 2 sin 2A cos 2A as a sum of two like terms.

17. Your sum in Exercise 16 can be written using one of the following. Circle your answer.

angle difference identity   angle sum identity   half-angle identity

18. Now write 2 sin 2A cos 2A as a single term.

2 sin 2A cos 2A = sin   = sin

Math Success

Check off the vocabulary words that you understand.

☐ identity   ☐ formula   ☐ double-angle identity   ☐ half-angle identity

Rate how well you can *use double-angle and half-angle identities.*

Need to review   0   2   4   6   8   10   Now I get it!